D1392768

ENGLISH LANGUAGE SERIES

TITLE NO. 14

The Rhythms of English Poetry

ENGLISH LANGUAGE SERIES
General Editor: Randolph Quirk

The Rhythms of English Poetry

DEREK ATTRIDGE
University of Strathclyde

LONGMAN
London and New York

Longman Group UK Limited
Longman House, Burnt Mill,
Harlow, Essex, CM20 2JE England
and Associated Companies throughout the world

Pulished in the United States of America
by Longman Inc., New York

First published 1982
Third impression 1992

British Library Cataloguing in Publication Data

Attridge, Derek
    The rhythms of English poetry. -(English language
    series; 14)
    1. English language – Versification
    I. Title   II. Series
    921'.009   PE1509   80-42114

ISBN 0-582-55105-6

Produced by Longman Singapore Publishers Pte Ltd.
Printed in Singapore.

Foreword

In one of the first books in this series, Ian Gordon was concerned with the claim that the style and rhythm, *The Movement of English Prose*, displayed a throb of continuity over a millennium and more. Dr Attridge in the present volume is concerned with no less a claim, no less grand a theme: the unity of tradition, extending over six hundred years, manifested by the main stream of English 'accentual-syllabic' verse. His exposition of this theme demands an initial examination of the partly distinct, partly intertwined theories that have informed critical approaches to poetics: and then – the bulk of this volume – a detailed analysis in turn of 'rhythm' and 'metre', themselves also partly distinct and partly intertwined, and demanding from the reader both a sensitive ear and an appreciation of technical, logical argument.

Dr Attridge brings to this daunting enterprise a well-practised expertise in the field. He won high acclaim – to give one outstanding example – for his book on Elizabethan classical verse, *Well-weighed Syllables*, which was published in 1974. But in that work, as in this, one is struck not only by the keen historical knowledge of poetic form but by the deep personal involvement in (and love of) poetry itself. Even these, though essential, are not sufficient. Derek Attridge has made himself expert in linguistics – historical, traditional, structural, and transformational. And all these aspects of his scholarship he is able to communicate with enthusiasm and conviction. As with some other successful books in this series, we have here an author who is a true 'philologist', effortlessly straddling literary values and linguistic technicalities, convincingly showing the relevance of each to the other, excitingly indicating analogies with music at one moment and basic relationships with ordinary speech at another.

Indeed, for all its artfulness and (sometimes strenuous) complexity, poetry is not disjunct from but intimately bedded in the most commonplace fundamentals of our everyday speech rhythm and grammar: even in the most everyday strategies of conversational discourse. For this reason alone, *The Rhythms of English Poetry* deserves a proudly central place in this series. As English has increasingly come into worldwide use, there has arisen a correspondingly increasing need for more information on the language and the ways in which it is used. The English Language Series seeks to meet this need and to play a part in further stimulating the study and teaching of English by providing up to date and scholarly treatments of topics most relevant to present-day English – including its history and traditions, its sound patterns, its grammar, its lexicology, its rich variety and complexity in speech and writing, and its standards in Britain, the USA, and the other principal areas where the language is used.

RANDOLPH QUIRK

University College London
January, 1982

Preface

If every book were prefaced by a description of its ideal reader, much of the public's time and effort might be saved; but this volume permits of no such convenient premonitory paradigm. The only requirements I can think of are an interest in the subject, sufficient patience to follow an extended argument, and some acquaintance with, and pleasure in, English poetry. Readers with an exclusively literary or exclusively linguistic background may find that occasionally they are asked to think in ways more characteristic of the other discipline, but advances in the study of poetic language depend on just such broadmindedness.

A single book on rhythm and metre can deal only with the most important features of the subject, especially if in its examination of those features it aims to take as little as possible for granted and to leave as little as possible unexplained. By and large, therefore, I have had to limit my scope to a single remarkably homogeneous body of poetry: the main tradition of regular accentual-syllabic verse in Middle and Modern English. This has meant keeping off some of the most picturesque byways of English versification, such as syllabic verse, classical imitations, concrete poetry, and the metrical experiments and theories of a host of individual writers, as well as avoiding the currently busy freeway of nonmetrical poetry; progress along these routes must wait upon an understanding of the central network from which they take their departure. It has also meant giving scant attention to other varieties of sound patterning like alliteration or rhyme, and leaving out of consideration altogether the wider manifestations of rhythm in the sequences of expectancy and satisfaction created by syntax, large-scale formal and generic conventions, and structures of meaning. And since my interest is primarily in the singleness of this metrical tradition – in the capacity, that is, of the modern reader to engage directly with rhythmic forms produced over the past six hundred years – I have deliberately ignored its historical dimension. Instead, I have drawn extensively and promiscuously on the poetry of writers with established reputations from Shakespeare to Yeats for most of my examples, because it is largely on familiarity with this body of poetry that the modern reader's metrical knowledge is based.

The book is designed to be read as a whole, but the interdependence of parts and chapters is balanced by a measure of independence which should enable readers to follow up particular topics without going through the entire work. Part One is a critical account of the major approaches to be found in discussions of English metre: its aim is not merely to summarise these approaches but also to ascertain the requirements of an adequate metrical theory, and it therefore adumbrates some of the main arguments that follow. The next two parts deal with the three main sources and determinants of rhythmic patterning in poetry: Part Two with the rhythmic characteristics of the English language and the nature of rhythmic form, and Part Three with the metrical conventions of the verse tradition. A proper understanding of the first two influences requires some forays into the domains of linguistics, psychology, and music, while the third demands close attention to the practice of poets, taking account not only of what they have written, but also of what they have chosen not to write. Finally, Part Four focuses on the critical implications of rhythmic form, considered generally in terms of its poetic functions, and specifically in a selection of verse examples. The more technical points of the book's argument are summarised in the Appendix.

Although (or perhaps because) the words 'rhythm' and 'metre' occur on virtually every page, and as the titles of two parts, I have no wish to differentiate between them by means of simple definitions. The connotations which they carry are basically those of common usage, not the more specialised meanings they are sometimes given in prosodic theory; and it is the business of the following pages to provide a justification and elaboration of those connotations. But if I were obliged to be more explicit, I would hazard the assertion that rhythm, although it can encompass all types of movement which display a tendency towards patterning, has special reference to patterns apprehended through ordinary habits of perception, whereas metre is dependent on habits acquired through familiarity with a particular tradition of verse.

Since the purpose of almost every example I quote is to illustrate a general point about English poetic rhythm, questions of provenance and textual detail are usually irrelevant; I have therefore been eclectic in my choice of texts, modernised spelling and punctuation freely, and in most cases left identification to the end of the book. Examples are numbered throughout each chapter, using the following conventions: (8), quotation identified in the list of sources; (*8*), repeated quotation; [8], invented construct; [8a], rewritten quotation or construct, relating directly to (8) or [8]. I have had to make frequent reference to a hypothetical (though never ideal) poet or reader; if these individuals are consistently masculine, it is only because I have found no practicable way of evading the established convention.

My work on this subject owes a great deal, both directly and indirectly, to my teachers and fellow-teachers, students and fellow-students (to use four categories that overlap considerably) during the course of many years. I can single out for individual thanks only a few of those who have responded willingly and helpfully to questions and drafts: Sidney Allen, John Birtwhistle, John Hollander, Samuel Jay Keyser, Frank Prince, Frank Stack, John Swannell, and Edward Weismiller. Nor can I list all the qualities Randolph Quirk has shown as an editor; despatch, meticulousness, and humour will have to suffice. I was fortunate to have in Heather King a typist who did not always assume that the author must be right. Various stages of this work were made possible by grants from the Fulbright-Hays Programme, the British Academy, and the Southampton University Advanced Studies Fund, and by the hospitality of Clare College, Cambridge, and the English Department of the University of Illinois at Urbana. I am grateful to the editors of *Essays in Criticism* for allowing me to use, in Chapter 9, material from an article published in that journal. Thanks, too, to Robert, Richard, Randy, and Penny for seeing me down the final straight.

Southampton University   DA
November, 1980

Contents

Acknowledgements

We are grateful to the following for permission to reproduce copyright material:
André Deutsch Ltd for 'Poem VII' by Geoffrey Hill *Mercian Hymns* 1971; Faber & Faber Ltd and New Directions Publishing Corp for the poem 'In a Station of the Metro' *Collected Shorter Poems* by Ezra Pound reprinted by permission of Faber & Faber Ltd. Ezra Pound, Personae. Copyright 1926 by Ezra Pound. Reprinted by permission of New Directions, New York.

In Memory of
Henry Lester Attridge
1903–1971

Part One: Approaches

Chapter 1

Traditional approaches

One kind of insight into the history of metrical study in English can be gained simply from a glance at the collections on the subject held by most large, long-established libraries. The shelves are dominated by fading volumes from the nineteenth and early twentieth centuries: unwieldy surveys thick with scanned quotations; elegant essays dabbling in this or that prosodic sidestream; scientific investigations of syllabic duration or vocalic quality; handbooks for the schoolroom parading lists of Greek terms and recherché metres culled from Swinburne and Bridges. Most of these works evince a deep passion for the subject: absolute truths are proclaimed in heavy capitals, opponents despatched in savagely civil footnotes, snippets of verse triumphantly displayed like newly-discovered zoological specimens. Very few fail to offer some illumination of a corner or two, or to provide some problematic example which demands an explanation; but by and large their undisturbed repose on the library shelves is not unmerited.

Within this vast demonstration of scholarly and critical ardour ranging from the comically idiosyncratic to the laboriously obvious it is possible to trace two main approaches to English metre, and these form the subject of this chapter. To categorise in this way is, of course, to over-simplify and misrepresent a complex web of arguments; but the survey that follows is intended not as a history of prosodic study, but as an examination of those ways of dealing with metre which have proved most tenacious in their hold on the English literary consciousness, and which are most likely to affect – whether we realise it or not – our present reading, teaching, and criticism of verse. This examination will have the double aim of providing an outline of the metrical assumptions which underlie most critical discussions of English poetry, and of assessing what is valuable and what misleading about these traditional accounts. While prosodic approaches of more recent origin, to be discussed in the next chapter, have begun to make themselves felt in literary criticism, it is still true to say that most comments on the rhythms of English poetry owe their existence to theories which bear the dust – or the patina – of centuries upon them.

1.1 THE CLASSICAL APPROACH

When, in the sixteenth century, English poets, scholars, and educators joined the general European revaluation of classical literature, and set the verse of Greece and Rome on the highest of pedestals, it was inevitable that the literary endeavours of Englishmen in their own language should come under fresh scrutiny, and equally inevitable (until the last quarter of the century) that in the ensuing judgement the home-grown product should be found wanting. One obvious respect in which English verse failed to match the high art of the ancients was in its apparent lack of metrical organisation and subtlety, since the only tools of analysis possessed by the early humanists were those of classical prosody, and these afforded no purchase on the lines of English poets. The syllables of the English language, unlike those of Greek and Latin, had not been definitively classified by means of minutely detailed rules and the hallowed example of great poets, and any attempt to scan English verse by the familiar procedures of classical prosody revealed only chaos. To be sure, the *sound* of English verse had a kind of crude regularity, but very few educated readers expected to find the principles of metrical patterning so obviously in what they heard: they read Latin verse with a mode of pronunciation which gave no aural embodiment to its metrical structure, and their sense of its fine artistic precision came from an intellectual perception of the ordered ranks of abstractly categorised syllables.[1]

One natural result of this dissatisfaction was the protracted endeavour by English poets to create in their own language an equivalent of classical metrical forms: the efforts of some thirty writers survive from between 1540 and 1603, including examples by Ascham, Sidney, Spenser, Greene, and Campion. Although some of this 'quantitative' verse achieved critical acclaim and a degree of popularity, by the end of the century it was evident even to the most diehard humanist that poetry in the native accentual tradition had come closer to equalling the achievements of Greece and Rome than any imitations of classical metres, and that a more valuable enterprise might be the study of the indigenous verse forms created by English poets without prosodic apparatus and scholarly effort. But in the absence of any phonetic analysis of the English language, or even any vocabulary with which to begin such an analysis, those undertaking the task naturally fell back on the only metrical terminology they possessed – that of classical prosody – and applied it to the native English forms. In doing this, they were drawing on procedures which the humanist education instilled at an early age: *Prosodia* formed the fourth section of Lily's grammar, on which the Elizabethan grammar school syllabus was founded, and it was the intention, as a 1612 handbook for teachers put it, to make all boys 'very cunning in the rules of versifying' and 'expert in scanning a verse' (Brinsley, p. 192).

Nevertheless, the exact manner in which classical terms and methods of analysis were to be transferred to English verse was far from obvious: George Gascoigne, the father of English metrical studies, is unusual in clearly perceiving the alternating stresses of English metre, but he identifies English stress with both 'grave' and 'long' syllables in Latin, thus combining the separate features of accent and quantity (1575, pp. 49–51). He initiates a long tradition by using the term 'foot' to refer to accentually-based subdivisions of the English line, and laments that only one type is employed by English poets; but he does not associate it specifically with the classical iambic foot. Three years later, however, Thomas Blenerhasset, commenting on the metre of his 'Complaint of Cadwallader', states that it 'agreeth very well with the *Roman* verse called *Iambus*' (1578, p. 450); and by 1586 William Webbe can remark that 'the natural course of most English verses seemeth to run upon the old Iambic stroke' (p. 273). And so the terms of classical prosody became lodged among the commonplaces of English metrical analysis, in spite of the sharp differences between the two languages and their prevailing metrical forms. The understanding of metre implied by these terms, which for convenience we can call the 'classical' approach, was not systematically elaborated for some time, however: the main tradition in prosodic theory until the end of the eighteenth century was based on syllables and accents rather than feet,[2] and only with the new interest in Greece and Rome in the nineteenth century did foot-scansion come into its own as a mode of analysis, accompanied by another round of experiments in English classical metres.

It is important to see this approach to metre in its historical context, and to understand how it came into being, so that its sheer familiarity does not confer on it any unwarranted authority. Latin is no longer a staple educational diet from an early age, and we should therefore find it easier than our forebears to question the appropriateness for English verse of terms and concepts borrowed from an ancient language, which were themselves a borrowing from an even earlier one. Nevertheless, because of its importance in the writing of both poets and critics, the outlines of the classical approach, at least, have to be mastered by anyone with an interest in English poetry. What follows is a mere sketch of its commonest form: upon this simple foundation much more elaborate theoretical edifices have been erected to take account of the huge variety in English metrical practice, but these should be consulted in their original presentations.[3]

The classical approach to English metre takes as its fundamental unit the *foot*, a group of syllables each of which is defined as *stressed* or *unstressed*, matching the 'long' and 'short' of the classical originals. Most English metres consist of the same foot repeated a fixed number of times, and the traditional names of the metres derive from the type of foot and the number of its occurrences in the line. The following list contains the essential vocabulary of the classical approach, x standing for an unstressed syllable, or nonstress, and / for a stress (a less misleading notation than those which retain one or both of the classical symbols for long and short syllables):

(a) *Types of foot*

x /	iambic foot or iamb
/ x	trochaic foot or trochee
x x	pyrrhic foot or pyrrhic
/ /	spondaic foot or spondee
x x /	anapaestic foot or anapaest
/ x x	dactylic foot or dactyl

(b) *Types of line*

monometer	one foot
dimeter	two feet
trimeter	three feet
tetrameter	four feet
pentameter	five feet
hexameter or alexandrine	six feet
heptameter	seven feet
octometer	eight feet

Since the English language is incapable of a long succession of either stressed or unstressed syllables, it will be obvious that of the six kinds of foot listed, only those which include syllables of both types can be used as the foundation of a simple metre, producing four main varieties of verse. Those which make use of the two-syllable feet are said to be in *duple* or *binary* metres, those which use three-syllable feet in *triple* or *ternary* metres. The following are examples of the four types of metre in differing line-lengths:

Iambic pentameter

$$\begin{array}{cccccccccc} & x & / & x & / & x & / & x & / & x & / \\ (1) & |\text{Enforced} & |\text{to seek} & |\text{some co} & |\text{vert nigh} & |\text{at hand} & | \end{array}$$

Trochaic trimeter

$$\begin{array}{ccccccc} & / & x & / & x & / & x \\ (2) & |\text{Higher} & |\text{still and} & |\text{higher} & | \end{array}$$

Anapaestic tetrameter

$$\begin{array}{ccccccccccccc} & x & x & / & x & x & / & x & x & / & x & x & / \\ (3) & |\text{When the voi} & |\text{ces of chil} & |\text{dren are heard} & |\text{on the green} & | \end{array}$$

Dactylic dimeter

$$\begin{array}{ccccc} & / & x & x & / & x & x \\ (4) & |\text{Happy and} & |\text{glorious} & | \end{array}$$

In order to relate these simple schemes to the much more varied lines which poets actually write, the classical approach has recourse to the notion of *substitution*, according to which the feet of the basic metre can be replaced by other feet. Thus a trochee can be substituted for an iamb, and vice versa; and a spondee or a pyrrhic for either. The following lines will serve as an illustration, the lower set of symbols indicating the basic metre, and the upper set the actual stresses and nonstresses of a possible reading:

$$\begin{array}{ccccc} & x & / & x & / & x & x & x & / \\ & x & / & x & / & x & / & x & / \\ (5) & |\text{Behold} & |\text{her, sing} & |\text{le in} & |\text{the field,} & | \end{array}$$

$$\begin{array}{ccccc} & x & / & x & x & \bar{x} & / & x & / \\ & x & / & x & / & x & / & x & / \\ & |\text{Yon so} & |\text{lita} & |\text{ry High} & |\text{land lass!} & | \end{array}$$

$$\begin{array}{ccccc} & / & x & x & / & x & x & x & / \\ & x & / & x & / & x & / & x & / \\ & |\text{Reaping} & |\text{and sing} & |\text{ing by} & |\text{herself;} & | \end{array}$$

```
        /   /   | x  /  | x   /
      x   /   | x  /  | x   /
     |Stop here,| or gent|ly pass!|
```

In the basic metre, three lines of iambic tetrameter are followed by an iambic trimeter. However, each of the three tetrameters has one pyrrhic substitution; the third line begins with a trochaic substitution (often called an *inversion*, and in this position an *initial inversion*); and the final line begins with a spondaic substitution. It is also possible to replace a duple foot by a triple foot; this is known as *trisyllabic* substitution, and its most common form involves the doubling of the unstressed syllable to replace an iamb by an anapaest, or a trochee by a dactyl. Thus in the following example the iambic tetrameters are varied by means of an occasional anapaestic substitution (I show only the substituted feet on the upper level):

```
                          x x   /
        x   /| x  /| x    /| x      /
   (6) |The Ba|bylo|nian star|light brought|
```

```
              x x   /
        x  /|  x    /|  x   /| x   /
     |A fa|bulous, form|less dark|ness in|
```

Triple metres are dealt with on the same principle, though less elegantly, since the many possible substitute feet demand further raids on the stock of Greek prosodic terminology.

Another classical term inherited by English prosody with a changed signification is *caesura*. In the analysis of English verse it is used to refer to a pause within the line created by the syntax; thus one can say that in (5) the first and the fourth lines have a prominent caesura, the former after the third and the latter after the second syllable. The term does not refer to anything in the *structure* of most English verse, however, and there is no reason to prefer it to 'pause' or 'syntactic break' in describing a line. Two other terms, of more value in metrical discussion, can be introduced here: a line which ends with a syntactic break is *end-stopped*, and one which does not is *run-on* (or *enjambed*). All the lines in (5) are end-stopped; the first line of (6) is run-on. It is also worth mentioning a metrical phenomenon which the classical approach does not easily accommodate: lines of iambic verse may have an extra unstressed syllable, or occasionally two, after the final stress; these are, respectively, *feminine* and *triple* endings (as opposed to the *masculine* ending which terminates the line on a stress), and have to be regarded as 'extrametrical'. We shall see in due course that the endings of much trochaic verse also create problems for the classical approach. What I have described is merely a mode of scansion, but it implies a particular conception of poetic rhythm: a simple underlying metre on which is superimposed a more complex pattern representing with greater fidelity the actual pronunciation of the words. Most modern defenders of the classical approach would argue that this picture of two levels, partly coinciding, partly conflicting, reflects what in fact happens as we read metrical verse, and reveals one source of its special character. Many attempts have been made to capture the level of actual pronunciation by means of an analysis more delicate than that provided by classical prosody, and we shall consider some of these in 1.2 and 2.1 below. But however the two levels are represented, the notion of the interplay, or counterpoint, or tension, between a simple metrical pattern and a more varied arrangement of stresses corresponding to the pronunciation of the line in one of the most suggestive features of the classical approach, and one to which we shall return.

Let us now subject the concept of the foot itself to closer scrutiny, without allowing ourselves to be awed by its classical pedigree. At the heart of the analysis of English verse in terms of feet is the understanding that the line is constituted by a series of repeated events, and that its character is determined in part by the number of those repetitions; thus a tetrameter has a distinctively different quality from that of a pentameter. English verse is shown by this means to be different from, say, French or Italian verse, in which there are no such repeated syllabic groups. So far so good; but the rub is that in offering this insight into the structure of the lines, the classical approach imports further assumptions which may not be justifiable. What is the difference between the following graphic representations of the stress pattern of an iambic pentameter?

x / x / x / x / x /
| x / | x / | x / | x / | x / |

Both indicate the quintuple occurrence of a nonstress and a stress which gives the line its character, but the second seems to imply in addition that the transition between a nonstress and the following stress is completely different from that between a stress and a following nonstress. This is not a distinction of which the reader is aware, unless perhaps he has through rigorous training developed the capacity to impose an abstract pattern on the words he reads. It is certainly not part of the rhythmic movement of the line, in which the transitions between syllables are governed not by the arbitrary divisions of scansion but by the natural links and gaps in the language. Thus in the following lines we are aware of the alternating pattern of nonstress and stress, and the fourfold grouping that underlies each line, but we do not perceive any division in the middle of 'chapel', 'organ's', or 'naked', nor any bond extending over the comma in the first line:

$$(7) \quad \text{|}\overset{\text{x}}{\text{The}} \overset{/}{\text{cha}}\text{|}\overset{\text{x}}{\text{pel,}} \overset{/}{\text{where}}\text{|}\overset{\text{x}}{\text{no}} \overset{/}{\text{or}}\text{|}\overset{\text{x}}{\text{gan's}} \overset{/}{\text{peal}}\text{|}$$

$$\text{|}\overset{\text{x}}{\text{In}}\overset{/}{\text{vests}}\text{|}\overset{\text{x}}{\text{the}} \overset{/}{\text{stern}}\text{|}\overset{\text{x}}{\text{and}} \overset{/}{\text{na}}\text{|}\overset{\text{x}}{\text{ked}} \overset{/}{\text{prayer}}\text{|}$$

Part of the rhythmic character – though not the metrical structure – of any line stems from the placing of word and phrase boundaries, creating rhythmic groups which may be *rising* (beginning with a nonstress) or *falling* (beginning with a stress), and an entire stanza or poem may be in a predominantly rising or falling rhythm, but this aspect of verse, though affected by the way lines begin and end, is not a product of any division into feet. Yet some writers on metre go further, predicating and analysing a 'counterpoint' between word-divisions and foot-divisions, as if the reader perceived both of these simultaneously.[4] Even those apologists for foot-scansion who argue that feet are only an analytical convenience are sometimes led into making statements which imply that they have some more substantial existence. One doctrine often to be encountered is that we are not able to make metrical comparisons across foot-divisions; so that in the following line, an example used by Wimsatt (1970, pp. 774–5), we supposedly perceive 'of' as metrically more prominent than 'sweet', since only the former is in the stressed position of the iambic foot:

$$(8) \quad \text{|}\text{When to}\text{|}\text{the ses}\text{|}\textit{sions of}\text{|}\textit{sweet si}\text{|}\text{lent thought}\text{|}$$

Only a reader for whom foot-divisions had become solid walls could fail to respond to the rhythmic progression from two roughly equal nonstresses to two roughly equal stresses in the four italicised syllables. That the foot should take on a substantial existence in the minds of its users need not surprise us, however; the bar-line in music frequently suffers the same fate, although that at least has the merit of occurring consistently in the same place relative to the main beats of the rhythm.

This reification of the foot is most evident in discussions of alternative scansions of a single metrical form. Consider the following lines, in a metre which occurs widely throughout the English tradition (the symbols here indicate the basic metrical scheme, not the actual stress pattern):

```
     /     x  /   x    /    x   /
(9) Here the anthem doth commence:
     /   x    /   x  / x     /
    Love and constancy is dead;
      /  x  /     x  /   x  /
    Phoenix and the Turtle fled
    /  x  /  x  /     x    /
    In a mutual flame from hence.
```

These lines cannot be divided into four identical units, yet one does not experience them as in any way metrically irregular or anomalous. For the classical prosodist, however, they pose a problem: are they to be divided into feet like this:

```
|  /    x| /    x |  /    x  |  /    |
| Here the| anthem| doth com | mence |
```

that is, as trochaic tetrameters with a missing final syllable, or like this:

```
|  /  |  x  /  |  x     /  |  x     /    |
| Here| the an| them doth | commence |
```

that is, as iambic tetrameters with a missing initial syllable? The question is without substance, of course, unless feet are regarded as having a real existence for the reader; if they are truly nothing but an analytical convenience, either scansion would suffice – though it is difficult to see what would be contributed to our understanding of the metre by the addition of foot-divisions. Yet prosodists frequently do pose such questions, and argue the pros and cons of this or that scansion. Two industrious exponents of the classical approach, Saintsbury (1910, pp. 79–81) and Hamer (1930, Ch. 2, *passim*), make attempts to classify particular examples of this seven-syllable metre as either iambic or trochaic, influenced apparently by the quite separate consideration of word-boundaries. Saintsbury consistently implies that decisions about scansion reflect (or give rise to?) different ways of reading, but it is not easy to see what these could be, other than the imposition of an artificial pattern on the natural movement of the lines. Nor do Wimsatt and Beardsley (1959, p. 593, n. 12), who remark that some examples of this metre 'may be susceptible of being satisfactorily read either as iambic or trochaic', say what the practical difference would amount to. Even a recent and widely-used introductory account of English verse form is so taken up with foot-scansion that it includes lines in this familiar metre among examples of 'initial trochaic substitution' (Fussell, 1979, p. 54).

When we turn to verse which does not observe strict control on the number of syllables, a category that includes much popular verse, we find the classical approach even less satisfactory. What is the basic foot in the following lines, in which I have indicated the stresses that would probably be emphasised in an exaggeratedly rhythmic reading?

          x / x x   / x /   x   /
(10) A little black thing among the snow,

        xx   /   /   x / x /
        Crying "'weep! 'weep!" in notes of woe!

        / x   x / x x   / x /
        "Where are thy father and mother, say?"

        x x   /   x / x x /   x /
        "They are both gone up to the church to pray."

One could choose almost any foot for the basic metre and explain the actual pattern of stresses in terms of substitutions; indeed, one of the weaknesses of the classical approach is that *any* succession of syllables can be divided into recognised feet. But the choice of a basic foot here would be an arbitrary one, not reflecting anything in the reader's experience, and the impression which such an analysis would give of a highly complex and deviant metre would be quite false. The rhythm is bold and strong, with the firm four-beat structure of the ballad or nursery rhyme. Some theorists would argue that such verse is not in the accentual-syllabic tradition in which the bulk of English poetry is written, and which imposes restrictions on both the placing of stresses and the number of syllables, but in a quite distinct form, closer to the strong-stress metre of medieval alliterative verse in its indifference to the number of syllables in the line; but to argue this is to drive a wedge between metrical types which shade into one another, and, by denying English literary verse its intimate links with the popular tradition, to ignore one of its great sources of vitality. We need a way of talking about poetic rhythm which will be useful for *all* varieties of English verse, which will reflect their interconnections and their dependence on the rhythmic characteristics of the language itself, and which will make sharp distinctions only where these are genuine perceptions experienced by the reader.

Even in its analysis of the type of metre most amenable to foot-prosody, in which the number of syllables in the line is strictly controlled, the classical approach and the theory of two distinct 'levels' is apt to be misleading. Consider the following lines from Shakespeare's Sonnet 29, shown with both the basic metre and substitutions:

$$
\begin{array}{c|c|c|c|c|c|}
 & /\quad \text{x} & \text{x}\quad / & \text{x}\quad / & \text{x}\quad\text{x} & /\quad / \\
 & \text{x}\quad / & \text{x}\quad / & \text{x}\quad / & \text{x}\quad / & \text{x}\quad / \\
(11) & \text{When in} & \text{disgrace} & \text{with For} & \text{tune and} & \text{men's eyes,}
\end{array}
$$

$$
\begin{array}{|c|c|c|c|c|}
\text{x}\ / & \text{x}\ / & \text{x}\quad / & \text{x}\quad / & \text{x}\quad / \\
\text{I all} & \text{alone} & \text{beweep} & \text{my out} & \text{cast state,}
\end{array}
$$

$$
\begin{array}{|c|c|c|c|c|}
 & & /\quad\ \ & & \\
\text{x}\quad / & \text{x}\quad / & \text{x}\quad\text{x} & \text{x}\quad / & \text{x}\quad / \\
\text{And troub} & \text{le deaf} & \text{heav'n with} & \text{my boot} & \text{less cries,}
\end{array}
$$

$$
\begin{array}{|c|c|c|c|c|}
\text{x}\quad / & \text{x}\ / & \text{x}\ / & \text{x}\quad / & \text{x}\ / \\
\text{And look} & \text{upon} & \text{myself} & \text{and curse} & \text{my fate}
\end{array}
$$

If metrical analysis is to be a valuable part of the criticism of these lines, it must show the contribution of the rhythm to the shifting emotional colours; it must capture, for instance, the heavy regularity of the second and fourth lines, with their inward-turning grief, and the contrasting rhythmic dislocation that accompanies the outburst of violent despair in the third line. The scansion shown here does indicate the metrical regularity of line 2 (though the division into feet contributes nothing to the analysis), and line 4 is almost as regular, if the second syllable of 'upon' is given some degree of stress. But the source of the third line's rhythmic power is obscured by the foot-scansion, which implies that the metrical variation here is the substitution of a trochee, 'heav'n with', for an iamb (I have used the spelling 'heav'n' to indicate the monosyllabic pronunciation common in Shakespeare's time). The reader responding directly to the verse is not conscious of any underlying, abstract nonstress in conflict with the actual stress of 'heav'n', nor of any notional stress challenging the unstressed 'with'. The tension is experienced not between two simultaneously perceived levels, but in the linear progression of the line: the stress on 'deaf' is immediately followed by a further stress carrying the next beat, which slows down the movement over both words and creates a point of rhythmic emphasis; and this in turn is followed by two lightly pronounced nonstresses. The rhythm therefore undergoes a temporary deformation – a slowing down of the syllabic movement, followed by a compensatory speeding up – which starts on the word 'deaf' and ends with a return to the regular pace on 'bootless'; and the five beats of the line, instead of being evenly distributed among the ten syllables, are irregularly dispersed.

The first line of the example, however, appears in a classical scansion to be even less regular than the third: three of its five feet involve substitutions. This hardly accords with one's experience of the verse, and again the culprit is the principle of the foot. What is classically called an 'initial trochaic substitution' or 'inverted first foot' is simply a line-opening with a stress, followed by two nonstresses instead of one; a relatively minor departure from regular alternation, involving no dislocating successive stresses. There is another extra nonstress in 'Fortune and', followed by a rhythmic effect similar to that of 'deaf heav'n': two adjacent stresses which attract two beats and momentarily retard the movement. Once again, a change in tempo in one direction receives compensation by a change in the other, but this time in the reverse order. These two patterns, $/ / \times \times$ and $\times \times / /$, make frequent appearances in strict verse, since they allow metrical variety and expressive rhythmic effects without any consequences for the syllable count; we shall discuss them fully in 7.6 and 8.6–7. In classical scansion, however, they are presented as completely distinct phenomena, the first involving trochaic substitution, or inversion, and the second involving two substitute feet which have no necessary connection. This would imply that the former is the simpler and more common variation in English poetry, but in fact the reverse is true; prosodists using the classical approach, however, often devote greater attention to the formation which is more easily accounted for by their theory. Some foot-prosodists have recourse to a four-syllable foot, the *ionic*, to take care of the $\times \times / /$ pattern, but this creates further complexities in scansion by reducing the number of feet in the line. The clear rhythmic structure of lines like those in (11) can be fully brought out in a reading that remains faithful to the normal pronunciation of English, and a metrical analysis should show this; foot-scansion obscures this fact by seeming to invite some audible manifestation of the ghostly divisions on which it is based, and by implying phonetic equivalences which are no more than theoretical. The classical approach tends to conceive of metre as a visual and spatial phenomenon rather than a dynamic one; it is satisfied if it can find five feet in a line by its analytical procedures, even if these do not coincide with the five recurring beats perceived by the reader.

Foot-prosody is less misleading in handling what it treats as pyrrhic and spondaic substitution, but to analyse these variations in terms of feet seems an unnecessary complication. Both are among the commonest deviations from strict alternation in duple verse, and do not strike the ear as markedly disruptive. Compare the following sonnet openings:

```
                      x   x                     x   x
      x   /   x   /   x  /  x   /   x  /
(12) |Not mar|ble, nor|the gil|ded mo|numents|

          x   x
  x   /   x   /   x  /   x    /   x   /
 |Of prin|ces shall|outlive|this power|ful rhyme|
```

```
                  /   /                     /
      x  /  x   /   x  /   x   /   x /
(13) |When I|have seen|by Time's|fell hand|defaced|

              /   /          /                /
   x  /   x   /   x  /   x   /   x  /
  |The rich|proud cost|of out|worn bu|ried age|
```

A description in terms of feet would state that three of the iambs in (12) are replaced by pyrrhics, and that three of the iambs in (13) are similarly replaced by spondees (assuming that we stress both syllables of 'outworn'), once more implying that in reading the lines we perceive at these points two different but simultaneous disyllabic patterns. But a more accurate account of what happens is that on three occasions in (12) we encounter a nonstress where we expect a stress, and on three occasions in (13) we encounter a stress where we expect a nonstress. When this occurs in mid-line, the result is a succession of three like syllables, x x x or / / /, the central one of which is encouraged by the rhythm of the whole line (and of the poem – and, as we shall see later, of the language itself) to function rhythmically as a syllable of the opposite kind. We are not invited to *read* these syllables in any special manner, or to experience a struggle between two levels, but to respond to the quickening of the rhythm in the first case and its slowing down in the second. Such tension as we do feel is the result of this hastening or retarding of the fundamental pulse; the poetic effect in these examples is to underline the vigorous confidence of (12) and the ruminative melancholy of (13).

The rhythmic quality of the variations in (13) is strikingly different from the effect of the pairs of stresses in example (11). In (11), each of the two stresses attracts one of the line's main beats, and the relationship between the pattern of ten syllables and five rhythmic pulses is disturbed; in (13) there is still a single syllable for each rhythmic alternation, and though there is an increase in weight and slowness, there is no dislocation. We can further illustrate this distinction by rewriting a familiar line: consider the different rhythmic character of the last two words in the following:

```
            x  /  x   /   x  /   /    /
    (14)   To walk, and pass our long love's day
            x  /  x    / x   x  /     /
   [14a]   To walk, and cherish our love's day
```

In the original, the natural rhythm of the language produces a smooth alternation, and the two words in question, though they effect a slowing down at the end of the line, create little sense of rhythmic dislocation; in the rewritten version both words require a strong emphasis to maintain the metrical structure of five beats, and a greater sense of disturbance is experienced as a result. Yet in the classical approach these are both regarded as examples of 'spondaic substitution'. Similarly, no distinction is made between the 'pyrrhics' of (11) or [14a] and those of (12), whereas their rhythmic function is quite different: the first type occurs *between* the beats of the line, the second type *includes* one of the beats.

An obvious task of any metrical theory is to make clear the distinction between lines which are acceptable as examples of a given metre, and those which are not. Apart from a few prohibited substitutions (such as trochaic substitution in the final foot of an iambic line), the classical approach has little to offer on this score. One should not expect a metrical theory to specify exact borderlines between 'acceptable' and 'unacceptable' lines, since such borderlines would not be a true reflection of the reader's experience, and in any case there are a number of factors, not all of them metrical, that affect our judgement of a line's rhythmic acceptability. But it should provide a framework which will allow the pinpointing of crucial metrical divergences in a line which is perceived as in some way anomalous. Classical prosody not only often fails to do this, but at times actually obscures the degree to which a line is irregular: we saw in example (11) that a line with three substitutions can be more regular to the ear than a line with one, and it is not difficult to invent lines which, in terms of feet, show only limited departures from the basic pattern, but which the ear registers as highly deviant. The following line, for example, has only two substitutions, but sounds clearly out of place in the context of regular iambic pentameter verse:

[15] | x / | / x / | / / | x / | x / |
      | When men | see by | Time's hand | the world | destroyed |

If we remove the foot-divisions, however, we can see why it strikes the ear so uncomfortably: it has six main stresses, all vying for the five main beats of the line: x / / x / / x / x / . At best, then, the division of lines into feet adds nothing, at worst it hinders accurate analysis of the metrical variations which all readers perceive.

In spite of its inadequacy as a way of analysing English metre, classical prosody has provided some commonly accepted terms which can be useful in metrical discussion if they are not misunderstood; there would be no point, for instance, in banishing the widely accepted term 'iambic pentameter' as a convenient label for a particular conventionalised metrical form much employed in the English tradition. The classical approach may also help us to understand certain features of verse written by poets who consciously adhered to such a view of metre, though their number is perhaps not very large. And in a more general way, this approach has been important in emphasising the distinction between a basic metrical pattern and the more varied rhythms of the spoken language, whether we think of this as another relatively simplified pattern, or as the fine gradations of speech itself. Of the terms used to refer to this distinction, and the expressive possibilities it offers the poet, the least helpful are those which imply that there are two levels of structure simultaneously perceived by the reader; Hopkins's influential borrowing of the term 'counterpoint' from music, for instance, gives the erroneous impression that the double structure is the equivalent of two voices in a polyphonic composition, each clearly perceptible, and each with a distinct character of its own. But what we are aware of in reading a metrical line is an onward movement which at times approaches a marked regularity and at times departs from it, constantly arousing and thwarting rhythmic expectations. It is in this sense that we can apply the term 'tension' to poetic rhythm, without implying foot-scansion and substitution, or the perception of two discrete patterns at different levels and a relationship between them, and we shall find it an invaluable concept in the chapters that follow. Tension arises out of the twin tendencies of language, towards variety and towards regularity: the voice, or rather the speech faculty of the human brain, enjoys its freedom to range over a finely gradated scale of intensities, timbres, pitches, and durations, but also feels the pull towards simple patterns and repetitions. This is a feature of all speech, perhaps of all human activity; but metre marks off the language of poetry from the language of daily existence by formalising and controlling this natural tension, and the classical approach to prosody has always shown an awareness of this central fact.

1.2   THE TEMPORAL APPROACH

Classical prosody may tempt the student of metre not by offering a body of useful terminology but by implying a simple theory of rhythm, and this too has had a marked influence on discussions of English metre from the sixteenth century to the present, sometimes in conjunction with the approach already described, sometimes in opposition to it. The feet of Latin verse were treated in classical accounts as simple durational units, the 'long' syllables taking twice the time to pronounce, in theory at least, as the 'short'. Most subsequent discussions of classical prosody have perpetuated this notion of a strictly temporal system, and, although it is far from adequate as an account of Latin metre[5] (or even of Greek metre, from which it is derived), it provides an attractively straightforward conception of rhythmic form. It is not surprising, therefore, that the Elizabethan commentators on English metre, lacking a conceptual framework within which to discuss stress patterns, fell back on the classical idea of 'quantity'. Both Gascoigne and Webbe, whose application of classical terms to English prosody we have already noted, describe English syllables as 'long' and 'short', and the attempt to naturalise classical metres at this time also assumes the existence in English of simple durational categories. Elizabethan readers, who made no systematic distinction between these two types of syllable in their pronunciation of Latin, would not have been perturbed by an equal lack of audible distinction in their own language; not for the last time in the history of prosodic study, the ear allowed itself to be governed by the mind. When, in the nineteenth century, the terms of classical prosody again became widely used in discussions of English verse, the associated theory of a strictly temporal metre once more found its supporters. (Saintsbury's approach to metre, a late bloom of the Victorian tradition, takes as its starting point the notion of 'long' and 'short' syllables in English – although Saintsbury resolutely, almost gleefully, refuses to give a theoretical account of this distinction.) Others, however, argued that because the feet of English verse use stress in place of quantity, durational relationships can be ignored; and it was, in fact, this hostility towards a strict temporal interpretation of feet which became more characteristic of the classical approach. As we shall see in the following chapter, it is a feature of some more recent approaches to metre as well.

But there have been many prosodists who have regarded it as axiomatic that rhythm is a phenomenon which occurs in the dimension of time, and yet have found the simple durational relationships of classical prosody too blunt an instrument to handle the subtleties of this aspect of English verse. For them, a more tempting analogy offers itself: the analogy with musical form. For the Renaissance prosodists, one valuable feature of the temporal theory implied by classical prosody was that it emphasised the close relationship of poetry to music, a relationship which was particularly appreciated and particularly fruitful during this period. Thus Sidney defends classical metres in his *Apologie for Poetrie* as 'more fit for music, both words and tune observing quantity' (1595, sig. L2^r),[6] and it may have been this relationship which led Thomas Campion, England's most accomplished writer of poetry and music united in song, to elaborate a quantitative theory of English verse in his *Observations in the Art of English Poesie* (1602). However, the pioneer of a more thoroughgoing musical approach, doing away with classical terminology altogether, was Joshua Steele, who used musical notation to describe the rhythms of spoken English in his *Essay towards Establishing the Melody and Measure of Speech* (1775), better known by the title of the second edition of 1779, *Prosodia Rationalis*. Steele's main interest was in the art of dramatic declamation, but his inclusion of specimens of English verse analysed by means of detailed durational symbols later exerted a strong influence in the field of prosody, and many similar projects have since been undertaken. The main body of work using a temporal approach can therefore be seen as an alternative tradition to the one already discussed, a tradition which can boast an equally long history and equally exorbitant demands on library shelf-space.[7] As in our discussion of the classical approach, it will be possible to extract and evaluate only its basic principles.

In its simplest form, temporal analysis using musical notation involves the representation of each syllable in the line of verse by a note-value, judged by the ear, producing scansions like the following:

(16) But hail thou goddess, sage and holy

By this means, something of the rhythmic variety of English verse – the way the voice hurries over certain syllables and lingers on others – can be shown in a manner impossible within the strict classical approach; and one could refine this notation further by adding such details as accent-marks above the stressed syllables, rests, pauses, and tempo indications. However, even with these additions, scansion of this kind offers very little insight into the metrical structure of the line, giving merely an impressionistic record of one possible reading of it. Most writers in this tradition make use of a further principle, fundamental to Western music from the seventeenth century to the twentieth century, by dividing the line into bars, or *measures*, of equal duration, and apportioning note-values accordingly. A possible notation for our example might be:

(*16*) But |hail thou |goddess, |sage and |holy |

As in music, the bar-lines always fall before the main beats, and therefore, unlike foot-divisions, make no distinction between iambic and trochaic, or anapaestic and dactylic, metres. In our example, classical scansion would hesitate between iambic or trochaic feet; musical scansion avoids this unreal dilemma by automatically inserting bar-lines in the appropriate positions.

What this notation implies, of course, is that the stresses function in the same way as musical beats, and that the line, when read, is divided into temporally equal units, each beginning with the onset of a stressed syllable. This constitutes a much stronger claim about the structure of the line than the previous example, and offers a clear alternative to the classical mode of analysing metre, though its connection with the durational theory of Latin prosody is obvious. Instead of two levels, involving 'substitution' and 'counterpoint', we have only one level, whose units are determined by the positions of the main stresses; thus the common sequence / / x x, for example, treated in the classical approach as an 'inversion', is regarded as a measure of one syllable followed by a measure of three, with the lengths of the syllables adjusted to make the two measures equal. Compare the following hypothetical musical analysis with the foot-scansion of the same line earlier in this chapter:

(*11*) And | trouble | deaf | heav'n with my | bootless | cries |

The use of standard musical notation implies a further principle: that the individual syllables, although not classifiable simply into 'long' and 'short', do bear simple durational ratios to one another, capable of being represented within the limited arithmetical system of note-values. Thus in (*11*) the claim is made that 'deaf' takes exactly one-and-a-half times as long to pronounce as 'heav'n'. In addition, accounts of English verse using this approach frequently introduce the idea that measurable intervals of *silence* function as an integral part of the rhythmic structure, as rests do in music; in both our examples, for instance, a rest at the end of the line extends the final bar to the same duration as the others. (The first syllable might be regarded as an anacrusis, or upbeat, or as the final part of a bar beginning in the previous line.) The underlying assumption of the whole approach is that the reader or hearer of verse perceives the durations of individual syllables, and that his sense of a rhythmic structure derives from the simple patterns in time that they create.

To carry the discussion of the temporal tradition further, we need to shift our attention to another branch of it, one which is often closely associated with the ideas we have been considering, but which takes as its starting point not the rhythms of music, but the rhythms of English speech. Many of the musical prosodists, from Steele on, argue that their analyses of syllabic duration are relevant to prose as well as to verse, and that poetic rhythm is merely a heightening of a natural tendency towards regularity in the language itself. This is a theoretical claim of the highest importance, although its application has often been hampered by an inadequate phonetic theory and the insights it promises obscured by too rigid an adherence to the musical analogy. Fundamental to this branch of the temporal tradition is the linguistic phenomenon known as *isochrony* or *stress-timing*: the tendency of the stressed syllables of certain languages to fall at perceptually equal time-intervals. The existence of this phenomenon as a perceived characteristic of English speech, at least under certain conditions, is easily demonstrated. Tap a finger on the syllables of a phrase like *Jóhn stánds*, spoken slowly but naturally, and then introduce an increasing number of unstressed syllables between the stresses, keeping the time-interval between the stresses the same: *Jóhnny stánds, Jóhnny withstánds, Jóhnny understánds, Jónathan understánds*. One does not feel that one is going against the natural rhythms of the language in doing this, at least until the number of nonstresses demands the introduction of a secondary accent; in other words, there is something in the way we pronounce sequences of syllables in English which encourages us to adjust the speed of utterance in order to keep the main stresses at roughly equal intervals. If we introduce another *stressed* syllable, however, and try to maintain the the timing of the original stresses, the result is a forced pronunciation: *Jóhnny Bláck withstánds* has the same number of syllables as *Jóhnny understánds* but normally takes longer to say, not because the sounds of the individual syllables are longer, but because there are three stresses instead of two, each demanding its own rhythmic space. We shall postpone to Chapter 3 an examination of the adequacy of an analysis of English speech rhythms which makes stress-timing its basic principle, but there can be no doubt that it is a phenomenon which speakers of the language perceive, and one which can scarcely be ignored in a full account of English poetic rhythm.

One of the clearest statements of the relation between the isochronic tendency of English speech and the metres of English verse is also one of the earliest: in his remarkably perceptive *Essay on English Metrical Law* (first published in 1857), Coventry Patmore asserts that 'metre, in the primary degree of a simple series of isochronous intervals, marked by accents, is as natural to spoken language as an even pace is natural to walking', and 'as dancing is no more than an increase of the element of measure which already exists in walking, so verse is but an additional degree of that metre which is inherent in prose speaking' (p. 224). Patmore sees isochronous intervals as a fundamental feature of the movement of spoken English and as the basis of English verse; but he also acknowledges that isochrony is not an exact and absolute phenomenon, but an approximate equality towards which speech tends, and that its rhythmic beats may occur mentally rather than materially.

Some phoneticians and prosodists, however, take very literally the notion of equal intervals in speech, and combine it with the musical analogy which we have already discussed. The view that stresses in English tend to be equally spaced in time does not, of course, imply that the syllables occurring *within* those intervals are of any particular duration; if there are two such syllables, for instance, they may divide the time in any proportion whatever and still fulfil the demands of isochrony. But a number of writers, influenced by the exact notations of music, have argued that these durations are in simple arithmetical proportion to one another.[8] Thus one common theory divides utterances into equally timed units consisting of a stress and all the following nonstresses, very like bars of music, and these units are held to be subdivided into time-lengths in simple ratios. A measure of two syllables, for instance, is said to exhibit only three kinds of proportion: 1:2, 2:1, or 1½:1½. Examples given by David Abercrombie (1964b) of each of these are, respectively, |*shilling*|, |*tea for* | *two*,| *limpid* |. Regular duple verse is then seen as a sequence of equal disyllabic measures, each of which is divided into one or other of these simple proportions. A further implication of this particular analysis is that the common 'iambic' or 'trochaic' metres of English are regarded as having a triple rhythm, since each measure is made up of three units. In order to preserve the equality of the measures in such an analysis, rests are freely used, and some writers in this tradition (for example Steele, 1775; David Abercrombie, 1964a, 1971) even allow for the occurrence of 'silent stresses', perceived in the gaps between pronounced sounds.

Several strands are thus twisted together in the temporal approach to English metre: the durational assumptions of classical prosody, the analogy with music, and the relationship of verse to the rhythms of English speech. The second and third of these general considerations, at least, have valuable insights to offer into the nature of metre, and we shall give them fuller consideration in later chapters; but the typical 'temporalist' account of verse, with its insistence on equal intervals and its detailed musical notations, provides only fitful illumination. An analysis in these terms proceeds as if the only structural principle in English verse were a temporal one: any number of syllables after a beat will sustain the metre as long as the total duration of the measure can be kept equal to that of the previous measures. What this fails to take into account is the tight control over the number of syllables in the line that characterises the main tradition of English verse. The classical approach, with its system of deviations from a fixed norm, does acknowledge this syllabic principle, but neither approach is wholly adequate to the reader's experience of verse, as may be seen by returning to one of the commonest variations in duple verse, the pattern x x / /. As we have noted, the classical approach views this as a fortuitous yoking of a pyrrhic and a spondee:

$$(11) \quad |\text{When in}| \text{disgrace} |\text{with For}| \overset{x}{\text{tune}} \overset{x}{\text{and}} | \overset{/}{\text{men's}} \overset{/}{\text{eyes}}|$$

Most musical prosodists, on the other hand, would treat it as a measure of three syllables followed by two measures of one syllable each:

$$|\text{When in dis}| \text{grace with} | \overset{/}{\text{For}} \overset{x}{\text{tune}} \overset{x}{\text{and}} | \overset{/}{\text{men's}} | \overset{/}{\text{eyes}}|$$

The latter is probably close to the experience of the unanalytical reader using normal pronunciation, since it shows how the final words both attract a rhythmic beat, but it fails to register the resulting disturbance to the regular alternations. What is more, it implies that there is complete freedom to add or drop unstressed syllables without metrical consequences. This is obviously not so, as the subtraction of one nonstress will show:

$$[11a] \quad |\text{When in dis}| \overset{/}{\text{grace with}} | \overset{/}{\text{Love and}} | \overset{/}{\text{men's}} | \overset{/}{\text{eyes}}|$$

Although this can still be scanned in five measures as shown (and in fact appears more regular than the original in this scansion), it would be an anomaly in pentameter verse, since it is more likely to be perceived as a line with four measures and a degree of triple movement:

$$|\text{When in dis}| \overset{/}{\text{grace with}} | \overset{/}{\text{Love and men's}} | \overset{/}{\text{eyes}}|$$

The cardinal difference between the rhythms of song and those of verse is that in the former it is the note-values which constitute the metrical structure, and the words are pronounced in accordance with that external authority, whereas in the latter the rhythmic properties of the words themselves provide the determining impulse, and musical notation can be used only as a graphic representation of the pattern they form. To *chant* poetry is to convert it from verse into a kind of song, in which the temporal values suggested by the words are allowed to become a determining grid acting upon them; but the approach we are considering proceeds as if all poetry were read in this way.

A distinction is sometimes made between 'song-verse', whose metrical structure invites recitation (and scansion) based on strict temporal proportions, and 'speech-verse', which is faithful to the rhythmic flexibility of the spoken language. It is a useful distinction if not pressed too far – a comparison of, say, Chesterton's 'Lepanto' and Donne's *Satires* would demonstrate its validity – but an adequate account of English metre needs to show how the two modes are blended in the central tradition of regular verse. The marriage is not to be effected, however, by describing speech itself in the terms provided by music; our sense of the rhythms of our language is a more complex matter than an awareness of temporal relations. That stress-timing, as a perceptual characteristic of language, does enter into the rhythm of spoken English is, as we have seen, demonstrable, but it need not be assumed that this is the only rhythmic principle at work in the language, nor that it implies objective temporal equality. While it is true that the syllables of *shilling* and *limpid* have different rhythmic structures, it is far from obvious that this is a matter of simple proportions in the time taken to pronounce them. The syllables of English speech cannot be measured and marshalled like the notes of music, and there is no reason why they should fall into elementary time-schemes, any more than one's paces in walking should cover distances of only x feet, $\frac{1}{2}$x feet, or $1\frac{1}{2}$x feet. Musical notation may be a useful way of highlighting the importance of time in the rhythms of speech and verse, but for all its complexity it imposes too rigid an analysis of temporal relations on the infinitely varied movement of language. Moreover, regular verse is experienced as a highly distinctive form of language, and it is impossible to explain this distinctiveness in the light of a theory that claims to find precise patterns in all speech. Language becomes metrical when, by observing constraints that heighten its natural tendency towards rhythmicality, it encourages the perception of rhythmic forms analogous with those found in music, and it is the task of a metrical theory to describe those rhythmic forms and to specify the constraints which bring them into being – something which cannot be done if the differences between verse and speech, or between verse and music, are blurred from the start.

There remains a fourth strand in the temporal approach, one that provides some evidence against which to test musical theories of verse rhythm: experimental measurements of the actual durations of the syllables of English in readings of prose and verse. There has been no lack of such laboratory work this century, from the early efforts of psychologists and phoneticians using the kymograph to recent investigations in sound spectrography.[9] The methods and aims of these experiments have varied, as have the detailed findings, but all the results point to one simple fact: objective measurement of the sounds of English verse does not reveal simple temporal relationships among syllables. Stressed syllables tend, not surprisingly, to be longer than unstressed syllables (though this is by no means an invariable rule); but there is no evidence of any preference for the simple ratios between the durations of syllables suggested by many temporal prosodists. More importantly, there is no evidence of exact isochrony as an objective characteristic of normal English speech; and in the reading of regular verse English speakers do not give identical durations to feet or measures, unless the lines are chanted in time to a precise beat.

These findings will surprise no-one who has listened carefully to English speech and English verse; whatever part is played by stress-timing in moulding the rhythms of the language, it obviously does not impose mechanical regularity upon it. Any account of metre based on the assumption that such objective regularity exists is without foundation; verse rhythm is not created by time-sequences measurable in centiseconds. But this does not mean that we can ignore the temporal dimension in discussing metre; it merely emphasises that the life of poetic rhythm resides not in physical patterns that a machine can register, but in the reader's subjective response to the totality of the text, a response which blends the perception of sheer sound – itself a far from mechanical process – with the intellectual and emotional apprehension of the structures of language embodied in that sound. From classical times to the present there have always been prosodists who have rightly insisted that the power of rhythm in poetry derives from the controlled movement of language through time, though it is only in this century that we have been made fully aware of the degree to which that vital movement is the product of the reader's own acts of perception. In responding to the metrical organisation of a poem, the reader is exercising a skill developed over a lifetime, through the daily experience of rhythmic movement in the actions of the body, in the use of language, and in the enjoyment of every level of sophistication of the arts of dance, music, and verse itself. That skill is intimately bound up with the perception of time, and whatever blind alleys the temporal tradition has wandered into, it has been true at least to that fundamental insight.

Notes

1. See Attridge (1974) for an account of the Elizabethan understanding of Latin metre, and its consequences in English literary practice.
2. See the studies of eighteenth-century prosody by Culler (1948) and Fussell (1954).
3. Among the more influential works published this century to have stated and built on the classical theory have been: Saintsbury (1906–10, 1910), Lascelles Abercrombie (1923), Hamer (1930), Brooks & Warren (1938), Thompson (1961), Gross (1964), Nabokov (1964), Shapiro & Beum (1965), Malof (1970), and Fussell (1979). Two frequently-cited articles in defence of the classical approach are those by Wimsatt & Beardsley (1959) and C. S. Lewis (1960). Countless studies of English poetry and poets make use of or imply the classical approach.
4. See, for instance, Roger Fowler (1966a, 1966b, 1968); and the further discussion in 4.6 below.
5. See, in particular, the discussions of Latin metre by W. S. Allen (1964, 1965, 1969, 1973) and Zirin (1970); a summary of current views is given in Attridge (1974, Ch. 1).
6. The other 1595 edition of this work, *The Defence of Poesie*, gives 'words and time', as does the standard modern text, but 'tune' makes the point clearer.
7. Among the more noteworthy contributions to the tradition of temporal analysis since Steele have been: Patmore (1857), Lanier (1880), Ruskin (1880), Omond (1921), Egerton Smith (1923), Thomson (1923), Croll (1929), Stewart (1930), Hendren (1936, 1959), and Classe (1939). A justification of the temporal approach within the framework of aesthetics is given by Prall (1929, Ch. 9; 1936, Ch. 4) and Perry (1965), and useful essays employing this approach have been written by Sapir (1921), Croll (1923), Baker (1960), Schwarz (1962), Calvin Brown (1965), Leech (1969, Ch. 7), and Stevenson (1970). An instructive account of the whole tradition is given by Hollander (1956); see also the summaries in Barkas (1934), Lightfoot (1970), and Sumera (1970).
8. See Jones (1960, Ch. 28), David Abercrombie (1964b), Halliday (1967), and Albrow (1968).
9. See, for example, Warner Brown (1908), Verrier (1909), Snell (1918–19), Scripture (1921), Schramm (1934), Classe (1939), Chatman (1956a), Shen & Peterson (1962), Bolinger (1965), Uldall (1971), Dillon (1976), and Funkhouser (1979); and the summaries by Jacob (1918, Ch. 10), Chatman (1965, Ch. 4), Lehiste (1977), and Adams (1979, Part I).

Chapter 2

Linguistic approaches

In the comprehensive collection of metrical studies which we have imagined burdening the shelves of some large library, two relatively short periods would be noteworthy for the space they demand: the decades around the beginning of the present century, which produced voluminous contributions to the two traditions we have discussed, and the years since about 1960, which have seen a flood of metrical investigation that shows no sign of abating. The latter proliferation is, of course, part of a general phenomenon in academic publishing, but it does not seem to be mere coincidence that during the same period there has been a huge expansion in a closely related discipline, linguistic science. In 1957, the publication of Chomsky's *Syntactic Structures*, like the launching of the first orbital satellite in the same year, opened up new realms for exploration, and though both events were signs of much broader intellectual advances in their respective fields, they deserve the symbolic status they have acquired. Inevitably, and quite properly, progress in linguistic theory has deeply influenced the study of the literary uses of language, and the effects have been felt nowhere more strongly than in the investigation of metre, whether manifested in defiant rejection or in rapturous embrace. Although the connection between the two realms has always existed, and has often proved profitable to both,[1] the explosion in linguistic theory produced by Chomsky's first book means that the student of prosody stands to lose more than ever by ignoring the sister discipline.

Linguistic theory has permeated metrical analysis in so many ways that the simplification involved in summarising its influence is even more gross than that which was needed to characterise the two main traditional approaches. Nevertheless, it will serve the purpose of introducing a complex subject, and will prepare the ground for arguments later in this study, if we once more pick out two threads from the intricate web that confronts us, though they will be more in the nature of specimens than generalisations. The first of these in fact takes us back to a linguistic approach which had its heyday prior to the Chomskyan revolution, though its main influence on metrical studies was delayed, and has outlived its pre-eminence within its own domain; it is as if the heightened status of linguistics as an intellectual discipline has opened the eyes of literary prosodists, but all they have seen, or been willing to see, are the relatively circumscribed linguistic approaches which prevailed before that status was achieved. Meanwhile, however, linguists themselves have not been slow to incorporate metrical study as part of their own intellectual enterprise, both as a means of investigating certain characteristics of language and as a subject in its own right, and the second section of this chapter will focus on some examples of metrical analysis made within the framework of contemporary linguistic theory. One other approach should be mentioned here, as a product of the application of quantitative methods to metrical study: the statistical analysis of bodies of verse. This tradition, largely Russian in origin, has produced some valuable information about those properties of English verse amenable to numerical description, which we shall make use of in Part Three (see the studies by Bailey, 1975b, and Tarlinskaja, 1976; and the collection of essays translated by G. S. Smith, 1980). The drawback of this approach, however, is that it is only as strong as the metrical theory from which it derives its categories, and this has tended to be of a strongly traditional cast.

2.1 THE PHONEMIC APPROACH

At the heart of modern linguistics lies the observation that what matters in any given language is not the multitude of physical distinctions between the actual sounds produced by individual speakers, but the very limited set of distinctions that constitute that language's phonological *system*, and the discrepancy we have already noted between instrumentally measurable sounds and perceived speech is one aspect of this wider insight. It finds its most telling expression in the theory of the *phoneme*, which has been one of the most powerfully suggestive linguistic concepts to have emerged this century, even if its status as an element in the language system has been questioned in recent years. Although a spoken utterance is physically a complex sonic continuum, which even the most finely detailed phonetic transcription cannot fully represent, it is interpreted by someone who knows the language as a sequence of familiar units of sound, selected from the small stock which that language makes use of. These units are the phonemes of the language, each of which may correspond to a range of physical sounds, but which acquires its identity by being in clear contrast to each of the other phonemes in the system. Alphabets constitute attempts to formalise and represent graphically the phonemes of a language, but are strongly affected by historical changes in pronunciation and by external factors; the list of phonemes produced by a modern linguist for English will bear an obvious resemblance to the English alphabet, but will not correspond exactly to it. The two sounds which the letter *c* can represent will be shown as different phonemes, usually indicated by the symbols / k / and / s / (though any agreed symbols would serve); while the first of these phonemes is also indicated by the letters *k* and *ck* in English spelling. On the other hand, a phonemic transcription will ignore the physical differences between the sounds represented by the letter *l* in *leaf* and *feel* respectively, which would be reflected in a detailed phonetic description, since they are irrelevant to the comprehension of English. Moreover, two speakers of English may have very different modes of speech, owing to differences in age, sex, physical endowments, regional and class background, even personality, but be able to understand one another without difficulty because they are using the same (or almost the same) set of phonemes.

In the 1940s and 1950s, the dominant school of American linguistics, often called 'Bloomfieldian' after one of its most prominent members, used the phonemic principle as the cornerstone of its linguistic enterprise, which was in large part the description of the languages of the world (and, for obvious reasons, the languages of North America in particular). When faced with a new language, they saw one of their major tasks as the enumeration of its phonemes, and much energy and ingenuity was devoted to the development of procedures enabling the linguist to deduce the phonemic structure of an unfamiliar language from a collection of utterances. Other labels attached to this school reflect its fundamental aims: 'descriptive', 'structuralist', and 'taxonomic' – the last applied by later linguists with a pejorative intention. It was a noteworthy chapter in the development of linguistics, but its methods have been superseded by those of more recent approaches, and it would not be necessary to introduce it here were it not that it has had a disproportionate influence on metrical studies.[2]

The concept of the phoneme, with its emphasis on the way the speaker of a language uses his acquired knowledge to make sense of a barrage of information, is a valuable one for the student of metre; for example, it helps one to distinguish between what Roman Jakobson (1960, pp. 364–6) has called *delivery instances*, the actual readings of a line on particular occasions, and *verse instance*, the metrical structure which underlies all readings of the line; and between verse instances and *verse design*, the metrical scheme that underlies all the lines in a particular metre. But at the level of specific linguistic detail, it was the extension of the phonemic principle to other features of the language which proved particularly attractive to metrists; and by far the most influential work in this field was *An Outline of English Structure* by George L. Trager and Henry Lee Smith (1951). In their attempt at a comprehensive and detailed description of spoken English, Trager and Smith propose several *suprasegmental phonemes*; that is, phonemes which are not themselves segments in the chain of sounds that make up the utterance, but features of pronunciation which affect these segments in a systematic way. They include pitch, juncture (the transitions between segments), and, most important for metrical study, stress. In dealing with stress, which they regard as a matter of loudness, the question that most concerns them is, 'How many significantly different degrees of stress are there in the system of English sounds?', and they conclude that it is necessary to postulate four distinct degrees to account for the stress contours which English speakers use. To these they allot four symbols: *primary* ´, *secondary* ˆ, *tertiary* ˋ, and *weak* ˇ. Every syllable in any English utterance, they claim, has one of these degrees of stress, determined by the phonological structure of the language. One of their examples, representing a normal pronunciation, will indicate the kind of stress contour which results from this theory:

Hôw dŏ thèy stúdŷ, nôw wè've gôt their bóoks?   (p. 44)

We need not take the Trager–Smith description any further; it will be evident already that a metrist who finds classical prosody, with only two categories of syllable, severely limited, and musical notation too impressionistic and too wedded to the notion of temporal relationships, might well be tempted by this system, apparently firm in its theoretical basis, objective in its application, and sensitive to the real fluctuations of the voice.

Most commonly, Trager–Smith analysis is used by prosodists in conjunction with classical prosody in order to show that an underlying metrical pattern, based on only two types of syllable, is in productive tension with the real variations of the voice, based on four types. Various attempts to systematise the relationship have been made, though no agreed correlation has been established; one proposition is that primary and weak stresses always function as metrical stresses and nonstresses respectively, while under certain circumstances tertiary stresses can be 'promoted' to function as metrical stresses, and secondary stresses 'demoted' to nonstresses. This ignores the fact that even weak stresses can function as metrical beats, and primary stresses can be demoted; but it does point the way to a fuller understanding of metrical tension than is provided by theories of substitution or attempts to relate metrical patterns to the minute variations recorded by the spectrograph. Unfortunately, however, a combination of classical and phonemic approaches can compound the errors of both. We noted in Chapter 1 that some prosodists using the classical approach invest the foot-boundary with such substance that they claim stress contrasts are not perceptible across it; when this doctrine is applied to lines analysed in terms of stress phonemes, it becomes even more misleading. An instructive example is the influential essay by Wimsatt and Beardsley (1959), which, although it takes a stand against the invasion of metrics by Trager–Smith phonology, uses the concept of graduated stress to argue that iambic feet have a real existence. For instance, the authors cite a line of Shelley's with indications of stress that can be converted to Trager–Smith notation as follows (pp. 593–4):

(1) Hail | to thee, | blithe Spi rit!

They then argue, in effect, that 'to thee' and 'blithe Spirit' are perceived as iambic feet because they contain contrasts between weak and tertiary stress in the first case, and secondary and primary in the second, and that the reader ignores the marked increase in stress between 'thee' and 'blithe' because it occurs over a foot-boundary. The prosodic cart seems to have got in front of the rhythmic horse here; metrical markings should reflect our perception of the movement of language and not determine it. Even a traditional classical scansion, innocent of phonemes and degrees of stress, is capable of reflecting the main stresses of this three-beat line more clearly, by means of an 'inverted foot' between two trochaic feet:

$$\acute{}\overset{\text{x}}{|}\quad\overset{\text{x}}{}\overset{\acute{}}{|}\quad\overset{/\text{x}}{|}$$

(*1*) Hail to| thee, blithe| Spirit!|

In most stanzas of the poem, at least two of the five lines begin with a stress and end with a nonstress, a pattern which lends itself, *pace* Wimsatt and Beardsley, to trochaic scansion.

This is by no means the most extreme instance of phonological theory imposing on aural reality, however. That honour probably goes to metrical analyses arising from another prosodic principle derived from Trager and Smith, stated as follows by the latter: 'When two instances of the same stress phoneme occur on syllables immediately following each other, the occurrence of the second in the sequence will be phonetically more "prominent" than the first' (introductory chapter to Epstein and Hawkes, 1959, p. 7). Not only is this 'fact of phonetics' unsupported by any evidence; it undermines what is valuable in the phonemic principle by implying that we respond to the rhythms of speech not at the level of language structure but at the surface, 'allophonic', level of mere sound. Nevertheless, it allows Smith to 'prove' in another article (1959) that all English verse is predominantly iambic, and gives Epstein and Hawkes (1959) the opportunity of demonstrating, in all seriousness, that there are 6,236 types of iambic foot in English. The old dilemma posed within the classical approach by 'ambiguous lines' is given a new sophistication by this theory, and a laborious analysis of Shakespeare's 'Full fathom five' enables the authors to pronounce that it is indisputably iambic. Since they have in effect devised their own definition of 'iambic verse', their conclusion has little relevance to anything outside their study; it certainly has no bearing on the fact that of the song's seven lines and implied eighth line of refrain, all but the first are examples of what the classical tradition normally regards as trochaic, that is, they begin on the metrical beat. Once again, the experience of the reader has been brushed aside in the imposition of a grid of theory on the syllables of the language.

But the failings of this approach are more fundamental (and more instructive) than the fact that it permits of such excesses; they lie in the nature of the linguistic traditions from which it derives. To conceive of the task of metrical theory as the exhaustive description of the lines of English verse, in the same way that the Bloomfieldian school saw the task of linguistics as the description of a corpus of utterances, is to offer little in the way of an explanation of metre and its poetic effects, and such an analysis can become meaningless when the descriptions only make sense in terms of the descriptive categories invented by the analyst. If one wishes to categorise and classify the lines of English verse, there are more adequate methods of linguistic description now available than the Trager–Smith system; but one needs to ask first if there are not more interesting and important tasks than this waiting to be undertaken in the field of metrical study.

2.2 THE GENERATIVE APPROACH

While literary critics with an interest in metre were absorbing (or reacting against) the phonemic theories of the Bloomfieldian linguists, the theories themselves were being strongly challenged by phonologists using the linguistic model put forward by Chomsky in 1957. It was Chomsky himself who, together with Morris Halle, made the most influential contribution to the study of English phonology within the new framework: their *Sound Pattern of English*, published in 1968, demonstrated the superficiality of a purely phonemic analysis of the sounds of language, and offered a fuller and more illuminating alternative. Before the publication of this work, one of its authors, Morris Halle, had co-operated with Samuel Jay Keyser to produce an account of Chaucer's iambic pentameter (Halle and Keyser, 1966) which marked the founding of a new school of metrical theory, soon to become the dominant linguistic approach to verse form in English, and the most rapidly proliferating of all branches of metrical theory.[3] Just as Chomsky had initiated his linguistic revolution by demonstrating the inadequacy of the theories then current, so many linguists writing on metre, catching something of his tone, dismissed the traditional approaches (or what they took to be representative examples of traditional approaches) and claimed to be putting forward for the first time theories which offered real insights into the nature of metrical form. Although these writers vary in the degree to which they make explicit reference to Chomsky's work, they all breathe the air of the new country he opened up, and to understand the kinds of dissatisfaction they express with earlier prosodic studies, and the alternative proposals they make, we need to have some notion of the fundamental shifts effected by Chomsky himself in linguistic theory.

As so often in intellectual revolutions, the heart of the change lay not merely in new answers, but in new questions. Chomsky argued that the real challenge to linguistic theory is offered not by the fact that a collection of utterances in a given language shows certain regularities capable of description, but that a native speaker's knowledge of his language goes beyond any such limited corpus: he can without difficulty produce and understand sentences which may never have been uttered before, and he can say of any utterance whether or not it is an acceptable or meaningful sentence in his language. What is more, every child rapidly and effortlessly acquires this ability on the basis of exposure to only a limited and fragmentary selection of linguistic specimens. Chomsky calls the implicit knowledge acquired by the child, the knowledge which underlies our use of language, *competence*, and he contrasts this with the actual process of speaking and understanding, which he calls *performance*. The main object of the linguist's attention is not the latter, the utterances produced on specific occasions and the physiological processes associated with them, but the former, the 'mental reality' underlying all speech. The linguist attempts to write a *grammar*, which is not merely a description of what is said in the language, but a formalisation, in terms of *rules*, of the knowledge which every speaker of that language possesses. These rules do not represent any process in the brain during the production or comprehension of language, but the underlying knowledge, the mental regularities and consistencies, upon which those processes are based. They specify in a highly formal and abstract manner all the possible ways in which the fundamental units of the language may be arranged in acceptable syntactic formations, and their output is therefore an indefinitely large set of utterances, all of which will be grammatical sentences of the language, and which will omit no possible grammatical sentence. The rules are thus said to *generate* the sentences of the language; in other words, any utterance which can be accounted for by the rules is grammatical, and any utterance which cannot be accounted for is ungrammatical. In generating a sentence the rules provide a structural description of it, and they may also indicate the ways in which an ungrammatical utterance deviates from grammatical correctness. The aim is a completely *explicit* account of the native speaker's knowledge of his language, which could be understood and applied by someone with no familiarity with the language at all (or, for that matter, by a powerful enough computer). The different varieties of grammar that have been proposed to achieve these perhaps impossibly ambitious ends are not our concern; what is important is the way in which linguistic theories based on these principles attempt to go beyond description to some kind of explanation, and that they do this by focusing on the *capacities* of the native speaker, rather than on the utterances he makes. This means approaching language at a level of abstraction even greater than that entailed by the phonemic approach, and leaving the actual sounds we utter to the very last stage in an elaborate analytical structure.

This new conception of the linguist's task has transformed all areas of linguistic theory, and phonology is no exception. An example from this branch of linguistics will illustrate the general shift in approach. On encountering a new word, let us say Lewis Carroll's *borogove*, Trager and Smith would ask how it is pronounced, and assign stress symbols accordingly: *bórŏgòve*. Chomsky and Halle, however, ask how it is that we are able to pronounce a word we have never seen before, and reply that we unconsciously apply to it the same rules which we apply to all the English words we use. A simplified outline of their analysis (which, it must be remembered, is *not* a description of any processes the brain might actually employ) would run something like this: a basic rule, which they call the Main Stress Rule, assigns primary stress to the final syllable because it contains a diphthong (indicated, of course, by a spelling convention); another rule, the Alternating Stress Rule, shifts the primary stress to the initial syllable, and at the same time weakens the final stress to a secondary; and lastly the Stress Adjustment Rule makes the final stress tertiary. The result is a stress contour which is indicated as *bŏrogŏve*. It is, of course, only because Carroll's coinage obeys the rules for English word formation that the stress rules can apply to it, but this is only another way of saying that we are able to pronounce it; had the word been *rbooovge* another branch of our linguistic competence would have excluded it immediately from the class of possible English words. When we encounter a new word in print, therefore, we use our phonological competence – our 'knowledge' of the stress rules – to derive its pronunciation from its spelling; we also constantly draw on that competence to speak, and Chomsky and Halle argue that we make full use of it in listening to speech as well: we will, for instance, tend to perceive the correct stress contours of utterances in our language even if they are not fully manifested in the sounds we hear. This feature of our perception of language, an extension of the phonemic principle and part of a much wider psychological phenomenon, is of fundamental importance in all responses to speech sounds, including, as we shall see, those of poetry.

Generative linguistics offers a promising model to the student of metre who is dissatisfied with the limited achievements of both the traditional approaches and the studies influenced by the phonemic approach of descriptive linguistics. But it also offers, in theories of generative phonology, specific and detailed accounts of that area of language most germane to metrical study: its patterns of stress. These two ways of drawing on recent linguistic theory are quite separate: it is perfectly possible to find the general theoretical model of linguistic competence and generative rules a fruitful one while rejecting the particular accounts of English stress offered by generative phonology; or one might, on the contrary, be doubtful about the validity of the general theory in its application to metre, but make use of some of the specific information about stress contours provided by generative phonologists. However, the phonological rules of English are at present the subject of much discussion, which will no doubt continue for an appreciable time, and it would therefore be premature to build a metrical theory on the fine detail of any one school of generative phonology, quite apart from the fact that it would certainly involve us in a complex and highly technical set of arguments. I am not, therefore, proposing to examine the competing rules of English stress that have been put forward, nor to discuss at any length the use made in metrical theories of these rules. Instead, I shall concentrate on the other avenue of approach, and examine the possibility of using the fundamental insights of generative linguistics as a model for metrical analysis, picking out three of the most important examples from the growing accumulation of such studies.

The metrical theory initially put forward by Halle and Keyser in 1966 has subsequently been modified and expanded, both by its authors and by others; what follows is only a bare outline of their account and of the assumptions on which it rests. Just as the native speaker of English can judge between grammatical and ungrammatical sentences of the language without being conscious of the rules which enable him to do this, so the experienced reader of English poetry can judge lines of verse to be acceptable or unacceptable examples of a particular metre without having a metrical theory at his fingertips. And just as the linguist tries to make explicit the rules which underlie the native speaker's judgements, so the generative metrist sees his task as formulating the rules which make judgements of metricality possible. The clues that lead to these rules do not lie in what the reader *thinks* he has imbibed, but in the actual judgements he makes of particular lines.

The rules should reflect all the consistent features of such judgements, and if two or more features can be accounted for by one rule, that rule has captured a significant generalisation, and may be a pointer to the basic principles on which metrical form rests. Thus the formulated rules for, say, iambic pentameter should be capable of generating all the lines which readers would accept as iambic pentameters without generating any lines which would not be accepted; and in so doing they should exhibit the metrical structure of the acceptable lines, as well as the ways in which the unacceptable lines deviate from metricality. Or, if we limit the task to a single author, we might attempt to formulate the rules of, say, Chaucer's iambic pentameter, which, let it be noted, would generate not only all Chaucer's iambic pentameters, but also all those pentameters which a reader thoroughly familiar with Chaucer would accept as being 'Chaucerian'. Traditional approaches to metre, which are confined largely to the description of metrical forms, cannot satisfy these demands: any line, however unacceptable to the ear, can be scanned as a succession of classical feet or musical measures.

Halle and Keyser approach this formidable task by proposing two components in the set of rules for any metrical form: an *abstract metrical pattern*, and *correspondence rules* (also called *mapping rules* or *realisation rules*) which relate that pattern to the stress contours of particular stretches of language. (This is, of course, a restatement of the familiar notion of a simple metrical base and a more complex pattern of stresses in the line of verse itself.) The metrical form most exhaustively analysed in these terms has been the iambic pentameter, and the following are the rules for that metre proposed by Halle and Keyser in the 1971 version of their theory (1971a, p. 169):

(a) ABSTRACT METRICAL PATTERN
(W)*S WS WS WS WS (X)(X)
where elements enclosed in parentheses may be omitted and where each X position may be occupied only by an unstressed syllable

(b) CORRESPONDENCE RULES
(i) A position (S, W, or X) corresponds to a single syllable
OR
to a sonorant sequence incorporating at most two vowels (immediately adjoining or separated by a sonorant consonant)

DEFINITION: When a fully stressed syllable occurs between

two unstressed syllables in the same syntactic constituent within a line of verse, this syllable is called a 'stress maximum'

(ii) Fully stressed syllables occur in S positions only and in all S positions

OR

Fully stressed syllables occur in S positions only but not in all S positions

OR

Stress maxima occur in S positions only but not in all S positions

The 'abstract metrical pattern' requires no comment, except to note that S and W stand for 'strong' and 'weak', and that the asterisk indicates an optional element which cannot be omitted without increasing the metrical complexity of the line. The first correspondence rule specifies the number of syllables which may occupy any one position in the metrical pattern, and constitutes a claim that what the classical approach calls 'trisyllabic substitution', the replacement of an expected single syllable by two, can occur only when the syllables in question meet certain phonetic criteria: their vowels must either be adjacent or be separated by / l /, / r /, / m /, or / n /. The definition that follows is in preparation for the second correspondence rule, which presents three possible ways in which the S positions in the line can be filled. The first two are stated in terms of 'fully stressed syllables', which consist for the most part of the main stresses of nouns, verbs, adjectives, and adverbs, and the third in terms of the previously defined 'stress maxima'.

These rules can be applied to any sequence of syllables and, it is argued, will distinguish between those which constitute acceptable iambic pentameters and those which do not. Moreover, they enable any acceptable line to be classified as a more or less complex example of the basic metre, both in terms of the abstract metrical pattern, where the omission of the first syllable increases complexity, and in terms of the correspondence rules, where the later the option that has to be invoked in order to account for the line, the more complex it is. Thus a line which uses only the first alternative of rule (i) is less complex than one which contains extra syllables in accordance with the second alternative. Similarly, the options of (ii) yield increasingly complex pentameters, beginning with the relatively rare type in which fully stressed syllables alternate throughout with unstressed syllables. The second option accounts for lines in which no stresses fall in weak positions, but one or more strong positions, where we expect stresses, are occupied by syllables that are not fully stressed. The third alternative requires a little more elucidation, as it involves the principle of the 'stress maximum', upon which Halle and Keyser lay great emphasis. This principle allows a line to be accepted as metrical even when one or more stressed syllables occur in weak positions, provided that they are not stress maxima: that is, provided that they are adjacent to another stress or to a syntactic break, or they fall at the beginning or end of the line. Such stresses are regarded as being 'neutralised' and as having no effect on the metrical acceptability of the line. Thus the following line fails to satisfy the first two alternatives of correspondence rule (ii) because it has an unstressed syllable in strong position and two fully stressed syllables in weak positions, but it does count as a pentameter of a complex type because the only stress maximum, on 'God', occurs in a strong position as required by the third alternative:

(2) Batter my heart, three-personed God, for you
     w   s   w s   w   s w   s   w s

The stressed syllables which fall in the first and third weak positions are not stress maxima, being neutralised in one case by the adjacent line-opening and in the other by the adjacent stresses and syntactic boundary. Halle and Keyser give the following example of a sequence of words which, though it has an appropriate number of syllables, cannot be accounted for by the rules, and hence is unmetrical (p. 171):

[3] Ode to the West Wind by Percy Bysshe Shelley
     w   s w s   w   s w s w   s w

The first syllable of 'Percy' constitutes a stress maximum, and it falls in a weak position, so even the third alternative of correspondence rule (ii) is not satisfied. (In examples illustrating generative theories, I underline any position in which the rules are contravened.)

The larger part of the set of rules proposed by Halle and Keyser is different from the traditional account of the iambic pentameter only in format and in the omission of foot-divisions; but the concept of the stress maximum is an original one, and is offered as a principle which captures a significant generalisation, and is therefore more explanatory than traditional accounts of the same phenomena. The third alternative of rule (ii) combines in one statement what traditional prosody regards as quite separate 'deviations' or 'licences' in iambic verse: the occurrence of inverted feet (or trochees), and the substitution of spondees for iambs. The stress maximum principle takes care of both of these, because in neither case is the 'deviant' stress a stress maximum, that is, a stress between two unstressed syllables. (At the same time, the second alternative allows nonstresses to occur in strong positions, thus accounting for pyrrhic substitutions.) If this principle does indeed allow the rules to generate all the stress patterns of acceptable iambic pentameters and only those stress patterns, it constitutes an important advance in metrical understanding; but it must, of course, be tested. One of the strengths of the generative approach to metre is that it offers a clear means of assessing the adequacy of any suggested set of rules: if counter-examples can be produced, whether taken from the verse tradition or invented for the purpose, to show that the rules fail to generate certain clearly acceptable types of line, or that they generate certain types of clearly unacceptable line, they cannot be said to capture the metrical organisation which readers intuitively recognise, in just the same way that syntactic rules must be found wanting if they fail to generate some acceptable types of sentence, or if they generate 'sentences' which would not be accepted as grammatical.

If we subject the Halle–Keyser principle of the stress maximum, and the rule which embodies it, to this kind of test, we find that, far from being an accurate reflection of the metrical knowledge that underlies particular judgements, it categorises as acceptable lines which a reader with any sensitivity to metre would immediately reject. A slight rewriting will convert the example of an unmetrical line given by Halle and Keyser to a line with no stress maxima, and hence, in terms of their theory, to an acceptable pentameter, though it does not strike the ear as any more regular:

[3a] Ode to the West Wind by James Elroy Flecker
    w   s   w   s   w   s w   s   w   s   w

Every stress in weak position is now neutralised by an adjacent line-boundary or stress. Notice, too, that such a line would be regarded as an acceptable example of *any* metre which allows lines of eleven syllables, since the only way a line can be finally rejected as a realisation of an abstract metrical pattern is if stress maxima occur in weak positions, and we have removed all the stress maxima. We could, therefore, exchange strong and weak positions and the line would still pass muster as a realisation, albeit a complex one, of the opposite metrical pattern. What is more, the rules make it very easy to avoid stress maxima: one merely has to keep stresses in pairs or at the extremities of lines:

[4] John is dead drunk and weeps tears from red eyes
    w   s   w   s   w   s   w   s   w   s

Halle and Keyser would accept this as an iambic (or for that matter trochaic) pentameter, whereas the only rhythmic context in which the ordinary reader of verse might find it tolerable is that of four-beat triple metre. Furthermore, the exclusion of stress patterns created by minor category words such as prepositions means that a line like the following, which to most readers would be a paradigmatic iambic pentameter, is regarded as having no metrical structure (or, what amounts to the same thing, *any* metrical structure):

(5) Before, behind, between, above, below

The neutralisation of stress maxima next to syntactic boundaries creates further anomalies, which I shall illustrate later in this chapter.

But the rules are not only too tolerant in what they accept; they are also too strict in some of the lines they exclude. One which Halle and Keyser quote is the following opening of a sonnet by Keats:

(6) How many bards gild the lapses of time!
    w   s w s   w   s <u>w</u> s w s

They try to explain the occurrence of this 'unmetrical' line by arguing that 'lapses of time' is a reference to unacceptable metres, and that the line therefore enacts its meaning. As the rest of the poem makes clear, the phrase refers in fact to the passage of the centuries, and the line, though exhibiting a high degree of deviation from the metrical norm, is recognisable as an iambic pentameter – that is to say, it has five clear beats, and the omission of the unstressed syllable after 'bards' is made good in 'lapses of'; or, in terms of feet, the line has inversions in both the third and fourth feet (and perhaps the first, as Halle and Keyser suggest). Such lines are not uncommon in certain styles of metre (see below, p. 185).

The metrical rule embodying the stress maximum principle fails, therefore, when put to the type of test which the generative approach invites; that the principle has been uncritically accepted in many recent studies of metre in spite of its inadequacy is perhaps a testimony to the widely-felt desire for a simple key to unlock the secret chambers of prosody.[4] While the failure of this particular set of rules suggests certain dangers inherent in the generative approach to metre, it does not discredit the whole endeavour. The proposals put forward by Halle and Keyser, however unsatisfactory in themselves, highlight some of the problems to be overcome in a satisfactory theory of metre, and clear the way for further attempts at an adequate formulation of the rules. Before we attempt to assess the generative approach as a whole, we shall look briefly at two such alternative proposals.

The first of these was put forward by Karl Magnuson and Frank G. Ryder (1970, 1971) as a counter-theory to that of Halle and Keyser. It also regards the metrical pattern as a sequence of weak and strong positions, and attempts to formulate rules which define the types of syllable possible in these positions. (I have slightly altered the terminology of the later theories I discuss in order to facilitate comparison.) But Magnuson and Ryder expose some of the weaknesses of the Halle–Keyser rules, and propose a different set of linguistic properties on which to base the rules; instead of a series of syllabic classifications progressing from unstressed syllables to stressed syllables to stress maxima, they make use of a set of binary features which, they claim, determine the degree of acceptability of a syllable in a weak or strong position. An example of such a feature is, of course, stress, which they indicate as [+ST] for a stressed syllable and [−ST] for an unstressed syllable. A syllable classed as [+ST] is said to be *affirming* when it occurs in strong position, because it reinforces the metre, and *nonaffirming* in weak position, because it contradicts it; and the converse is true for [−ST]. As in all generative accounts of metre, the aim is to deduce rules which will capture as many generalisations about the positioning of syllables as possible; in effect, this entails a claim that the shorter and simpler the set of rules, the more likely they are to constitute a correct account of the principles underlying the metrical diversity of English verse.

In order to illustrate the kinds of rule used in this approach, I shall sketch the account given by Chisholm (1977) as a modification of the somewhat more complicated rules proposed by the original authors.

Chisholm makes use of three features in his rules; besides [+ST] and [−ST], he classifies syllables as [+WO] ('plus word-onset') or [−WO] ('minus word-onset'), that is, occurring at the beginning of the word or occurring elsewhere in the word; and [+PT] ('plus phrase-terminal') or [−PT] ('minus phrase-terminal'), that is, occurring at the end of the syntactic phrase or occurring elsewhere in the phrase. To propose these particular features within the theory is, of course, to claim that they play a part in determining whether a syllable is affirming or nonaffirming in a given position, or, to put it more generally, that both word-divisions and syntactic boundaries have a role in metrical structure. The status of the former is one of the trickiest problems of English metrics; Halle and Keyser ignore word-boundaries, while the theory that we shall consider next places a strong emphasis on them. Syntactic boundaries, on the other hand, play a part in all generative theories of metre, though they have no structural role in traditional foot-prosody.

Chisholm suggests three types of rule making use of these features. Firstly, he postulates a *prosodic transformation rule*, whose function is to convert the linguistically-defined categories of the language into those categories which are distinctive in metre; this is a recognition of the fact that metre does not use all the features of the language in all their diversity. Secondly, there is a *base rule*: this is the fundamental metrical rule, stating the constraints which govern the placing of syllables in the weak and strong positions of the line. Finally, Chisholm suggests two *positional rules*, which reflect the fact that not every position in the line accommodates syllables in the same way. Once again, the iambic pentameter is the main focus of attention, and Chisholm's rules are framed by means of the formal conventions of generative phonology: each set of square brackets represents a syllable possessing the features indicated within those brackets, and the rule constitutes a statement that the syllable to the left of the arrow must have (or, in the prosodic transformation rule, is given) the feature to the right of the arrow, when it occurs in the environment shown after the slash:

1. Prosodic Transformation Rule:
   $[+WO, -PT] \rightarrow [-ST] / - [+ST, +WO]$
2. Base Rule:
   $[F] \rightarrow [-ST] / x [-PT] -$

3. Positional Rules:
   a. $[F] \rightarrow [+ST] /$ ₃,₉ $[+ST]$ —
   b. ₁₁ $[F] \rightarrow [-ST]$ (p. 150)

Rule 1 states that any syllable which is word-initial and not phrase-terminal, and which occurs before a syllable which is stressed and also word-initial, is regarded, for the purposes of the metre, as unstressed. Or, more simply, a stressed monosyllabic word before another stressed syllable within the same phrase loses its stress. The rule depends, of course, on the prior analysis of the language into stressed and unstressed syllables, and into syntactic phrases, a far from automatic process, but one which need not be discussed here. Some examples will be more useful: in the phrase *the green tree*, 'green' is changed from $[+ST]$ to $[-ST]$; in *the man spoke*, however, both stressed syllables retain their stress, since they occur, according to standard generative syntactic theory, in different phrases, a Noun Phrase and a Verb Phrase. In *swaying tree* and *renowned tree*, of course, the rule does not apply since in the first of these the stresses are not adjacent, and in neither is the first word a monosyllable.

The base rule states that for a line to be metrical any syllable (represented by $[F]$) must be unstressed if it occurs after a syllable in strong position (shown by x) that is not the final syllable of a phrase. Or, looking at it the other way round, a stressed syllable can occur in a weak position only if it constitutes the beginning of a new phrase. Thus the following sequences are regarded as acceptable iambic pentameters:

> [7] He struck at the tall cook with heavy blows
>   w   s   w   s w   s   w   s w   s

> [8] The weeping man fell to his knees in pain
>   w   s w   s   w s w   s w   s

In [7], 'tall' loses its stress by the prosodic transformation rule, and so does not contravene the base rule; and in [8], the stressed syllable which occurs in weak position, 'fell', is the start of a new phrase, and is therefore permissible. But the base rule classes the following sequences as unmetrical:

> [9] He struck the amazed cook with heavy blows
>   w   s   w s w   s   w   s w   s

$$\overset{/}{\text{They}} \underset{w}{} \overset{}{\underset{s}{\text{sent}}} \overset{/}{\underset{w}{\text{the}}} \overset{/}{\underset{s}{\text{huge}}} \overset{}{\underset{w}{\text{man}}} \overset{/}{\underset{s}{\text{to}}} \overset{}{\underset{w}{\text{his}}} \overset{/}{\underset{s}{\text{knees}}} \overset{}{\underset{w}{\text{in}}} \overset{/}{\underset{s}{\text{pain}}}$$

[10] They sent the huge man to his knees in pain
     w   s   w   s   w   s   w   s   w   s

In the first of these, 'amazed' does not lose its stress as it is not monosyllabic; and in neither is the stressed syllable in a weak position the start of a new phrase. In making these distinctions, Chisholm is aiming at a subtler embodiment of readers' judgements than Halle and Keyser, for whom all these lines would be metrically similar. There is no doubt that the differences are perceptible, though one might wish to question a theory which draws such a sharp line between metrical and unmetrical lines; both [9] and [10] would be acceptable in some metrical styles.

Finally, there are the two positional rules, the first of which reflects a tendency often noted in classical treatments of the iambic pentameter: the avoidance of inversions in the second and fifth foot. It requires that a stress in the third position or the ninth position of the line be followed by another stress, thus creating a 'spondee' instead of the forbidden 'trochee'. The second positional rule prohibits stressed syllables in the eleventh position; that is, feminine endings can only be unstressed. Chisholm claims that his set of rules 'will generate over 97 per cent of the actually occurring iambic pentameter lines in the English tradition [from Shakespeare to the onset of the Romantic period] without generating any unmetrical lines' (p. 150). We shall test this claim in due course.

The other noteworthy contribution to the generative approach to English metre that we shall consider is one made by Paul Kiparsky in 1977, a much-revised version of a theory first put forward in 1975. Besides being an interesting restatement of the basis of English metre, this is the most fully worked-out attempt to map precisely the differences in metrical practice of various English poets (chiefly Wyatt, Shakespeare, Milton, and Pope) by means of generative rules, and has much to offer the student of metrical style. It would be even more misleading than in the case of the other theories to attempt a summary, not only because Kiparsky's account is more complex, but also because it is based on a specific theory of English stress elaborated by Liberman and Prince (1977) as a counter-proposal to Chomsky and Halle's *Sound Pattern of English*. (One aspect of this theory is touched on below in 3.3.) A rather general description of Kiparsky's method, with one or two examples, will have to suffice. Like Chisholm, he makes a distinction between rules which determine what features of the language are relevant to the metre, which he calls *prosodic rules*, and rules which determine the ways in which those features may be arranged, which he terms *metrical rules*. Although the prosodic rules occupy the same place in the theory as Chisholm's prosodic transformation rule, their content is different: the subordination of a monosyllabic stress to a following stress which is the substance of Chisholm's rule is for the most part regarded as a phonological feature of the language itself, and the only examples of prosodic rules which Kiparsky discusses are those which allow certain syllables of English to be discounted for metrical purposes, making it possible, for instance, for words like *poetry*, *victory*, or *envious* to be treated as either trisyllables or disyllables.

Kiparsky's method of analysing a line of verse involves matching its phonological structure, as determined by the procedures suggested by Liberman and Prince, with its metrical structure, the familiar succession of W and S positions with the addition of brackets corresponding to the feet of the classical approach. In most cases there will not be a perfect match, but Kiparsky draws a distinction between permissible and impermissible mismatches, the former rendering the line more complex, but only the latter rendering it unmetrical. Various combinations of mismatches are examined in an attempt to state precisely what departures of the phonological structure from the metrical pattern render a line unmetrical for a particular poet. Like Chisholm, Kiparsky focuses on the conditions under which a stressed syllable may or may not occur in a weak position. To simplify his argument drastically, the most fundamental type of unmetricality in iambic verse is created when the stressed syllable in a weak position is too closely connected with a preceding weak syllable in strong position, either as parts of the same word or, for many poets, as parts of a single phrase which contains only one lexical item (for example, a preposition with a noun or an auxiliary with a verb). Example [9] above is classed as unmetrical for most poets because the stressed syllable in a weak position and the preceding weak syllable are part of the same word, 'amazed'; [10], on the other hand, is more acceptable, because 'huge', though classified as weak, is lexically separate. Kiparsky quotes some examples from Shakespeare which suggest that in this case his rules are more accurate than Chisholm's: the following line from the *Sonnets*, for instance, has a similar structure to [10] and would be unmetrical by Chisholm's rules:

(11) Resembling strong youth in his middle age
      w s   w   s   w   s w   s   w s

To be fair to Chisholm, however, such lines are rare in Shakespeare; the problem is not that these theories place the boundary of metricality at different points, but that both assume that a strict metrical boundary can be fixed at all.

Kiparsky also examines the restrictions on what *follows* a stressed syllable in weak position (although his approach to the subject masks the symmetry of what he is doing, and in some ways his examples are more instructive than his analysis), and finds that it is common for poets to avoid too close a link in this direction as well. Thus by his rules the following line would not be acceptable in Shakespeare's verse:

[11a] Resembling strong anger in middle age
       w s   w   s   w s w   s   w s

Milton's metrical style seems to be distinguished from Shakespeare's, and that of many other poets, by its occasional acceptance of such lines (though the picture is complicated by uncertainties about pronunciation). Kiparsky cites only one example, and regards it as exceptional; but there are a few others, like the following:

(12) By policy, and long process of time
      w s w s w   s   w s   w s

(13) With many a vain exploit, though then renowned
      w   s   w   s   w   s   w   s   w s

As Kiparsky observes, the spanning by a single word of a stress in a weak position and a following nonstress is more common in Milton when the preceding syllable is not stressed; that is, when the pattern is not that of traditional 'inversion', / / x x, but the rarer sequence x / x x:

(14) To the garden of bliss, thy seat prepared
      w s   w   s   w   s   w   s   w s

A possible reason for this will be considered in 8.7, where we shall place the question in a different context from that which Kiparsky provides. All such lines, whether of the type represented by (12) and (13) or by (14), would be regarded as unmetrical by Chisholm.

Kiparsky and Chisholm are, however, agreed that restrictions on stressed syllables in weak positions apply only if the stress in question is not preceded by a phrase-boundary. Shakespeare has many lines like the following, where the stressed syllable in weak position begins a new phrase:

$$
\begin{array}{ccccccccc}
& & & & / & & / & & \\
\text{(15)} & \text{At} & \text{random} & \text{from} & \text{the} & \text{truth} & \text{vainly} & \text{expressed} \\
& \text{w} & \text{s w} & \text{s} & \text{w s} & & \text{w s w} & \text{s}
\end{array}
$$

These restrictions on the positioning of word-boundaries and phrase-boundaries constitute a fact about English metre which demands explanation, but which has largely been ignored in traditional accounts. Unfortunately, Kiparsky tries to explain it by reintroducing the concept of feet into metrical analysis, implying that readers expect word-boundaries and foot-boundaries to coincide, and that when they do not the metre is rendered less regular. His observations have some bearing on the question of metrical style (see the discussion of rising and falling rhythms in 4.6), but we have already noted the problems involved in making feet part of the structural description of English metre (see 1.1). In fact, Kiparsky's examples show that the same kind of prohibition is as common *within* foot-boundaries as across them: many poets avoid lines like [11a] as much as lines like [9]. There is more to be said about the problems posed by word-boundaries, and we shall return to the question in 8.7.

Kiparsky pursues distinctions such as these through the metrical styles of his chosen poets in an illuminating fashion, and it is regrettable that his work will not be easily followed by readers without some familiarity with current linguistic theory. To say this is not merely to lament the gap between the two cultures; by moving straight from the abstract metrical pattern to the complexities of a particular metrical theory, Kiparsky obscures that aspect of metre which concerns the ordinary reader: its creation of satisfying and expressive rhythmic forms. Widely different rhythmic phenomena are treated as identical because they can be captured in a single rule, and so satisfy the demands of generative theory. For instance, Kiparsky (like Chisholm) follows the classical approach in treating as equivalent the occurrence of paired stresses in very different rhythmic contexts, giving the following as instances of the same metrical pattern (p. 208):

(16) But, like a *sad slave*, stay and think of naught

(17) Better becomes the *grey cheeks* of the east

In the first of these, the pair of stresses is followed by a third stress, creating a succession in which only the first and third are felt as beats, while in the second both stresses in the pair take beats (see the discussion of examples (14) and [14a] in Ch. 1). The reader's experience of two distinct kinds of movement here is something that should be reflected in the metrical rules, not masked by them; it is as much a part of metrical 'competence' as judgements about the acceptability of particular lines within a given metre.

Both these further generative theories capture the details of English metrical practice more accurately than any of their predecessors, but once again their rules fail to reach the goal at which a generative approach aims: they may come close to generating all the acceptable lines in this or that variety of English metre; they do not, however, generate *only* such lines. This is, of course, the stiffer test: it is not difficult to devise a rule which will account for every line in a given metre (virtually all iambic pentameters would be covered by a rule that stated, 'A line has 9 to 12 syllables'); it only becomes a meaningful rule if it distinguishes between the lines that occur and those that do not occur. The Halle–Keyser rules, as we saw, allow some lines to be classed as acceptable examples of *any* metre, and this will always be at least a theoretical possibility when metricality is defined in terms of the absence of certain offending features rather than the presence of certain positive features. So although Chisholm and Kiparsky provide a means of demonstrating the unacceptability in most metrical styles of a line like [11a], which has no violations of the stress maximum principle but does have a strong syllable in a weak position that fails to satisfy their criteria, they allow syntactic boundaries the same power to neutralise metrical violations as Halle and Keyser do – if not more, since they accord this power to less marked boundaries. All these theories would regard as acceptable sequences of short phrases which bear very little relation to the rhythm of the iambic pentameter, as in:

[18] Harold – look! Enemies! Beat it! Run home!

I have underlined the weak positions which are filled by stressed syllables, but in every case there is a preceding boundary which allows the mismatching to occur. It is a simple matter to construct pure trochaic lines which are accepted as iambic (or anything else) by these theories (again I underline weak positions with neutralised stresses):

[19] Harold, Charlie, Carol, Sidney, Horace
　　　w s　　w s　w s　w s　　w s

Chisholm's second positional rule does, it is true, rule out the last inversion, but none of these theories indicates that the rhythm of the line runs precisely counter to that implied by the metrical pattern. Dactylics which these theories would accept as iambic are equally easy to invent:

[20] Jittery Caroline, skittery Lil
　　　w s w　s w s　　w s w　s

This exaggerated importance given to syntactic breaks seems to stem in part from a desire to treat such boundaries as equivalent to line-boundaries, so that both can be subsumed under a single rule; but this is a 'generalisation' which has been forced on the material, since the two kinds of boundary play a different role in metrical structure. Again, all these theories are very lax in their treatment of monosyllabic adjectives, which are regarded as metrically innocuous when they occur before another stressed monosyllable. A line like the following is regarded as a fairly simple iambic pentameter instead of, at best, a highly complex one:

[21] Long hours on a hard chair at a broad desk
　　　w　s　w s w　　s w s　w　　s

There are no stress maxima here by the Halle–Keyser rules, and the three adjectives are regarded as weak, and therefore metrically unoffending, by both Chisholm and Kiparsky, the former by his prosodic transformation rule and the latter as a result of the phonological theory he is using.

　The fact that such counter-examples can readily be invented points to a curious feature of the generative approach to metrical analysis: it has not made full use of one of the most distinctive and powerful procedures of the linguistic method from which it is derived. A linguist attempting to formulate the grammar of a language will constantly test the output of his rules against the competence of a native speaker; if he is working on his own language, this will usually, at least in the first instance, be himself. But there has been only limited evidence of this procedure in generative studies of metre, which have tended instead to concentrate on a corpus – Chaucer's iambic pentameters, Shakespeare's *Sonnets*, *Paradise Lost* – and to aim at rules which will generate all the lines in this corpus. What is missing is close scrutiny of the other types of line which will be generated by the proposed rules. The result has been, as we have noted, theories which are far too accommodating in what they accept as metrical. The kind of appeal to the sensitive reader that I am suggesting is, of course, subject to the accusations which are sometimes levelled at the equivalent procedure in linguistics, such as its lack of objectivity and scientific rigour, and I shall discuss some of the problems involved in transferring the notion of 'competence' from linguistics to metrics in Chapter 6, but it remains true that generative metrics has so far failed partly because it has not taken full advantage of one of the major insights of the Chomskyan theory from which it originates.

The process of testing, recasting, and refining the rules of generative metrics will undoubtedly continue, and may eventually produce a set of rules which will meet the objective of generating all the acceptable lines of, say, iambic pentameter within a given metrical style, without generating any unacceptable lines. The qualification, 'within a given metrical style', is important, because rules which would generate all the lines acceptable within Donne's metrical practice would, as Kiparsky's work makes clear, fail to distinguish between acceptable and unacceptable lines in the metrical tradition exemplified by Pope. Another way of saying this is that an experienced reader does not simply make judgements of the type, 'this is an acceptable iambic pentameter', but 'this line would be out of place in Wordsworth's poetry but not in Yeats's'. The rules should also reflect the reader's awareness of varying degrees of complexity or tension in the line, which might be the same as the scale along which poets can be ranged, from the freedom of Donne to the strictness of Pope, but might show interesting differences. The process of arriving at such rules is likely to be a prolonged one, if only because their correct formulation depends on the correct formulation of the rules of English phonology. Nor will they be simple rules; there is no reason to suppose that the capacity possessed by readers of English verse is explicable in terms of one or two general principles, any more than one can suppose that the apparently natural and effortless use of language is the result of a few elementary grammatical rules. One of the achievements of generative linguistics is to have revealed just how complex is the system of language we learn so easily in childhood, and similarly, after the failure to find a philosopher's stone in the earlier attempts at a generative theory of metre, the work of prosodists like Magnuson and Ryder, Chisholm, and Kiparsky has begun to reveal an equivalent complexity in metrical systems, beyond the reach of the simple categories of the traditional approaches to the subject.

But even if such a set of rules were to be formulated, there would remain some fundamental questions to be asked about the whole approach. The assertion is frequently made in generative metrical studies that an *explanation* is being given for what had hitherto only been, at best, *described* – a claim which echoes Chomsky's similar claims in linguistic theory. But can generative metrics be said to have brought us any closer to understanding why particular metrical forms are common in English, why certain variations disrupt the metre and others do not, or why metre functions so powerfully as a literary device? The answer, as Kiparsky acknowledges at the end of his 1977 article, is no. Readers of poetry with no expertise in linguistics will find it a laborious and often frustrating task to get to grips with generative metrics, and they may find when they have done so that no attempt has been made to solve the problems which most interest them, and no set of tools has been provided to analyse the expressive power of rhythmic forms in the verse they enjoy. One of the unsatisfying features of the generative approach is that, for all the valuable insights it has thrown up about the permissible or forbidden arrangements of syllable-types, it has lost touch with the material out of which verse is fashioned: the sounds of the language moving rhythmically through time, or, to be more accurate, the reader's perception of that rhythmic activity. Fundamental to the iambic pentameter, for instance, is its fivefold structure; it is this which clearly distinguishes it from longer or shorter metrical forms in duple metre, and approaches in terms of classical feet or musical measures usually reflect this. But generative theories operate at a much higher level of abstraction; the criterion by which rules are judged is that they generate the correct sequence of syllables, in as economical a manner as possible, but not necessarily that they embody the rhythmic perceptions of the reader or hearer. To regard the metrical base as a sequence of abstract positions determined by a numerical count from the start of the line (in the Magnuson–Ryder theory they are actually called 'Odd' and 'Even' slots) is to ignore the fact that the perception of metre is the perception of rhythmic beats, a matter not of arithmetic but of the rhythmic characteristics of the language. We have also noted that these theories concentrate not on what positively creates an acceptable line, but on what renders a line unacceptable; the actual movement of the words in a series of rhythmic alternations is never brought to the centre of attention. Many of the types of unacceptable line which these sets of rules erroneously generate are lines which fail in an elementary way to satisfy the reader's demand for five rhythmic peaks. Thus the Halle–Keyser rules, by permitting any position to be filled by two syllables, will generate lines with far too many syllables and stresses to be remotely acceptable as iambic pentameters. There is no need to invent an example, since they provide one themselves (1971a, p. 178):

```
      /        /         /    /                 /    /              /
    Billows, billows, serene mirror of the marine boroughs, remote
      w    s     w       s   w      s     w           s
            /
         willows
         w  s
```

For Halle and Keyser, this is an iambic pentameter, albeit one which is too complex ever to be used, because it is accepted by their rules; an alternative interpretation might be that a metrical theory which can generate such a monstrosity needs some reconsideration.

In Chapter 6 we shall consider in more detail the value and the dangers of using generative linguistics as a model for metrical studies; the point I wish to emphasise here about the proposals we have been discussing is that while they have rightly increased the demands made upon any metrical theory, they have failed themselves to satisfy those demands, through their over-reliance on certain aspects of their model. To write metrical verse is not just to select arbitrarily an abstract pattern and give this a material embodiment in a sequence of sounds, as if it might be equally well represented by beads on a string, or by an arrangement of words with odd and even numbers of letters; it is the ordering of those sounds themselves in ways which are determined by the nature of the language and by the general aesthetic and psychological properties of rhythm. We shall return in Part Three to the problem of formulating adequate rules of English metre, but before we consider how they can best be expressed, it is essential that we make a study of the medium in which they function and the general principles according to which they operate. This means asking some fundamental questions about the rhythmic structure of the English language itself before it is subject to the organising procedures of metre, and then about the principles of rhythmic form which guide that ordering process.

Notes

1. Many of this century's developments in metrical study were foreshadowed in a short paper by the philologist Otto Jespersen, first published in Danish in 1900. Though his reliance on absolute degrees of stress leads to some implausible explanations of metrical phenomena, his approach is a model of intelligent enquiry.
2. A Kenyon Review symposium on 'English Verse and What It Sounds Like' in 1956 included fanfares for phonemic analysis as a metrical tool from Harold Whitehall and Seymour Chatman, and it has been employed in many subsequent studies, including Sutherland (1958), H. L. Smith (1959), Epstein & Hawkes (1959), Chatman (1960), Wells (1960), Thompson (1961), Hawkes (1962), Fowler (1966a, 1966b), Fraser (1970), Hewitt (1972), and Dougherty (1973). The fullest and most useful work in this tradition is Chatman's *Theory of Meter* (1965). As late as 1971 one finds the then twenty-year-old Trager–Smith analysis of phonology described by a metrical commentator as 'the most exhaustive available' (Hawkes, p. 887).
3. See Halle & Keyser (1971a, 1971b), Keyser (1969a, 1969b), and Halle (1970). The underlying assumptions of this approach have been made most fully explicit by Beaver (1968a); see also his restatements of the theory, with some modifications (1968b, 1969, 1971a, 1971b, 1973, 1974, 1976). Among the many other contributions to this approach have been those of Freeman (1968, 1969, 1972), Hascall (1969, 1971), Levin (1973), Newton (1975), and Wilson (1979). The Halle–Keyser theory has been applied to Romance languages by Roubaud (1971) and Lusson & Roubaud (1974).
4. See, however, the criticisms of the Halle–Keyser approach by Wimsatt (1970), Cable (1972, 1973, 1976), Youmans (1974), Standop (1975), Devine & Stephens (1975), Barnes & Esau (1978, 1979), and Groves (1979).

Part Two: Rhythm

Chapter 3

The rhythms of English speech

In the course of an ordinary day we perform a multitude of tasks that require highly complex skills of which we are scarcely conscious, and of these the production and comprehension of speech is one of the most remarkable. In order to employ language, we do not need to understand how it works, any more than we need to understand the musculature of the leg to be able to walk; but in order to conduct a meaningful discussion of its use, including its use in poetry, we have to subject what we do so effortlessly and unselfconsciously to a very deliberate examination. When we learn to speak, we learn not only the grammar of a language, but also a particular way of employing the speech apparatus – lungs, vocal cords, tongue, lips, and so on – to create the sounds of that language; and because different languages require different ways of using that apparatus, a new one will always present an adult learner, to whom the sounds of his own language seem 'natural', with problems of pronunciation. Even if he succeeds, by dint of effort and practice, in getting his tongue and lips to behave in the manner demanded by the new language, he will probably find that there are some kinds of muscular activity that are so little under conscious control that he cannot alter their habitual movements, ingrained since childhood. This is especially true of the more fundamental processes in the production of speech, such as the action of the muscles controlling the lungs, and the relationship between this pulmonary activity and the movements of the speech organs higher up the vocal tract – David Abercrombie (1967, p. 36) notes that the deep-rootedness of these processes is reflected in certain types of aphasia in which these are the only features of speech production to survive brain damage. This fact is of crucial importance in our investigation, since it is these fundamental processes which determine the rhythmic features of the language: its patterns of stress and intonation, its pauses, its control of speed, and its modes of emphasis. And it is upon the rhythmic characteristics of the language that metrical form is founded. In the discussion of these characteristics that follows, it will become clear that our understanding of them is far from complete, but what is known has important consequences for the study of verse. It will be necessary to make one initial simplification: I shall ignore the fact that there exist rhythmic differences among the varieties of English spoken both now and in the past. There is a homogeneity about the tradition of English verse which suggests that it will not be too great a falsification to relate poetry written at different times and in different places to a single mode of speech rhythm; and in fact that homogeneity itself provides evidence for the continuity and uniformity of the English language's deeper articulatory processes.

3.1 THE SYLLABLE

A language can be analysed into syntactic units of varying scope, these into words and morphemes, and these in turn into phonemes and distinctive features, to provide an account of the abstract structures by means of which meaning is conveyed. The syllable, however, is the smallest *rhythmic* unit of the language; like the step in walking, it is the repeatable event which keeps the utterance going, the carrier of all the elements in the linguistic system. Its rhythmic character is clearly revealed by what we do if we wish to count the syllables in a word or phrase: we pronounce them in a strong, regular rhythm, perhaps accompanying each with a muscular movement. Doing this comes quite naturally, whereas counting individual phonemes, or whole words, by means of the same procedure creates the feeling of an unnatural rhythm being foisted on the language. The syllable has been the subject of much linguistic debate; its status in relation to the language-system is not settled, and there is disagreement about its precise phonetic constitution.[1] Most of this discussion is of little importance for the study of rhythm, but it will be worth giving some attention to the articulatory basis of the syllable, and to the perception of syllables in speech, as these are directly relevant to our purpose.

All speech is created by the forcing of air under muscular pressure through the orifices of the vocal tract, the differing configurations of which produce different qualities of sound. It is primarily the deflation of the lungs which produces the airstream on which speech-sounds are imposed by the higher organs, and it is possible to record the action of the muscles which effect this deflation by means of an experimental technique known as electromyography. So far, no indisputable physiological basis for the syllable in English has been discovered with this technique, but some of the evidence suggests that it can be understood as the product of a minimal stretch of pulmonary muscular activity (see Catford, 1977, pp. 88–91). It has also been argued that the syllable is the fundamental unit in the organisation of language by the brain (see Fry, 1964; and, for a similar proposition with regard to Russian, Kozhevnikov and Chistovich, 1965). Further experimentation will be necessary before we can say with certainty to what degree syllables correspond to neuromuscular activity, and how this relationship varies from language to language, but it tallies with subjective experience to regard the sequence of syllables as the product of rhythmically-controlled releases of energy.

Turning from production to perception, we need to be aware that although the native speaker can 'hear' the syllables of his language very clearly, this is not merely a matter of the brain's processing certain acoustic properties in a mechanical way. The perception of the syllable, like all acts of perception, depends on the knowledge we bring to it. Someone hearing a series of spoken sounds will interpret them within the framework of his own language, unconsciously inferring from them the speech-activity which he would have used to produce them. If they happen to be the sounds of another language, with a different way of using the speech apparatus, his analysis will probably go awry; thus according to Bloch (1950, p. 92) a Japanese speaker hearing a careful pronunciation of the English word *asks* will hear five syllables, since he would have to utter five syllables to produce a similar sequence of sounds in his own language. In other words, when we think we are hearing a very distinct succession of units objectively present in the sound sequence, we are in fact interpreting a complex stream of sounds in terms of the language we know, and its characteristic ways of using the speech musculature. This does not make syllables any less real; on the contrary, as far as our use of language is concerned, it is only this subjective reality that matters. It does, however, emphasise how irrelevant the instrumental measurements discussed in 1.2 are to an understanding of how language – and poetry – work.

There are no established English metres in which the number of phonemes or words is controlled, but in all verse from Middle English to the present the syllable plays a significant rhythmic role, frequently observing strict rules as to number and disposition, and it should be evident that this is no accident. It is important, however, that we recognise the syllable for what it is – a perceptual unit of rhythm, probably originating in the neurological and physiological production of language – and that we do not transform it into something merely acoustic, or merely visual, or merely theoretical.

3.2 STRESS

When we hear a burst of spoken language we do not hear an undifferentiated sequence of syllables; we are aware of larger structures created by variations in the prominence and duration of the syllables, and by the occurrence of pauses between them. Such features were christened 'suprasegmental phonemes' in the structuralist analysis of language (see 2.1 above), because they functioned over units of language greater than a single segment; they are also known as *prosodic* features, a term which can be useful if it is not confused with the use of 'prosody' to mean 'versification'. These features are an essential part of language, and the ability to use them is learned at a very early age, as will be evident to anyone who has heard a young child imitating the continuous patterns of intonation and rhythm in adult speech before the acquisition of any vocabulary. Poetic form relies on the moulding and ordering of such features of speech into patterns more aesthetically interesting, and more expressive, than those of ordinary language.

In English verse, the most important prosodic feature is the prominence given to certain syllables in the sequence. Discussion of this subject is often hampered by terminological confusion, and it is important to make clear in what sense the common terms are being used. I shall use both 'accent' and 'stress' to refer to this relative prominence, distinguishing between them only in so far as the former can refer to *any* means whereby syllables are rendered salient, while the latter refers specifically to the means used by the English language (and certain other languages with similar sound-characteristics) to achieve this end. As most of the discussion is concerned with English, this distinction will not be of great importance; what the student of metre needs to be aware of is that some commentators use 'stress' more narrowly to refer to degrees of intensity or loudness in contrast to such features as pitch or duration. As the ensuing discussion will make clear, my use of 'stress' does not imply that loudness is its sole, or even its primary, determinant. I shall use the term 'nonstress' for syllables which do not possess this salience in the sequence. As is the case with the syllable, explorations of the physical nature of stress can proceed in two directions: one, the province of articulatory phonetics, is the examination of the way in which it is produced by the speech apparatus; the other, the province of acoustic and auditory phonetics, is the study of the sounds produced and their perception as stress by the hearer. To the composite picture which they provide must be added the insights of phonology, the study of the linguistic system which is embodied in the physical sounds.

Experimental evidence is fullest in the field of acoustic and auditory phonetics, and several studies have been made of the perceptual cues which signal stress in English (see the summaries in Lehiste, 1970a; and Adams, 1979, Ch. 3). Our perception of a syllable as stressed is based on one or more of three major features: its pitch, its duration, and its amplitude. Of these, pitch has long been considered the most effective cue: experiments have shown that the stress pattern of individual words is largely determined by pitch-changes, and it is easy to test the role of pitch by reading a sentence like the following aloud, first with the final word stressed on its initial syllable, then on its second syllable:

Stress is the subject of much controversy.

The intonation contour rises sharply on the syllable that is stressed, and then falls for the remaining syllables of the sentence. A number of studies have suggested that the next most effective cue is duration, though some recent work on the subject points to its being, at least in connected speech, even more important than pitch (see Liberman and Prince, 1977, p. 250; Gay, 1978; Adams, 1979). A syllable that is longer than its neighbours will tend to be perceived as stressed, if other parameters are held constant (which is what happens, for instance, when a prayer is intoned on a single note and at a constant volume). The organisation of a chain of syllables into sequences of varying length (or speed in utterance) is therefore crucial to the perception of stress; and this means that durational patterns and stress are intimately connected, a point to which we shall return in section 3.4 below. The third perceptual cue is the one that uninstructed speakers often assume to be of paramount importance: loudness. Experiments have repeatedly shown that the degree of intensity with which a syllable is uttered, though in isolation it will signal stress, can be overridden by pitch-change and duration. We have no difficulty in perceiving the rhythmic configurations of music played on a harpsichord or organ, though these instruments do not make use of variations in volume for rhythmic purposes. There is a fourth feature which plays some part in the perception of English stress: sound-quality. In particular, the reduced vowel [ə] (as in the second syllable of *docker*) occurs only in unstressed syllables in most varieties of English, and is therefore a reliable cue for nonstress, and helps give English its distinctive contrast between stressed and unstressed syllables. All four of these cues interact in signalling stress, and their relative importance in any given instance depends in part on the acoustic and syntactic context in which the syllable occurs (see McClean and Tiffany, 1973; and Gay, 1978). Because stress can be manifested in these different ways, the speaker has some choice in the matter – he can, for instance, convey the stresses in a whispered sentence without using pitch, or do without changes in volume when shouting at the top of his voice. This is of some importance in the reading of verse, since the various cues have different effects on the rhythmic character of the utterance: changes in duration, for example, will obviously have a more direct effect on the rhythmic pattern than changes in pitch. We shall discuss this topic further in 8.2.

Do these different cues for stress constitute an arbitrary feature of the particular language system? Or, to put it another way, would it be equally possible for a language to signal prominence by low-pitched, or short, or quiet sounds? Intuition suggests that the answer is no, and, more reliably, the occurrence of similar combinations of cues for accent in other languages implies that there is some intrinsic appropriateness. Music shows that a sudden change of pitch, especially to a higher level, or a sudden increase in duration or loudness, are effective ways of creating a rhythmic beat. But we can also turn to the other area of investigation mentioned above, the production of language by the articulatory apparatus, for an explanation. Speech is produced by variations in muscular effort, and the stress cues we have noted are usually the product of an increase in such effort, both in the muscles which contract the lungs and in those that increase the tension of the vocal cords. It seems likely, therefore, that stress in English is produced by a neural signal which creates a burst of energy in the speech musculature, resulting in a number of related changes in the vocal signal.[2] If the interpretation of the syllable as a unit of energy-release is correct, stress is an additional charge of energy superimposed on this basic pulse, to create a peak in the rhythmic chain.

This conclusion sends us back to the hearer, to ask why these vocal characteristics should be perceived as syllabic prominence, and what exactly 'prominence' means in this context. Is it the same as the prominence of a red bead in a black necklace, or a piccolo note against low trombones? It might seem so to an intelligent being without the human speech apparatus, who responded only to the acoustic differences observable between stress and nonstress, but it is likely that someone who speaks a language will interpret the sounds of that language partly in terms of the muscular energy needed to produce them. In a similar way, the spectators at a pole-vaulting event interpret the visual signals they receive as indicating the expenditure of intense muscular effort at certain moments. It may even be that pole-vault spectators and language-hearers alike experience minimal muscular movements in sympathy with the activity which they infer from the perceptual cues they receive. Our response to a pas-de-deux is very different from our response to an aerobatic display; the former we comprehend as a series of muscular tensions and relaxations, a pattern created, ultimately, out of energy, while the latter is a fascinating visual event – unless our own experience in a cockpit enables us to empathise with the pilot's muscular endeavours.

Such a view of the stress contours of a language, which can be called the *motor theory* of stress, carries considerable explanatory force as well as intuitive conviction; and it is one which provides a valuable basis for the study of rhythm in speech and poetry. As with syllables, we count stresses by instinctively exaggerating their rhythmic function, turning them into beats at equal intervals, and often accompanying each stress with a muscular movement. There is also a certain amount of experimental support for the motor theory: some electromyographic studies have suggested that stress does tend to be accompanied by an increase in muscular effort (Ladefoged et al., 1958; Netsell, 1970; Catford, 1977, pp. 84–5), though certain aspects of this finding have been challenged by other workers in the field (see Adams, 1979). Furthermore, this theory helps to explain why our perceptions fail to match acoustic reality: Draper, Ladefoged, and Whitteridge (1959) have shown that perceived loudness in speech correlates not with objectively measured intensity, but with air-pressure in the lungs. In other words, listeners do not assess the acoustic properties of the sounds they hear, but take account of the pressure needed to produce those sounds. It seems reasonable to assume that the same is true of the other cues for stress, and that what we perceive as equal pitches or durations in an utterance are felt to be equal because they require similar activity in the speech musculature, not necessarily because they are objectively so.

The kind of prominence that is manifested by stress, then, is one which engages physical as well as mental responses in the reader; it is not merely an abstract phenomenon induced by contrast, like the red bead in the black necklace, but an empathetic response based on a shared way of using the speech apparatus. This view of stress is particularly associated with the name of R. H. Stetson, who elaborated a theory of language production and perception based on recordings of the speech musculature in action (see Stetson, 1905, 1945, 1951). Stetson's work has been criticised by later experimenters using more sophisticated equipment, but some aspects of his theory have considerable explanatory power in the analysis of stress contours, as has been shown by W. S. Allen (1973, pp. 40–45, 62–82, 191–9). For our purposes, it is sufficient to note that Stetson's theory, as developed by Allen, suggests a classification of English stress into two types, depending on whether the muscular movement which produces the stress is arrested within the stressed syllable, usually by means of a long vowel (or diphthong) or a final consonant, or whether a following unstressed syllable is used in the arrest of the stress, usually when there is a single consonant between the syllables. The first type of stress, which occurs in words like *keeper*, *lazy*, *camping*, can be called *self-arrested* stress; the second, in words like *kipper*, *Lizzie*, *coming*, can be called *disyllabic* stress. Such an analysis would suggest that the relationship between adjacent syllables is often determined by the muscular activity which produces them, creating different kinds of rhythmic sequence. It is interesting to note that Ladefoged *et al.* (1958, p. 6) cite *pity* as an example of a word they found to be accompanied by a single burst of muscular activity, and that Bridges (1909, p. 100) gives as examples of quantitative pyrrhics (feet of two short syllables) *habit*, *very*, *silly*, *solid*, and *scurry* – all cases of disyllabic arrest. The distinction made by David Abercrombie (1964b) between disyllables with durational ratios of $1\frac{1}{2}:1\frac{1}{2}$ and $1:2$ (see above, p. 23) is based on the same difference in syllabic structure, though we have already noted the dangers of specifying arithmetical ratios for these perceived rhythmic relationships. When we move beyond the word, the picture becomes even more complex; there is, for instance, a clearly perceptible rhythmic difference between 'Take Grey to Leeds' and 'Take Greater Leeds', though the sound-qualities may be identical and the stresses are self-arrested in both cases.

One weakness of most attempts to analyse these relationships is the use of a basic unit consisting of a stress and all the following nonstresses: this 'foot' is as artificial a subdivision as that created by the metrical foot in verse. A more promising approach is that adopted by Knowles (1974), who examines the relationship between a stressed syllable and the unstressed syllables which are rhythmically linked to it, whether before or after; these smaller units he regards as parts of larger rhythmic hierarchies. It will be useful, using such an approach, to focus on just one question, which will have a bearing on our later discussion: in a rhythmic unit of two syllables, what difference is made by the position of the stress? It seems that if the stress falls on the first syllable of a disyllabic word (*shilling*, *limpid*, *Greater*) we tend to perceive that syllable as shorter than or about the same length as its unstressed partner, and the same is true of a stressed monosyllable followed by a closely connected nonstress (*hop it*, *sock him*). If, on the other hand, the stress is on the second syllable, this syllable will usually seem longer (*instead*, *believe*, *for two*, *to Leeds*). These differences are implied in Abercrombie's categories of 'foot', and objective confirmation is provided by the results of an experiment conducted by Warner Brown (1908). Brown asked subjects to pronounce sequences of two syllables in 'rising' and 'falling' rhythms, for example, 'pápa papa papa . . .' and 'papa pápa papa . . .', and found that in the first the stressed syllable was two or three times as long as the other, while in the second the stressed syllable was the shorter (pp. 55–6). It is not the exact durations that matter, however, but the perceived rhythmic differences, and there is ample scope for further study of this aspect of speech rhythm and its embodiment in verse.

3.3 STRESS HIERARCHIES

The linguistic investigation of English phonology has demonstrated that the patterns of sound which characterise English speech are no less systematic than the patterns of syntax. In particular, generative accounts of phonology, in Chomsky and Halle (1968) and subsequent studies, have emphasised that a stress contour is a direct reflection of linguistic structure, and that a native speaker of English can predict, without conscious effort, the pattern of stress in any given word or sentence. Several competing analyses of English stress contours have been proposed in recent years, and this is not the place to consider them, but there is one fundamental principle implied by a number of these studies which is particularly illuminating for the study of verse rhythm: the idea that the stress contour of an English utterance is a hierarchical organisation involving relative stress values, rather than a simple concatenation of syllables with different degrees of stress.

A familiar example in phonological discussions is the contrast between the noun phrase *black bird* and the compound *blackbird*. Whatever sound-features we use to distinguish between them, and whatever symbols we use to indicate the difference, the basic contrast is between a structure in which the first word is felt to be subordinated to the second, and a structure in which the reverse relationship obtains. A similar distinction exists between a *white house* one might see by the roadside, and the *White House* where the American President lives; or between *Harley Road*, which we treat as if it were a phrase, and *Harley Street*, in which the second word is the subordinate member, as if it were a compound. If we now insert such a two-part unit into a larger structure, the pattern is repeated; thus in the phrase *blackbird pie*, *blackbird* is now subordinated to *pie* but retains its internal structure of subordination, and the resulting pattern can be shown in a hierarchical tree-diagram:

blackbird pie

This indicates that at the lowest level of the hierarchy, *black* is the strong member and *bird* the weak, while at the next level, *blackbird* is the weak member and *pie* the strong. This procedure can be extended to larger structures, producing a complex tree-diagram which gives every syllable a place in the hierarchical order.[3]

There is no need to go into further detail: what is important is the general view of the stress contour as a set of relationships extending over, and reflecting the linguistic structure of, an entire syntactic unit, in contrast to the rather myopic view prevalent in metrical studies (fathered perhaps by Jespersen in his 1900 essay) which considers only contrasts between adjacent syllables. However, it is worth noting two specific tendencies in speech rhythm which are highlighted by this approach. One is a general tendency for a stress to be subordinated to a *following* stress within a syntactic unit, whether or not any unstressed syllables intervene. An adjective is subordinated to a following noun (*black bird*, *yellow carnation*) and a verb to its object (*admire birds*, *relish carnations*); and within the phrase, the last stress normally takes the strongest emphasis. This is, of course, subject to the use of emphatic stress on a particular word, which needs special attention in metrical analysis, as does the stress pattern of compounds (see 8.2 and 8.8 below). The other tendency which is implied by many studies based on this approach is that the stress hierarchies are fundamentally binary in character, a point which we shall take up in the following section of this chapter.

One beneficial result of regarding a stress contour as a hierarchical organisation is that it does not create the false impression of a series of syllables, each with a distinct, objective, 'degree of stress' which is somehow manifested by the speaker in his pronunciation. My sense of the stress contour of a sentence I hear is not a matter of the exact phonetic weight given to each syllable, but of the total structure of the sentence and of the relationships within that structure; and as long as the speaker does not grossly deviate from the normal pronunciation of the language, I will perceive the hierarchy of stresses which reflects that structure. A simple test is to read the following two sequences of syllables with volume, pitch, and syllabic duration held constant:

[1] Eng-lish-is-marked-by-its-strong-use-of-stress

[2] Its-use-of-strong-stress-is-what-marks-Eng-lish

Although the stress contour is given no physical manifestation, an English speaker cannot but feel its presence in the places dictated by the linguistic structure, and will register the first sequence as rhythmically more regular than the second. Listening to them read in this way, he may even perceive stresses which are not objectively present. On the other hand, someone unfamiliar with English would hear a similar sequence of ten equal sounds in each case.

What we hear in an English sentence, then, is not simply a series of pitches, volumes, and durations, but a group of syllables held together in a linguistic structure which determines their patterns of subordination to one another. It seems likely that the perception of a hierarchical structure is in part a reflection of the way syllables are produced in sequence by the speech apparatus; we have already seen how the syllables in a word like *pity* may constitute a particularly close rhythmic group as a result of the way in which they are produced, in contrast to those of a word like *lazy*, and similar distinctions may operate over larger units. Experimental work on the timing of speech-segments supports the view of utterances as temporally organised wholes, not merely concatenations of syllables; for example, it has been found that altering the duration of one item in a syntactic unit can affect the duration of later items, suggesting that the whole sequence is preprogrammed as a single temporal unit by the brain (see Lehiste, 1970b; Shockey, Gregorski, and Lehiste, 1971; Huggins, 1972; Wright, 1974). The point to be emphasised, however, is that we will sense these relationships among syllables even when they are not fully manifested in the speech-signal itself, because knowing the language means having established intimate connections between certain features of an abstract system and certain kinds of muscular behaviour. In trying to understand an utterance in a language with which we are not familiar we need all the physical cues we can get, and a slow, precise enunciation is a great help; but in listening to our own language we can dispense with many of the signals and still grasp the meaning, and the rhythmic structure which makes that meaning communicable.

3.4 ALTERNATION AND STRESS-TIMING

In our discussion of the hierarchical analysis of English stress contours, we noted that a fundamental principle of most studies using this approach is the existence of binary structures, and at the level of syllables, alternation between strong and weak is an easily observable preference.[4] For instance, it produces the characteristic stress pattern of English polysyllables: *rhythmicality, independence, interpretation*. Furthermore, there are a number of English words in which the position of the stress is not fixed, but is influenced by the rhythmic context in which the word occurs: many speakers will say *outdoor activities* but *outdoor sports, thirteen bananas* but *thirteen elephants*, thus avoiding successive stressed syllables. An alternating pattern may even be perceived in stresses which the normal phonological rules specify as equal: Chomsky and Halle (1968, p. 117) cite *tired old man* as a sequence in which *old* may be perceived as less stressed than *tired*; and Liberman and Prince (1977, p. 327) remark that the second word in *John's three red shirts* may receive additional stress to create an alternating rhythm. The converse can occur in sequences of unstressed syllables: in a phrase like *carried with the wind* there is a tendency to hear *with* as having a slightly stronger stress than its neighbours, whereas the two nonstresses in *gone with the wind* are perceived as equal. Yet another way in which the preference for alternation manifests itself is in the choices English speakers make among possible phrasings; thus Bolinger (1965) notes that we tend to say *a free and easy manner* in preference to *an easy and free manner*, or *bright and shining eyes* rather than *shining and bright eyes*. He also suggests that certain words retained from earlier stages of the language have survived because of their alternating rhythms, so that we prefer the form *drunken sailor* to the clashing stresses of *drunk sailor*, and will say *shrunken skin* but *the skin had shrunk*. Perhaps the final *−e* of Middle English, whose disappearance has been the subject of much debate, survived longest as an optional feature which could be used in just this way to prevent successive stresses, exactly as it does in Chaucer's poetry. The significance for English verse of this alternating tendency in the language is obvious: the overriding preference poets have shown for duple metres can be understood as a preference for a rhythm that heightens a phenomenon already fundamental to the language but only imperfectly realised in normal speech, and thus not only makes possible the fullest use of natural English sentences in regular verse, but at the same time can create the illusion of a purified and perfected language. However, it should be noted that English speech is not hostile to an alternation between stresses and pairs of nonstresses, and that triple metres, though attended by certain disadvantages (to be discussed in 4.4), are consequently within the constraints set by the language.

This preference for the alternation of stressed and unstressed syllables should not be thought of as merely a patterning of two contrasting units of language: we are dealing, rather, with a natural product of the muscular processes which underlie all speech. It is a matter of common observation that we prefer to use our muscles in a rhythmic way for repeated actions, like breathing or walking, and we should not be surprised to find that a regular sequence of energy expenditure and relaxation forms the basis of our speech activities. What we are examining is not just a tendency towards an alternating pattern, but a tendency towards a particular dynamic organisation of the language: the occurrence of stresses at equivalent intervals to create a rhythmically regular progression. We have already noted the importance of this feature of the language in the temporal tradition of metrical analysis, within which it is usually referred to as 'isochrony', though the alternative term, 'stress-timing', which does not carry the implication of exact intervals, is preferable. We also noted that instrumental studies have shown that the intervals between stresses in English speech are not objectively equal; stress-timing, like every other aspect of speech, depends on the hearer's perception as well as the speaker's physical activity. In listening to the utterances of another speaker of English, I relate the physical signals I hear to the sequence of muscular actions needed to produce them, a sequence which is rhythmic in character, with its peaks on the bursts of energy that create stressed syllables, and its troughs on the weaker activity that produces unstressed syllables. The neural signals which trigger this muscular activity may be rhythmically very precise, but the physical demands of the speech apparatus introduce irregularity (see Kozhevnikov and Chistovich, 1965, pp. 104–18; and Boomsliter and Creel, 1977); even so, G. D. Allen (1975, pp. 81–2) cites studies which suggest that the measurable variations in speech-timing are similar to those in any rhythmic muscular activity, and Lehiste (1977, 1979) has shown that these variations are often not large enough to be perceived by the hearer. One can conclude, then, that although an instrument or a native speaker of another language might detect no rhythmic regularity in English speech, a speaker of English perceives stresses as rhythmic pulses, and the intervals between them as rhythmically equivalent (though not necessarily as equal). This impression is not affected by changes in *tempo*, when the overall speed of utterance is increased or decreased, and can survive the occasional suspension of the rhythm in a *pause*.

Stress-timing as a perceived characteristic of English has often been discussed by phoneticians,[5] and a contrast is frequently drawn with other languages, such as French and Japanese, which are described as 'syllable-timed'; that is to say, the speaker perceives the *syllables*, not the intervals between the stresses, as being rhythmically equivalent. One obvious reflection of this difference is that in the versification of syllable-timed languages the number of syllables in the line is more important than the number and arrangement of stresses. Spectrograph recordings made by Delattre (1966) of German, English, Spanish, and

French utterances show that English has by far the greatest durational ratio between its longest and shortest syllables, and Adams (1979) has demonstrated that native speakers of syllable-timed languages have difficulty in achieving the correct timing of English speech, however good their command of other aspects of the language.

But if stress-timing were the only rhythmic principle in English, or one that overrode all others, there would be no way of explaining the preference for an alternation between stressed and unstressed syllables: the number of nonstresses between stresses could vary freely without affecting rhythmic regularity. We have already noted, however, that the syllable is itself a rhythmic unit, and although it is clearly secondary to stress, its part in English speech rhythm should not be overlooked. It has been found that whatever objective tendency to stress-timing exists in the language decreases as the variation in number of nonstresses increases; Uldall (1971), for instance, found evidence for isochrony in one subject's speech as long as the number of nonstresses between stresses remained below three. (One reason for this is the preference for rhythmic alternation itself: as we noted earlier, when the number of nonstresses reaches three, the middle one will tend to take on some of the characteristics of a stressed syllable, thus lengthening the interval.) English speech rhythm is therefore characterised by a certain degree of tension between two rhythmic principles, and the preference for an alternation between stressed and unstressed syllables that the language exhibits can be understood as a way of minimising that tension, since only if the number of nonstresses between stresses is held constant can the two principles be brought into harmony. Alternation between single stresses and single nonstresses is clearly the simplest form of rhythm that can achieve such a marriage. Other factors prevent this from being any more than a general tendency in the language at large, but it lies at the heart of English metrical form, which capitalises on both the satisfying sense of regularity produced by bringing the two rhythmic tendencies into accord, and the expressive possibilities inherent in the conflict between them.

It would be more accurate, therefore, to describe English as a language in which stress-timing dominates syllable-timing, rather than one which is wholly stress-timed. The dominance of stress-timing can sometimes emerge in the daily use of language: for instance, we may impose a regular rhythm on an utterance for special purposes (see Crystal, 1969, p. 163; Quirk *et al.*, 1972, p. 1043). The pressure of an emotion like exasperation or resignation may produce exaggerated regularity; as an example, imagine the following being spoken through clenched teeth with heavy, evenly-spaced stresses:

/   /   /   /   /
For God's sake, all I want is some attention!

In doing this, the frustrated speaker is merely heightening the natural stress-timing of the English language; it would be unnatural to give an evenly-spaced emphasis to every syllable. Another way in which stress-timing can be illustrated is by means of 'choral reading': if a group of English speakers is asked to read a passage together they will tend to exaggerate the natural rhythmic tendencies of the language to make unison pronunciation possible. Boomsliter, Creel, and Hastings (1973) found that the intervals between stresses in the recitation of verse come much nearer to being equal when such choral reading is performed. The more closely an utterance approaches to isochrony, the more fully the stressed syllables are experienced as *beats*; and although this term is frequently used in phonetic studies to refer to the function of stressed syllables in all utterances, it is most appropriate when the regularity of the stress pattern is such that a clear rhythmic structure of alternations is perceived. When this occurs, the rhythm becomes self-reinforcing, since we instinctively give the beats more emphasis, and control the duration of the intervals between them to heighten the regularity.

The movement of English speech, then, is determined by two rhythmic phenomena, the syllable and stress, and most regular verse in English acknowledges this in its control of the number and disposition of both these in the metrical line. The poet writing in English is not handling an infinitely malleable substance; the language has its own highly distinctive rhythmic character, which the skilful artist will exploit to the full, as a sculptor brings out the natural forms and textures of his material. But regular verse involves the shaping of those linguistic features into structures that obey more general principles of rhythmic form, and it is to these that we turn next.

Notes

1. For a valuable discussion of the debate over the syllable, see W. S. Allen (1973, pp. 27–73).
2. See the hypothesis advanced by Öhman (1967) that stress should be understood as

'the addition of a quantum of "physiological energy" to the speech production system as a whole ... distributed (possibly unevenly) over the pulmonary, phonatory, and articulatory channels'.

3. This approach to stress contours derives from the notion of the 'transformation cycle' proposed by Chomsky & Halle (1968), and two different uses of it, from quite disparate points of view, can be found in Martin (1970, 1972) and Liberman & Prince (1977). The latter theory is valuably developed by Giegerich (1980).

4. The preference for alternating sequences is an important feature of the study of stress patterns in polysyllabic words by Arnold (1957), and is embodied in an 'Alternating Stress Rule' by Chomsky & Halle (1968) and in the stress rules proposed by Schane (1979a, 1979b). Schane also incorporates a 'rhythm rule', which reflects the tendency to avoid successive stresses in phrases, as do Liberman & Prince (1977) in their theory of stress hierarchies; see also Gimson (1970, pp. 289–90) and G. D. Allen (1975, pp. 80–81). For a pioneering exploration of the way in which choices between alternatives in pronunciation and phrasing are guided by the rhythmic context see van Draat (1910, 1912).

5. See, for example, Classe (1939), Pike (1945, pp. 34–5), David Abercrombie (1964a, 1964b), Gimson (1970, pp. 260–61), G. D. Allen (1975), Lehiste (1977), and Catford (1977, pp. 85–88).

Chapter 4

The four-beat rhythm

When we apply the word 'rhythm' to speech we are referring to its characteristic movement in time, as perceived by the speaker and hearer; and we saw in the previous chapter that although spoken English has an underlying tendency towards regularity, this is seldom fully achieved in normal usage. The 'rhythm' of a song or a dance, on the other hand, or 'rhythm' as a psychological phenomenon, both of which we are concerned with in this chapter, carry much stronger connotations of regular patterning. The two notions are close – if the language had no principle of regularity at all we would refer merely to its 'movement', not its 'rhythm' – but the gap between them must not be ignored, since it is the function of metre to bridge that gap, and in so doing to shape the linguistic material into the lively and subtle forms of verse. The general principles of rhythm, as manifested in music as well as in poetry, operate in metrical verse at several levels, and in our discussion of them in this chapter we shall move from the deeper levels to those nearer the surface; that is, from the simple rhythmic forms which underlie the variety that exists in metrical practice to the rhythmic features which make that variety possible. The one exception to this order will be the final section on dipodic rhythm, which takes us back once more to elementary rhythmic processes. This chapter deals exclusively with the four-beat rhythm in its various guises, as the most fundamental rhythmic form in verse, but the framework developed in the course of the discussion is relevant to all regular forms, and will be the basis of the account of the five-beat rhythm in the chapter that follows.

4.1 THE PERCEPTION OF RHYTHM

To perceive a regular rhythm is to comprehend a sequence of events as a pattern in time, with two mutually reinforcing features, *repetition* and *periodicity*.[1] That is to say, a series of stimuli is understood as the *same* stimulus occurring again and again; and these repetitions are felt to be occurring at equal, or at least equivalent, temporal intervals. It is not an objective, measurable phenomenon, but a perceptual one: if the stimuli are of the right kind, they need not be identical, nor need they fall at equal intervals, in order to establish a regular rhythm in the mind of the perceiver. But what constitutes the 'right kind' of stimulus? The most powerfully rhythm-inducing events, some kinds of sound, for instance, appear to be those which involve discharges of energy that can be directly interpreted in terms of muscular activity. The natural response to rhythmic sound is muscular participation, whether in the tapping of a finger or the movement of the whole body in a dance. One of the reasons for the supremacy of the drum as a rhythm-marking instrument is that we are able to relate the sound very immediately to the muscular movement of the arm that produces it; by contrast, electronically synthesised music, unless it mimics the imprint of human energy, is likely to be rhythmically inert. Visual stimuli alone are less often felt as strongly rhythmic: the satisfaction in watching classical ballet comes from the manifestation in movement of the rhythms we *hear*. Perhaps the only rhythms as commanding as those of sound are those directly induced by kinetic or muscular stimuli, such as we feel (or used to feel) when the train-wheels beneath us pass over the line-joints, or when we become hyperconscious of our own heartbeats.

Rhythm in its most elementary form, then, is the apprehension of a series of events as a regularly repeated pulse of energy, an experience which has a muscular as well as a mental dimension. The strongest perception of rhythm, however, comes not from a simple succession of stimuli, but from the repeated alternation of a stronger pulse and a fixed number of weaker pulses, usually one or two. The mind prefers to organise its perceptions in such alternating patterns, as is clear from the way in which we hear a clock's succession of identical ticks as a rhythm of stronger and weaker sounds. The strong impulses in such a rhythmic sequence are usually called *beats*, and I shall retain this term, and its opposite, *offbeats*, in referring to the fundamental alternations of verse rhythm.

Given this description, the reasons why patterns of stressed and unstressed syllables in English speech constitute such a powerful source of rhythm are not far to seek. We saw in Chapter 3 that syllables can be understood as rhythmically-controlled releases of energy, and that the most satisfactory account of stress sees it as a burst of increased energy on particular syllables, manifested by such features as change in pitch and increase in duration or volume, and interpreted by the hearer in terms of the muscular activity needed to produce them. We noted also that it is the muscular basis of speech production which creates the tendency towards rhythmic alternation and periodicity in the sequence of syllables. And we emphasised that a native speaker of English will, because of his knowledge of the patterns of stress placement in the language, perceive the stress contour even if the cues are only partially present, or sometimes in their absence altogether. It is hardly surprising, therefore, to find that stressed and unstressed syllables are very readily perceived as rhythmic beats and offbeats, and that they can function as such even when they do not form an objective, measurable pattern of equal intervals and peaks of energy.[2] The strongest rhythms that can occur in English, therefore, are created by the simple alternation of stress and nonstress, or stress and double nonstress, in sequences like these:

```
     /  x    /   x / x      /
(1)  Go, and catch a falling star
```

```
     /   x  x / x  x   /  x  x   /
(2)  Sweet be thy matin o'er moorland and lea
```

In these arrangements of syllables, the stress-timed character of the language is most fully brought out, and whatever the objective durations may be, we experience the stresses as falling at equivalent time-intervals. When we read regular verse aloud, we participate directly in the muscular rhythmic activity that underlies metrical form, and when we listen to it we participate empathetically.

Once established, a regular rhythm has a tendency to self-perpetuation, a momentum like that of motion in a straight line: the producer of a rhythm will be inclined to impose it on further material, and the perceiver will be inclined to go on hearing it if it is possible for him to do so, if, that is, the physical reality does not depart too far from the established norm. Rhythm thus projects itself strongly into the future, and the occurrence of one rhythmic event, while it satisfies a previous expectation, simultaneously generates a fresh one. This creation of rhythmic expectancy, affecting the interpretation of following stimuli, is a form of what is known in the psychology of perception as *set*, a concept aptly introduced into metrical theory by several writers (for instance, Chatman, 1965, p. 121; R. Fowler, 1968, pp. 150–51; Harding, 1976, Ch. 3 and 4), and one which we shall find very useful in discussing the rules of metre in Part Three. In general terms, it makes possible a clearer account of the notion of metrical *tension*, which we touched upon in 1.1. In the perception of rhythm, tension may be regarded as the psychological experience produced by a local failure to satisfy completely an established regular rhythmic set. It is felt only if the stimuli come close enough to their expected form to be interpreted as at least a partial fulfilment of the set, and it has the effect of heightening the perceiver's attention to the rhythmic substance (whereas an absolutely regular rhythm often works to exactly the opposite effect), and, by creating a demand for a return to the momentarily thwarted regularity, of increasing the sense of forward propulsion. There are therefore two principles of onward movement involved in rhythm: underlying patterns of expectation and satisfaction, and sequences of tension and relaxation produced by variations in the degree to which that satisfaction occurs. In many cases the two cannot be separated, of course: the relaxation attendant on a return to strict rhythmic regularity, for instance, acts to heighten the sense of fulfilled expectation. Tension can also inhere in the relations *between* rhythmic and other levels of the verse, and complete relaxation occurs only if the patterns of expectation and satisfaction at every level coincide. We shall return to the question of tension frequently in the pages that follow; see in particular 7.10 and 9.5.

It should be clear from this discussion that in whatever medium a rhythm occurs, it always takes place in the dimension of time, albeit psychological rather than objective time. 'Rhythm' is, of course, often used metaphorically – the rhythms of a painting, or chimney pots against the sky – but one must not lose sight of the fact that such uses *are* metaphorical; and that we use the word unmetaphorically when discussing speech and poetry, which occur in time, and in which sequential and dynamic relations are of the utmost importance. It is difficult to escape from the tyranny of the sense of sight, and many of the terms one falls back on in describing rhythm – 'groups', 'structures', 'positions', even 'lines' – have spatial origins. I can only hope that in what follows they will not be construed as having spatial implications, but simply as a reflection of the poverty of the lexical store on which one draws to refer to the richly various qualities of movement through time.

4.2 UNDERLYING RHYTHM

One might say that the tendency of a rhythm to continue once established is a consequence of its escape from the normal limitations of time, since it converts a succession of different events into a repetition of the same event, and part of its fascination may lie in this illusory triumph over mutability. But an art-form requires a shape, not a series extending into infinity; middles should feel like middles, and ends like ends (and surprises are only possible if these norms have been established). Hence in verse, as in music, rhythm is always organised, and it is with the elementary forms which provide this organisation that we are now concerned. As we are investigating the basic elements from which sophisticated literary works are built, we shall give much of our attention to anonymous, popular verse in which a prevalent rhythmic phenomenon is more likely to be a reflection of a fundamental property of rhythm than a literary convention. Not that separation of the two is easy to achieve; even in looking at conventional aspects of form it is pertinent to ask why certain poetic choices have become established conventions and others have never been made a second time, and the answer may be that only the former coincide with something in the nature of the medium itself. And if we find elementary patterns repeated again and again in popular verse from medieval times to the present, and reflected in a large body of more literary verse, we can assume that there are reasons for this recurrence which lie deeper than convention. Just as myth and folk-tale reveal in stark form the plots which may be disguised in more self-conscious novels, so nursery rhymes and ballads, which are not the product of a single conscious artistic act (or if they are, have been taken up by audiences because they conform to the popular tradition), present the simplest rhythmic forms in clear outline. One must not, of course, conclude that the reader's or critic's task is done when he has released the popular form from its sophisticated envelope; as we shall see, the artist's problem is in part the *avoidance* of the ever-tempting elementary forms, which his readers, consciously or unconsciously, will be only too ready to find. But without grasping the nature of those elementary forms, we cannot hope to understand the achievement of the complex work of art which builds on them or finds ways round them.

Rhythmic pulses in verse (and in music) tend to fall into groups, each of which the mind perceives as a whole, with a beginning and an end;

we can call such a group an *underlying rhythm*. (One could use the term 'Gestalt', though its usefulness in this context is limited by its connotations of visual configuration.) The most common underlying rhythm in English popular verse is the group of four beats, and examples come readily to hand from all periods:

(3) Adam delved and Eve span;
B   B   B   B
Who was then the gentleman?
B   B   B   B

(4) It was a lover and his lass,
B   B   B   B
With a hey, and a ho, and a hey nonino
B   B   B   B

(5) She was poor but she was honest,
B   B   B   B
Victim of the squire's whim.
B   B   B   B

(6) High o'er the fence leaps Sunny Jim,
B   B   B   B
'Force' is the food that raises him!
B   B   B   B

Nor is it confined to the English tradition: Ker (1928, 205–12) traces four-beat rhythms in verse written in Sanskrit, classical and modern Greek, classical and medieval Latin, French, Provençal, and German; and while his examples are not all equally convincing, his evidence does suggest that this form occupies a special place in Western European verse. Burling (1966) goes even further afield in his examination of children's verse in various languages, and finds four-beat rhythms in the Peking dialect of Chinese, Bengkulu (a language of South West Sumatra), Yoruba, Cairo Arabic, and some North American Indian languages. The four-beat phrase is also, of course, one of the fundamental units in Western musical structures, popular and sophisticated. Indeed it is sometimes argued that four-beat patterns in verse owe their existence to the music with which the verse was originally associated; but I shall proceed on the assumption that Burling is right to feel that 'we have general rules of rhythm, which are neither predominantly musical nor predominantly poetic, but stand equally behind both music and spoken verse' (p. 1425).

One can only guess at the reasons for the repeated occurrence of this form. Burling's appeal to our 'common humanity' does not get us very far, and neither does Ker's assertion that 'this type of verse is natural because it runs in periods of 4, 8, 16, which one may call the natural rhythm for the human race' (p. 206). His hint at the importance of the four-beat rhythm's capacity to enter into larger structures is a valuable one, however, and is taken further by Tovey (1910–11), who states that we have a 'natural tendency to group rhythmic units in pairs, with a stress on the first of each pair; and hence, if our attention is drawn to larger groups, we put more stress on the first of the first pair than on the first of the second; and so with still greater groups' (p. 279). As we shall see later, it is somewhat artificial to isolate the four-beat line as the most fundamental pattern; what seems to be at the heart of simple rhythmic structuring is, as Tovey suggests, the existence of rhythmic pairs, arranged in hierarchies, each pair joining another pair to form a four-unit whole. We can leave aside as unproven the question of whether this is a truly universal characteristic of rhythm. Studies of 'primitive' music and verse have found a wide variety of rhythmic patterning (see, for instance, Nettl, 1956, Ch. 5; and Finnegan, 1977, pp. 90–102), but there is no reason to assume that such art is any less complicated in its elaboration of simple underlying forms than our own. Burling's use of children's verse in his cross-linguistic study is a more useful pointer to what might be considered 'rhythmic universals'. One can safely say, at least, that for reasons which go beyond the separate domains of music and poetry the four-beat rhythm has been a recurrent feature in the rhythmic arts of Western Europe; and it seems likely that this is a reflection of something fundamental in the faculty of rhythmic production and perception itself.

It will be evident that each pair of lines quoted above forms a single unit; the sense of completion after the second line is appreciably stronger than after the first. It is reinforced by the different kinds of syntactic break at these points, though it is clearly not *caused* by these breaks. And if we examine a typical nursery rhyme, we find a second pair of lines complementing the first pair, and producing another fourfold structure (I indicate the main beats):

(7) Ride a cock-horse to Banbury Cross,
   B   B   B   B
    To see a fine lady upon a white horse;
     B   B   B   B

Rings on her fingers and bells on her toes,
B   B   B   B
She shall have music wherever she goes.
B   B   B   B

Here we have fully realised what we can call an *underlying rhythmic structure*: four lines of four beats each, which I shall abbreviate as 4 × 4. This is by far the commonest rhythmic structure in popular song (as well as being used, of course, in more elaborate musical works), and, as we shall see, it occurs in, or underlies, nearly all popular verse in English.[3] Burling, in the study already mentioned, finds evidence of it in children's verse in several languages. It is also common in the literary tradition:

(8) Come live with me, and be my love,
B   B   B   B
And we will all the pleasures prove,
B   B   B   B
That hills and valleys, dales and fields,
B   B   B   B
And all the craggy mountain yields.
B   B   B   B

Though the 4 × 4 structure manifests itself in several guises, it is immediately recognisable by its distinctive rhythmic swing, and the way in which it binds a series of lines together (almost always with the assistance of rhymes). An ear accustomed to the rhythms of English verse responds to the presence of this structure immediately, even though in a complex stanza some analytical effort may be required to unearth it.

This rhythmic form is, of course, a direct product of the hierarchical character of rhythm already mentioned, a pair of pairs of pairs of beats. In its simplest manifestations it has a typical intonation pattern, which emerges clearly when one recites a nursery rhyme like (7) to a child *con amore*: each beat is signalled partly by a pitch change, producing four different contours for the four lines, and different degrees of finality at the line-ends. A musical equivalent would be a series of cadences: interrupted cadences at the ends of lines 1 and 3, a half-close on the dominant at the end of line 2, and a full close on the tonic to complete the pattern. (Popular melodies often bear a resemblance to this scheme, in fact; see Hendren, 1936, Ch. 1.) Thus, for instance, the third line has a very characteristic pitch contour with a strong sense of 'penultimateness' about it: starting high on the first beat, dropping on the second, rising again on the third, and dropping again to a tone of anticipation and suspension on the fourth. (This contour reinforces strongly the division of the line into two, a third-line feature to which we shall return.) Like other aspects of metrical form, such intonation patterns are a stylisation of the patterns we use in normal speech, though this subject has been something of a Cinderella among studies of metre, as Crystal (1975) points out. Intonation is, of course, one of the most important features in signalling stress in English, as we noted in 3.2, so it is hardly surprising that it has an important part to play in the rhythms of verse.

Not only the syntax of (7) but also the rhymes – *aabb* – reinforce the main structural division. Other common rhyme-schemes for the 4 × 4 structure are *abab* and *abcb*, which, rather than emphasising the correspondence between the two lines of each half-stanza, emphasise that between the two halves, giving the whole quatrain a fuller sense of cohesion. The following two ballad stanzas will illustrate both of these more cohesive schemes:

> (9) He took the halter frae his hose,
>   And of his purpose did na fail;
>   He slipt it oer the Wanton's nose,
>   And tied it to his gray mare's tail.
>
> But on the morn, at fair day light,
>   When they had ended a' thier chear,
> King Henry's Wanton Brown was stawn,
>   And eke the poor old harper's mare.

In the literary tradition, the rhyme-scheme is sometimes counterpointed against the rhythmic structure, as, for instance, in Tennyson's *In Memoriam* stanza, which achieves its special character by postponing a sense of finality until the last word by means of an *abba* rhyme-scheme; but it is more typical of popular verse that the various aspects of form should reinforce one another, allowing the simple hierarchical organisation of the 4 × 4 structure to be fully experienced.

4.3 METRICAL PATTERNS AND UNREALISED BEATS

So far there has been no need to differentiate between the underlying rhythmic structure of a stanza and the way it is actually manifested as a set of lines. However, the 4 × 4 structure is not always realised as a four-line stanza, and it is important to keep the specific arrangement of lines in a particular stanza-form distinct from the common underlying structure it realises. We shall call this specific arrangement the *metrical pattern*, and abbreviate it by stating the number of beats in each line; thus the stanzas we have so far considered are examples of a 4.4.4.4 metrical pattern. (Later we shall consider the more detailed specification of the metrical patterns of individual lines.) In moving to this level we are moving away from a very general rhythmic form found in several languages and in music, towards the particular manifestations of that form found in the English verse tradition; but at this level, too, there are many cross-linguistic similarities. An interesting example of a metrical pattern not confined to English is given by Ker (1928, pp. 219–27), who cites examples in medieval verse in the Irish, Welsh, and German traditions, in Irish songs, and in *Don Giovanni*, as well as in *A Midsummer Night's Dream* ('Ercles' vein') and in poems by Byron and Swinburne. As normally printed, it looks like this (I give only eight lines of the Byron example):

(10) Could love for ever
       Run like a river,
       And Time's endeavour
       Be tried in vain –
       No other pleasure
       With this could measure;
       And like a treasure
       We'd hug the chain.

The infectious rhythmic swing to this indicates immediately that it is related to the 4 × 4 structure, since there is no other rhythmic form in English which carries such a strong sense of beats organised into a complete whole. It could be written as follows:

[10a] Could love for ever run like a river,
          B   B   B   B
       And Time's endeavour be tried in vain –
         B   B   B   B
       No other pleasure with this could measure;
        B   B   B   B
       And like a treasure we'd hug the chain.
         B   B   B   B

While altering the distinctive rhythmic flavour imparted by the metrical pattern, this rearrangement reveals clearly the underlying 4 × 4 structure, and helps explain why the rhyme word 'chain' is reached with such a feeling of resolution: it is, in fact, the crucial closing rhyme of the familiar *abcb* scheme.

There are many other metrical patterns which realise this basic structure, and the structure can be extended to create an effect of suspension or prolongation. One example is the 'Burns stanza', in which two two-beat lines are inserted in the pattern, and the whole form bound together by an *aaabab* rhyme-scheme:

> (11) Ha! whare ye gaun, ye crowlin ferlie!
>   B   B   B   B
> Your impudence protects you sairlie:
>   B   B   B   B
> I canna say but ye strunt rarely,
>   B   B   B   B
> Owre gauze and lace;
>   B   B
> Tho' faith, I fear, ye dine but sparely
>   B   B   B   B
> On sic a place.
>   B   B

Again, such variations are typical of the literary use of a popular form.

The metrical pattern which fully realises the 4 × 4 structure – four lines of four beats each – is to be found throughout the corpus of popular and literary English verse and song, and is provided with a convenient label in the traditional classification of hymn-forms (of which, as one would expect, it is one of the most widely used types): 'long metre' or 'long measure'. But the following nursery rhyme also has an easy, natural rhythmic shape:

> (12) Mary had a little lamb,
>   B   B   B   B
> Its fleece was white as snow;
>   B   B   B
> And everywhere that Mary went
>   B   B   B   B
> Her lamb was sure to go.
>   B   B   B

Instead of four lines of four beats each, we have a metrical pattern of 4.3.4.3, and this too is a form we find frequently in nursery rhymes, as well as in hymnody (where it is known simply as 'common metre'). Moreover, ballads occur in this form more frequently than in any other: Gerould (1932, pp. 125–6) notes that of the 305 ballads in Child's collection, 179 have this form, while 111 have the full long metre form, and Hendren (1936, p. 78) puts the proportion at roughly half of all ballads in common metre, and only a quarter in long metre. The form is, in fact, often known simply as the 'ballad-stanza':

> (13) She's laid her down upon her bed
>   B   B   B   B
>   An soon she's fa'n asleep,
>   B   B   B
>   And soon oer every tender limb
>   B   B   B   B
>   Cauld death began to creep.
>   B   B   B

The literary tradition has made much use of it, perhaps most commonly when an effect of simplicity is desired:

> (14) She dwelt among the untrodden ways
>   B   B   B   B
>   Beside the springs of Dove,
>   B   B   B
>   A maid whom there were none to praise
>   B   B   B   B
>   And very few to love.
>   B   B   B

A metrical form which became very popular in the sixteenth century, at a time when rhythmic regularity was at a premium, and has been used sporadically since then, is the 'fourteener'; this is exactly the same pattern, manifested as couplets of seven beats each, and exhibiting a strict syllable count (yielding fourteen syllables per line):

> (15) No image carved with cunning hand, no cloth of purple dye,
>   B   B   B   B   B   B   B
>   No precious weight of metal bright, no silver plate give I.
>   B   B   B   B   B   B   B

Here one can feel the strong pauses after four beats, corresponding to the line-ends in the four-line form.

Do all these examples represent a rhythmic form distinct from the 4 × 4 structure? Careful introspection as one reads shows that the answer is no. If one chants (12) very rhythmically, beating time as one does so, one finds that it is much more natural to follow the second line with a beat in silence, giving the line four beats, than to go straight on to the next line; and the final line obviously follows the same pattern, making up the full 4 × 4 structure. We need not be disturbed at the last beat's occurring in the silence after the end of the stanza, since music provides clear parallels; Cone (1968, p. 18) comments that the first movement of Beethoven's Fifth Symphony forces the listener 'to add a silent measure after the last one notated – a measure that is as essentially a part of the composition as those actually written'. Alternatively, one might choose to extend the last syllable of the shorter line over two beats in pronunciation, without affecting the basic form. Hendren (1936) demonstrates that there is only one fundamental type of ballad melody – four phrases of two double measures each – whether the verse is in long metre or common metre, and such musical settings show clearly the extra beat after the three-beat lines. Anyone who has recited nursery rhymes in their normal social context will be familiar with the chant-like delivery that gives the underlying four-beat structure full emphasis, but if objective evidence is desired, the experiment in 'choral reading' mentioned earlier (Boomsliter, Creel, and Hastings, 1973) provides it. (Choral reading, it will be recalled, induces each individual to adjust his pronunciation to a norm shared by others, thus bringing out the common underlying rhythms more clearly.) The group of subjects was asked to recite in chorus a stanza by Emily Dickinson in common metre; the recorded syllable durations indicate that in such a reading unrealised beats at the ends of lines 2 and 4 occupy the full time of realised beats. We can therefore show the underlying rhythmic structure of this type of stanza as follows (using square brackets to indicate unrealised beats):

(12) Mary had a little lamb,
      B   B   B   B
      Its fleece was white as snow;
      B   B   B   [B]
      And everywhere that Mary went,
      B   B   B   B
      Her lamb was sure to go.
      B   B   B   [B]

In this pattern, the division of the four-line unit into two pairs is emphasised by the absence of a realised beat at the end of the second line, a structure which is reflected graphically when the verse is set out as a fourteener couplet. However, the further subdivision of the seven-beat group into two will always make itself felt, and one of the difficulties in writing (and reading) fourteeners is the pause or intonational cadence demanded after four beats. If this is reflected in the syntactic structure of the line, any advantages of the long line as a vehicle for meditative or narrative verse are lost, since the units of composition remain short, and the 4 × 4 structure, with its associations of song-form, remains prominent. If, on the other hand, the syntax overrides the medial break, the result is rhythmic awkwardness, and fourteeners which consistently do this, like those of Chapman's Homer, avoid monotony only at the cost of rhythmic incoherence.[4]

How is it that we are able to accept the absence of an audible beat so easily, and why only in very limited positions in the 4 × 4 structure? The answer lies, in part at least, in the hierarchical patterning of elementary rhythms: a four-beat line tends to resolve into two units, the four beats being perceived as alternately stronger and weaker, even if there is no phonological reason to stress the syllables in this way (see Tovey's comment quoted above, p. 82). Each two-line unit, therefore, represents on a larger scale the same basic four-beat form that underlies the single line, which is what gives four-beat couplets their strong feeling of cohesion. We shall discuss this 'dipodic' alternation among beats in section 7 of this chapter, but what must be noted here is that the main rhythmic weight of a four-beat line is carried by the first and third beats, making the fourth beat the least important in the structure of the line. If it is not physically manifested, we are likely to provide a silent substitute; and that this should happen most easily at the end of the second and fourth lines is not surprising, since the third beat of these lines is also the fourth and final main beat of the larger two-line unit. If an example of common metre is read with exaggerated stresses on the first and third beats of each line, the larger structure (indicated here by upper-case B's) will be evident, with the last realised beat of lines 2 and 4 conveying a strong feeling of finality:

(16) Hard is her heart as flint or stone,
     B   b   B   b
     She laughs to see me pale;
     B   b   B   [b]
     And merry as a grig is grown,
     B   b   B   b
     And brisk as bottled ale.
     B   b   B   [b]

The syllables on these beats invariably rhyme, and we rarely find the *aabb* scheme familiar in long metre, which would produce an awkward linking of a weaker beat in the fourth position of the line with a stronger one in the third position.

It is perhaps as well to emphasise again at this point that what we are trying to discover is the fundamental rhythmic organisation that gives rise to our sense of a unified whole in which temporal relations are controlled and ordered, and that we are not attempting a transcription in some kind of musical notation of what we actually hear. One can read straight on from line 2 to line 3 in stanzas like (12) or (13) without destroying the perceived underlying rhythm, the line-break being signalled partly by the intonation contour which the syntactic structure demands; but a performance of these lines as a chant, or a strict musical setting, will reveal the importance of the unrealised fourth beat of line 2. On the other hand, one cannot add an extra beat to the first or third line without disrupting the rhythm altogether. One must of course distinguish sharply between an unrealised beat, the equivalent of a bar or half-bar rest in music, which occurs in only a few very strictly defined positions in the 4 × 4 structure, and a *pause*, effected in performance either by lengthening a syllable or by a silence, which temporarily suspends the underlying rhythmic movement, but does not enter into its organisation or affect its coherence. As we noted in 1.2, some writers with a musical approach to English metre make free use of unrealised beats (or 'silent stresses') in all parts of the line, but in doing so they are moving from the basic rhythmic form to possible performances of the verse. Pauses are an important element in the sensitive reading of a poem; unrealised beats are part of its structure.

As in the case of long metre, this 4.3.4.3 pattern may be varied and extended, especially within the literary tradition. One recurring form is *rime couée*, in which the long lines are doubled, creating a form which still has the satisfying unity of common metre, but with a rhythm which is less likely to overpower the sense:

(17) From hence, ye beauties, undeceived,
           B   B   B   B
      Know, one false step is ne'er retrieved,
          B   B   B   B
       And be with caution bold.
       B   B   B   [B]
      Not all that tempts your wandering eyes
      B   B   B   B
      And heedless hearts is lawful prize;
       B   B   B   B
        Nor all that glisters gold.
         B   B   B   [B]

The finality of the fourth line can be countered by an extension of the pattern, producing sometimes the effect of a repeated refrain, sometimes a further climax, more powerful than the one already experienced. Coleridge is a master of both effects:

(18) And I had done a hellish thing,

　　　B　　　　B　　　　B　　　　B

　　　And it would work 'em woe:

　　　B　　　　B　　　　B　　　[B]

　　　For all averred, I had killed the bird

　　　B　　B　　　　　B　　　　B

　　　That made the breeze to blow.

　　　B　　　　B　　　　B　　　[B]

　　　Ah wretch! said they, the bird to slay,

　　　B　　　　B　　　　B　　　　B

　　　That made the breeze to blow!

　　　B　　　　B　　　　B　　　[B]

(19) Like one, that on a lonesome road

　　　B　　　　　B　　B　　　　B

　　　Doth walk in fear and dread,

　　　B　　　　B　　　　B　　　[B]

　　　And having once turned round walks on,

　　　B　　B　　　　　B　　　　B

　　　And turns no more his head;

　　　B　　　　B　　　　B　　　[B]

　　　Because he knows, a frightful fiend

　　　B　　　　B　　　　B　　　　B

　　　Doth close behind him tread.

　　　B　　　　B　　　　B　　　[B]

Though long metre and common metre are the two realisations of the 4 × 4 rhythmic structure most frequently to be met with, the same structure can be manifested in other metrical patterns. Occasionally only the last line has an unrealised beat, creating a 4.4.4.3 pattern which, in children's verse, is especially common in counting-out rhymes, where the rhythmic climax is delayed until the very last syllable, at which point the victim is selected – one can imagine the expression of his chagrin replacing the final unrealised beat. Iona and Peter Opie record several variants of one such rhyme (1951, p. 223), incidentally illustrating how nonsense formations which observe the morphological and phonological principles of English are perfectly capable of establishing a strong rhythm, thanks to our knowledge of stress rules and our receptivity to elementary rhythmic structures. One version runs:

(20) Inter, mitzy, titzy, tool,

　　　B　　　B　　　B　　　B

　　　Ira, dira, dominu,

　　　B　　B　　　B　　　B

　　　Oker, poker, dominoker,

　　　B　　　B　　　　B　　　B

　　　Out goes you.

　　　B　　　B　　　B　　[B]

The short last line, with its distinctive rhythm, can be used in literary verse as a haunting refrain:

(21) But who hath seen her wave her hand?
      B   B   B   B
      Or at the casement seen her stand?
      B   B   B   B
      Or is she known in all the land,
      B   B   B   B
      The Lady of Shalott?
      B   B   B   [B]

Our ear seems to need the reassurance of a fully-realised four-beat line from time to time, and stanzas in which all four lines have unrealised beats, a metrical pattern of 3.3.3.3, are not very common in popular verse (Gerould, 1932, pp. 127–8, notes only four examples in Child); once again, it is a more consciously artistic mind that experiments with such patterns and the slight tensions they create. Theodore Roethke is fond of this metre, which suits the tendency of much of his poetry to move forward one line at a time. He also uses its interrupted progression for comic effect:

(22) The whiskey on your breath
          B   B   B   [B]
      Could make a small boy dizzy;
      B   B   B   [B]
      But I hung on like death:
      B   B   B   [B]
      Such waltzing was not easy.
      B   B   B   [B]

The continuous use of six-beat lines occurs occasionally in the literary tradition, and such lines usually resolve into two groups of three realised beats plus one unrealised beat; Drayton's *Polyolbion*, Swinburne's *Hymn to Proserpine*, and Morris's *Sigurd the Volsung* are examples of this metre, all of which show the medial hiatus in the line's structure.

A more common pattern, however, is one in which only the third line of a quatrain is fully realised as four beats:

(23) Hickory dickory dock,
      B   B   B   [B]
      The mouse ran up the clock;
      B   B   B   [B]
      The clock struck one, the mouse ran down,
      B   B   B   B
      Hickory dickory dock.
      B   B   B   [B]

The unrealised beats in this pattern are clearly manifested in a choral reading (Boomsliter, Creel, and Hastings, 1973). It is a pattern familiar from the limerick, though there the long third line is usually printed as two (we have already noted that the typical intonation contour of the 4 × 4 rhythmic structure encourages this division of the third line). It is also common among hymn-stanzas, and is to be found in a few ballads:

(24) She's tyed it in her apron
      B   B   B   [B]
      And she's thrown it in the sea;
      B   B   B   [B]
      Says, 'Sink ye, swim ye, bonny wee babe!
      B   B   B   B
      You'l neer get mair o me!
      B   B   B   [B]

As with common metre, Tudor poets in search of metrical regularity liked to run the pairs of lines in this pattern together, resulting in lines of six and seven beats alternately, or, given a strict syllable count, twelve and fourteen syllables. The couplet was called 'poulter's measure', because of the generosity – or carelessness – of sixteenth-century poulterers, whose eggs came in dozens of twelve and fourteen (see Gascoigne, 1575, p. 56). Once again there is a tendency to pause at the rhythmic break in the line, which is even more of a problem than in the case of the fourteener, since the first line now has a full metrical rest in the middle.[5] The following is an example attributed to Queen Elizabeth, which does not rise above the mediocrity characteristic of such verse.

(25) The doubt of future foes exiles my present joy,
      B   B   B [B] B   B   B   [B]
      And wit me warns to shun such snares as threaten
      B   B   B   B   B
      mine annoy.
      B   [B]
      For falsehood now doth flow and subject faith doth ebb,
      B   B   B [B]   B   B   B   [B]
      Which would not be if reason ruled or wisdom weaved
      B   B   B   B   B   B
      the web.
      B   [B]

In this 3.3.4.3 realisation of the 4 × 4 structure, which we can conveniently refer to as 'short metre' thanks once more to hymnodic classification, the main rhyme is again between lines 2 and 4, but an *abab* scheme is rendered unlikely by the different lengths of lines 1 and

3; hence the favouring of the limerick rhyme-scheme, which links all the three-beat lines, and marks off the four-beat line with its own internal rhyming.

Why has this particular arrangement of 3.3.4.3 emerged as a popular one, rather than other apparently equivalent patterns? We have seen that because of the underlying dipodic tendency the second and fourth lines can most easily dispense with a final realised beat, and that this contributes to the sense of finality about their endings; but it is not as easy to see why, say, a quatrain of 4.3.3.3 should not be as popular and rhythmically acceptable as the short metre form. To answer this question, we need to step back and take in the whole group of lines as a single rhythmic unit. Whereas the 4.3.4.3 pattern is a clear binary structure, the 3.3.4.3 pattern presents itself more obviously as a rhythmic whole. The second half of the pattern does not merely repeat the first half, but fills it out, supplying in the third line what was missing in the first two, and rounding off the rhythmic shape with an unbroken succession of seven realised beats. The characteristic intonation pattern of the third line mentioned earlier is preserved (or even, since this is the only intonation contour which is allowed to spread itself over four beats, given special emphasis), conveying a strong sense of an approaching conclusion. This line obviously occupies a crucial place in the scheme, as it does in the other realisations of the 4 × 4 structure, constituting a rhythmic and intonational climax before the movement returns to that of the opening line. Example (23) emphasises this pattern verbally and semantically; the third line *is* the climax of the piece, and is given additional prominence by the internal rhyme and the subdivision it enforces; while the final line is quite literally a return to the opening.

It will be worth devoting some attention to this pattern as an example of the second controlling influence on metrical form mentioned in the Preface: aesthetic tendencies with wider scope than the literary tradition alone. The 3.3.4.3 structure exemplified by the limerick, short metre, and poulter's measure is probably related to a common rhythmic form, found in music as well as verse, which we can indicate as a sequence of four bars, though it occurs over large time-spans as well as small:

| ♩ | ♩ | ♩♩ | ♩ |

The doubling of notes in the third bar of this pattern, while maintaining the regularity of the rhythm, gives that bar a special salience, fills it more fully with physical material, as it were, and transforms four separate units into a single rhythmic whole. It does this by implying an internal structure: a new phase begins at bar 3 which is and yet is not the same as the first phase, and as a result the fourth bar comes as a clinching repetition of bar 2 after the slight disturbance. One has only to try rearranging the order of the units to test the crucial function of this third bar.

We find variants of this rhythmic pattern in many individual lines of nursery rhymes, where the third beat is followed by a larger number of syllables than the other beats:

(26) See-saw, Margery Daw
      B   B   B   B

(27) Humpty Dumpty sat on a wall
      B   B   B   B

(28) Ding dong bell, pussy's in the well
      B   B   B   B

A similar principle can be seen at work in the ballad tradition:

(29) He's mounted on his berry-brown steed
      B   B   B   B

(30) And thrice he has kissed her cherry, cherry cheek
      B   B   B   B

Another version of this pattern is found in the long line of the accentual sapphic:

(31) Come, let us sound with melody the praises
      B   B   B   B

This is a form which has recurred in the Western literary tradition from medieval (and perhaps Roman) times; for a discussion see Needler (1941) and Attridge (1974, pp. 211–16). And we shall see at the end of the following chapter that the rhythms of the iambic pentameter are also related to this pattern. It does not seem unlikely, therefore, that the same fundamental rhythmic tendency underlies both the shaping of many individual lines and the 3.3.4.3 structure of the short metre stanza.

This rhythmic formation is, in fact, a small-scale example of one of the commonest ways of effecting closure in an aesthetic form, usefully discussed by B. H. Smith (1968, pp. 44, 65–6): the return to an established norm after deviation. A single repetition is the minimum required to set up a norm, which is followed by one deviant element, and one re-establishing element; and this is the fundamental principle of the ubiquitous *AABA* form, to be found at all levels of musical structure, from the four-phrase melody in which the third phrase deviates from the pattern of the other three (Beethoven's setting of Schiller's 'Ode to Joy' is a simple example), to the structure of whole movements or works.[6] It may also be relevant to note that metrical designs are often characterised by a more explicit manifestation of underlying patterns towards the end of the line; the classical dactylic hexameter, for example, does not allow the substitution of a spondee for a dactyl in the fifth foot, and the Latin hexameter is further characterised by coincidence of quantity and accent in the last two feet. One might say that what makes the 3.3.4.3 form a particularly strong Gestalt is that the third line is both a deviation before a final return, and a realisation, at a crucial point in the structure, of implicit form. In fact, it is far *too* prominent a rhythmic shape for most literary purposes, capable of less variety in its handling than long metre and common metre, and hence likely to be avoided by any poet wishing to exploit the most subtle aspects of the four-beat rhythmic structure.

4.4 OFFBEATS; DUPLE AND TRIPLE RHYTHMS

So far we have been concerned only with the beats of the underlying rhythmic structure and their realisation in metrical patterns, and have proceeded as if what happens between the beats is irrelevant. As far as the basic architecture of verse form is concerned this assumption is valid, but once we start trying to characterise the different qualities of movement that can be built upon this foundation, it becomes important to examine the effect of syllables which function in the sequence of rhythmic alternations as offbeats. As we have seen in our discussion of stress-timing, our sense of the movement of English speech, whether we are speaking it or hearing it, depends primarily on the fully stressed syllables, and there is a tendency to lighten and quicken the unstressed syllables between these rhythmic focal points. We should not be surprised, then, to find that we perceive stresses as beats (that is to say, as repetitions of a rhythmic pulse) not only if the number of syllables between each stress is constant, but also if the variation in their number is kept within certain limits. Thus Coleridge can write:

(32) Higher and higher every day,
      B   B   B   B
    Till over the mast at noon
    B   B   B   [B]

and our perception of the four realised beats of the first line and the three realised beats of the second line is in no way hindered by the presence of sometimes one, sometimes two, unstressed syllables between them. The stress-timed rhythm of English will, under certain conditions, allow even successive stressed syllables to be read as two beats:

(33) O lang, lang may their ladies sit,
      B   B   B   B
    Wi thair fans into their hand.
    B   B   B   [B]

Here we will be inclined to give the first 'lang' enough weight and duration to allow the next beat to fall on the second 'lang', and in the following line 'into' can be given its normal stress contour if 'fans' is drawn out a little in pronunciation. (In so reading it, we are not going against the natural speech rhythms of English; at most, we are bringing out one possibility in the language at the expense of another.) Many of the examples discussed earlier in this chapter exhibit a similar freedom as regards the realisation of offbeats. However, we noted in the previous chapter that unstressed syllables also have a rhythmic identity of their own, and as the variation in the number of syllables between beats increases, the underlying structure becomes blurred; thus the assigning of beats in the following example can only be tentative:

(34) Never the least stir made the listeners,
    B   B   B   B
    Though every word he spake
        B   B   B   [B]
    Fell echoing through the shadowiness of the still house
    B   B   B   B
    From the one man left awake.
    B   B   B   [B]

Offbeats play no part in the underlying rhythm, which, as the simplest and most fundamental rhythmic form, is merely a series of beats; they are best regarded as an aspect of the various metrical patterns which may realise that underlying rhythm. It is a fundamental principle of English verse that beats are always separated by offbeats: one phase of relaxation cannot follow another without an intervening energy pulse, since it would merely extend that phase. An underlying rhythm of four beats, therefore, always has three offbeats between the beats, which we can show as follows:

B o B o B o B

It may have, in addition, an offbeat before the first beat and/or one after the last beat. In the line of verse itself, the offbeats of the metrical pattern can be manifested in various ways: as one syllable (*single offbeat*), which we shall indicate in scansion by o; as two syllables (*double offbeat*), indicated by ŏ; or occasionally as three syllables (*triple offbeat*), indicated by ̆, though we have already noted the tendency of three unstressed syllables in English to be interpreted as a beat with an offbeat on either side. Offbeats can also be implied in the rhythm but not realised in the language, and we shall indicate this by ȯ. A fuller scansion of (33) is therefore as follows:

(*33*) O lang, lang may their ladies sit
    o B ȯ B   ŏ   B o B

We should not think of the unstressed syllables in English verse as having no other function than to keep the stresses at roughly equal intervals; they clearly contribute to the nature of the rhythmic movement itself, and this has important expressive consequences. Consider the following stanzas from one of Auden's literary ballads:

(35) Victor looked up at the mountains,
      B ŏ   B ŏ   B o   [B]
The mountains all covered with snow;
  o B   ŏ B   ŏ   B [o B]
Cried; 'Are you pleased with me, Father?'
  o   B o B   ŏ   B o   [B]
And the answer came back; 'No'.
  ŏ   B   o B   o   B   [o B]

Victor came to the forest,
  B o B   ŏ   B o   [B]
Cried; 'Father, will she ever be true?'
  o   B   ̆   B ŏ   B   [o B]
And the oaks and the beeches shook their heads
  ŏ B   ŏ   B o B   o B
And they answered; 'Not to you'.
  ŏ   B   o   B o B [o B]

The chilling finality of the replies is conveyed in part by the shift in the last line of each stanza from a light and rapid movement created by double offbeats to a weightier alternation of beats and single offbeats (a change which in the second stanza begins in the nightmarish headshakes of the penultimate line). This can be demonstrated by noting the lightening effect of rewriting the last two lines with double offbeats throughout:

> [35a] And the oaks and the beeches all twisted their heads,
>   And they answered him; 'Never to you'.

It is, of course, the stress-timed rhythm of English, in co-operation with the regular verse form, which speeds up the syllables when there are two nonstresses between beats, and slows them down when there is one. It might be noted in passing that in the first stanza Auden leaves a final beat unrealised in the relatively rare position of the third line, thus emphasising the tense pause after the question, while in the same position of the second stanza the inescapable reply fills the full four-beat structure; and also that the anguished cry in the second stanza achieves its effect partly by the unusual use of a triple offbeat.

The various methods of realising offbeats can be used in this way for local rhythmic effects; if, however, a poet makes consistent use of either single or double offbeats in a poem, another kind of general rhythmic principle is introduced: the special character of duple and triple rhythms. Two of Blakes's *Songs of Innocence* will illustrate this familiar distinction:

> (36) When the voices of children are heard on the green
>   ŏ   B   ŏ   B   ŏ   B   ŏ   B
>   And laughing is heard on the hill,
>   o   B   ŏ   B   ŏ   B   [o B]
>   My heart is at rest within my breast
>   o   B   ŏ   B   o B   o   B
>   And everything else is still.
>   o   B   ŏ   B   o   B   [o B]
>
> (37) To Mercy, Pity, Peace, and Love
>   o   B   o   Bo   B   o   B
>   All pray in their distress;
>   o   B   o   B   o   B   [o B]
>   And to these virtues of delight
>   o   B   o   B   o   B   o B
>   Return their thankfulness.
>   o B   o   B   o   B   [o B]

In the first of these, the occurrence of single offbeats does not upset the fundamentally triple rhythm established by the first line, with its characteristic qualities of rapidity and lightness; while the second example has the somewhat heavier movement of duple verse. A line like the last one in (36) could occur in duple verse, but we would experience its rhythm differently in that context: the double offbeat would merely be a substitute for the expected single offbeat, instead of a reminder of an established triple rhythm. It is important to note that the *metrical pattern* of these two examples is identical, and that the distinction between duple and triple rhythms occurs not as a structural principle, but in the surface realisation; it is for this reason that there is no clear dividing line between the two. In composing a bleak counterpart to (36) for the *Songs of Experience*, Blake is able to create a more ambiguous rhythm after the first line by slightly increasing the proportion of single offbeats:

(38) When the voices of children are heard on the green
      ŏ   B   ŏ   B   ŏ   B   ŏ   B
      And whisp'rings are in the dale,
      o   B   ŏ   B   o   B   [o B]
      The days of my youth rise fresh in my mind,
      o   B   ŏ   B   o   B   ŏ   B
      My face turns green and pale.
      o   B   o   B   o   B   [o B]

Most traditional ballads have a fundamentally duple rhythm, but show much freedom in the numbers of unstressed syllables between beats, rather in the way that triplets can occur in a basically duple-time piece of music (though the tempting musical analogy is, as we have seen, a dangerous one; a poet is under no obligation to specify or keep to a time-signature). The freedom to spice one kind of rhythm with touches of another, or to avoid the characteristics of either, is a freedom on which the power and delicacy of rhythmic effects depend. We are, in fact, probably more sensitive to these details of a poet's metrical style than we realise: Harding (1976, pp. 41–3) shows how Swinburne's use in many poems of a double offbeat at least once in each line rapidly establishes a perceptual set which makes a strictly duple line seem out of place, even though a fully triple rhythm is never established.

Duple rhythms are much commoner than triple in the English literary tradition, and it is worth asking why this should be so. We can approach the question in terms of the three sources of metre mentioned in the Preface: the nature of the language, the principles of rhythmic form, and the conventions of the poetic tradition. One feature of English speech that we noted in 3.4 was the tendency towards an alternation of stronger and weaker stresses; verse in duple metre embodies this tendency as its basic rhythmic principle, and is therefore able to draw on the full resources of the spoken language, accommodating polysyllables and stretches of monosyllables with relative ease. Triple metres, on the other hand, have to work against this tendency in order to create an alternative rhythmic pattern, which can tolerate certain words only by suppressing their natural stress contours. Moreover, duple verse matches the two rhythmic principles of English, the stress-timed rhythm and the syllabic rhythm, by providing one syllable for a rhythmic peak and one for a trough; triple verse, on the other hand, favours stress-timing, both in its implied equivalence of one strong to two weak syllables, and in its overriding of the alternations of the language. This alliance with the stronger, and probably more fundamental, rhythmic principle produces a prominent rhythm that tends to simplify the contours of speech.[7] A strong triple rhythm will often force a bad poet (or even tempt a good one) to subordinate semantic and syntactic choices to metrical choices, producing verse which is more gesture than expression, poems like 'The Charge of the Light Brigade' or 'The Cloud', which lodge in the mind less for what they say than for the rhythm in which they say it. We shall see in Part Three how often a particular feature of duple metre can be explained as a stratagem to keep the powerful triple rhythm at bay.

Turning next to the influence of rhythmic form as a general principle, we may observe that a duple rhythm *per se* is simpler than a triple rhythm; all it requires is an alternation between a relatively stronger and a relatively weaker signal, where a triple rhythm demands two approximately equal signals perceived as weaker than the signals on either side. If the distinction between strong and weak is not rigorously observed, the integrity of the rhythm is threatened, and this is no doubt one reason why we experience a triple rhythm as peculiarly insistent. This again makes it less suited to poetry which imitates the flexibility of speech, and more common in poetry associated with music: nursery rhyme, ballad, song itself.

As for the part played by convention, it is, as always, difficult to assess, and we shall take up the subject again in 9.3. Any tendency for triple and duple rhythms to be used in the different ways outlined above, as a result of their inherent qualities, will be strengthened as the literary tradition grows and metres acquire conventional associations. Tedford and Synnott (1972) tested these associations experimentally, and found that their subjects linked verse in duple metre with the adjectives 'heavy', 'sad', 'earnest', 'tragic', and – interestingly –

'outdoor', whereas verse in triple metre was 'light', 'happy', 'playful', 'humorous', and 'indoor'. But one can only guess at the degree to which these subjects were responding to some direct evocation of emotion by rhythm, and the degree to which their responses resulted from associations they had learned either in their encounters with poetic form, or more generally in their experience of rhythm.

4.5 LINE-OPENINGS, LINE-ENDS, AND LINE-JUNCTURES

We have now considered the main beats in the simple rhythmic structure, and the effect of differing kinds of offbeat between those main beats, but what of the offbeats that may occur before the first beat and after the last: to what extent do they influence the movement of the line? That they do not have the same role in maintaining duple and triple rhythms is suggested by the fact that popular verse forms show even freer variation in these positions than between beats. It is very common for lines to begin with the first realised beat and to end with the last, whatever the arrangement of syllables in between, with an effect of simplicity and directness, as in the openings of many of the nursery rhymes already quoted:

(7) Ride a cock-horse to Banbury Cross
    B   B   B   B

(12) Mary had a little lamb
     B   B   B   B

(23) Hickory dickory dock
     B   B   B   [B]

Also common is a single offbeat at the opening of a line, whose rhythmic function is very similar to an opening upbeat, or anacrusis, in music, providing a gentler introduction:

(39) There was an old woman who lived in a shoe
       o   B   B   B   B

(40) As I was going to St Ives
    o B   B   B   B

(41) The king sits in Dumferling toune
     o B   B   B   B

In ballad melodies, the anacrusis is more often than not at a lower pitch than the accented syllable that follows, reflecting its introductory character; and many ballads begin with an unstressed 'O', serving little purpose except to give the musical anacrusis a vocal realisation (see Hendren, 1936, p. 62). The difference between lines with and without an initial offbeat can have a marked effect on our experience of the rhythmic character of the verse, however. Take, for example, the contrast Marvell establishes between the hectoring voice of Created Pleasure and the gentle confidence of the Resolved Soul by giving only the latter an initial offbeat:

(42) PLEASURE: Thou in fragrant clouds shall show
                 Like another god below.
     SOUL: A soul that knows not to presume
                 Is heaven's and its own perfume.

A double offbeat is a more complicated way of opening a line than a single offbeat, and is less common in popular verse, even when a triple rhythm has been established. It is largely in literary examples of triple verse that we find the opening syllables insisting on the rhythm:

(43) And the rose like a nymph to the bath addrest,
     ŏ   B   B   B   B
     Which unveiled the depth of her glowing breast
     ŏ   B   B   B   B

All these examples have had beats at line-end, but a less resounding culmination is achieved by ending on an offbeat (traditionally, a feminine ending):

(44) Little Miss Muffet sat on a tuffet
     B   B   B   B o

(45) Three little kittens they lost their mittens
     B   B   B   B o

Such endings do not provide as strong a sense of closure as masculine endings, and are less common in all English verse, whether popular or literary. The difference may result not only from the fact that in a masculine ending there is no extra syllable to complicate the pattern: we may recall that in one view of English speech rhythms a final stress is 'self-arrested' (see 3.2), and this would contribute to the impression of completed movement. It is noteworthy that feminine endings in nursery rhymes often involve an internal rhyme, as in (44) and (45), which produces its own sense of resolution at the end of the line. The second and fourth lines of the 4 × 4 structure, requiring a stronger closure than the other two, seldom have a feminine ending, a point to which we shall return in due course. In popular verse, however, one must be careful to distinguish between the genuine feminine ending and the common phenomenon of a normally unstressed syllable taking the final beat of the line, or at least going some way towards giving substance to an unrealised beat:

(46) Goosey, goosey, gander,
       B   B   B B
       Whither shall I wander?
       B   B   B   B

The occurrence of a double offbeat at the end of a line, as at the beginning, is rare, one problem being that the alternating rhythm (both of the language and of duple metre) tends to invite a beat on the last syllable. Once again, most examples are for self-conscious literary effect. They usually rely on the prior establishment of a triple rhythm, which prevents the last syllable from being interpreted as a beat:

(47) Touch her not scornfully;
       B   ŏ   B   ŏ
       Think of her mournfully;
       B ŏ   B   ŏ
       Gently and humanly
       B   ŏ   B   ŏ

We cannot, however, consider single lines in isolation when dealing with the question of their openings and endings. In metrical forms built on the 4 × 4 structure, there is a continuous rhythmic sweep from the beginning to the end of the stanza, and perhaps even the entire poem, so it is necessary to re-examine the status of syllables at the beginning and end of each line in this larger context. Let us return to the familiar realisation of the 4 × 4 structure in lines with initial beats:

(48) Golden haired and golden hearted
       B   B   B   B   o
       I would ever have you be,
       B   B   B   B
       As you were when last we parted
       B   B   B   B   o
       Smiling slow and sad at me.
       B   B   B   B

Why is alternation between feminine and masculine endings so common in this form? At least part of the reason must be the fundamental division of such a quatrain into two pairs of lines. The offbeat at the ends of lines 1 and 3, followed immediately by the opening beat of the next line, is part of the smooth flow of rhythm from the first to the eighth beat, and from the ninth to the sixteenth. But there is no unstressed syllable to bridge the gap between 'be' and 'As', and the result is a pause, not as great as that created by an unrealised beat at this point, but marked enough to impart a distinctive rhythmic character to the stanza. If we introduce a final offbeat here, the change is very noticeable:

> [48a] Golden haired and golden hearted
> I would ever have you standing,
> As you were when last we parted
> Smiling slow upon the landing.

The rhythm becomes wooden, and the strong outline of the whole stanza is clouded, merely by adding two unstressed syllables. The rhythm of the original is also affected if we omit the final offbeats of the first and third lines:

> [48b] Golden haired and golden souled
> I would ever have you be,
> As you were in days of old,
> Smiling slow and sad at me.

The loss of two unstressed syllables has now made the movement more abrupt, the lines more self-contained. We could return to something like the original rhythm by adding unstressed syllables at the *beginning* of lines 2 and 4:

> [48c] Golden haired and golden souled
> Would I for ever have you be,
> As you were in days of old,
> Departing sad and slow from me.

One might say that the exact position of the line-boundary with respect to the offbeat is relatively unimportant to the metrical pattern, though it does affect the rhythmic flavour of the poetry. Musical settings of 4 × 4 verse clearly demonstrate this continuity: an unstressed syllable occurring at the beginning of a line other than the first is most likely to form part of the final bar of the previous line.

Nursery rhymes, too, exhibit the continuity between lines very plainly. We have seen that a common opening line is one which begins and ends on a beat; the second line, however, does not usually repeat this pattern, being more likely to begin with an offbeat to smooth the transition from the final beat of the previous line, as in examples (7),

(12), and (23). But in those cases where the initial line ends with an offbeat and the rhythm is duple, the next line tends to begin with a beat:

> (49) Doctor Foster went to Gloucester
>   B   B   B   B   o
>   In a shower of rain
>   B   B   B   [B]

If the rhythm is triple, however, a final offbeat followed by an initial offbeat will sit very happily together, creating the expected double offbeat:

> (50) Hey diddle diddle, the cat and the fiddle,
>   B   B   B   B   o
>   The cow jumped over the moon
>   o   B   B   B   [B]

Lines later than the first and second show similar tendencies, the transition between lines 3 and 4 being more likely to demand realisation of offbeats than that between 2 and 3.

These characteristics are, of course, manifested only when smoothness of rhythm is at a premium; nursery rhymes passed on by oral delivery to children are likely to develop in the direction of smoothness, though sometimes a more abrupt rhythm becomes part of the distinctive character of a particular rhyme. But even in sophisticated uses of the four-beat rhythm, the continuity between the units of the underlying structure is an important aspect of the form, to be used or challenged by the poet. For instance, feminine endings before initial offbeats can be used to increase the integrity of the individual line and inhibit the onward thrust of the 4×4 structure. When an alternation of feminine and masculine endings occurs in an iambic quatrain, such an effect is produced at the end of the first and third lines (where the interlineal momentum is strongest), and the last syllable of the stanza is given a satisfying finality:

> (51) And not by eastern windows only,
>   B   o
>   When daylight comes, comes in the light,
>   o   B
>   In front, the sun climbs slow, how slowly,
>   B   o
>   But westward, look, the land is bright.[8]
>   o   B

One aspect of the relationship between the metrical pattern and the language in which it is realised is the degree to which the metrical structures coincide with the syntactic structures, and the point at which this is most obvious is the juncture between lines: the line-boundary may coincide with a syntactic boundary to create an end-stopped line, or the line may be run-on. This distinction is not black and white, of course; syntactic breaks vary in strength (often reflected by the punctuation), and a run-on which occurs between, say, a noun and the verb of which it is the subject is less strong than one between an adjective and the noun it qualifies. One might expect the continuity between lines in the 4 × 4 form to favour run-ons, but we must remember that for all its cohesion the rhythmic structure is very clearly articulated into four units, and that we experience a distinct sense of transition between these units, manifested in part by the intonation contour described earlier. If the syntactic units, which have their own intonation patterns, do not coincide with this structure, the result is a tension uncharacteristic of popular verse, and inappropriate in any literary verse which aims at lyrical smoothness. This is especially true of structures with unrealised beats, of course, since an unrealised beat is a very strong marker of the break between lines. We find, therefore, that the endings of four-beat lines in the 4 × 4 structure usually coincide with a syntactic boundary of some kind; and we can construct a paradigm in which the strongest syntactic break, marked, say, by a full stop, does not come till the end of the stanza; the next strongest, marked by a semicolon, falls halfway through; and there are weaker boundaries, marked by commas, after the first and third lines. Many four-beat stanzas do in fact have this type of structure:

(52)   There lived a wife at Usher's Well,
      And a wealthy wife was she;
    She had three stout and stalwart sons,
      And sent them oer the sea.

Here the characteristic 4 × 4 intonation contour discussed earlier is close to the intonation contour suggested by the syntax. (The break which occurs when a four-beat unit is divided into two short lines is, of course, a different matter; the sense of a hiatus in the rhythm is much weaker, and a run-on much more natural.) Another aspect of the way lines end is the use of rhyme, and we have already noted that the most common rhyme-schemes of the 4 × 4 structure reflect the subdivisions and relationships of the basic form. A striking fact about four-beat verse is that rhyme is almost never absent, and this is something we shall consider when we compare it with its five-beat counterpart in the following chapter.

4.6 RISING AND FALLING RHYTHMS

The following stanzas are both from poems by Samuel Johnson:

> (53) Condemned to Hope's delusive mine,
>   As on we toil from day to day,
>   By sudden blasts or slow decline,
>   Our social comforts drop away.

> (54) When the bonny blade carouses,
>   Pockets full, and spirits high,
>   What are acres? What are houses?
>   Only dirt, or wet or dry.

Although both are fully realised 4 × 4 structures, they have strikingly different rhythmic qualities. In sensing this, we are not responding merely to the presence in one and absence in the other of an initial offbeat to smooth the way into the line, although this is an important factor; we seem to be encouraged (and not just by the subject-matter) to read the second with a jauntier rhythm, the beats and offbeats occurring in a more sharply emphasised alternation. These two kinds of rhythm, traditionally called *rising* and *falling*, spring from the way in which we group stressed and unstressed syllables, or beats and offbeats; if there is a strong tendency to link the offbeats with the following beats, the rhythm will be perceived as rising, and if the offbeats are felt as completing the movement started by the beats which precede them, we will experience a falling rhythm. The most obvious influence at work in shaping the line into rising or falling groups is the structure of words and phrases. In (54), the words 'bonny', 'pockets', 'spirits', 'acres', 'houses', and 'only' are themselves falling units, and in the third line there is a break after an offbeat, traditionally called a 'feminine caesura' by analogy with feminine line-endings, which emphasises this rhythm. By contrast, most of the words and phrases of (53) consist of an offbeat followed by a beat; line 2, for instance, is rising throughout:

As on we toil from day to day

(The symbol used to indicate the rhythmic groups here is not in any way systematically applied and is not part of the scansion, whose purpose is to indicate structural and rule-governed features.)

It is not merely fortuitous, however, that all the lines of (53) have a metrical pattern that begins with an offbeat and ends with a beat, while those of (54) begin with a beat and twice end with an offbeat. To start lines consistently with an offbeat leading to a following beat is to encourage the reader to perceive a rising rhythm in what follows, and to end with a rising unit is to reinforce this tendency. The reverse is true of lines that begin consistently with a beat linked to a following offbeat, especially if they have feminine endings. Moreover, a poet who wishes to establish a strong rising or falling rhythm is likely to match the openings and endings of the line with appropriate words and phrases within it.[9] And in short lines, the extremities may limit the choices available: in (47), for example, there is scarcely any room for the triple falling rhythm of the opening and close of each line to be contradicted. A general correlation is therefore to be expected between, on the one hand, rising rhythms and metrical patterns that begin with an offbeat (traditionally classified as iambic and anapaestic, though I shall call them *offbeat-initial*) and, on the other, falling rhythms and patterns that begin with a beat (trochaic and dactylic metres, or *beat-initial*). However, it is important not to confuse this general tendency with the claim made by many metrical theorists that the distinction between rising and falling rhythms is part of the metrical *structure* of English verse. To scan a line as iambic, in terms of classical foot-prosody, is merely to show that its metre is duple and that it begins with an offbeat; it provides no information about the rising or falling nature of the rhythm, except in so far as the line is subject to the general tendency already noted. There is nothing structurally anomalous about an iambic line with a predominantly falling rhythm, or a trochaic line with a predominantly rising rhythm – indeed, many lines traditionally classed as trochaic end with a beat, like the second and fourth lines of (48) and (54). The last line of (54) moves into a rising rhythm without any sense of dislocation, while (53) contains many falling groups. To equate 'iambic' and 'anapaestic' with 'rising', and 'trochaic' and 'dactylic' with 'falling', is to confuse metrical structure with metrical style, and to diminish greatly the usefulness of the two descriptive terms we are discussing.[10] Similarly, analysts of musical rhythm – like Stetson (1923), Cooper and Meyer (1960) – point out that conventional bar-lines are no guide to the way in which rhythmic units in a piece of music group themselves. We should remember, too, that the continuity within the 4 × 4 structure noted in the previous section diminishes the rhythmic effect of initial and final offbeats on the line.

Whether a line or stanza has a rising or falling tendency is not an aspect of the metrical pattern nor of its realisation as a series of stressed and unstressed syllables, let alone of the underlying rhythm, and would not normally be noted in the scansion. However, the placing of word-boundaries and phrase-boundaries can, like other surface details, be a crucial factor when the rhythm reaches the borders of metricality, as we shall see in 8.7. It is often illuminating to examine a poet's use of the rhythmic grouping of words and phrases, though there is a dangerous temptation to be oversubtle in such analyses. Perhaps one reason why the final line of the following stanza comes as a climax is that it falls into a strong rising rhythm, after three lines which resist both rising and falling tendencies:

(55) Old yew, which graspest at the stones

That name the underlying dead,

Thy fibres net the dreamless head,

Thy roots are wrapt about the bones.

If the last two lines are exchanged, and the altered rhyme-scheme ignored as far as is possible, the stanza seems to end with less emphasis and finality. (Sinfield, 1971, p. 178, observes that Tennyson favours falling rhythms throughout *In Memoriam*, so this rising rhythm is also somewhat unusual in the context of the whole poem.) Attempts have been made at a systematic analysis of word and phrase placement, and its effect on rhythm (for example, R. Fowler, 1966a; Cummings and Herum, 1967; Beardsley, 1972), but such accounts usually suffer from unsatisfactory theories of 'counterpointing' between words and feet (see above, p. 10), and from the general poverty of our knowledge about the finer details of English speech rhythm.

The first three lines of (55) are by no means untypical; a large proportion of the lines of English verse (roughly 45 per cent, according to Stewart, 1930, p. 38) cannot be classified as either rising or falling. Even lines which begin consistently on a beat need not favour a falling rhythm; Sidney, the poet who pioneered such verse in English, provides an example:

(56) Only joy, now here you are,
     Fit to hear and ease my care:
     Let my whispering voice obtain
     Sweet reward for sharpest pain.[11]

Here it would be hard to say whether the rhythm is predominantly rising or falling; like much good poetry, it is written in a flexible metrical style that can draw on the expressive potential of both types of movement. Verse which consistently maintains either a rising or a falling rhythm will of course be perceived as more insistently rhythmical than verse which varies between them or remains neutral.

The difference in character between marked rising and falling rhythms in duple verse has often attracted comment; Hascall (1971, p. 225) observes that there is an 'all but universal subjective impression that trochaic verse has a rhythm which is more insistent, more distinct'. The mere fact of perceptually grouping syllables in one way rather than another says nothing about the rhythmic effect of such groupings; but not much has been offered by way of further explanation. Chatman (1965, p. 141) states that 'the trochaic mode more easily violates normal prose accentual patterns; it quite insists on dominating the rhythm', but he ascribes this to convention, commenting that 'the sophisticated smoothness of iambic verse has been long in developing' (n. 34) – as if Chaucer's pentameters were 'unsophisticated'! Cummings and Herum (1967), using a Gestalt approach, also regard convention as the only cause of the reader's tendency to group syllables into iambic rather than trochaic patterns. For whatever reason, verse in rising rhythms is far more common than its opposite in the English tradition: Stewart (1930, p. 38) has calculated that about 45 per cent of English verse is rising, and only 10 per cent falling. (This preference is of course not the same thing as the overwhelming preference for iambic over trochaic metres, though the two are undoubtedly related.)

If we recall the discussion of the rhythmic character of English words and phrases in 3.4, we can perhaps throw more light on the issue. We saw, for instance, that a word or phrasal unit consisting of a stressed syllable followed by an unstressed syllable tends to be more evenly divided in duration between the syllables than the reverse grouping, in which the stressed syllable takes up a greater part of the duration of the whole. This means that falling words and phrases help impart to the rhythm the characteristics we have noted: a steady, march-like movement, with beats and offbeats tending towards equal duration, though the beats, unprepared for by any lead-in, come with a sharp emphasis. On the other hand, where stressed syllables tend to follow unstressed syllables in words and phrases, the beats will take up a longer time, and the offbeats will be shorter, resulting in a more varied movement, often perceived as smoother than a falling rhythm because the short offbeats lead naturally into the longer beats. Some writers have made a distinction between a characteristically 'duple' timing for falling disyllables or disyllabic phrases (♪ ♩) and 'triple' timing for rising one (♪ ♩), but while this reflects a genuine difference between the rhythms, it implies a strict temporal basis for verse, which, as we have seen, is a misleading interpretation; there is little in common between waltz-rhythm and iambic metre.

This rhythmic difference between rising and falling groups may, as we noted in Chapter 3, be an outcome of the physiological processes of stress-production; however, psychological studies suggest that it may also be a manifestation of a more widely occurring feature of rhythmic perception (though this in turn is probably based on the fundamental properties of muscular action). For example, Woodrow (1909), in a series of experiments in which subjects were asked to report on their rhythmic perception of a sequence of sound stimuli, found that there is a general tendency for alternating loud and soft sounds to be perceived in falling groups, but for alternating long and short sounds to be perceived in rising groups; a strong falling rhythm is therefore likely to be characterised by durational equality and contrasts in intensity, while a strong rising rhythm will be relatively even in intensity but varied in duration. A similar relationship is observable in music: Stetson (1923, p. 184) notes that a falling rhythm is usually in the form ♪ ♩, sometimes ♪ ♩, and only rarely is the accented note longer, ♩ ♪; while the common alternation of long and short notes is in fact perceived in rising groupings, whatever the bar-lines might suggest: ♪|♩♪|♩♪|♩. Meyer (1956, pp. 104–9) provides further musical illustrations of the tendency for durational differences to result in 'end-accented' rhythms, and for intensity differences to result in 'beginning-accented' rhythms. It seems likely, therefore, that the association between, on the one hand, falling groups and a strongly-marked, evenly-divided rhythm, and, on the other hand, rising groups and a more flowing, unevenly-divided rhythm, is a general property of rhythmic perception as well as a specific property of the English language. In addition, a falling rhythm, *qua* rhythm, appears to be perceptually more salient (see Wallin, 1911–12, pp. 114–15), and would be likely, once established, to play a more prominent part in the reader's experience.

Rising rhythms in English verse are commonly experienced not just as more flexible and pleasing in themselves, however, but as more 'natural'. At first sight, this may seem surprising: English words exhibit falling stress contours more often than rising ones, and it has been argued that a 'trochaic' grouping is fundamental to the stress patterns of English words (Allen and Hawkins, 1978; Schane, 1979a, 1979b). But it is at the level of phrases and sentences that we respond to the rhythms of poetry, and here a rising rhythm seems the more common one: unstressed words are more frequently linked to what follows than to what precedes them, and if one stress is subordinated to another, it will usually be to a later one (see 3.3 above). If it is true that verse in a falling rhythm emphasises something basic to the structure of the language, it does so at the cost of the more complex higher-level patterns to which a predominantly rising rhythm is more sensitive. (See note 7 to this chapter for a similar point with respect to duple and triple rhythms.) This would help account for the widely-felt experience of falling verse as imposing itself upon the language in a way that rising verse does not; it has often been noted, for instance, that trochaic verse makes use of fewer metrical variations than iambic (see the statistics presented by Newton, 1975; and for further discussion, 7.8 below). In triple rhythm, the distinction between rising and falling is perhaps less clear than in duple, and one would hesitate before classifying most examples of such verse as one or the other; the insistent movement of a triple rhythm tends, anyway, to override the rhythms of speech.

The distance which a continued falling rhythm puts between itself and the natural rhythms of speech, and the restraints it imposes on the poet's choice of language, make it a rare bird in the literary tradition. Its regular, chant-like movement can, it is true, be put to evocative use if it is varied with an occasional rising group, as in this blessing from *The Tempest*, which does not need to be sung to reveal its ritualistic beauty:

(57) Honour, riches, marriage-blessing,
       Long continuance, and increasing,
       Hourly joys be still upon you!
       Juno sings her blessings on you.

>Earth's increase, foison plenty,
>Barns and garners never empty;
>Vines with clustering branches growing;
>Plants with goodly burthen bowing [...]

But if a rigorous falling rhythm is maintained by all the means at the poet's command, the result is the monotonous, inflexible, and eminently parodiable music of *Hiawatha*:

(58) O'er the water, floating, flying,
      Something in the hazy distance,
      Something in the mists of morning,
      Loomed and lifted from the water,
      Now seemed floating, now seemed flying,
      Coming nearer, nearer, nearer.

4.7 DIPODIC RHYTHMS

In considering the 4.3.4.3 pattern of common metre (section 4.3 above) we noted the tendency for rhythmic beats to alternate between stronger and weaker. This is part of a general tendency in the perception of rhythm; Woodrow (1951, p. 1233) reports experimentation showing that 'in a subjective grouping by four, with the first member accented, the third member is apt to be given a lesser, secondary accent'. Such an alternation in verse is called a *dipodic* rhythm, and we can refer to the two kinds of beat as *primary* and *secondary*. As is the case with all underlying rhythms, dipodic alternation can function without the reader being aware of it; the easiest way to become conscious of its role in a 4 × 4 structure is to tap twice in each line during a normal reading, allowing one's rhythmic instincts to choose the most natural places. This will usually turn out to be on the first and third beats, suggesting an underlying dipodic rhythm which we can indicate by upper and lower case as follows:

(59) Her skirt was of the grass-green silk,
      B   b   B   b
      Her mantel of the velvet fine,
      B   b   B   b
      At ilka tett of her horse's mane
      B   b   B   b
      Hung fifty silver bells and nine.
      B   b   B   b

As we saw earlier, the large-scale dipodic structure underlying the 4 ×

4 organisation is especially clear when the final, weaker, beat is
unrealised:

(60) The cock he hadna crawd but once
      B   b   B   b
      And clappd his wings at a',
      B   b   B   [b]
      When the youngest to the eldest said,
      B   b   B   b
      'Brother, we must awa.'
      B   b   B   [b]

Nursery rhymes, with their blatant use of elementary rhythmic
forms, are often dipodic, and an example will help to make clear the
rhythmic hierarchies which are responsible for the alternation of
primary and secondary beats. The following rhyme can be read in the
manner implied by either of these scansions:

(61) Baa, baa, black sheep,
      B   B   B   B
      Have you any wool?
      B   B   B   [B]
      Yes, sir, yes, sir,
      B   B   B   B
      Three bags full.
      B   B   B   [B]
      One for my master,
      B   B   B   B
      And one for my dame,
      B   B   B   B   [B]
      And one for the little boy
      B   B   B   B
      Who lives down the lane.
      B   B   B   B   [B]

(61a) Baa-baa black sheep, have you any wool?
      B   B   B   B
      Yes sir, yes sir, three bags full.
      B   B   B   B
      One for my master and one for my dame,
      B   B   B   B
      And one for the little boy who lives down the lane.
      B   B   B   B

The first scansion implies a relatively slow, emphatic reading, with a
beat for every stressed syllable, and reveals two 4 × 4 structures; the
second takes the whole as one 4 × 4 structure, and implies a faster
reading with half as many beats. Neither, however, is a full description
of the rhythm which the reader experiences in any reading, fast or
slow; the first masks the large-scale organisation that binds the whole

rhyme together into a single unit, while the second masks the subsidiary rhythmic patterning that is felt between the beats. We could indicate a dipodic rhythm in both scansions: the primary beats in (61) would be the ones that correspond to the beats shown in (61a), and the primary beats in (61a) would form a giant four-beat couplet. But a full scansion would have to show the interaction of these different levels of rhythmic organisation, perhaps by means of a diagram of hierarchies like those sometimes used in the analysis of musical rhythms (see Cooper and Meyer, 1960):[12]

And one for the little boy who lives down the lane

The result may look complex, but the doubling rule which generates the structure could hardly be more elementary, and has a clear relationship with the binary, hierarchical nature of English stress-patterns brought out by Liberman and Prince (1977) (see 3.3 above).

It is tempting to enlarge the hierarchical diagram to include an alternation between lines and pairs of lines (see, for instance, the discussion by Croll, 1929, pp. 420–21), but whether one should use the same term for the alternating structures at such different levels is a debatable point. Tovey considers the same issue in music (1910–11, p. 279): 'As rhythm is contemplated in larger measures, it becomes increasingly difficult to say where the sense of rhythm ends and the sense of proportion begins. The same melody that may be felt as a square and symmetrical piece of proportion in four-bar rhythm if it is taken slowly, will be equally rational as a single bar of "common time" . . . if it is taken very quickly; and between these two extremes there may be insensible gradations.' Thus the analogy between the relationship of the first and second pairs of lines in a 4 × 4 stanza and the relationship of a stressed and unstressed syllable in a falling rhythmic unit may be a tenuous or merely metaphorical one; but the different kinds of relationship shade into one another, and it would be unwise to assume that any particular level of the hierarchy is primary. Patmore (1857) and Croll (1929) regard the dipodic alternation between beats as the most fundamental of all English rhythms, even of verse rhythm in all languages, but to argue this is to isolate artificially one element in an interrelated network, as well as to lose sight of the fact that most verse moves a long way from the simple forms of elementary rhythms.

Dipodic rhythms are most likely to be perceived in strongly rhythmic verse occurring in 4 × 4 structures, especially if the content encourages a chant-like mode of delivery. It is less common in triple verse than in duple, no doubt because the triple units discourage a hierarchical structure based on binary units. Something else which brings out the dipodic structure is the omission of realised offbeats and beats in appropriate positions: the first line of (61) has no offbeats, and we are quite likely to give the four solitary beats an alternating emphasis; while the unrealised fourth beat in alternate lines increases the emphasis on the third beat. The varying degrees of stress in the language can also be used to create a dipodic rhythm by using stronger stresses for alternate beats; Stewart (1924, 1925a) found that popular verse in four-beat rhythm tends to foster dipodic rhythms by this means, while literary verse in the same rhythm, unless it is very overtly dipodic, does not. There is no need to imagine conscious artistry in such manipulations of the accentual contours of the language; a poet who has the basic dipodic rhythm running in his head will be likely to produce this configuration of stresses without realising it, just as it is possible to read such verse without becoming conscious of the nature of the rhythm to which we are responding. Another practice which encourages dipodic alternation is the combining of four-beat units into eight-beat lines, since we are induced to read the whole line as a four-beat structure: such lines are often found in writers like Browning and Kipling, who favour dipodic rhythms for special effects. If a regular and strong dipodic rhythm is set up by these means, the result is usually a rapid, insistent rhythm particularly suited to light verse; W. S. Gilbert's patter-song lyrics make much use of it, for instance. This is a well-known example by Chesterton:

(62) A merry road, a mazy road, and such as we did tread
      B   b   B   b   B   b   B   [b]
      The night we went to Birmingham by way of Beachy Head
      B   b   B   b   B   b   B   [b]

Traditional prosodists often label such verse as 'paeonic', regarding its basic foot as a paeon, $/ \times \times \times$, but this of course obscures the importance of the secondary beat, which is felt even when it is not realised by a stressed syllable.

In all the examples given so far, it is the first beat of the line that is primary, reflecting what seems to be a general rhythmic principle – see, for instance, Tovey's comments quoted above (p. 82), and the experiment by Woodrow mentioned at the beginning of this section. But it is possible to create in verse a dipodic alternation that begins with the secondary beat; this is achieved by starting the line with two relatively weak syllables, which are interpreted, once the general rhythmic scheme has been established, as a secondary beat and offbeat respectively:

(63) Oh Galuppi, Baldassaro, this is very sad to find!
      b   B   b   B   b   B   b   B
      I can hardly misconceive you; it would prove me deaf
      b B   b   B   b   B   b
         and blind
          B

Apart from the running together of the pairs of lines, the pattern of beats and offbeats here is identical to that of the common 4 × 4 beat-initial stanza (as in (48) and (54)), but this example is given a lighter, more lilting, movement by the secondary–primary alternation. Notice, too, that having begun on the secondary beat, the line ends satisfyingly on a primary beat without any use of unrealised beats, and hence with a smoother transition to the next line.

Taranovsky (1971) has formulated two laws which operate in Russian verse to determine the strength of the beats, and which may have some applicability to English, since they aim to encapsulate general rhythmic principles. Putting them in the terms we are using, they state that the beat after the first offbeat of the line tends to be primary (this would apply to the first beat in (62) and the second beat of (63)), and that the last two realised beats of the line tend to be weak and strong respectively, creating an alternation which extends regressively back through the line (again, (62) and (63) illustrate this principle). The two principles may conflict to weaken the dipodic alternations, as in the full 4 × 4 stanza with initial offbeats (see (59)), or coincide to create a strong dipodic rhythm, as in the 4.3.4.3 equivalent considered as two seven-beat units (see (60)). These principles would help account for some of the features of dipodic rhythm that we have noted, though the greater tolerance in English verse of lines ending with weak beats means that the fundamental preference for a primary–secondary rhythm can override them both, as often happens in the 4 × 4 beat-initial stanza.

Some lines of Byron's will illustrate the distinction between the two types of dipodic rhythm, and the way in which the reader's response is coloured by them:

> (64) Though the ocean roar around me,
>   Yet it still shall bear me on;
>   Though a desert should surround me,
>   It hath springs that may be won.

How are we to read this? Two ways present themselves, depending on the degree of stress we give to the first word in each line. If we emphasise it by means of a strong stress, a heavy rhythm is established, which moves the verse on with a regularity and insistence which, it might be felt, is appropriate to the poet's empty posturing. If, on the other hand, we give it very little weight, and allow the first strong stress to fall on the third syllable of each line, the rhythm loses much of its march-like solidity, and moves with an elasticity which permits a greater variety of tone, including a sense of self-awareness and self-amusement. Why is it that this slight difference in reading has such a marked effect?

The answer lies in the two varieties of dipodic rhythm. Stressing the first syllable creates the conditions for the common primary–secondary rhythm, familiar from nursery rhymes, and if the stanza is chanted with alternating stronger and weaker stresses, this rhythm will emerge in an exaggerated form:

> Though the ocean roar around me,
> B   b   B   b
>   Yet it still shall bear me on;
>   B   b   B   b
> Though a desert should surround me,
> B   b   B   b
>   It hath springs that may be won.
>   B   b   B   b

The result is a rhythm which tends to dominate the language, and give unnatural weight to words like 'Though', 'Yet', 'should', and 'may', as if the speaker were heavily underlining the connectives and auxiliaries to make his meaning plain to a dull-witted audience. The other reading, if we exaggerate it, produces the rarer and less dominating secondary–primary dipodic rhythm:

> Though the ocean roar around me,
> b   B   b   B
>   Yet it still shall bear me on;
>   b   B   b   B

Though a desert should surround me,
b   B   b   B
It hath springs that may be won.
b   B   b   B

The switch from the perception of one of these rhythms to the other is rather like the switch between the two interpretations of a visually ambiguous figure: it may take some time before the alternative interpretation is grasped, but when it does appear, all the perceptual evidence suddenly coheres in a fresh way, the rabbit entirely displacing the duck. That Byron was alert to these rhythmic qualities, and that the second of these readings (in a muted form) is the correct one, is made clear from the first stanza of the poem, where the initial weak beat is omitted altogether from the first line, making the wrong reading impossible, and establishing a rhythmic configuration which a sensitive reader will allow to carry him through the poem:

(65) My boat is on the shore,
      [b] B   b   B
      And my bark is on the sea;
      b   B   b   B
      But, before I go, Tom Moore,
      b   B   b   B
      Here's a double health to thee!
      b   B   b   B

Statistics furnished by Tarlinskaja (1976, p. 260, Table 25) and Bailey (1975b, Ch. 4) show that in literary uses of four-beat verse (with all beats realised) it is the second and fourth beats which are most often given full stress, suggesting that this is just one example of a widespread tendency in sophisticated poetry to counter the more insistent type of dipodic rhythm.

We have noted that the omission of offbeats and beats in appropriate places increases the tendency towards a dipodic rhythm; and the establishment of a strong dipodic rhythm in its turn makes possible the omission of many syllables from the verse line. Kipling is a poet who takes full advantage of this freedom, and the following lines, beneath which I have set out the full implied structure, are typical:

(66)   The days are sick and cold, and the skies are grey and old,
        [b] o B o   b o   B ô b   o B o   b o B [o]
        And the twice-breathed airs blow damp;
        b   o B ô b   ôB ô b ô B   [o b o B o]
        And I'd sell my tired soul for the bucking beam-sea roll
        b   o B   o b o B ô b   o B o   b   o B [o]
        Of a black Bil-ba-o tramp
        b o B ô b ô Bôb ô B   [o b o B o]

The way the underlying rhythm is realised in these lines is not arbitrary: the implied offbeats after the second primary beat in lines 1 and 3 help, like the internal rhyme, to divide the line into its component halves, and the sequences of five omitted syllables in lines 2 and 4 allow the line to end on the third primary beat, establishing the familiar 4.3.4.3 pattern on a larger scale, and implying the same kind of higher-order dipodic alternation among the primary beats themselves that we observed in (61). The climactic effect of the second and fourth lines is further enhanced by the omission of all the offbeats after the first, creating an unhindered succession of five beats, especially remarkable when a word with only one stress – 'Bilbao' – realises three beats. The complexity of this rhythmic structure is not a perceptual complexity; the simple, vigorous movement is something we respond to with great immediacy, and we do not need to be able to analyse it in order to appreciate it. In verse which is not overtly metrical, we may not even be conscious of the rhythm; probably not many admirers of Pound's 'In a Station of the Metro' are aware of the dipodic structure, very similar to that of (66), which contributes to its memorability:

(67) The apparition of these faces in the crowd;
      o b   o B o   b   o   B o b   o   B
      Petals on a wet, black bough.
      B o   b   o B ồ   b ồ B

Kipling's virtuoso handling of the four-beat rhythmic structure, however, has different objectives from the metrical endeavours of most poets in the English tradition; instead of creating delicately modulated lyrical sequences or imitating the expressive rhythms of speech, he draws on the most elementary rhythmic resources, those of the nursery, the parade-ground, the labour-gang, to forge a strong, unsubtle, but highly memorable verbal shape that exploits to the limit the simple forms we have been examining in this chapter.

Notes

1. In the earlier part of this century, there were a number of experimental investigations of rhythm, including those of Warner Brown (1908), Woodrow (1909), Wallin (1911–12), and Isaacs (1920). Prall (1929, 1936) provides an aesthetic foundation for the study of rhythm, and there are discussions of musical rhythm which have a bearing on verse in Langer (1953, Ch. 8), Meyer (1956), and Cooper & Meyer (1960). A useful introduction to the psychological background is given by Harding (1976, Ch. 1), and surveys of the field are provided by Chatman (1965, Ch. 2) and W. S. Allen (1973, Ch. 8).

2. For experimental confirmation of the functioning of stresses as rhythmic beats, see G. D. Allen (1972) and Lunney (1974).

3. An over-sophisticated ear or an over-abstract approach can sometimes miss this simple underlying structure, however: see the scansions by Gross of 'Old Mother Hubbard' (1964, pp. 90–91) and by Halle & Keyser of 'Ride a cock-horse' (1971a, pp. 145–6). The Halle-Keyser approach proves more of a hindrance than a help to Guéron (1974) and Napoli (1978) in their studies of nursery rhyme metres, and enables Freeman (1972) to find iambic pentameters in Emily Dickinson's four-beat verse.

4. But for an interesting defence of the fourteener as used by Golding in his translation of the *Metamorphoses*, see Braden (1978, pp. 22–54).

5. Thompson (1961, pp. 33–6) gives a valuable account of the weaknesses of poulter's measure.

6. Compare Lotman's statement of the 'law of three-quarters': 'If one takes a text, which on the syntagmatic axis is articulated into four elements, then we shall find, almost universally, that the first two quarters establish a structural inertia while the third violates it, and the fourth re-establishes the original pattern, preserving, however, some token of its deformation' (1976, p. 50).

7. Schane (1979a, 1979b) regards the syllabic sequence *strong–weak–weak* as the most fundamental unit in English phonology; if this analysis is correct, the peculiar insistence of triple metre may result partly from the overriding of surface stress-patterns (on which subtleties of expression rest) by a more elementary rhythm.

8. See also the valuable comments by Nowottny (1962, pp. 108–111) on line-junctures in the 'Elegy on the Countess of Pembroke'.

9. This may not happen very often, however: Stewart (1925b) found that although there is on average a higher percentage of falling words and phrases in trochaic verse than in iambic, the difference is not very marked, and even in trochaic verse there are usually more rising units than falling.

10. An essay which keeps these terms distinct, and provides some interesting statistics on poets' use of rising and falling rhythms, is Creek (1920).

11. Robertson (1960, pp. 121–2), using a traditional prosodic approach, notes that a smooth reading of the 'trochaic' poems of *Astrophil and Stella* depends on taking the first syllable as an anacrusis.

12. Beardsley (1972, p. 245) uses a similar model for the purpose of metrical analysis, but with somewhat different aims.

Chapter 5

The five-beat rhythm

In the last chapter, we reached some firm conclusions about the rhythmic structure that underlies the types of verse that were our prime concern there. Almost all nursery rhymes, ballads, hymns, and other forms of popular verse and song use the four-beat rhythm as the basis of their metre, most often in groups of four lines or in simple variations on this basic structure. Lines with three main stresses usually imply a fourth, unrealised, beat; and lines with six main stresses usually resolve into two units of three, each with an unrealised fourth beat, as, for instance, in the first line of the poulter's measure couplet. Similarly, lines of seven main stresses are for the most part felt as two four-beat groups, with a final unrealised beat, as in fourteeners or the second poulter's measure line. Eight main stresses are interpreted as four plus four, though it is unusual to find lines of this length unless the rhythm is dipodic, making the whole line a larger-scale four-beat unit. The metrical pattern which realises the basic four-beat group is sometimes divided, as in the limerick, where the third group appears as two and two; and occasionally two-beat lines occur alone with the rhythmic effect of a half-line.

When we turn to poetry of less popular origins, we find that a large part of it makes use of the same elementary rhythms, though the underlying form may not be as clearly manifested. There is, for instance, less reliance on the 4 × 4 structure; many poems are written in a continuous series of four-beat rhyming couplets, or in stanza forms more elaborate than the popular four-line one. Restrictions on the number of syllables in a line are usually tighter, and a regular duple rhythm with only a limited degree of variation is common. One line, however, which is to be found in a large proportion of literary verse from Chaucer to the present day, and which is the medium of many of the greatest achievements in English poetry, is very rare in popular verse, and cannot be seen as a realisation of an underlying four-beat rhythm:

(1) To ferne halwes, kowthe in sondry londes
     B   B   B   B   B

(2) Since brass, nor stone, nor earth, nor boundless sea
     B   B   B   B   B

(3) Some natural tears they dropped, but wiped them soon
     B   B   B   B   B

(4) Yet let me flap this bug with gilded wings
     B   B   B   B   B

(5) The solid mountains shone, bright as the clouds
     B   B   B   B   B

(6) The salmon-falls, the mackerel-crowded seas
     B   B   B   B   B

The fundamental reason why poets over the centuries have turned to
the five-beat line for their most ambitious verse is an obvious but
frequently overlooked one: it is the only simple metrical form of
manageable length which escapes the elementary four-beat rhythm,
with its insistence, its hierarchical structures, and its close relationship
with the world of ballad and song.

The difference in rhythmic character between the four-beat and the
five-beat line is often blurred in metrical studies, but some writers have
commented on it, and perhaps even overstated it: Ker (1928,
pp. 205–6) claims that the four-beat measure 'agrees with certain
common tendencies or habits in the human mind, and is in a sense
more natural, more easily found out and appropriated, than, say, the
ten-syllabled line, which is often difficult to understand and imitate',
and both Lewis (1938) and Burling (1966; 1970, Ch. 10) assert that
whereas four-beat structures are appreciated without instruction, the
five-beat rhythm requires training before it can be perceived. Malof
(1964) argues that the four-beat line is a 'native' English pattern to
which the language is 'naturally attracted', as opposed to the 'foreign'
pentameter tradition (p. 586); but while this may throw some light on
the history of English metre, it is misleading as a synchronic
description: as we have seen, it is precisely the 'naturalness' of the
four-beat line as an elementary rhythmic form that lies at the heart of
its relative insensitivity to the distinctive rhythms of a particular
language. Literary criticism is perhaps too eager to ask what the formal
(and other) properties of poetry manage to get into language;
sometimes it is more enlightening to take note of what they succeed in
keeping out. To understand the special character of the five-beat line,
therefore, it is essential to be aware of the properties of the four-beat
rhythm which it escapes, and to examine its strategies of evasion.

What is remarkable about the five-beat line is not only the success with which it has been used over a wide range of poetic kinds, but the tight constraints observed by the poets who have used it. It is worth quoting Ruskin's comment on this point, the classical vocabulary of which is easily translatable into other terms:

> Upon adding the fifth foot to our gradually lengthening line, we find ourselves fallen suddenly under hitherto unfelt limitation. The verses we have hitherto examined may be constructed at pleasure of any kind of metre – dactyl, trochee, iamb, or anapaest. But all at once, we now find this liberty of choice refused. We may write a pentameter verse in iambs only.
>
> A most notable phenomenon, significant of much more than I can at present understand, – how much less explain; [. . .] the historical fact being quite indubitable and unalterable, that no poet has ever attempted to write pentameter in any foot but the iamb, and that the addition of another choreus [trochee] to a choreic tetrameter – or of another dactyl to a dactylic one, will instantly make them helplessly prosaic and unreadable. (1880, pp. 55–6)

At least two of Ruskins's contemporaries had attempted – not wholly without success – these 'unreadable' metres (see below, pp. 130, 131); but the essential validity of the observation remains. In this chapter we shall examine the distinctive characteristics of the five-beat rhythm by comparing it with the four-beat form already discussed. In asking to what extent these characteristics reflect the nature of the five-beat rhythm itself, rather than literary convention, we can hope to reach a fuller understanding of its special status in the English poetic tradition.[1]

5.1 UNDERLYING RHYTHM AND METRICAL PATTERN

That a five-beat rhythm is a less simple and less salient perceptual form than a four-beat rhythm scarcely needs demonstrating; if experimental evidence is required, Woodrow (1951, p. 1234) reports that subjects find rhythmic groups of five more difficult to impose on a sequence of undifferentiated sound stimuli than groups of two, three, four, or six. Or if we attend to the elementary rhythms of popular music, we find that a five-beat bar or a five-bar phrase is rarely to be encountered. The reason for this difference is equally obvious: a four-beat rhythm, and its manifestation in different line-lengths, is the product of the fundamental doubling principle discussed in the previous chapter, whereas a five-beat group cannot be divided into rhythmically equal components larger than its five subdivisions. From these elementary facts spring most of the differences in poetic potential between the two rhythmic forms.

The five-beat line does not bring with it the sense of a strong underlying rhythm; it observes the heightened regularity of movement created by the alternation of stressed and unstressed syllables, without those rhythmic pulses grouping themselves consistently – and insistently – into twos and fours, and without any tendency for dipodic rhythms to make themselves felt. For this reason it strikes the ear as more faithful to the natural rhythm of speech: it is not that five-beat groups are in any way indigenous to English, but that such groups impose themselves less strongly on the movement of the language. In other words, five-beat lines exhibit a different relationship between the two rhythmic principles that collaborate in the creation of metrical form: the rhythm of language speaks louder, the elementary rhythmic form more softly. This is not to say that four-beat verse in the literary tradition encourages the reader to use unnatural pronunciations to bring out the rhythm, but that the rhythm, established by the normal movement of the language, is perceptually stronger and is more likely to influence those aspects of pronunciation where variation or choice is possible. This difference can be strikingly reflected in the way a poet writes: Byron's verse in five-beat lines, for instance, tends to be much more subtle in its rhythmic variety and emotional colouring than his verse in four-beat forms, while Wyatt writes more smoothly and lyrically in four-beat forms than in the longer line.

The hierarchical organisation of four-beat verse is not confined to the individual line, as we have seen; the doubling tendency produces pairs of lines, and pairs of pairs in the ubiquitous 4 × 4 structure. But the five-beat line, itself not generated by such a process, is less likely to generate it over a larger span; the quatrain, therefore, does not hold pride of place among five-beat stanza forms as it does among four-beat, and the five-beat line has an independence as a rhythmic unit which makes it the ideal medium for the poet who wishes to avoid the stops and starts of stanza forms altogether. And by not taking part in the rhythmic swing of the 4 × 4 structure, with its emphatic beats and dipodic tendency, the five-beat line is, once again, more able to reflect the rhythm of the spoken language. Although we can refer to underlying rhythmic structures of, for example, 5 × 2 or 5 × 4, these do not have the same cohesion as the 4 × 4 structure, and the true underlying rhythm of five-beat verse is always the single five-beat unit.

The metrical patterns which realise four-beat verse can, as we have seen, vary a great deal; certain beats can be unrealised, for instance, and the line-divisions need not coincide with the four-beat groups. The five-beat rhythm, on the other hand, can only be manifested as five realised beats. (Because of this, the term *pentameter* is less misleading than such terms as 'trimeter', 'tetrameter', or 'heptameter', which tend to mask the unity beneath the various realisations of the four-beat rhythm.) This difference is another result of the relative weakness of the five-beat group as a rhythmic Gestalt. To omit the final beat of a pentameter is to deliver it over to the four-beat pattern which is always waiting for an opportunity to gain dominance, whereas to do the same in the 4 × 4 structure may, as we have seen, serve only to strengthen the underlying rhythm. Nor does the five-beat line break naturally into two; its rhythmic unity is not strong enough to survive division, especially since an uneven distribution of beats is unavoidable. The following example is from a broadside ballad, in which the literary tradition has clearly influenced the popular one:

(7) Intomb'd he now doth lye,
   B   B   B
    in stately manner,
      B   B
'Cause he fought valiantly,
     B   B   B
    for love and honour:
      B   B
That right he had in you,
    B   B   B
    to me he gave it:
     B   B
Now since it is my due,
   B   B   B
    pray let me have it.
     B   B

A sequence of four five-beat lines has been divided by syntax and rhyme into an eight-line stanza of three-beat and two-beat lines in alternation. Although the three-beat lines carry echoes of the popular four-beat pattern, any such expectations are constantly being frustrated by the shortness of the two-beat lines. Instead, we remain aware of the five-beat groups, with the only true pauses occurring after every second line; and the break enforced by lineation, syntax, and rhyme after three beats imparts a clipped, staccato movement to the verse. Five-beat lines are, of course, often divided internally by syntactic breaks, but it is one of the advantages of the pentameter as a vehicle for long poems that the rhythmic structure does not create pressure for one particular subdivision. The most rhythmically balanced line results, it is true, from a pause after the second or the third beat, and poets favouring regularity usually prefer one of these positions if the line is to have only one break; this was incorporated into prosodic theory by some eighteenth-century poets and critics (see Dillon, 1977). But even this allows variety, and does not result in the perception of the line as an edifice built up from smaller blocks.

The traditional stanza forms in which five-beat verse has been successfully written all use undivided pentameters, sometimes with an occasional six-beat line; and because each five-beat line is rhythmically independent, rhyme plays an active role in binding lines together. When a poetic style demands tightness of organisation together with the freedom to employ speech rhythms, the pentameter couplet offers the ideal combination: the adjacent rhymes create strong formal units larger than the line, while the five-beat rhythm remains a flexible medium for the spoken language. Not surprisingly, therefore, the couplet form seems more appropriate to the controlled wit of *The Dunciad* than to the free-ranging fantasy of *Endymion*. On the other hand, because the five-beat line is under no rhythmic pressure to form four-line groups, it lends itself more fully than the four-beat line to the creation of complex stanza forms. These are capable of combining a sense of large-scale freedom almost as great as that of blank verse with a formal orderliness unmatched by any other metrical form (and in this case Keats furnishes some of the finest examples). Because such forms do not have an underlying rhythmic structure with a natural end, they often make use of some special device to achieve a feeling of closure, such as the couplet with new rhymes in the rhyme royal stanza (*ababbcc*) and the ottava rima stanza (*abababcc*), or the final six-beat line in the Spenserian stanza (*ababbcbcc*). Simple stanzas of four lines do, of course, occur in five-beat verse, the most famous example being Gray's *Elegy* (which has provided the name *elegiac quatrain* for the stanza), and the usual rhyme-scheme of this stanza, *abab*, can, especially if the syntax emphasises the divisions between lines and pairs of lines, induce something of the continuity, and the rising and falling intonation, of the 4 × 4 structure:

(8) Let not Ambition mock their useful toil,
     Their homely joys and destiny obscure;
     Nor Grandeur hear, with a disdainful smile,
     The short and simple annals of the poor.

In such verse, the five-beat line is brought back to the lyrical symmetries from which it is more usually the means of escape, and the weightiness of the longer line is blended with the formal completeness of the metrical structure to create a meditation free from the rough rhythms – and one might add, the rough emotions – of real speech.

5.2 DUPLE AND TRIPLE, RISING AND FALLING RHYTHMS

The greater sensitivity of the five-beat line to the rhythms of speech, and its consequent use in the literary tradition by poets who wish to capitalise on the expressiveness of those rhythms, goes part of the way towards explaining its other characteristic features in English verse. Where there is a choice to be made between different realisations of an underlying rhythm, a poet who has already chosen the five-beat rhythm for this reason will opt for those realisations which increase rather than diminish its capacity to evoke the spoken language; and we have seen from our discussion of four-beat verse that this will mean duple rather than triple rhythms, and rising rather than falling rhythms. Run-on lines, an absence of rhyme, and the avoidance of dipodic alternation, are also features which minimise the connection with song, and so are likely to characterise five-beat verse. And since the same choices have been made by generations of poets, they have become established accompaniments to the pentameter. To regard this as a full explanation of the limitations in the use of five-beat verse, however, is to cast poets too completely in the role of servants rather than masters of literary convention. Who knows how many attempts to fashion other varieties of five-beat verse have never reached the light of day because their inventors sensed that something deeper than poetic convention was being challenged? It is worth at least asking to what extent their choices have to do with the rhythmic properties of the form itself rather than the example of previous poets.

We have seen that the four-beat rhythm not only manifests itself in a variety of metrical patterns (with unrealised beats and divided or combined lines), but that those metrical patterns can in turn be variously realised in the lines of poetry by means of different types of offbeat, whether to create one of many possible fixed forms, or to achieve variation in a single poem. But the five-beat rhythm, as Ruskin observed, is realised, with rare exceptions, in only one way: as a five-beat, duple, offbeat-initial line. Certain limited deviations are possible, and will be discussed in Chapter 7, but they are experienced as temporary departures from the basic scheme. We can call this form, with its strictly controlled variations, *iambic pentameter*, as long as this is not taken to imply any analogy with classical verse or subdivision into feet. In so doing, we are referring to a highly particularised metrical form that occupies an important place in the English tradition, as distinct from using a more general descriptive category like 'five-beat line' or 'rising rhythm'.

Let us consider first the preference for duple over triple rhythms, that is, the realisation of offbeats by one rather than two syllables. We have seen that triple rhythms have a characteristically insistent movement, setting up a strong and regular pulse. When we experience such an insistent rhythm, we are naturally led to expect the most elementary rhythmic form, the four-beat line, and if there are five beats instead of four, the movement becomes strained: the pronounced rhythm impels us towards simple song forms, the pentameter structure pulls away from these to more complicated rhythms and more isolated lines. Compare Byron's original with my rewriting:

(9)   The Assyrian came down like the wolf on the fold,
         And his cohorts were gleaming in purple and gold;
         And the sheen of their spears was like stars on the sea,
         When the blue wave rolls nightly on deep Galilee.

[9a]   The Assyrian came down in his might like the wolf on the
             fold,
         And his galloping cohorts were gleaming in purple and gold;
         And the sheen of their spears was like stars on the silvery sea,
         When the blue wave rolls nightly in thunder on deep Galilee.

It is not, despite Ruskins's assertion to the contrary, an impossible form (Browning uses it for *Saul*, for instance, and Swinburne for one of the *Atalanta* choruses; while Lawrence develops a free form of it in several of his *Rhyming Poems*); but it has not become an accepted part of the tradition, for reasons to do with the pentameter's distinctive rhythmic character rather than any accident of taste.

Turning to the question of line-openings and line-ends, we find that regular five-beat verse with very few exceptions observes the conventions of iambic metre. These allow some freedom in the use of offbeats at the beginning and end of the line, under strict conditions which we shall examine in 7.7; for the purposes of the present discussion, it is sufficient to say that they encourage a rising rather than a falling rhythm. This avoidance of metrical formations which produce falling rhythms can be explained in a similar fashion to the avoidance of triple rhythms: both kinds of rhythm have an insistent quality which sets them at some remove from the natural movement of speech and arouses expectations of a four-beat rhythm. A fifth beat will therefore be likely to cause some rhythmic confusion, as the recast stanza below indicates:

(10)　　Had we never lov'd sae kindly,
　　　　Had we never lov'd sae blindly,
　　　　Never met – or never parted,
　　　　We had ne'er been broken-hearted.

[10a]　Had we never, never lov'd sae kindly,
　　　　Had we never, never lov'd sae blindly,
　　　　Never met – or never sadly parted,
　　　　Jeanie, we had ne'er been broken-hearted.

Again, the coherence of the quatrain is diminished, and the feeling of a simplicity – almost starkness – of rhythm created by Burns's falling groups lost, when the line is extended by one beat. Perhaps the only considerable achievement in this rhythm is Browning's 'One Word More', a metrical tour-de-force that capitalises on the feeling that the recalcitrant language (at the level of syntax as well as rhythm) is being forced into submission to the metre's demands:

(11)　　Rafael made a century of sonnets,
　　　　Made and wrote them in a certain volume
　　　　Dinted with the silver-pointed pencil
　　　　Else he only used to draw Madonnas.
　　　　These, the world might view – but one, the volume.
　　　　Who that one, you ask? Your heart instructs you.

As I have mentioned, it is relatively unusual even in four-beat forms to find lines which imply a falling rhythm both at the beginning and at the end in this way; more often the line concludes with a beat, allowing rising rhythms greater freedom to assert themselves. With such endings, a beat-initial pentameter reads more easily, though the contrast between four-beat and five-beat forms is still marked:

(12) Queen and huntress, chaste and fair,
        Now the sun is laid to sleep,
     Seated in thy silver chair,
        State in wonted manner keep.

[12a] Queen and huntress, ever chaste and fair,
        Now the weary sun is laid to sleep,
     Seated smiling in thy silver chair,
        State in wonted manner do thou keep.

Again, the lines become more independent of one another, and the lucid rhythmic flow of Jonson's lines gives way to a more hesitant movement. At the same time, the effect of the initial beat becomes more pronounced, because it is perceived each time not as part of a continuous rhythmic pattern extending over several lines, but as a new beginning.

Five-beat lines therefore usually begin with an offbeat, keeping the powerful tread of the falling rhythm and its associated four-beat structures at bay. This is not to say that pentameter verse is always strongly rising; the longer line in fact allows great flexibility in the grouping of syllables, and a poet who uses a marked rising rhythm is exercising an artistic choice:

(13) A heap of dust alone remains of thee;
     'Tis all thou art, and all the proud shall be!

More often, the five-beat line is characterised by its rhythmic variety, allowing the natural movement of speech to be imitated or heightened as the poet determines.

5.3 LINE-JUNCTURES AND BLANK VERSE

One area where five-beat verse seems to be under weaker rather than stronger constraints than four-beat verse is in the relationship between metrical structures and syntactic structures: some poems observe the same tendency as four-beat verse to end lines at syntactic boundaries, while others make use of run-on lines, including strong run-ons across close syntactic links, in a way which is rare in the shorter form. The character of the transition from one line to the next is clearly different in the two forms, and this demands careful examination.

In the 4 × 4 structure, the end of each four-beat group is perceptually very distinct (even if it does not coincide with the line-end), but it is not until the end of the fourth group that we experience a full sense of finality. The different degrees of closure at the end of each line are controlled by the overall pattern, resulting in both continuity and a clear articulation into subdivisions. The pentameter line, as we have noted, is a more independent form, and does not have a strong tendency to become part of a larger whole; even when it is organised by rhyme into stanza forms, the lines retain their separate identity as five-beat groups. This means that when we reach the end of the line there is no compelling pressure from the larger structure to register the completion of a rhythmic unit and to move on to the next one. Instead, the syntax has a more powerful voice – another example of the five-beat rhythm's less dominating relationship with the language – and will determine whether we pause or read straight on to the following line. Pentameter verse which consistently encourages us to pause at line-end will, of course, be marked by stronger rhythms, since the five-beat units will be highlighted; the liberal use of run-on lines, on the other hand, will create a continuous movement in which the line-divisions may not be very apparent – Johnson's complaint that Milton's verse is verse only to the eye is not without foundation. The latter form comes as close to natural speech rhythms as is possible in a regular metre, and dramatic pentameter verse is able to take full advantage of this fact.

It is sometimes suggested that five-beat lines should be understood as six-beat units with a final silent beat (see, for example, Bracher, 1947; David Abercrombie, 1964a, p. 23; Leech, 1969, Ch. 7), but the freedom to pause at the end of a five-beat line if the syntax demands it should not be confused with the metrical rest produced by an unrealised beat in a four-beat structure. Careful introspection should be enough to demonstrate the difference; compare, for instance, the effect of the run-on at the end of the three-beat second line of the following stanza with the rewritten five-beat version that follows:

(14)   And if I pray, the only prayer
       That moves my lips for me
       Is – 'Leave the heart that now I bear,
       And give me liberty.'

[14a] And if I come to pray, the only prayer
That dimly moves my feeble lips for me
Is – 'Leave the heart that now I sadly bear,
And give me once for all my liberty.'

There is a greater feeling of tension in the original, because the run-on occurs over an unrealised beat; we may even be tempted to treat the first word of the following line as the fourth beat. But a six-beat unit has none of the rhythmic primacy of a four-beat unit, and is not likely to be intuitively felt when it is not physically present. The most that can be said is that occasionally a writer with a penchant for dipodic rhythms will use alternating stronger and weaker beats in a pentameter to call up the ghost of a line with four primary beats, as in Kipling's 'If –' (which also alternates feminine and masculine endings in a manner more typical of four-beat verse):

(15)   If you can keep your head when all about you
         B   b   B   b   B   [b B]
       Are losing theirs and blaming it on you
         B   b   B   b   B   [b B]

The relative discontinuity between pentameter lines is also illustrated by the greater freedom to introduce a final offbeat. We noted above (p. 106) that in strict duple verse in a 4 × 4 structure a final offbeat followed by an initial offbeat is usually avoided, since it creates a momentary dislocation in the continuous rhythm, but the same does not hold true for pentameter verse (though we have already noted that femine endings are, for other reasons, less common than masculine). The difference can be observed if we rewrite masculine endings as feminine in both types of line:
Four-beat:

(16)   How vainly men themselves amaze
       To win the palm, the oak, or bays

[16a] How vainly men do fret and quarrel
       To win the palm, the oak, or laurel

Five-beat:

(17)   Oh be thou blest with all that Heav'n can send,
       Long health, long youth, long pleasure, and a friend

[17a] Oh be thou blest with all that Heav'n doth treasure,
       Long health, long youth, a friend, and lasting pleasure

Although both the original couplets depend on an epigrammatic pointedness for their effect, the four-beat lines are bound more closely together by their underlying rhythmic structure, and the feminine ending produces a double offbeat between the beats of this larger pattern, which slightly disrupts the flow of the rhythm, enforcing a separation between the lines. The pause at the end of the pentameter, however, is in a sense extrametrical, and the presence of an additional syllable has a less marked effect on our perception of the rhythm. If there is a close *syntactic* link between pentameter lines, however, the extra offbeat can be disruptive, and Kiparsky (1977, p. 234) claims that both Shakespeare and Milton avoid feminine endings when there is a strong run-on.

It is this greater freedom at the end of the line which gives pentameter run-ons a different quality from those in four-beat lines, especially such lines occurring in 4 × 4 structures. A comparison will suggest something of the difference. I have rewritten a quatrain by Herbert with run-ons, first retaining the 4 × 4 structure, then extending the lines to pentameter length.

(18)   I got me flowers to straw thy way;
   I got me boughs off many a tree;
  But thou wast up by break of day,
   And brought'st thy sweets along with thee.

[18a]   I got me blooming flowers to straw
   Thy way; and boughs off many a tree
  Did break; but thou wast up before
   The dawn, and brought'st thy sweets with thee.

[18b]   I got a thousand blooming flowers to straw
   Thy way; and leafy boughs off many a tree
  Did break; but thou, O Lord, wast up before
   The dawn, and brought'st thy sweets along with thee.

Though the sense of simplicity on which the stanza relies for much of its power disappears as soon as the correspondence between the underlying structure and the rhythm of the language is disrupted, the run-ons seem less jarring in the five-beat version than in the four-beat one. If we pause slightly at line-ends in reading [18a], the underlying rhythmic structure makes itself felt, imposing on the fourth beat a final cadence which goes against the sense; if on the other hand we ignore line-ends altogether, we lose the rhythmic coherence of the stanza.

[18b] is easier to manage: no dominating rhythmic structure imposes itself if we pause slightly at line-ends, and the suspension in the unfolding of the sentence is experienced as a natural lingering; or if we choose to read without pauses, allowing the line-lengths to register mentally, the more variable and less insistent five-beat rhythms emerge of their own accord.

In the nonstanzaic uses of four-beat lines, however, enjambment is more common, and the effect is often to create a rhythmic freedom which is closer to that of the pentameter; the lyrical or epigrammatic potential of the line is played down, and conversational or meditative registers of speech evoked:

> (19) Dear friend Elizabeth, dear friend
> These days have brought me, may the end
> I bring to the grave's dead-line be
> More worthy of your sympathy
> Than the beginning; may the truth
> That no one marries lead my youth
> Where you already are and bless
> Me with your learned peacefulness.

The same pentameter-like flexibility can be created by similar means in three-beat or six-beat lines; see the discussion of Yeats's 'Easter 1916' in 10.2 for an example.

One of the most obvious differences between four-beat and five-beat lines in the literary tradition is that it is only the latter which occur widely without rhyme; yet this is a fact which has received scant attention in literary criticism. The existence of unrhymed pentameters is obviously related to their more frequent use of run-ons; both features encourage fluid forms determined more by the language itself than by underlying rhythmic structures. The use of one may encourage expectations of the other, as Charles Elton noted in 1812: 'In blank measure, the pause is judiciously shifted to different syllables in different successive lines: because if the sense were to close with the verse, as is too generally the case in the poem of *The Seasons*, the absence of rhyme would be felt' (preface to Habington's *Castara*, cited by Wasserman, 1940, p. 252, n. 39). Though we might expect to find weaker rhythmic forms using rhyme to mark the ends of each unit, and stronger forms doing without it, the relationship is in fact the reverse: the more perceptually salient the rhythmic units, the more they seem to demand a closing rhyme, while a less prominent form like the run-on pentameter arouses no such expectation. We have already noted that where rhyme is used in pentameter verse, it is less a reflection of an underlying structure than a way of organising the lines in the absence of such a structure. The four-beat rhythm, on the other hand, with its emphatic line-endings and propensity to participate in larger groupings, strongly invites rhyme; in the 4 × 4 structure there is a definite sense that the third line is a repetition of the first, and the fourth of the second, and this experience is clinched by an *abab* rhyme scheme.

Even outside its common stanza forms, the insistence of the four-beat rhythm seems to invite a special marking of the final beat. Some four-beat couplets of Sidney's, rewritten without rhymes, will indicate what is lost when they are absent:

> (20) What tongue can her perfections tell
>   In whose each part all pens may dwell?
>   Her hair fine threads of finest gold,
>   In curléd knots man's thought to hold,
>   But that her forehead says, 'In me
>   A whiter beauty you may see.'

> [20a] What tongue can her perfections tell
>   In whose each part all pens may stay?
>   Her hair fine threads of finest gold,
>   In curléd knots man's thought to trap,
>   But that her forehead says, 'In me
>   A whiter beauty you may find.'

In the rewritten version, the rhythmic organisation, supported by the syntax, encourages the reader to group the lines in pairs, but the absence of rhyme contradicts this, and the result is a sense of expectation frustrated. But rewrite the unrhymed lines as pentameters, and they lose that awkwardness; each line stands on its own as a rhythmic whole, and relates both to what went before and to what will come after:

> [20b] What human tongue may her perfections tell
>   In whose each part all pens may ages stay?
>   Her shining hair fine threads of finest gold,

> In curléd knots man's straying thought to trap,
> But that her candid forehead says, 'In me
> A whiter beauty you may chance to find.'

The lines have now escaped the structuring pressure of the four-beat form, and enjoy a more relaxed and flexible rhythm, which brings them closer to speech. Four-beat verse without rhyme is occasionally attempted, and the strong rhythmic structure can still be felt, but the sense of anticlimax at line-ends is hard to evade – indeed, it can be put to good use:

> (21)   There was a young man of St Bees
>   Who was stung on the arm by a wasp;
>   When asked 'Does it hurt?'
>   He replied, 'No it doesn't;
>   It's a good thing it wasn't a hornet.'

5.4 SYLLABIC RHYTHM

Given their sensitivity to speech rhythms, one might expect five-beat lines to allow free variation in the number of unstressed syllables between beats. This is not so, however, even within the literary tradition; while the four-beat line has often been used with this kind of variation (Coleridge's 'Christabel' is perhaps the most self-conscious example), the pentameter has usually been distinguished by a more rigorous control of the number of syllables, its preference for duple rhythms and initial offbeats producing in strict metrical styles a count of ten, or eleven if a feminine ending is used, and only slightly more variety in freer styles.

To understand this difference, we need to look a little more closely at the role of the syllable in the rhythms of English verse. While there are external reasons for the emphasis in different periods of literary history on a fixed syllable count, these cannot explain the success of this metrical principle in English; the achievements of Shakespeare, Spenser, Milton, and Wordsworth can hardly rest on a metre which is foreign to the language in which they wrote. It will be recalled that in Chapter 3 we found evidence for regarding the syllable as an elementary rhythmic unit of language, and it is likely, therefore, that apart from acting as the carrier of stress patterns and creating duple or triple rhythms, it can play a metrical role in its own right. The stress rhythm of English is too dominating for this role to be a major one, as it is in French verse, but we have already noted that the tendency towards isochrony in English is circumscribed by the rhythmic effect of the syllables between stresses. We can gauge the relative importance of the two rhythmic principles by attending to purely syllabic verse, in which the number and position of the stresses is allowed to vary freely while the syllable count is fixed:

> (22) Bare-throated profile with the tumbled bright young hair,
>   Full face with shining eyes, and the rose-leaf and gold
>   Granted by our complaisance to the monochrome:
>   Well, thank the American that with both hands he took
>   And offered us 'God's vulgar lyric *Rupert Brooke*'.

Most readers find it difficult to distinguish the rhythmic effect of such verse from that of free verse, although more than one poet who has written extensively in syllabics has reported that one can become habituated to the syllable count, and recognise instinctively when, say, the twelfth syllable has been reached. We can conclude, then, that the syllables of the language exert a subsidiary rhythmic influence, but that this is most likely to be felt within the framework of a regular stress pattern.

In 7.6 we shall consider the effects of the syllabic principle on the rules of metre, but our immediate question is, why does it appear to be of more importance in five-beat verse than in four-beat verse? The distinction is not between a metrical form which is based on the syllable count and one which is based on stress-timing, as is sometimes argued; five-beat verse clearly reflects the stress-timed rhythms of the language while much four-beat verse observes a fixed syllable count. It does appear, however, that the rhythmic character of the pentameter line demands a degree of syllabic strictness which the shorter form can dispense with. The four-beat line, especially in the 4×4 structure, rapidly sets up an insistent rhythm: we are very ready to interpret a few rhythmic signals in terms of that simple structure if we are at all able to do so, just as we can understand a frequently-heard sentence-type from only a few fragments. And as long as the verbal material does not deviate too far from that pattern, we will continue to perceive it. But the five-beat rhythm is not as deeply embedded in our mental habits: it is a relatively less prominent form, a weaker Gestalt, and if a writer wants to maintain a sense of the underlying pattern, he has to exercise careful control over the disposition of rhythmic elements. Or as

Johnson put it in his *Life of Milton*: 'The music of the English heroic line strikes the ear so faintly that it is easily lost, unless all the syllables of every line co-operate together'. So where four-beat verse can tolerate varying numbers of syllables between the beats without any disturbance to the underlying rhythm, and indeed thrives on such variation because the principle of stress-timing is thereby strengthened, poetry in five-beat lines is more likely to observe the rule of one syllable realising one offbeat, departing from this only when compensation earlier or later in the line maintains the syllable count.

The result is verse in which the rhythmic function of the syllable is relatively more important, and any marked degree of variation in the realisation of offbeats dissolves the rhythmic structure and produces what is really a form of free verse. As such, it still has a great deal of potential, and can draw on many of the strengths of the pentameter (as in some of Hopkins's experiments in 'sprung rhythm', for instance), but it is far less closely related to the regular five-beat line than, say, 'Christabel' is to duple four-beat verse. This difference can be illustrated by taking examples of both line-lengths with a strict syllable-count, and introducing a few variations between the beats:

Four-beat:

(23) Sweet, be not proud of those two eyes,
　　　　 B　　　　 B　　　　 B　　　　 B
　　　Which star-like sparkle in their skies;
　　　　 B　　　　 B　　　　 B　　　　 B
　　　Nor be you proud that you can see
　　　 B　　　　 B　　　　 B　　　　 B
　　　All hearts your captives, yours yet free.
　　　　 B　　　　 B　　　　 B　　　　 B

[23a] Sweet, be not boastful of those two eyes,
　　　　 B　　　　 B　　　　 B　　　　 B
　　　Like stars sparkling in beauteous skies;
　　　 B　　 B　　　　 B　　　　 B
　　　Nor be proud that you can see
　　　 B　　 B　　　 B　　 B
　　　All are your slaves, you yet free.
　　　 B　　　 B　　　 B　　 B

Five-beat:

(24) In sober mornings do not thou rehearse
　　　　 B　　　 B　　　 B　　　 B　　 B
　　　The holy incantation of a verse;
　　　 B　 B　　 B　　　 B　　 B

But when that men have both well drunk and fed,
  B   B   B   B   B
Let my enchantments then be sung or read.
  B   B   B   B   B

[24a]   In dull mornings do not thou rehearse
             B   B   B   B   B
        The magical incantation of a verse;
           B   B   B   B   B
        When that men have both well drunk and fed,
         B   B   B   B   B
        Let Herrick's delights then be sung or read.
      B   B   B   B   B

The alterations are not sufficient to destroy either the four-beat or the five-beat rhythm, but the difference between the pairs is more marked in the second case: the cultivated urbanity of Herrick's pentameters is more damagingly affected than the graceful lyricism of his four-beat lines.

But while the number of syllables between beats is more strictly controlled in the pentameter than in the four-beat line, the number of beats in the line is probably slightly less crucial. An extra beat anywhere in the 4 × 4 pattern will upset the entire structure, but in a succession of pentameter lines, a line with one beat more or less will have only a local effect; it may not even be noticed, provided that the regular alternation of beat and offbeat is maintained. The fundamentally five-beat movement of Spenser's verse in *The Faerie Queene* is not upset by the six-beat final lines of the stanzas, nor do Dryden's heroic couplets lose their rhythmic character as a result of the occasional Alexandrine; and the four-beat lines that occur sporadically in Shakespeare's blank verse are not fatal to the rhythm. This is in part a consequence of the isolation of the five-beat line – it is less likely to affect what occurs before and after it – and in part a result of the less prominent rhythmic pattern of five units. In other words, the distinguishing feature of five-beat verse is that it observes the continuous alternation of beat and offbeat as a result of the strict control of stressed and unstressed syllables, and not because it is carried along by a strong underlying rhythm. If the motto of the characteristic four-beat rhythm might be said to be 'Take care of the beats and the offbeats will take care of themselves', there is perhaps some appropriateness in regarding the motto of the pentameter as being the reverse.

5.5 FIVE-BEAT AND FOUR-BEAT RHYTHMS

In discussing these features of the pentameter I have, of course, been emphasising the differences between four-beat and five-beat rhythms. We shall examine in the rest of this book the rather more complex picture that emerges when these basic patterns are put to use in poetry, but it should perhaps be stressed once more that both forms are capable of huge variety, and that four-beat lines can be made to work in ways very similar to the typical five-beat line, as in (19) above, while pentameters can occur in four-line and other simple stanzaic patterns, as in (8), or with a hint of dipodic structures, as in (15), to evoke some of the rhythmic associations of the alternative form. Much of the four-beat verse in the literary tradition, in fact, does not make use of the freedom we have noted, but is written in a strict accentual-syllabic metre (for which the traditional term *tetrameter* is appropriate). Because it is shorter, and because too many variations would produce the more insistent rhythms to which the four-beat line is prone, the literary tetrameter actually tends to observe somewhat *stricter* syllabic restraints than the pentameter (see Tarlinskaja, 1976, pp. 144, 151).

A further link between the two forms is that the ease with which the four-beat pattern is established means that it is sometimes experienced as a kind of sub-rhythm in the pentameter, imparting a little of its rhythmic insistence to the gentler line. Byron furnishes a useful example:

(25) For dance, and song, and serenade, and ball,
     And masque, and mime, and mystery, and more.

While these are perfectly normal pentameters, the rhythms of the language create within the pentameter framework a distinctive pattern which is heightened by being repeated in the second line. The first two stresses of each line are strong, and followed by a pause; the third stress initiates a polysyllable and so speeds up the rhythm; the fourth stress is weak; and the final one is emphatic once more. The resulting rhythmic pattern could be formalised (and of course its symmetricality exaggerated) in musical notation:

♪ | ♩. ♪ | ♩. ♪ | ♫♫♩ | ♩.

Not only is this a four-beat rhythm, but it conforms very closely to the particularly common type of four-beat rhythm which we discussed in 4.3, where the third measure is given special status by an increase in constitutive elements. Now while it is obvious that the lines quoted do not change the poem's rhythm from five-beat to four-beat, they do possess a distinctive rhythmic spring; and that this is the result of the pattern I have described can easily be shown by a rearrangement:

[25a]   For dance, and serenade, and song, and ball,
        And masque, and mystery, and mime, and more.

They now sound clumsy instead of sprightly, and yet as iambic pentameters are still unexceptionable.

Our earlier observation of a general preference for mid-line pauses among poets favouring rhythmic regularity can therefore be sharpened: a pause after the fourth syllable is likely to create a special kind of balance, with two heavier beats before it and three somewhat lighter ones after it. Gascoigne (1575, p. 54), Puttenham (1589, p. 75), and Campion (1602, p. 299) all recommend that the pause in the pentameter should occur after the first four syllables; and Oras (1960) presents statistics to show that the earlier Elizabethan poets had an overwhelming preference for a pause in this position, and no further pause until the end of the line. On the other hand, writers who wish to escape a four-square rhythmicality and bring their verse closer to speech may prefer pauses in other places; Oras's evidence shows Shakespeare moving in the later plays from the typical use of fourth position pause to a strong preference for a break in the sixth position, which is less likely to awaken echoes of the four-beat rhythm, though it divides the line into the same proportions. Few poets and fewer readers have been conscious of the existence and importance of this aspect of the pentameter, though this is far from saying that they have not exploited and responded to its particular rhythmic and expressive potential. We shall consider one example by Pope in 10.3.

One feature of a writer's pentameter style, then, will be the prominence and frequency with which a subsidiary four-beat organisation of the line is allowed to emerge: Chaucer, for instance, seems closer to four-beat rhythms than most, partly because the light final $-e$ diminishes the effect of unstressed syllables, partly because his rhyming, end-stopped verse encourages the perception of lines in pairs, and partly, perhaps, because the four-beat line was the most common verse form of his time. But this is not to say that the four-beat rhythm is part of the pentameter's structure, as has sometimes been claimed (most influentially by Frye, 1957); it is precisely because the writer is free to make use of it as he wishes, or to avoid all suggestions of it, that it is a valuable rhythmic resource in five-beat verse. In Chapter 7 we shall see that our experience of the pentameter is determined by strict restraints on the number and disposition of syllables, and to think of it as a four-beat rhythm with extra syllables is to fail to appreciate the sensitivity to metrical detail possessed by the ordinary reader.

Mixed forms, using both four-beat and five-beat patterns in a regular scheme, do of course occur, and it is worth noting that such a mixture usually results in something closer to the pentameter movement, since the four-beat hierarchies are inevitably disrupted (we do not, however, experience the shorter lines as five-beat lines with unrealised beats):

(26) Up with the day, the sun thou welcom'st then,
   B   B   B   B   B
    Sport'st in the gilt plaits of his beams,
     B   B   B
    And all these merry days mak'st merry men,
    B   B   B   B   B
    Thyself, and melancholy streams.
     B   B   B   B

Indeed, it might in some respects be more accurate to make a distinction between four-beat and non-four-beat forms, rather than between four-beat and five-beat, since many of the features of the pentameter which we have discussed are in fact characteristic of any verse which succeeds in escaping the four-beat rhythm. But of the various ways of making this escape, the pentameter is the one with by far the greatest poetic potential, as it retains the simplicity of an elementary rhythmic form while remaining open to the rhythm of the spoken language, and in this way manages to combine aesthetic shapeliness with expressive power.

Note

1. Not much has been made in metrical studies of the distinctive rhythmic qualities of the iambic pentameter, and the particular dangers it courts as a metrical form. The most perceptive comments on this topic are probably those by Fitzroy Pyle, made in the course of several essays (1939, 1968, 1973). A valuable survey of discussions of the iambic pentameter is given by Weismiller (1975, pp. 259–83).

Part Three: Metre

Chapter 6

What is a metrical rule?

The distinction we have drawn between the rhythm of the language and elementary rhythmic forms is to some extent a misleading one: our experience of rhythm as a general phenomenon may well be coloured by our deeply-ingrained habits of speech production and perception, and the rhythms we create and hear in language are certainly conditioned by more general rhythmic principles. Nevertheless, the two do have an existence independent of each other: the movement of normal English speech does not exhibit regular rhythmic forms, and patterns of rhythm are perceptible in media other than language. Regular verse is a wedding between the two, and like any good marriage, involves compromises on both sides: the language has to give up its freedom to arrange syllables in whatever patterns the sense requires, and to submit to a new set of principles, while the rhythmic forms have to give up the perfect regularity and symmetry they possess in their ideal state, and accept the distortions to be expected from union with the unruly material of speech. These compromises are made easier by the underlying compatibility already mentioned, however, and by a set of established conventions giving precise expression to that compatibility. The formal statement of those conventions – the marriage contract, one might say – is the set of metrical rules.[1]

A poet writing in regular verse organises the syllables of the language in such a way as to bring them within reach of one of the underlying rhythms that readers are predisposed to perceive. In Part Two we took for granted this arrangement of syllables in lines of verse, but it is time to ask what patterns of stress the poet may use, how close the language needs to come to the form of an underlying rhythm before the reader will perceive the connection, and to what degree the natural rhythms of speech can be retained, or perhaps even heightened, within the resulting regularity. To attempt to formulate the rules of English metre is to undertake a map of this region of interaction, giving concrete representation to the principles which not only guide the poet, but also enable the reader – any reader who speaks the language and has some acquaintance with rhythmic form – to perceive in a sequence of syllables the orderly processes, and the expressive possibilities, of regular verse. We shall begin in this chapter with some general considerations concerning the task ahead.

6.1 RULES OF METRE AND RULES OF LANGUAGE

Metrical form is an aspect of poetry that has always attracted discussion in terms of rules, and this reflects an abiding intuition that the activity of the writer in constructing verse, and of the reader in responding to it, is far from haphazard, and rests on shared principles which are capable of being formally stated. There is a clear parallel here with the activity of producing and understanding the sentences of a language: this activity, too, has always been discussed in terms of rules, on the basis of similar assumptions. The traditionally accepted equivalence of the two kinds of rule is reflected in the Latin grammars produced for Tudor schools, and their successors in the following three centuries: after such sections as 'Orthography', 'Etymology', and 'Syntax', each with its appropriate set of rules, came 'Prosody', with its own awesome array of rules governing the quantity of Latin syllables and their arrangement into lines of verse. But with metre as with language there is no need to have any conscious knowledge of the rules if one has assimilated them in a more direct manner: the Elizabethans formulated few rules of English grammar and fewer rules of English metre, but their conversation and their poetry in the vernacular were not thereby impaired. It is usually only when we are faced with a foreign language or verse form that we have to rely on the mechanical use of explicit formulations; and we then find ourselves envying those who have never experienced the need to learn them as rules. Renaissance scholars who were able to scan Latin verse only by dint of long labour marvelled at Cicero's description of the uneducated Roman populace jeering at an actor who committed a metrical blunder.[2]

To set out to formulate the rules of one's own language, therefore, is to attempt to make explicit what one already knows, in some sense of that slippery word 'know'; and to propose rules of metre for a body of verse with which one is deeply familiar is to do something very similar. There is therefore a theoretical justification for the time-honoured practice in metrical study of taking one's own judgements as the primary evidence in the construction of metrical rules, and inviting readers to test these proposed rules against their own internalised knowledge of metrical principles. Unfortunately, the sense of conviction that frequently accompanies a metrical judgement can lead to dogmatic attitudes that paralyse debate, just as it is all too easy to elevate one's own sense of what is grammatically acceptable into an absolute. It is important, therefore, to make use of any available evidence of the metrical judgements of others, whether in the present or the past: both direct comments by experienced readers, and the judgements implied by the metrical choices of poets themselves.[3] Some writers on metre, especially those fired with a Wittgensteinian hostility to definitions, deny the possibility of formulating rules to account for their sense of metrical form. Robinson (1971, p. 54) rightly observes that all the iambic pentameters in the language are related by a 'complex web of likenesses' with which we gradually become familiar, and that there is no underlying 'core of iambicity' which can be captured in a definition; he fails, however, to consider the possibility that this web could be represented in an appropriately complex set of rules. If one's judgements of metre are not capricious, they must be the product of consistent, if unconscious, principles; moreover, if there is widespread agreement in such judgements, those principles must be shared, and learned – through experience – by each successive generation. The question is not 'Are there such things as metrical rules?' but 'How can metrical rules be adequately formulated?'

Because of the similarities between our ability to use language and our ability to respond to metrical organisation, it is tempting to transfer the methods and concepts used in the study of one to the study of the other. But great caution is needed in doing so: the general similarity does not underwrite any particular correspondence, and every procedure or category transferred from one domain to the other needs separate justification. In 2.2. we discussed some examples of the metrical approach which draws its inspiration from the generative school of linguistics, noting that it fails in some ways to take full advantage of its model, while in other ways it is too dependent on it. At the very least, generative theory suggests certain features which an ideal set of metrical rules should possess. They should not merely describe a body of verse; they should distinguish between acceptable and unacceptable lines within any given metrical style. In so doing, they should provide a structural description of the acceptable lines, and indicate in what ways other lines are deviant. They should not be formulations of the conscious metrical principles to which poets may have adhered – we might as well base an account of Jonson's syntax on the quaint theories of his *English Grammar* – but of the principles which actually governed their practice, as they govern the reader's response. They should reflect the capacity of the reader to appreciate the rhythmic qualities of a metrical style or a line – its regularity or irregularity, its speed or slowness, its energy or inertness – and to recognise the particular metrical characteristics of a poet or period. The rules should aim at explicitness; that is, they should not rely on the reader's acquired sense of metre, since this is precisely what they are intended to explain: Saintsbury is posing, not solving, the problem when he says with reference to a proposed metrical rule, 'The ear must decide whether the substitution is allowable' (1910, p. 32). In the attempt to satisfy such requirements as these, the analogy with generative linguistics serves as a useful stimulus; but it must not be allowed to obscure a fundamental difference between grammatical and metrical rules. This will be most clearly demonstrated if we consider a situation – unlikely but theoretically possible – in which two alternative sets of rules both satisfy the requirements I have sketched. How do we decide which set is better or more correct?

The task of the generative linguist is to produce an entirely abstract system of rules to represent the implicit knowledge which underlies the use of language; or, in the terms introduced earlier, the 'competence' which underlies all 'performance'. His main criterion in choosing between two sets of rules will be economy; not merely out of respect for Occam's razor, but on the assumption that the most economical statement of the rules will capture the generalisations of the language system itself, those generalisations which guide the child in the acquisition of language. A metrical system, on the other hand, is not a set of abstract relations, as we have seen; its features are a direct reflection of the nature of language production and of rhythmic perception. In choosing between our hypothetical sets of rules, therefore, we should be guided primarily by the degree to which they represent these rhythmic realities, and it is perfectly conceivable that this may result in a preference for the less economical alternative. Unlike the generative linguist, the student of metre is concerned with what we actually experience when we speak or listen to speech; it is only by focusing on this that we can understand, and perhaps enhance for other readers, the functions of metre in poetry. An abstract system of rules that predicts what collocations of syllables will be regarded as metrical without relating those patterns to the rhythms that readers perceive has very little meaning: it exists only as a convenient formulation which might be used to programme a verse-reading computer. Another way of putting this is that a sharp distinction between competence and performance is an obstacle to the formulation of metrical rules. The way in which the rules of metre are governed by principles of rhythmic form and by the rhythmic characteristics of the language has its closest linguistic analogy, perhaps, in the way the sentences we utter are governed by the properties of sound and the nature of the articulatory organs; and this is classed in generative theory as an aspect of performance, to which relatively little theoretical attention has been given. Even here the analogy is far from exact, since the physical and psychological constraints on speech still permit thousands of different languages, whereas the equivalent constraints on the metrical forms in a particular language allow only limited freedom to the poet. In the field of performance, it may be that linguistics has more to learn from metrics than the other way round.[4]

To be both useful and explanatory, therefore, metrical rules should be a formalised statement of the ways in which we perceive a regular rhythm when we read, or hear, metrical verse. They should operate neither on the minutiae of phonetic detail (which are a property of individual performances) nor on purely abstract categories, but on the perceptual realities of linguistic rhythm. The rules should also imply a general theory of rhythmic form in the language concerned, by specifying which linguistic features can be used in metre; thus a theory of English metre should suggest why strictly quantitative verse has never been successful, or why verse forms based on intonation patterns have never – as far as I am aware – been attempted, and should offer some insight into borderline areas like syllabics. The phonetic and phonological systems of English, together with the nature of rhythm, prevent us from inventing new modes of sound organisation at will, and also from proposing metrical theories with complete abandon. The rules which govern the rhythms of regular verse are not, therefore, conventions in the strict sense; they have deep roots in human physiology and psychology. Nevertheless, in turning from underlying rhythmic principles to metrical rules we are engaging with that aspect of the subject in which convention plays the greatest part. The more strictly literary the verse, the more important will be the conventions of the metrical tradition, and in order to examine their role, we shall devote particular attention to the iambic pentameter as a firmly established literary form. We shall find that, far from being arbitrary impositions, they usually serve a specific purpose – often the purpose of evading the simple and insistent forms that result from the most elementary realisations of rhythm in language.

The rules proposed in the following chapter, therefore, should not be thought of as strictly analogous with generative rules of syntax or phonology. Though they are presented in terms of a framework which might suggest that analogy, and can be said to 'generate' lines of metrical verse, they are concerned not with underlying competence but with perceptual experience. The most economical way of presenting rules of this kind is in terms of formal conventions, by means of which simplicity of formulation can be used as an index of a rule's generalising power; but the search for algebraic elegance can all too easily take precedence over the need for accurate representation, and achieve only empty abstractions. In the following chapter, I give the rules in the form of verbal statements, though I have used the Appendix on 'Rules and Scansion' to suggest a possible system of formal conventions, drawing on, but differing significantly from, the conventions of generative linguistics. The rules which I propose are intended to be more explicit than those of most metrical theories, but, unlike linguistic rules, they do not aim to be wholly so: there comes a point where rhythmic distinctions are too fine to be captured in manageable rules, and one has to say with Saintsbury, 'The ear must decide'. Critical utility may be more valuable than theoretical rigour or economy of formulation, and the goal of expository clarity more worthwhile than the dream of total explicitness.

6.2 METRICAL SET

The word 'rules', in the context in which I have been using it, is somewhat misleading; it suggests an instruction which poet and reader are obliged to follow, inscribed like Mosaic tablets somewhere apart from the verse they write and read. Perhaps a better word would be 'regularities', for the rules are simply statements of consistencies in the behaviour of poets and readers, those habits of mind and speech-apparatus which make the creation and appreciation of metrical form possible. A reader finds a poem metrical when he perceives in its movement an underlying rhythm of the kind discussed in Part Two, and the metrical rules specify how certain arrangements of syllables and words give rise to this perception. They are therefore statements about relationships with which the reader becomes familiar; fundamentally, relationships between the beats and offbeats of the metrical pattern and the stressed and unstressed syllables of the language.

A useful way of approaching the reader's familiarity with the rules is in terms of the notion of psychological *set* (see above, p. 78). A set is an expectation which involves a predisposition to interpret stimuli in a particular way; and we can borrow (and somewhat extend) the term to distinguish between *rhythmic set* and *metrical set*. The former is the widespread disposition to perceive rhythmic structures in sound stimuli; an example noted earlier is the perception of alternating patterns in objectively undifferentiated sounds like the ticks of a clock. When a simple underlying rhythm is directly embodied in the language (in a chanted nursery rhyme, for instance), the hearer's rhythmic set enables him to perceive the regular form, whether or not he knows the English language. But as the underlying rhythm grows more complex, its embodiment in language less direct, and the element of convention more significant, the role of metrical set increases. Through experience, the reader grows familiar with this or that metrical form in his language, until he responds readily to the rhythms it creates. He can then be said to have acquired a set for that metre; if one were using a linguistic analogy, one would say he had internalised its rules. Moreover, any given poem in a regular metre will establish its own highly specific metrical set, which in most cases will be a more sharply-defined version of a common metrical set. It should be obvious that any metrical set is built on, and embodies, a more fundamental rhythmic set, and that the two kinds of set correspond roughly to the underlying rhythm on the one hand, and on the other to the metrical pattern together with the principles by which it may be realised in a sequence of stressed and unstressed syllables.

The full statement of the rules of English metre can be thought of as an attempt to represent the basic metrical set which every reader who is familiar with the language and the verse tradition brings to the poetry he reads. We can call this the *general set* for English metrical verse, referring both to the psychological set itself and to the set of rules which represents it, rather as 'grammar' can refer both to the speaker's internalised rules and to the linguist's formulation of them. To propose such a general set is to make the claim that all English verse that we recognise as rhythmically regular falls within the framework it provides, and can be described in its terms. Any invented metre which cannot be so described is not likely to be perceived as rhythmic. A particular metrical style, or single poem, or individual line, will make use of only some of the possibilities provided for by the general set, and the choice it makes from the available options is a reflection of its metrical character. One of the important tasks of a metrical theory is to make it possible to specify the relationship between the patterns and rules of a particular metrical form and the general rules of the verse tradition. When we start to read a poem in an orthodox regular metre, we very rapidly attune our reading to its metrical form; in other words, the specific metrical set for that poem is quickly established. What makes this possible is the fact that it falls within the general set with which we are already familiar, and it normally takes only a few lines to determine the particular subset of rules that is being used. An analogy would be the rapidity with which a piece of music written according to the conventions of the Western tonal system establishes in the mind of a listener familiar with those conventions a sense of its key (which does not entail the ability to name that key). But an atonal work will not immediately signal a place in the key-system, nor will, say, purely syllabic verse in English fall into place in the reader's set of expectations.

Any metrically homogeneous body of verse will have associated with it a metrical set, whether we are talking of a traditional form like the iambic pentameter, an author's distinctive use of that form, such as Milton's iambic pentameter, or the metrical style of a particular poem, such as the iambic pentameter of *Paradise Regained*. The more homogeneous the verse, the more precisely defined the metrical set will be, excluding a greater number of the options included in the general set. The metrical set of a poem can of course be momentarily challenged by an exceptional line, like a deliberate dissonance in music, or can undergo transformation, like modulation from one key to another.

The general set for English verse, and the sets for individual metres and poems, can be given a formal statement under four headings: the *underlying rhythm*, the *metrical pattern*, the *realisation rules*, and, in some cases, the *conditions*. The first two have already been introduced: the underlying rhythm indicates the most basic rhythmic grouping in the poem, and the metrical pattern shows how this underlying rhythm is manifested in a particular configuration of beats and offbeats, arranged in lines. The realisation rules exhibit the possible ways in which the metrical pattern (and through it the underlying rhythm) can be embodied in a sequence of stressed and unstressed syllables. Finally, in some metres, notably those which are the product of the literary tradition, we shall find certain constraints placed upon the operation of the realisation rules, which are formalised as conditions. A correct formulation of the general set and its subsets in these terms will not only show how English metre is constituted, but will relate it to the fundamental properties of rhythm, and should suggest reasons why these rules, rather than any others, have taken root in the tradition. Scanning a line is a process of using the realisation rules to relate its stress contour to a metrical pattern; if any combination of rules within the set for the metre in question will permit a realisation of the metrical pattern, the line is an acceptable example of that metre. A similar procedure is involved in the normal reading of a line, but it happens rapidly and for the most part unconsciously, and the rules, although they are intended to reflect the perceived relationships on which the apprehension of rhythm is based, make no attempt to represent the actual psychological processes of reading in the order in which they occur.

One aspect of the reader's understanding of metre which the rules should reflect is his sense that certain lines are less direct realisations of the metrical pattern than others. Generally speaking, the more complex the realisation, the greater the feeling of metrical tension, though we shall have cause to qualify this statement in the fuller discussion in 7.10. If we place the rules in an order which reflects increasing deviation from the simplest realisation, we can say that the more often a later rule is made use of, the more complex is the metre. It is worth noting, incidentally, that in discussing such features as complexity and tension, we have no option but to appeal to the reader's subjective experience of verse. It is not sufficient to base assessments of complexity on frequency of appearance in the verse tradition, as is sometimes done by metrists who wish to avoid an appeal to their own judgements, since a type of line which occurs rarely need not be complex – it may, for instance, be too simple to be used with any frequency.

We have seen that the realisation rules specify the relationships between the beats and offbeats of the metrical pattern on the one hand and the stresses and nonstresses of the line of verse on the other, which means that the rules of metre and the rules which govern the stress contours of English speech interlock, and other linguistic rules play a part in this complex web as well. However, the study of metre and the study of phonology can be kept separate without grave damage to the former, because it is possible while discussing a metrical rule to rely on the reader's implicit knowledge of the phonological structure of his own language; for instance, the assignment of stresses and nonstresses in a line of verse need not be explicitly justified in terms of phonological rules if readers agree on their position in a normal pronunciation. By making this separation the study of metre can be kept safely out of the continuing debates in the field of phonology, and made accessible to those whose main interest is in literature, not linguistics. Moreover, we thereby avoid the possibility of circularity that creeps into some accounts of metre within a generative framework, where interpretations of metrical and phonological phenomena are used to justify each other. Our rules will therefore make use of nothing more complex at the level of phonology than a classification of syllables as stressed or unstressed; with the implication that in any given metrical example, a syllable will function as either one or the other, even if it occupies an intermediate place in the stress hierarchy of the phrase or sentence. This simplifying assumption (which has been a feature of most traditional accounts of metre) will facilitate the statement of the metrical rules, and probably corresponds to an actual process of simplification which occurs in the perception of regular rhythm. However, it leaves unsolved a number of questions about the relationship between metrical form and the movement of spoken English, some of which will be taken up in Chapter 8, where we shall investigate the final level in the metrical edifice: the relationship between the simplified stress contour – we can call this the *stress pattern* – employed in the rules of metre and the huge variety in sound and movement that characterises the language we use.

Notes

1. A clear statement of the interaction between linguistic material and abstract patterns is given by Žirmunskij (1925, Ch. 1), though like many other writers on verse form, he identifies the latter with *metre* and calls the result of the interaction *rhythm*, thereby overlooking the important role of elementary rhythmic forms in determining what patterns are possible.

2. See Erasmus (1528, pp. 110–11) and Ramus (1564, fol. 53^v). These passages are discussed in Attridge (1974, pp. 80–81).

3. One possible approach would be the use of elicitation experiments to test readers' metrical responses, though carefully designed and controlled experimental procedures would be necessary, as is shown by Quirk & Svartvik (1966) and Greenbaum & Quirk (1970).

4. Within linguistic theory, the absolute dichotomy between competence and performance has often been questioned, and the importance of the latter emphasised: see, for instance, Fodor & Garrett (1966), Wales & Marshall (1966), Fromkin (1968), Whitaker (1968), Bever (1970), Campbell & Wales (1970), R. Fowler (1970), Turner (1970), Derwing (1973, Ch. 8), Lakoff (1973), and Kates (1976). It has recently been argued that the temporal dimension, usually regarded as an attribute of performance only, should enter into phonological descriptions (see Coates, 1980; and C. A. Fowler, 1980): the importance of this suggestion for metrical theory is obvious.

Chapter 7

The rules of English metre

We come now to the task of formulating as rules the consistent relationships observable in English metrical verse between the elementary properties of rhythmic form and the rhythmic features of the English language. We are concerned primarily with the general set that underlies the tradition as a whole, but we shall look for a way of stating it which will allow us to specify the rules that constitute any particular metre, or that govern any particular poem. A summary of the rules proposed in this chapter, including alternative statements by means of formal conventions, is given in the Appendix (p. 357).

7.1 UNDERLYING RHYTHMS AND METRICAL PATTERNS

The metrical set for any poem in regular verse includes an underlying rhythm, usually four-beat or five-beat, and a metrical pattern which embodies that rhythm in lines or groups of lines. We have already discussed these features of metrical form in some detail, and the main object of our attention in this chapter is the way in which they are related to the stress patterns of the language, but a résumé may be useful at this point.

The metrical pattern indicates the number and position of beats and offbeats in the line of verse. We can specify a particular metrical pattern as follows:

    B o B o B o B

This represents four-beat verse with no initial or final offbeats (or a single line in that metre). Since beats are automatically separated by offbeats, this metrical pattern can also be fully characterised as 4B. Four-beat verse which regularly opens and closes with an offbeat can be shown as:

    o B o B o B o B o

and abbreviated as o4Bo. Optional offbeats at the beginning or end of the line can be indicated by means of parentheses; thus optional feminine endings can be shown as:

o B o B o B o B (o)   or   o4B(o)

Note that, unlike the earlier examples, this could not be a representation of a single line, but must refer to a sequence of lines (and to the expectations aroused by that sequence); the metrical pattern of any individual line will be either o4B or o4Bo. The same conventions will serve to state the metrical pattern of verse that uses lines of differing lengths, though in this case more than one line has to be indicated.

A common metrical form, which traditional prosody has always found awkward to deal with, is the four-beat line with optional opening and closing offbeats:

(o) B o B o B o B (o)   or   (o)4B(o)

As the metrical pattern indicates, it is not some anomaly stranded between 'iambic' and 'trochaic' metres, but the freest use of the options available in the four-beat form, which accounts for its aura of simplicity and naturalness. Another feature of the metrical pattern discussed in Chapter 4 is the occurrence of unrealised beats; these, it will be recalled, are most commonly experienced when the fourth beat of a four-beat line is absent. Unrealised beats are indicated in the metrical pattern as follows:

B o B o B [o B]   or   3B[oB]

(Here the previous offbeat is also unrealised, which is frequently the case in four-beat lines.) If unrealised beats are optional within a poem, the usual bracketing is used: 3B([oB]). A way of representing a dipodic metrical set has also been introduced:

B o b o B o b

However, I shall make no attempt to formulate rules to account for the establishment of anything as elusive as dipodic rhythms.

The psychological set established by a body of verse can include very fine detail, and metrical features often interlock with syntactic or lexical features, making a completely explicit description impossible. We may wish, however, to be a little more precise in the representation of optional offbeats, in order to reflect the fact that our expectations are sometimes strong and sometimes weak. In such cases, we can employ different types of bracketing: the ordinary parentheses as above when the expectation is neutral, an angled bracket to show that the stronger expectation is for the presence of an offbeat, and a double bracket for the reverse:

(o) B o . . .   ⟨o⟩ B o . . .   ((o)) B o . . .

This variety of symbols is useful only in representing the metre of a body of verse, and the expectations derived from it; when it comes to assessing the acceptability of any single line, all that matters is that an offbeat is permitted but not obligatory. It is probably as well not to attempt a more precise definition than this of degrees of expectation; while being very specific in some respects, metrical sets are relatively indeterminate in others, and their fuzzy edges should not be artificially trimmed.

7.2 BASE RULES AND DOUBLE OFFBEATS

An underlying rhythm manifested in a metrical pattern exerts a simplifying pressure on the complex stress contour of the language, so that the reader of regular verse perceives not a multiply-gradated hierarchy of stresses, but a pattern made up only of two kinds of syllable, relatively strong and relatively weak, or stressed and unstressed (using these terms in a way not exactly consonant with their use in phonology), which we shall indicate as +s and −s respectively. (The experience of reading most verse is in fact somewhat more complicated, but we shall postpone consideration of these complications to Chapter 8.) The general set for English metre includes all the possible ways in which the beats and offbeats of a metrical pattern can be realised by a simplified stress pattern of this kind, though a particular poem or metrical style may make use of only a selection of these realisation rules.

We have already discussed the naturalness with which the stressed syllables of English are perceived as rhythmic beats: they act as peaks of energy in the utterance, and have a tendency towards periodic occurrence. The most fundamental metrical rule, therefore, is one which embodies this fact: it is the first of the two *base rules* of English metre, and we shall call it the *beat rule*:

Beat rule

A stressed syllable may realise a beat

It must be remembered that a rule of this kind is intended to reflect the perceptual realities of performance rather than the abstract relations of competence: it states that a syllable which is perceived as stressed may be perceived as the beat of a metrical pattern, and hence of an underlying rhythm. It is important, too, to note that the rule specifies a *possible* realisation, not an obligatory one; we shall see later that under certain conditions stressed syllables can play a different role in the metre. Realisation rules are therefore to be understood as optional: in the reader's attempt (usually unconscious) to find a rhythmic organisation in the line of verse, he may make use of any of the rules in the set for that metre; or, to put it another way, every realisation rule has attached to it the implied condition: 'when by so doing the appropriate metrical pattern is realised.' Since the beat rule includes no special environment in which this realisation occurs, no other condition applies to it; in other words, *any* stressed syllable may realise a beat if the metrical pattern requires it.

We need a second base rule to state that the simplest realisation of an offbeat is a single unstressed syllable, reflecting the preference in the language for alternations of stress and nonstress, and the rhythmic simplicity of a single weak pulse between the peaks of energy. However, we have seen that freer metrical forms, especially those of popular verse, allow a single nonstress to be replaced by two nonstresses, creating a *double offbeat*, and that because of the stress-timed character of English, this does not disturb the underlying rhythm to any great degree:

$$\overset{-s}{} \quad \overset{-s}{}$$

(1) 'O have they parishes burnt?' he said
                         ŏ

Rather than formulate two separate rules, it seems truer to rhythmic reality to include this option within the offbeat rule:

Offbeat rule

One or two unstressed syllables may realise an offbeat

As in the statement of the rules as a whole, the statement of an individual rule implies an order of increasing complexity in the realisation of the metrical pattern; thus the second option of this rule –

allowing two unstressed syllables to realise an offbeat – is slightly more complex than the first. Once again, the rule includes no specific environment, implying that any nonstress or pair of nonstresses may realise an offbeat. The demands of the metrical pattern of course impose restraints on this freedom: thus a pair of nonstresses could never realise two offbeats, although the rule on its own might seem to permit this, because no metrical pattern includes adjacent offbeats. Note that the rule allows initial and final offbeats to be double, as in these examples:

(2) As the king one day a hunting was

(3) The noblest kind of love is love Platonical

However, in many types of verse strict conditions are imposed on the use of double offbeats, and we shall discuss these in section 6 of this chapter.

We have been considering the offbeat rule with reference to the general set for English verse, but a given metrical form is likely to make use of it in a more limited way. In the very strictest duple verse, the optional second nonstress would be omitted entirely, and the rule would simply state that one unstressed syllable may realise an offbeat; in strict triple verse, on the other hand, the first option would be omitted, and the rule would allow only *two* nonstresses to realise an offbeat. There are, of course, many gradations between these extremes: almost all duple verse allows occasional double offbeats (often under the specific conditions referred to above), and some triple verse allows single offbeats. These variations, too, can be suggested in the statement of the rule: as given above, it implies a metre which varies freely between single and double offbeats, but we can bracket the second option to show that it is only occasionally used:

Offbeat rule (duple verse)

One (or two) unstressed syllables may realise an offbeat

We shall consider the form of the rule appropriate to triple verse in 7.9.

I have said that a double offbeat is a more complex realisation than a single offbeat, but it should be noted that this does not mean that it always creates metrical tension: if the rule indicates a strong preference for double offbeats, they will be experienced as an expected and natural part of the metre. (The relationship between complexity and tension will be discussed in 7.10.) We have also encountered a few examples of *triple* offbeats, as in the line from Auden's 'Victor':

$$\overset{+s}{\text{ }} \quad \overset{-s}{\text{ }} \quad \overset{-s}{\text{ }} \quad \overset{-s+s}{\text{ }}$$

(4) Cried; 'Father, will she ever be true?'
     B   ŏ   B

This is probably too rare an occurrence to justify inclusion in the general set, but if we wished to do so, a third option in the rule would allow for it. As in the examples quoted, we scan a line by showing the stress pattern above it and the metrical pattern beneath it, giving the symbol for a double offbeat if the second option of the offbeat rule is utilised. The presence of this *deviation symbol* shows at a glance that the line is more complex at this point. It is unnecessary in such examples to give the stress pattern, since it is fully indicated by the symbols below the line, B implying +s, and o (or ŏ) implying −s (or −s −s). I shall continue to show it where it might be helpful, however; and in the following chapter we shall consider ways of refining the representation of the rhythm at this level.

When one of the unstressed syllables has a vowel which tends to disappear in pronunciation, and thereby to lose its rhythmic force as a syllable, the result is more like a single offbeat than a double one. This is an aspect of phonetic structure which we shall consider in the following chapter, under the heading of *elision* (8.4), but it is necessary to introduce it here as it has a bearing on the treatment of double offbeats. We could scan the following line with a double offbeat:

(5) And never a spray of yew
  o   B   ŏ   B   o   B

Or we could assume that the pronunciation of 'never' approaches that of a monosyllable, which is a natural result of stress-timing and the phonetic character of the sequence, and show it as a single offbeat. Neither reading involves a wholly simple realisation: the first implies a degree of complexity in the relationship between the syllables and the metrical pattern, the second a slight compression of the syllables themselves. The metrical style of the work is usually the best guide; other lines in Arnold's poem make it clear that double offbeats are acceptable, especially after the first beat:

(6) Strew on her roses, roses
   B   ŏ   B   o   B   o

(7) She bathed it in smiles of glee
     o B   ŏ   B   o   B

On the other hand, where a poet observes strict principles preserving the syllable count, it is best to assume that elision is intended. In any case, the reader seldom has to make a conscious choice; the two phenomena shade into one another, and the stress-timed rhythm of English, together with the metrical set, provide an unnoticed but efficacious guide to pronunciation.

7.3 PROMOTION

Relatively few lines achieve metrical regularity through the operation of the base rules alone. Consider the following:

(8) They'll turn me to a flash of fire
(9) Balanced on her wings of light
(10) The Pilot and the Pilot's boy

Each of these is clearly experienced as a four-beat line, yet each has only three fully stressed syllables. When we read such lines, the extra beat is provided by the words 'to', 'on', and 'and', even though we do not need to pronounce these words with any special emphasis. We can of course chant the lines, in which case we convert the felt beat on these words into a vocally manifested one by stressing them, but if we are reading naturally the only extra stress we might give is the product of the language's own tendencies towards alternation (see 3.4 above), perhaps encouraged by the metrical set established in earlier lines. (Ruskin's mother spent three weeks training him not to stress the preposition when reciting 'The ashes of the urn'; *Praeterita*, Ch. 2). Were we to encounter any of lines (8)–(10) in a context which created a strong expectation for three realised beats, and not for a strict alternation of syllables, we would no doubt be able to accept them, the stress-timed rhythm of English coming to our aid to speed us over the group of three nonstresses.

It is not the case, however, that any nonstress in a line can function as a beat. The following lines, for example, both have four main stresses and ten syllables, but only in the first can one of the nonstresses carry a fifth beat; the second has to be read as a four-beat line:

(11) For always roaming with a hungry heart

[11a] For always roaming with hungry demands

We must conclude that an unstressed syllable can function as a beat only under rigorously defined conditions; specifically, as our examples suggest, when it occurs between two other unstressed syllables. [11a] indicates clearly that an unstressed syllable cannot realise a beat if there is an unstressed syllable on only one side; neither '-ing' nor 'with' reveals any inclination to function as a beat. This can be tested by the rather crude method of imposing a pattern of beats on the line as one reads it: to give either of these syllables a strong stress creates an intolerable wrenching of the rhythms of the language, whereas to stress the appropriate syllables in (8)–(11) is much less unnatural. A nonstress between two stresses is even less able to realise a beat, as the rhythm of the language will insist on its playing its natural part as an offbeat between two beats.

We arrive, therefore, at the first of the *deviation* rules, which allow the elements of the metrical pattern to be realised in ways other than the simple ones enshrined in the base rules. In formulating deviation rules, we shall for the time being confine ourselves to duple metre, and discuss later the extent to which modifications are necessary to account for triple metre. The type of deviation we are at present concerned with can be termed *promotion*, as a nonstress is promoted to the role normally held by a stress. We shall need to extend the rule later, but we can tentatively state it as follows:

Promotion rule (first version)

An unstressed syllable may realise a beat when it occurs between two unstressed syllables

In scansion, we can show the operation of this rule by a deviation symbol consisting of a horizontal line above the beat in question; this symbol will always imply −s at the level of stress pattern:

(9) Balanced on her wings of light

$$\overset{+s-s}{\text{Balanced}} \overset{-s}{\text{on}} \overset{-s}{\text{her}} \overset{+s}{\text{wings}} \overset{-s}{\text{of}} \overset{+s}{\text{light}}$$
$$\text{B} \quad \text{o} \quad \overline{\text{B}} \quad \text{o} \quad \text{B} \quad \text{o} \quad \text{B}$$

The scansion here shows that by the application of the base rules and the promotion rule, the stress pattern of the line can realise a four-beat metrical pattern; and that it can do so with only one application of a deviation rule (and a simple one at that) indicates that it is not a very complex line, rhythmically speaking – which is, of course, consistent with one's response to it. We should not, however, allow the scansion to suggest that a beat is clearly perceived as falling on the middle of the three nonstresses; all it implies is that this pattern of three nonstresses is capable of functioning as the rhythmic equivalent of offbeat, beat, offbeat, thanks to the expectations set up by the duple verse and the alternating tendency in the language. It may be psychologically more accurate in many cases to say that the beat is *blurred* rather than being precisely located, or that the rhythm is suspended – but not contradicted – over this stretch of syllables. (An equivalent in music might be the perception of a beat during a held note.) Notice, incidentally, that the way a syllable is perceived depends not only on what has gone before, but also on what is to come; this will be puzzling only if one believes that the spoken language is produced and understood syllable by syllable, rather than, as is amply testified by experimental evidence, by means of constant forward scanning.

An unstressed syllable at the beginning of a line is also very easily promoted to take a beat:

(12) Of his bones are coral made
     B̄   o   B   o   B o   B

This is, of course, most likely to happen when we expect a beat at the start of the line; otherwise we will be inclined to treat the two unstressed syllables as an initial double offbeat. To put it more formally, the metrical pattern (which is part of the reader's metrical set) will determine how two initial nonstresses are perceived. In a five-beat line, with its relatively weaker metrical set, two such syllables are most likely to receive a double-offbeat interpretation – which is a further reason for the avoidance of trochaic metre in the pentameter noted in 5.2. Sometimes, promotion in this position can be thought of as an example of the type already considered, with a line-juncture intervening in the sequence of three nonstresses:

(13) Now, like moonlight waves retreating
                                  B o

     To the shore, it dies along
     B̄   o   B

But it can occur just as well without a run-on line or a preceding offbeat, and we therefore need to extend our promotion rule to include syllables that fall after a line-boundary and before a nonstress. We also need to include a mirror image of this environment, because promotion is common at the end of the line as well:

(14) Here swallowed up in endless misery
                                     B o B̄

Once again, there are instances where a run-on may make the environment very similar to that of the promotion rule as already stated:

(15) Me only cruel immortality
                            B o B̄
      Consumes
       o   B

But it is clear that a line-boundary before or after a nonstress can function on its own like another nonstress in allowing promotion, and we can therefore state the full rule as follows:

Promotion Rule

An unstressed syllable may realise a beat when it occurs between two unstressed syllables, or with a line-boundary on one side and an unstressed syllable on the other

(Notice that we do not specify whether the line-boundary falls before or after the syllable.) The ordering of the options in the rule implies that the environment of two nonstresses produces a somewhat less complex realisation than the environments at line-opening and line-end. None of the options, however, contributes very markedly to metrical tension, though it is interesting to note that if the metrical set includes a strong expectation for double offbeats, promotion may not occur so smoothly. Gross (1964, p. 43) cites an example:

(16) We called her the Hack of the Parade
       o   B   ŏ   B   o   B̄   o B

Here the double offbeat earlier in the line inclines us to treat 'of the' as a further double offbeat, an inclination strengthened by the verbal similarity, and a degree of special attention in reading is required to bring out the third beat of the line. The rhythm runs more smoothly if we omit the extra nonstress:

[16a] We called her Hack of the Parade
        o   B   o   B o   B̄ o B

To conflate the three environments for promotion within a single rule as we have done is to imply that the generalisation captured in so doing is a metrically significant one; that the three processes are in fact versions of the same process. It is not difficult to see the basis for this: promotion occurs when the metrical set encourages the perception of a nonstress as a beat, and this can only happen if there is no competing adjacent stress to attract that beat. In fact, if elegance were the prime criterion, one could phrase the rule in those terms: an unstressed syllable may realise a beat when it is not adjacent to a stress in the same line.

7.4 DEMOTION

Some further examples will suggest another elementary rule in English metre, applicable to sequences of three stressed syllables:

(17) Then out bespoke the brown, brown bride
(18) Thy rapt soul sitting in thine eyes
(19) But where the ship's huge shadow lay

These examples read easily as four-beat lines, even though 'brown' (on both occurrences), 'soul', and 'huge' receive full stresses. To utter the second 'brown' with any less force than the first would be to go against the normal pronunciation of English, and the equivalent words in both the other lines demand a strong semantic emphasis. Yet there is no sense of strain when we encounter lines like these in four-beat verse, as we frequently do. We can call the rule which operates here the *demotion rule*, and a tentative formulation would state that a stressed syllable may realise an offbeat when it occurs between two stressed syllables. Again, metrical practice is a reflection of a tendency we have already noted in English speech rhythms (see pp. 70–1 above): in a sequence of three stressed syllables, the middle one is often perceived as playing a subsidiary rhythmic role. (An analysis of this pattern in classical terms, incidentally, could only be made in terms of 'spondaic substitution', which would obscure the part played by the sequence of three stresses.)

   This rule is the converse of the previous one, and the two could be combined by means of a simple formal convention. To do this would be to claim that they have the same rhythmic origin, and one might justify this by arguing that they are both a product of the tendency to perceive an alternating rhythm in the language: where there are three syllables of equal weight, the middle one will function as a rhythmic contrast to its partners. Sequences of syllables do occur in which it is impossible to make a choice between demotion of one or promotion of another (see Ch. 8, example (4)), and in such cases our conflated rule would be useful; but for the most part the generalisation it captures holds only at an abstract level, and is not a matter of similar physical or psychological processes. This will become clearer if we examine the other environments in which demotion can occur. Of the following two lines, only the first is metrically acceptable as a four-beat line:

(20) Full fathom five thy father lies
[20a] Fathoms five thy father lies drownéd

Whereas promotion can occur at the beginning of the line and at the end, demotion is possible only at the beginning. It cannot be said that a stress may realise an offbeat when it is not adjacent to a nonstress, and the demotion rule is therefore not a strict mirror image of the promotion rule.

The full statement of the demotion rule, then, includes the line-initial environment, as exemplified by (20):

Demotion rule

A stressed syllable may realise an offbeat when it occurs between two stressed syllables, or after a line-boundary and before a stressed syllable

The implication of the ordering of options is that line-initial demotion is the more complex realisation, which seems generally true. In scansion we can use a dot above the offbeat to indicate demotion:

$$-s \quad +s \quad\quad -s \quad +s \quad\quad\quad -s \quad +s \quad\quad\quad\quad +s \quad\quad\quad +s$$
(*17*) Then out bespoke the brown, brown bride
  o   B   o   B   o   B   ȯ   B

$$+s \quad +s \; -s \quad +s \quad\quad\quad -s \; +s \; -s \; +s$$
(*20*) Full fathom five thy father lies
  ȯ   B   o   B   o   B   o   B

Once again, it is strictly unnecessary to show the stress pattern, since the deviation symbol for demotion will always imply +s.

Why does demotion occur at the beginning of the line and not at the end? In our discussion of stress hierarchies in 3.3 we noted that a stressed syllable is more likely to be subordinated to a stress which follows it than to one which precedes it; this means that if a line ends with two stresses, the last one will probably be perceived as a beat, as in

[20a], rendering demotion impossible. The same tendency encourages demotion of an initial stress when it is followed by another stress, as in (20). This is not the whole story, however, since examples of initial demotion frequently occur in which both stresses require emphasis:

(21) Wee, sleekit, cowrin, tim'rous beastie
      ŏ   B o

(22) Hail, King! tomorrow thou shalt pass away
     ŏ   B   o

It is more accurate to say that in such cases we accept – perhaps partly through convention – a suspension of the rhythm, treating the first syllable as outside the rhythmic structure of the line, and experiencing the start of the alternating rhythm on the second stress. At the end of the line, however, the rhythm is fully in action, and exerts pressure on any additional stress to act as a beat.

Something like demotion appears to occur in one other context not provided for in the demotion rule. Consider the following examples:

(23) Drawn of fair peacocks, that excel in pride
(24) Flows in fit words and heavenly eloquence
(25) Damn with faint praise, assent with civil leer
(26) Deep as first love, and wild with all regret

To emphasise the five-beat rhythm in each of these lines, one has to reduce the stress on the third word; one might wish to say, therefore, that these are demoted stresses occurring as part of a double offbeat. Such lines are interesting because they bring us to the bounds of strictly metrical analysis, and lead us into the area which is the subject of the following chapter: the interlocking of metrical rules with the phonological properties of the language. The similarity of all the lines quoted suggests that this metrical formation is very limited as to the place of its occurrence in the line and the verbal structure which makes it possible. It is in fact rare at any point other than the one at which it occurs in these examples, and it almost always involves a stress which is syntactically subordinated to a following stress, most often an adjective before a noun. What this implies is that when special rhythmic and linguistic conditions are met, it is possible to push deviation from the metrical pattern further than usual. But to attempt to account for it in a metrical rule, allowing any nonstress and stress to function as a double offbeat in duple verse, would be to open the floodgates to a welter of unmetrical lines, while to hedge it in with detailed restrictions as to position and linguistic content would be to introduce a rule of a very different kind from the other rules, which are characterised by the generality of their application. For this reason, we shall regard it for the time being as an exception to the rule, and discuss it fully in section 3 of the following chapter.

Promotion and demotion are of great importance in the achievement of rhythmic expressiveness, as they allow the line to move away from completely regular alternations without threatening the metrical pattern or affecting the syllable count. It is worth emphasising that promoted and demoted syllables do not demand special pronunciation; rhythm is a matter of perception, and it is possible to perceive a syllable as both light and yet playing the part of a beat, or heavy and yet functioning as an offbeat. Each occurrence of promotion will speed up the line, as the nonstress will be quicker and lighter than the stress it replaces, and stress-timing will encourage the trio of nonstresses to pass rapidly in order to reach the next stress:

> (27) I sent it in a letter to the Editor
>   o B   o B̄ o B o   B̄   o B o B̄

This can have expressive and structural consequences, reinforcing (or qualifying) the meaning, and diverting attention away from a relatively unemphasised part of the line. Demotion, on the other hand, will slow the verse down as a result of the extra stress, both because of its inherent length, and because the stress-timed rhythm will tend to separate the three stresses:

> (28) And strains from hard-bound brains eight lines a-year
>   o   B   o   B   ŏ   B   ŏ   B   o   B

Of the two phenomena, demotion is somewhat more disruptive of the steady movement of the rhythm, which is why we have treated it as a later rule in the general set. However, the precise effect of these deviations on the rhythm depends on the actual words being used, and we shall take up this question in 8.5.

To a certain extent, these effects of speed and slowness can be achieved in free verse, since they spring from the nature of English speech rhythm. In a line of metrical verse, however, something else happens: the underlying rhythm itself moves more quickly or slowly. The acceleration we experience when a beat is realised by a promoted nonstress is not just a quickening in the rate at which the syllables are pronounced; it is a quickening in the underlying rhythm, which moves faster when a beat is realised with so slight an expenditure of energy. And our sense of a ritardando when demotion occurs comes in part from the momentary holding up of the underlying rhythm. When we talk of the tension created by such variations, then, it is not so much a tension between the metrical pattern and the actual syllables, as our scansion rather misleadingly suggests, but the result of a regular rhythmic movement being slowed down and speeded up, or, to use a spatial metaphor, stretched and compressed. The alternative view, that the underlying regular metre ticks away independently of the actual line, and that the tension we experience arises from the distance between the two, is not very different from the inadequate notion of 'counterpoint', and is unconvincing as a psychological model. Though it remains true that the easiest way to talk about rhythmic tension is in terms of the relationship between an underlying metre and a verbal realisation, one should be fully aware that this does not imply two independent psychological levels, but a single complex experience.

7.5 IMPLIED OFFBEATS

We have seen (3.4) that speakers of English instinctively avoid sequences of two stresses when alternative pronunciations or phrasings are possible, unless there is a third stress to allow demotion. Nevertheless, opportunities for evasion are limited, and pairs of stresses remain a common feature of English speech. Any verse which relies on the incorporation of speech rhythms, therefore, needs a way of accommodating this pattern, even though it challenges the alternating rhythms both of the language and of the metre. The natural tendency in a careful reading of such a sequence is to let each syllable function as a beat, allowing the stress-timed rhythm of English to interpose an offbeat. Where stress-timing is reinforced by an insistent underlying rhythm, as in nursery rhymes, this happens frequently and easily, the offbeats being literally realised as pauses (most naturally by prolonging the first stressed syllable of the pair). We have already introduced a deviation symbol to indicate such implied offbeats:

(29) Tom, Tom, the piper's son
     B ô B   o B o   B

(30) Four-and-twenty blackbirds
      B   o   B   o   B   ô B

(31) Yes, sir, yes, sir,
      B ô B ô B ô B

      Three bags full
      B ô B ô B

A similar effect is sometimes found in literary verse:

(32) Break, break, break
      B   ô B   ô B   [o B]
      On thy cold gray stones, O Sea!

It can even become a fixed part of the metre in a four-beat line:

(33) Over hill, over dale,
      B o   B ô B o   B
      Thorough bush, thorough briar,
      B o   B   ô B o   B
      Over park, over pale,
      B o   B   ô B o   B
      Thorough flood, thorough fire
      B o   B   ô B o   B

More commonly, however, implied offbeats are used in the literary tradition to create a minor disruption in the rhythm, an eddy in the smooth flow of the verse:

(34) Perchance thee lie withered and old
                     B ô B

(35) For I am every dead thing
                     B   ô B

(36) Thy brother death came, and cried
             B   ô B

Here the absence of a realised offbeat markedly increases metrical tension, since we do not impose a regular rhythmic grid on such lines and therefore do not supply a pause fully equivalent to an offbeat. The second beat falls sooner than we expect, while the actual syllables move more slowly (just the opposite of the simultaneous acceleration or deceleration at both levels that occurs in promotion and demotion). The rhythmic sequence does not heighten the latent tendency towards alternation possessed by the language as it does when following the base rules, nor does it exploit that tendency in order to maintain a smooth rhythm, as in the two earlier deviation rules; instead, it insists on contravening it by bringing two emphasised stresses together.

Our final deviation rule, therefore, permits implied offbeats between successive stresses:

Implied offbeat rule

An offbeat may be implied between two stressed syllables

The similarity between the environments of the demotion and implied offbeat rules is not a coincidence; it reflects the fact that the rhythmic structure of the line is largely determined by the stresses, and that two stresses functioning as beats can induce varying kinds of phonetic material between them to act as an offbeat – not only one or two unstressed syllables, but also a stressed syllable, or nothing at all.

As the most disruptive of all the accepted deviations in regular verse, this rule is placed last; some metrical styles make no use of it at all. It not only threatens the vital alternations of the rhythm, but also upsets the relationship between the metrical pattern and the syllable count. For this reason, its use in the literary tradition is usually controlled by conditions which enforce some degree of syllabic compensation, and these are the subject of the following section. Five-beat metres are particularly strict in this respect (see 5.4): implied offbeats ungoverned by conditions are largely confined to some dramatic pentameter styles (the so-called 'monosyllabic foot'). The disruptiveness of the implied offbeat is also reflected in the infrequency of its occurrence early in the line, before the rhythm has had a chance to establish itself; in the iambic pentameter, for instance, it seldom occurs in the earliest position in which it is theoretically possible, though the following is a notable exception, announcing a poem that is going to challenge more than just metrical conventions:

(37) Of man's first disobedience, and the fruit
    o   B   ô B

Classical treatments of English metre often note the infrequency of this variation, which is termed 'second-foot inversion'; and in the generative metrical theory proposed by Chisholm (see above, 2.2) it is forbidden by a special rule. Tarlinskaja (1976, p. 283, Table 43) finds only 17 examples in about 1,300 lines of nondramatic iambic pentameter. Another traditional prohibition is that applied to initial inversion in trochaic verse, which produces an implied offbeat in the same position:

(38)   The pale yellow woods were waning
　　　　o　B　ᐭ B

(Initial inversion in iambic verse of course produces no implied offbeat, and there is therefore no reason to avoid it.) Even more disruptive in duple verse, and therefore even rarer, is an implied offbeat after an initial beat:

[38a] Pale, yellow, the woods were waning
　　　 B　ᐭ B

An initial stress before another stress is, as the ordering of the rules suggests, usually demoted.

It is important to note that the operation of the implied offbeat rule can overlap with that of the demotion rule, producing lines like the following:

　　　　　+s　　 +s　　 +s　　　　+s
(39)   I have a faint cold fear thrills through my veins
　　　 B　　ŏ　 B　ᐭ B　　　　 ̆　 B

Here the stress on 'fear' functions as part of the environment permitting the demotion of 'cold' and as part of the environment permitting an implied offbeat before 'thrills'. The result is a series of four strong stresses, beating like Juliet's pulse; yet the line remains perceptibly duple in its rhythm.

7.6 PAIRING CONDITIONS AND SYLLABIC RHYTHM

We have now established five realisation rules – two base rules and three deviation rules – which will account for all the normal metrical variations in duple metre. Verse which observes these rules, and no other metrical restraints, will not be characterised by a fixed syllable count, since they permit the free occurrence of implied or double offbeats in place of single offbeats. Such verse, sometimes called *strong-stress verse*, is characteristic of the popular tradition, and springs immediately from the most predominant feature of English speech rhythm, its stress-timing. But a large proportion of literary verse, traditionally, and accurately, called *accentual-syllabic verse*, observes a strict control over syllables, and allows implied and double offbeats only under special circumstances. We can capture these in the metrical set by the formulation of *conditions*. The resulting framework of realisation rules and conditions represents the union in the mainstream of English verse of the two rhythmic principles of English speech: the stress principle and the syllabic principle. In shifting the balance in the direction of the latter, the imposition of conditions also represents a modification of the metrical principles derived directly from the linguistic and rhythmic sources already discussed by the somewhat different demands of literary convention. In this and the following two sections we shall examine some of the ways in which poets writing in the accentual-syllabic tradition have superimposed the constraints of a fixed syllable count on the stress-dominated rhythms that constitute the foundation of English verse.

Since implied offbeats are the most disruptive deviation in regular metre, they are the most frequently subject to metrical conditions. In a great deal of poetry, an implied offbeat can occur only when it is immediately preceded or followed by a double offbeat:

> (40) Beside a pool bare to the eye of heaven
>   B   ŏ B   ŏ

> (41) As a huge stone is sometimes seen to lie
>   ŏ   B   ŏ B

We have already observed the widespread use of the two metrical formations exemplified here, and we have also noted that the classical approach to prosody, and some linguistic approaches, obscure the close relationship between them, and are unable to explain the frequency of their occurrence. We shall regard them as manifestations of the same metrical phenomenon, and call them *stress-initial* and *stress-final pairing*.

The limitation on the occurrence of implied offbeats can therefore be stated in the first of two *pairing conditions*:

Implied offbeat condition (first version)

An implied offbeat may occur only when it is immediately preceded or followed by a non-final double offbeat

Scansion makes it obvious if this condition has been observed, since every occurrence of ŏ should be accompanied by an occurrence of ŏ, as in the examples above. 'Non-final' has to be stipulated in the condition, or lines like the following would be permitted in strict duple verse:

> [42] So when you find a rule you like, follow it.
>   B   ŏ B   ŏ

At the beginning of the line, however, two nonstresses function easily
as a double offbeat, leading into the first beat, as in (41). The implied
offbeat condition also prohibits what is regarded in the classical
approach as inversion of the final iambic foot:

[43] So when you find a rule you like, break it
                                    B   δ B   o

There is no double offbeat accompanying the implied offbeat, so the
line is classed as unacceptable in any metrical style that observes this
condition. In both classical foot-prosody and the generative theory
proposed by Chisholm, this pattern has to be proscribed by a special
rule (and in the other generative theories discussed earlier it is
ignored).

A few poets occasionally contravene the pairing condition at the end
of the line while observing it elsewhere; it is something of a trademark
in Keats's verse, for instance:

(44) O soft embalmer of the still midnight
                                  B   δ B   o
(45) Or on the rainbow of the salt sand-wave
                                B   δ B   o

Such line-endings are felt as contradictions of the metrical norm, and
the momentary discord is heightened by the occurrence of a rhyme on
an unstressed syllable. Keats may be echoing a common ballad ending:

(46) But all was for this fair ladie

but here the musical setting would normally allow the last two syllables
to receive equal weight ('fair la-dee'). Similar endings in Chaucer's
verse usually provoke speculation about changes in pronunciation;
whether or not these are justified, such a response does indicate how
ingrained the prohibition is in our sense of the iambic pentameter. It
may in fact be derived from more general rhythmic principles; Baum
(1952, pp. 96–7) found in a sample of 3,400 clause and sentence
endings in written English prose that the pattern +s −s +s was more
than four times as common as +s +s −s.

Not all verse which limits the use of implied offbeats in this way
exerts similar control over double offbeats; Browning's pentameter
lines, for example, make frequent use of double offbeats without
adjacent implied offbeats, but the latter seldom occur without the
former (see Hatcher, 1928, Ch. 6 and 9). In the strictest form of duple
metre, however, double offbeats also occur only in pairing formations.

In such verse, a second pairing condition is observed:

> *Double offbeat condition (first version)*
>
> *A double offbeat may occur only in observance of the implied offbeat condition*

The form of the rule indicates that this condition is observed only if the implied offbeat condition is observed; that is to say, there is no natural metrical form which restricts double offbeats and not the more disruptive implied offbeats. When both conditions are observed, neither ◌̇ nor ◌̆ may occur in the scansion without its complementary partner, and leaving aside the question of optional offbeats at the beginning and end of the line, which will be discussed in the following two sections, the syllable count remains constant. A further point to note is that even strict accentual-syllabic verse will usually permit elision, so to state that a poem observes the offbeat condition is to claim that every instance of two successive nonstresses functioning as an offbeat is either accompanied by an implied offbeat, or is phonetically (or at least conventionally) capable of being regarded as one syllable.

One difference between rules and conditions is that the latter may not overlap; in determining whether a line meets a pairing condition, that is, we cannot allow the same offbeat or double beat to count more than once. Take the following construct:

[47] The slow syllables sailed gently past
      o B ◊B   ŏ B   ◊B o B

Although each implied offbeat is adjacent to a double offbeat, it is the same double offbeat; the line therefore fails to meet the first pairing condition, and is a syllable short – and the ear registers it as an irregular pentameter. Similarly, the following exceptional line by Browning observes the first but not the second pairing condition, though an illusion of compliance is almost created:

(48) By the straight cut to the convent. Six words there
    ŏ , B ◊B ŏ B o   B ◊   B

On the other hand, successive occurrences of pairing are acceptable within verse that observes the conditions:

(49) Of the wide world, dreaming on things to come
   ŏ   B ◊B ◊B   ŏ B   o B

Here the stress on 'world' is part of the environment for implied offbeats on either side, which is allowable, and the pairing conditions are fully observed in the two double offbeats. A pairing formation can also overlap with demotion or promotion, though careful handling of the syntax is required to save the reader from getting lost in the four successive stresses or nonstresses which this produces; (39) is an example of the former, and the following line shows the latter:

(50) Antiquity from the old schools of Greece
    o B o B̄   ŏ B ŏ B o   B

The bulk of English literary verse maintains control over the number of syllables in the line by observing both pairing conditions, though there is more than one way of interpreting this fact. Sometimes it is seen primarily as a conventional feature of English metre, an imposition on native accentually-based rhythms of the external principle of a fixed syllable count. It is certainly true that historically the triumphs of this principle reflect foreign influence: the poets who have, at various stages in the history of accentual verse, influentially tightened the restrictions on the syllable count have usually been well acquainted with French or Italian models, whether we think of Chaucer in the fourteenth century, Wyatt and Surrey in the sixteenth, or Waller and Dryden in the seventeenth. In eighteenth-century England, as Culler (1948) and Fussell (1954) have shown, the prestige of French verse was such that English poetry with any pretensions had to imitate its syllabic strictness, and influential handbooks like Bysshe's *Art of English Poetry* (1702) enshrined and propagated the syllabic principle. (On the other hand, poets who have taken English verse in the other direction, like Coleridge and Hopkins, have usually appealed to native precedent.) Syllable counting as a metrical principle may sometimes have won favour for a different kind of external reason: it is more amenable to the formulation of metrical rules than patterning of stresses, and therefore has a particular appeal to the technically self-conscious artist. Thus Elizabethan attempts to describe English metre frequently ignore aural rhythms and concentrate on the visually more obvious properties of syllable count and rhyme (see Attridge, 1974, Ch. 7). The very names 'fourteener' and 'poulter's measure' testify to a conception of metre rooted in the counting of syllables; and Peter Quince's name for the ballad stanza, we may recall, is 'eight and six'.

But our discussions of the rhythmic function of the syllable in 3.1 and of the syllabic strictness of the pentameter in 5.4 suggest that the control of syllables by means of pairing also reflects a rhythmic principle of the language itself. This view is supported by the widespread occurrence of pairing in English verse; for instance, the implied offbeat condition is commonly observed in ballads:

> (51) Oh lang, lang may their ladies sit
>   B   ồ B   ŏ
>
> (52) His corpse was laid in the cauld clay
>   ŏ   B   ồ B

And its use in the literary tradition is not confined to verse which fixes the number of syllables in the line: Milton employs it, for example, in *L'Allegro*, which has lines of seven, eight, and nine syllables:

> (53) And, singing, startle the dull night
>   ŏ   B ồ B

Pairing also appears fully-fledged in early accentual-syllabic verse; it seems to come naturally to Chaucer, the founder of the strict pentameter in English:

> (54) Or if men smoot it with a yerde smerte
>   ŏ   B ồ   B
>
> (55) The Millere was a stout carl for the nones
>   B   ồ B   ŏ

and to Surrey, who reintroduced this metre in the sixteenth century:

> (56) For my lord's guilt thus faultless bide I pain
>   ŏ   B   ồ B
>
> (57) The hart hath hung his old head on the pale
>   B   ồ B   ŏ

And the importance of the syllabic principle goes back even further: four-beat lines with a fairly strict syllable count occur in the twelfth century (in *Ormulum*) and in the thirteenth century (in *The Owl and the Nightingale*). It seems likely, therefore, that pairing has a rhythmic function in its own right, reflecting the role of the syllable as a rhythmic unit in the language since at least early Middle English, and this function requires explanation in terms of its local effects as well as its effects on the syllable count of the whole line.

If one thinks of a regular duple rhythm as the matching of a beat–offbeat alternation with a syllable-by-syllable progression, thereby satisfying both stress and syllabic principles, an implied or double offbeat constitutes a mismatch between the two types of rhythm. But this misalignment can receive some compensation if an implied offbeat is followed by a double offbeat, and vice versa. This process of compensation can also be seen in terms of the underlying rhythm: an implied offbeat momentarily speeds up the underlying rhythm, as we have seen, and the slight postponement of the following beat created by a double offbeat is perhaps sensed as a return to regularity. The reverse would, of course, happen in the case of stress-final pairing. This should be thought of in rhythmic, not temporal, terms, however; it is not an adjustment made against an absolute temporal standard, but a perceptual experience of a hastening followed by a slowing, or vice versa. (In the chanted recital of a nursery rhyme, the underlying rhythm itself controls the speed of the syllables, and is not subject to slowing down or speeding up; there is therefore no need for compensation, and such verse does not observe the pairing conditions.) A double offbeat produces less disruption than an implied offbeat, since two nonstresses are rhythmically more like a single nonstress than is the complete absence of nonstresses; hence the former is less rigorously controlled in English verse. Generally speaking, the imposition of syllabic conditions increases the potential not only for a heightened sense of metrical control, but also for expressive variation, since promotion and demotion can be more extensively used in the context of a strictly syllabic metrical set, while double and implied offbeats are more strongly experienced as challenges to an established rhythm.

There is one more way of looking at the phenomenon of pairing. The classical approach regards stress-initial pairing in iambic verse as 'inversion', and in fact both types of pairing can be seen as the result of switching a stress and a nonstress: $-s -s +s +s$ can be derived from $-s +s -s +s$, and $+s +s -s -s$ from $+s -s +s -s$, by exchanging the middle two syllables. This view suggests a further respect in which pairing reflects the natural rhythm of English, since the exchanging of a strong and weak stress to maintain an alternating pattern is part of the normal processes of the language (see 3.4). For instance, Liberman and Prince (1977, pp. 316–20), in their discussion of the rules of English pronunciation, suggest an optional 'iambic reversal rule' to allow such exchanges, and Beaver (1971b, 1973) proposes 'stress exchange rules' for a similar purpose. We are sometimes faced with a choice between two realisations of the metrical pattern which derives from this feature of the language; the opening of the iambic line, in particular, encourages such alternatives, since inversion in this position does not produce the disruption of an implied offbeat:

(58) And in the narrow rent at every turn
$\bar{\text{B}}$ ŏ   B

or   o $\bar{\text{B}}$ o   B

Consider, too, the pairing to be found in ballads, as in (51) and (52): the melody, based on regular alternation, will often enforce a reversal of stress which, in this context at least, the language seems to survive:

(*51*) Oh lang, lang may their ladies sit
+s   −s   +s   −s

(*52*) His corpse was laid in the cauld clay
−s   +s −s   +s

This is not to say that in most examples of pairing we experience any inclination to reverse the stresses in order to produce smooth alternation; but it may be that our familiarity with reversible forms enters our experience in some way, perhaps by a slight blurring of the rhythm between the adjacent nonstress and stress, especially when there is no syntactic break between them. Nabokov (1964, p. 20) is referring to this feature of pairing when he says that its beauty lies in 'a certain teasing quality of rhythm . . . [which] owes its subtle magic to the balance it tends to achieve between yielding and not yielding – yielding to the metre and still preserving its accentual voice'. Other metrists have called it a 'hovering accent', and it is presumably what lies behind the assertion by Jespersen (1900, p. 125), Winters (1957, p. 94), and Wimsatt (1970, p. 775) that there is a steady increase in the stresses of sequences like:

(59) When to the *sessions of sweet si*lent thought

The effect is not unlike that of some occurrences of syncopation in music, in which the misplaced accent is strong enough to attract the beat without permanently dislocating the metrical grid. It is noteworthy that in all the examples quoted above the adjacent stress and nonstress are monosyllables; we shall return to this point in 8.7, where we shall examine the role of word-boundaries in the pairing formations.

We have been considering the two types of pairing as rhythmically equivalent, but there are bound to be differences between a sequence that moves from two nonstresses to two stresses, and one that does the opposite. A difference with important consequences is that each type is associated with a distinctive rhythmic phrase, and these two phrases have found a place among the expectations involved in reading accentual-syllabic verse in duple metre. In stress-final pairing, the phrase consists of the four syllables directly implicated: −s −s +s +s. This progression from double nonstress to double stress is easily recognisable, and its introductory double upbeat and concluding pair of beats give it a firm structure. The double upbeat helps it to function successfully as a line-opening, and it occurs readily in this position:

(60) With a huge empty flagon by his side

It also occurs not infrequently at line-end, where the emphatic strength of its two stresses is as appropriate as the beguiling weakness of its two nonstresses is at line-opening:

(61) O for a beaker full of the warm South

One of Marvell's most memorable rhythmic inventions is simply a pair of these units:

(62) To a green thought in a green shade

This four-syllable pattern has become an accepted part of the metrical tradition, and although it has not been given much attention in the classical approach, because it is inexplicable in terms of feet, it is much more common than stress-initial pairing. Tarlinskaja's figures (1976, pp. 283–6, Tables 43 and 44) reveal that in the iambic pentameters of most poets it is at least twice as frequent; in Keats it occurs more than six times as often, and it is the only type of pairing used by Pope in her sample.[1]

Its fellow pattern is more damaging to the smooth flow of the line: instead of a double offbeat to lead into the rhythmic variation, a disruptive implied offbeat is sprung upon the reader without warning. As a result, the pause enforced by the successive beats is more marked, and the most effective way of minimising the tension it produces is by allowing it to coincide with a syntactic break. We shall consider some of the consequences of this in 8.6 and 8.7, but one result which is relevant here is that stress-initial pairing does not tend to create a separate rhythmic unit extending over the two pairs of syllables. Such a group is not a natural whole, in any case, for exactly the reasons that the reverse form is: it begins with a climax and then peters out. But its occurrence does tend to push into prominence a different, and equally satisfying, four-syllable rhythmic phrase, beginning *after* the pause between the stresses:

$$\overset{+s}{}\qquad\overset{-s}{}\qquad\overset{-s+s}{}$$

(63) The rustic youth, brown with meridian toil
          B   ŏ   B   ŏ   B

This +s −s −s +s grouping has a distinctive and cohesive form which we might indicate musically as ♩ ♫ ♩. .[2] Its quantitative equivalent, —ᴗᴗ—, is the core of aeolic verse, a staple form for Greek and Latin lyrics. And it is especially familiar in the iambic tradition because it has become a favoured way of opening the line, which will be discussed in the following section of this chapter. (The same pattern can be isolated in stress-final pairing, of course, but it usually does not emerge as a perceptual unit, since there is nothing to signal its beginning, and its end usually blends with the following beat.) Compared with the pattern −s −s +s +s, this rhythmic shape is more clearly perceived as a substitute for the expected alternating contour, and is less likely to induce the sense of a blurred rhythm; there is no tendency in (63), for example, for rhythmic energy to spread from 'brown' to 'with'. In a sense, therefore, the traditional term for this pattern, 'inversion', is more appropriate for its opposite, which relies more on the reversability inherent in some of the language's phrasal configurations.

A type of line which is occasionally to be encountered in regular duple verse is the following:

(64) Your business is not to catch men with show
        o   B   ŏ B   o B   ŏ B   o   B

As the scansion indicates, the pairing conditions are not observed: although there is both a double offbeat and an implied offbeat in the line, they are not immediately adjacent. The result is a metrical form which is experienced as deviant, though not wholly beyond the bounds of the pentameter rhythm. The syllable count is maintained, and the five beats are perceptible; but the way the line totters on the edge of unmetricality shows the importance of the immediate recovery of the rhythm in the normal pairing formations. We can call this variation *postponed pairing*, and a metrical style which employs it as a regular feature can be indicated by omitting the qualification 'immediately' in the statement of the pairing conditions. Any metrical theory which regards the syllables of the line as filling a series of abstract positions is bound to rule postponed pairing out of court, since it appears to produce a complete mismatch of metrical positions and stress contour. The line by Keats which Halle and Keyser regard as unmetrical (see above, p. 42), is a straightforward example of postponed pairing:

(65) How many bards gild the lapses of time!
        o   B o B   ôB   o   B   ŏ   B

Donne uses it together with a normal pairing in a line which gives Beaver (1976) much trouble:

(66) To believe all: change thy name: thou art like
        ŏ   B   ôB ŏ   B   o   B   ŏ   B

Like ordinary pairing, postponed pairing can be used in conjunction with promotion or demotion; the following line illustrates the former:

(67) A gaze blank and pitiless as the sun
        o B   ô B   o   B ŏ   B̄   o B

Postponement seems more acceptable in stress-initial pairing, as in (65)–(67), than in stress-final pairing, as in (64); the occurrence of an implied offbeat establishes an expectation for a double offbeat, which can still be at least partially satisfied after two beats, whereas a double offbeat is more likely to be accepted as a local variation and not an announcement of an implied offbeat to follow. A virtuoso example to the contrary is the double postponed stress-final pairing by Donne, for which Grierson, in introducing his *Metaphysical Lyrics*, was unable to offer a satisfactory scansion:

(68) Both the year's and the day's deep midnight is
        ŏ   B   ŏ   B ôB ô B o   B

The degree of disruption caused by pairing depends a great deal on the actual linguistic content of the formation, and this is the subject of 8.6–7. As for the uses to which poets can put pairing, we shall investigate some examples in Chapter 10, but it is worth looking now at one example which shows how the contravention of even the double offbeat condition can have powerful expressive effects in verse which sets up expectations of strict syllabic control. Tennyson's 'Mariana' begins with an 8-line stanza in impeccably syllabic four-beat verse with masculine endings, observing both pairing conditions; and this is followed by a refrain:

> (69) She only said, 'My life is dreary,
>   o B o B   o B o   B o
>   He cometh not,' she said;
>   o B o   B   o B   [o B]
>   She said, 'I am aweary, aweary,
>   o B o B̄ o B ŏ B o
>   I would that I were dead!'
>   o   B   o B o   B   [o B]

The first tremor in the rhythm occurs with the feminine ending of the first line, creating a double offbeat over the line juncture. The effect is then repeated much more disturbingly *within* the third line, where the syntactic pause in the double offbeat increases its rhythmic disruptiveness and momentarily suspends the rhythm; this gives the repeated 'aweary' an emotionally charged emphasis, as the movement of the line drags against the underlying rhythm, to fall back into the heavy, inescapable alternation of the final statement. One only has to substitute monosyllables for 'dreary' and the second 'aweary' – say 'bad' and 'sad' – to realise how much expressive force the refrain would lose if it maintained the strict syllabic form of the stanza.

It may be thought that verse which exerts control over the syllable count by means of the pairing conditions is more distant from the movement of speech than verse based entirely on stress-rhythms, but this is not so; in being less dominated by the stress-timed rhythm of the underlying beats, syllabically strict verse can be more subtle in its reflection of speech, as the vivid imitation of spoken language in accentual-syllabic verse by writers like Shakespeare and Browning testifies. Whereas strong-stress verse observes only the stress principle of English rhythm, syllabics only the syllabic principle, and free verse, while using both stress and syllabic rhythms, turns its back on elementary rhythmic forms, accentual-syllabic verse exploits to the full all three of these rhythmic resources.

7.7 IAMBIC VERSE

As we have observed, the beginning and end of the line are points of relative metrical freedom: the metrical pattern may or may not have offbeats in these positions, or may have optional offbeats which permit variation from line to line. However, in verse which observes a strict control of syllables, this freedom at line-opening and line-end is necessarily curtailed. It is by means of different kinds of restriction at these points that the traditional categories of duple verse, *iambic* and *trochaic*, are distinguished; and when I use these terms I am referring specifically to this distinction. It should be remembered that the distinction between *rising* and *falling* rhythms is a separate one, even though such rhythms are influenced by the way lines begin and end (see 4.6).

The following are types of opening that occur frequently in traditional iambic verse:

(70) With loss of Eden, till one greater man

(71) In the beginning how the heav'ns and earth

(72) Hurled headlong flaming from the ethereal sky

(73) Nor the deep tract of hell, say first what cause

(74) Regions of sorrow, doleful shades, where peace

On the other hand, the following openings do not normally occur:

[75] Nor the deep domain of hell, say first what cause

[76] Dens of sorrow, doleful shades, where peace

[77] Regions of despair, and shades, where peace

[78] Hurled headlong aflame from skies above

[79] Hurled God flaming from the ethereal sky

or

As (74) shows, it is possible for an acceptable iambic line to start with a beat: this is the familiar 'initial inversion', which I shall continue to call by its traditional name. One way of handling this variation might be to say that in this case the expected initial offbeat of the metrical pattern may be implied, in the same way that an offbeat may be implied between two stresses; and to extend the implied offbeat rule to allow for this additional environment. In a more abstract treatment of metre, this might be the most elegant solution, since it would provide the implied offbeat rule with an environment identical to that of the demotion rule, and the two could be conflated into a single rule permitting an offbeat to be demoted *or* implied between two stresses or between a line-boundary and a stress. However, we need to test this suggestion against the experience of reading the two kinds of line; and it is evident that initial inversion does not create the same rhythmic tension as an implied offbeat within the line (which is, of course, why the former is more common). In the case of a strong run-on from a final stress to an initial stress the effect is certainly closer to that of an implied offbeat, but even here the pause induced by the line-end takes the place of the missing offbeat and creates a different rhythmic experience. Somewhat more complicated are line-junctures in the 4 × 4 structure, in which a pair of lines may function rhythmically as a single unit; our metrical theory and system of scansion need to be sensitive to the whole range of possibilities in this form, from tightly organised stanzas in which an offbeat is required between lines (and must be implied if not realised) to looser groupings in which the lines have greater independence and it is possible to regard final and initial offbeats as optional. Confining our attention to the line as a single rhythmic unit, however, we may conclude that the opening of the traditional iambic line, as experienced by the reader, is more accurately represented by a metrical set with an optional initial offbeat than by one with an obligatory initial offbeat that is sometimes implied rather than realised. If a fuller indication of the status of that initial offbeat is required, we can use the bracketing convention introduced earlier to show that its presence is strongly preferred: $\langle$o$\rangle$ B o B... This makes it clear that (70) is the simplest realisation of the metrical pattern, using no deviation rules and including the initial offbeat.

This metrical pattern, together with the rules and conditions so far discussed, would allow an exceptional line like [76], but would not allow the common variation exemplified by (74), which contravenes the double offbeat condition as given above. In some styles of iambic pentameter, lines like [76] are in fact accepted; the following examples are by Chaucer, Surrey, Shakespeare,[3] Keats, and Browning respectively:

(80) Twenty bookes, clad in blak or reed
(81) Norfolk sprang thee, Lambeth holds thee dead
(82) Stay, the king hath thrown his warder down
(83) Thea, Thea, Thea, where is Saturn?
(84) Steadied him a moment, set him straight

To account for stricter forms of iambic pentameter, however, which constitute the bulk of writing in that metre, we need a condition which will exclude lines like these, but accept the omission of the initial offbeat in lines like (74):

Initial inversion condition (iambic opening)

An optional initial offbeat may be omitted only if the first beat is immediately followed by a double offbeat

Observance of this condition is the feature which distinguishes strict iambic metre from any other metre that includes an optional initial offbeat. However, initial inversion breaks the double offbeat condition as provisionally formulated, necessitating an extension of this condition for iambic verse:

Double offbeat condition

A double offbeat may occur only in observance of (i) the implied offbeat condition, or (ii) an initial inversion condition

These conditions, together with the implied offbeat condition, will distinguish accurately between the acceptable and unacceptable lines given above. Examples (70)–(72) realise the more common metrical pattern by means of an initial single offbeat; (73) has an initial double offbeat, acceptable under the double offbeat condition because it is followed by an implied offbeat; and (74) is allowed to drop the optional offbeat becuase of the following double offbeat, which is itself permitted under the extended double offbeat condition. [75] on the other hand, fails to observe the double offbeat condition; [76]–[78] and the first reading of [79] fail to observe the initial inversion condition, since the initial beat is not followed by a double offbeat, and the alternative reading of [79] fails to observe the implied offbeat condition. The injunction that conditions may not overlap also prohibits a line like the following in strict iambic verse:

[85] Here is my hand; keep it firmly held
      B   ŏ   B   ô B   o   B   o   B

The same double offbeat cannot be used to satisfy both the initial inversion condition and the implied offbeat condition.

Pentameter verse which permits headless lines like (80)–(84) does not, of course, consistently observe the initial inversion condition, since in such lines an initial beat is not always followed by a double offbeat. However, verse of this kind usually makes use of lines with initial inversions as well, so the second part of the double offbeat condition will remain valid, though we have to understand the phrase 'in observance of the initial inversion condition' as applying to the individual line, which has, as it were, chosen to abide by this restriction when some of its fellows have not. (If, however, double offbeats are used freely throughout the line, the double offbeat condition does not apply at all.) The same freedom to omit an optional initial offbeat with or without a following double offbeat occurs in some four-beat metrical styles; the following lines are characteristic of the verse of Milton's *L'Allegro* and *Il Penseroso*, which, with a metrical pattern of (o)4B(o), observes the full double offbeat condition consistently but the initial inversion condition only intermittently:

(86) And ever against eating cares,
      o   B   ŏ   B   ôB   o   B

      +s   −s−s +s   +s −s−s +s

      Lap me in soft Lydian airs,
      B   ŏ   B ô B ŏ   B
      Married to immortal verse
      B   o   B̄ o   B   o   B
      Such as the meeting soul may pierce
      B   ŏ   B   o   B   o   B

All these lines except the first omit the optional opening offbeat. But lines 2 and 4 do so with, and line 3 without, a following double offbeat. (Line 2 continues with stress-initial pairing, giving the line a highly apt lilt, whose symmetry is revealed in the stress pattern.) Since the experienced reader takes in the lines of this verse form at once, rather than syllable by syllable, the variability of its openings causes few difficulties in performance; but it has acquired the reputation of a highly problematic variety of metre because of its unsusceptibility to scansion in terms of classical feet (see the survey and discussion by Weismiller, 1972, pp. 1029–33).

One further type of line which occasionally turns up in iambic pentameter verse is the following:

(87) Teach me how to repent, for that's as good
    B   o B   ŏ B   o   B o B

This pattern, which we can call initial inversion with *postponed compensation*, is the equivalent of postponed pairing: the omitted initial offbeat is made good (and the syllable count preserved) by a double offbeat which does not occur immediately, but later in the line. Like normal initial inversion, it does not produce an implied offbeat, and it is therefore more common than postponed pairing: Bridges (1921, p. 56) finds 11 examples in *Samson Agonistes*, and Hatcher (1928, pp. 82–4) notes that postponed compensation after the second beat is 'everywhere in Browning', and that it is sometimes delayed until after the third (and occasionally even the fourth) beat:

(88) All which work takes time: till to-morrow, then
    B   o   B   o   B   ŏ   B o   B

(In fact, Browning's use of the double offbeat is so free that it is perhaps best to consider his iambic pentameters as not observing the double offbeat condition at all.) One of Shakespeare's best-known lines is an example of postponed compensation (together with pairing in the second part of the line):

(89) Let me not to the marriage of true minds
    B o B   ŏ   B   ŏ   B ŏ B

Postponed compensation is usually regarded in metrical analysis as highly anomalous – the *Norton Anthology of English Literature* (Fourth Edition, I, 2547) has it that (89) is 'neither pentameter nor in any way iambic' – but all that is required is that we extend the initial inversion condition to allow the omission of an initial offbeat if the first *or second* beat is immediately followed by a double offbeat, or, for metrical styles that allow later compensation, that we leave out the qualification 'immediately' from the condition. However, such lines can usually be regarded as momentary expansions of the metrical limits; they do not condition the reader's metrical set for the whole poem, and there would be little point in including them in the general set. What is important is that their relationship to the basic rules and conditions should be capable of precise specification.

When we turn to the ending of the iambic line, we find less stringent restraints: most styles of iambic pentameter, for instance, allow an occasional offbeat at the end of the line, even though this produces lines of eleven as well as ten syllables. The metrical pattern of such verse is therefore ⟨o⟩ B o B o B o B o B ((o)). The influence of verse in other languages may have had a part in the development of this trait: in French the alternation between feminine and masculine rhymes is built into the structure of the Alexandrine couplet (though the terms mean something different in the rhythmically very different language – see Attridge, 1979), while in Italian the hendecasyllable can have ten, eleven, or twelve syllables, depending on the stress pattern of the final word. But it is also no doubt a reflection of the fact that the very end of the line is less crucial in determining the character of its rhythm than the opening.

The licence to use initial inversion can be explained as a way of allowing the first syllable to take a beat without detriment to a fixed syllable count, or alternatively, as the only way a double offbeat can be introduced without necessitating the relatively complex deviation of an implied offbeat. The aesthetic benefits of rhythmic variety at line-openings are obvious, but it is also significant that this licence greatly extends the range of words that can be used in a highlighted position at the beginning of the line. If we look again at examples (70)–(74), we shall see that every type of monosyllable and disyllable is possible, and nearly every type of trisyllable or trisyllabic phrase. Without the acceptance of initial inversion, no disyllables with an initial stress could occur, and any stressed monosyllable would have to be followed by another stress. The freedom at the end of the line, too, allows the poet to use words and phrases with a wide variety of stress patterns:

$$-s+s$$
. . . believe
   o B

$$+s\ \ -s$$
. . . happen
   B   o

$$+s\ \ -s\ -s$$
. . . happiness
   B   ŏ

$$-s\ \ -s\text{-}s\ \ +s$$
. . . to disappear
  o B̄ o B

$$+s\text{-}s\ \ \ \ -s\text{-}s$$
. . .melancholy
  B o   B o

$$+s\ \ -s\ \ -s\ +s$$
(90) . . . voice of the shade
    B   ŏ   B

$$-s\ -s\ +s\ \ \ \ +s$$
(91) . . . in a green shade
    ŏ B ŏ B

It is surely no accident that the rules and conditions of the most widely used and versatile English metre have developed in such a way as to provide the poet with a firm rhythmic structure which at the same time allows him the greatest possible freedom to use the verbal resources of the English language. A further consequence of the rules that govern the opening and closing of the iambic pentameter is that they make the establishment of a strong falling rhythm unlikely: the line cannot begin with the pattern +s −s +s, except in the rare case of postponed compensation, and it most commonly ends on a stress. This hostility towards the more insistent of the two types of duple movement is of a piece with many of the other features of the iambic pentameter, such as its avoidance of the dominating four-beat rhythm, its use of duple metre rather than the more insistent triple metre, and its dependence on a fixed syllable count and pairing formations to keep the powerful stress-timing principle in check. All these features prevent the strong, simple, fundamental rhythmic forms from taking precedence over the more variable patterns of living speech, and go a long way towards explaining the remarkable predominance, and repeated reinvigoration, of this metrical form in the literary tradition from Chaucer to the present.

7.8 TROCHAIC VERSE

Like iambic verse, trochaic verse is distinguished by the opening of the line; whereas the metrical set for the former includes a strong expectation for an initial offbeat, that for the latter stipulates the occurrence of an opening beat. Strict trochaic verse therefore has a metrical pattern which begins B o B o . . . It is this strong opening which gives it its characteristic rhythmic quality, and it frequently affects the rhythmic organisation of the rest of the line, encouraging a falling rather than a rising movement (see 4.6). We have discussed the tendency for trochaic verse in a falling rhythm to be more regular than verse in rising or varied rhythms; and this strictness is reflected in its use of the rules of the general set. The promotion and demotion rules are used (though less often than in iambic verse), but implied and double offbeats are relatively rare, and almost always controlled by the pairing conditions. Kiparsky (1975, p. 608) notes that there are only two examples of 'spondaic feet' in the 194 eight-beat trochaic lines of Tennyson's 'Locksley Hall', and only one of these involves an implied offbeat (the other being an example of demotion, which Kiparsky's foot-analysis does not keep distinct):

(92) Catch the wild goat by the hair, and hurl their lances
in the sun

And there is only one example of an 'iambic foot', that is, the pattern −s −s +s +s:

(93) Summer isles of Eden lying in dark-purple spheres of sea

Even in these examples, the strong metrical set encourages the reader to give extra weight to the monosyllables 'by' and 'in' to reduce the rhythmic dislocation.

The initial inversion condition as we have formulated it is of course not relevant to trochaic line-openings, but the equivalent phenomenon does occasionally occur, producing an implied offbeat without a balancing double offbeat:

(94) To more virtue than doth live

(95) For whole centuries of folly, noise and sin!

To describe verse in which this occurs, we need a metrical pattern beginning with an optional offbeat, though with an indication that its absence is preferred: ((o)) B o B ... The conditions under which this optional offbeat can be included may then be stated as a second inversion condition:

Initial inversion condition (trochaic opening)

An optional initial offbeat may be included only if the first beat is immediately followed by an implied offbeat

And the implied offbeat condition must be extended to allow for this possibility:

Implied offbeat condition

An implied offbeat may occur only (i) when it is immediately preceded or followed by a non-final double offbeat, or (ii) in observance of an initial inversion condition

As with the double offbeat condition, the implied offbeat condition in its extended form can operate in verse which does not consistently observe the corresponding inversion condition, though this is much less common. Tennyson's *Lady of Shalott* includes the following passage, in which the third and fourth lines have the optional initial offbeat, but only the third follows this with an implied offbeat:

(96) By the margin, willow-veiled
　　　 B̄   o   B   o   B   o   B
　　　 Slide the heavy barges trailed
　　　 B   o B o B   o   B
　　　 By slow horses; and unhailed
　　　 o   B ô B o   B̄   o B
　　　 The shallop flitteth silken-sailed
　　　 o   B o   B o   B o B

Most trochaic verse avoids initial inversion, however, and it is easy to see why. Although, like initial iambic inversion, it increases the range of words possible at the beginning of the line, it does so at the cost of introducing the most disruptive of the deviations, an implied offbeat. Trochaic verse tends to avoid implied offbeats in any case, and their occurrence after the first beat creates a markedly complex line, especially when there is no compensating double offbeat. When trochaic inversion does occur, the line usually begins with two monosyllables, and quite often allows a reversal of stress:

(97) Or who cleft the Devil's foot
　　　 o　　 B ô   B

　　　 B̄　　 o　　 B

(98) And find naught but pride and scorn
　　　 o　　 B　 ô B

　　　 B　　 ȯ　　 B

Initial trochaic inversion is a tribute to the strength of the syllable count as a convention; it may have arisen as a conscious counterpart to initial iambic inversion, but it is hardly surprising that it has not become a familiar part of the metre in the same way. An equally disruptive opening is stress-initial pairing; we shall consider an instance in Chapter 10, example (7).

In the classical approach to English metre, a strictly trochaic line requires a final offbeat, in order to create a final trochaic foot. My use of the term to refer only to characteristic line-openings is consistent with ordinary usage, however, since what is usually called trochaic verse does not demand feminine endings; we saw in 4.5–6 that the line beginning and ending on a beat is a common one, and that trochaic verse which insists on feminine endings, like *Hiawatha*, is rare and difficult to handle successfully. Free variation between masculine and feminine endings, as in iambic verse, is perfectly acceptable, and represents a metrical pattern with an optional final offbeat:

> (99) Like a Poet hidden
>   B   o
>   In the light of thought,
>   B
>   Singing hymns unbidden,
>   B   o
>   Till the world is wrought
>   B

Since most trochaic verse is in a four-beat rhythm, the line-endings are often controlled by the needs of the 4 × 4 structure, as in this example, which may be compared with examples (48) and (54) in Chapter 4.

For most trochaic verse, then, the metrical set consists of the five realisation rules and the two pairing conditions in their unextended form, together with a metrical pattern showing an obligatory opening beat and an optional final offbeat; while the strictest trochaic verse will make use of only the first four rules, omit the double offbeat option of the second base rule, require none of the conditions, and realise a metrical pattern with an obligatory final offbeat. The only kinds of line-opening available to a poet who avoids trochaic inversion and stress-initial pairing are the following:

>   +s −s +s
> (100) Only joy, now here you are
>   B o B

>   −s −s +s
> (101) In a cowslip's bell I lie
>   B̄ o B

>   +s +s   +s
> (102) Wrote one song – and in my brain I sing it
>   B ȯ   B

Of these, the third is rare, no doubt because the line has not had a chance to establish its strong alternating rhythm. The constraints on the poet in terms of verbal choice are therefore much greater than is the case in iambic or free duple verse, and the rhythmic experience of the reader more likely to approach monotony. Once again, the metrical choices of English poets are vindicated.

7.9 TRIPLE VERSE

Up to this point, we have concentrated our attention on duple metre, by far the commonest form in the English tradition, but it will be valuable to see how far the framework thus established needs to be altered to take care of triple metre. There are two ways in which one could capture the distinctive character of triple verse: one would be to specify double offbeats in the metrical pattern and to rewrite the rules accordingly; the other would be to use the same metrical patterns as for duple verse, but stipulate in the realisation rules that double offbeats are the norm. Although the former method has the advantage of emphasising by means of different metrical patterns the different character of the reader's metrical set in the two types of rhythm, it obscures the close relationship between them. There is no point at which the inclusion of one more double offbeat will switch the rhythm from duple to triple; we have already seen that there is a spectrum of rhythmic types between the two extremes. It would be imposing our own categories on a natural continuum if we tried to class the following lines as either duple or triple; nor is it accurate to call the metre 'ambiguous' if this suggests some complex perceptual experience involving alternative readings:

(103)   Alack, it was I who leaped at the sun
　　　　　To give it my loving friends to keep!
　　　　Nought man could do, have I left undone:
　　　　　And you see my harvest, what I reap
　　　　This very day, now a year is run.

We shall therefore keep the same metrical patterns, which reflect a deeper rhythmic principle than the disposition of stressed and unstressed syllables, and characterise the different metrical set established in triple verse by means of the realisation rules.

In its generalised form, the offbeat rule makes provision for both single and double offbeats; the strictest triple metre, of course, is represented by a rule which states only that *two* nonstresses may realise an offbeat. However, verse in which there is a preponderance of double offbeats and a sprinkling of single offbeats is still perceived as triple, and this can be suggested by reversing the order of the options in the statement of the rules:

Offbeat rule (free triple verse)

Two unstressed syllables (or one) may realise an offbeat

In scansion, the presence of a triple rhythm will be indicated by the consistent, or at least predominating, occurrence of the symbol for the double offbeat, without accompanying implied offbeats:

(104) Under the blossom that hangs on the bough
   B ŏ B ŏ B ŏ B

Very occasionally, three syllables may realise an offbeat in triple verse, but only if a strong, song-like rhythm has been established:

(105) When that I was and a little tiny boy
    B ŏ B ŏ B o̬ B

Because this is a song, the rhythm is to some extent under external control, and we are prepared to modify our pronunciation to emphasise 'when' and 'was', and to lessen the stress on 'tiny'; though this last variation might be more accurately described as a shift to a rapid, duple, dipodic metre with a subsidiary beat on the stress of 'tiny'. (Notice how similar this example is to the ballad lines quoted in Chapter 4, examples (29) and (30).) A more usual explanation of three syllables realising an offbeat is that elision enables one of them to be suppressed:

(106) In spite of myself, the insidious mastery of song
  o B ŏ B   ŏ B ŏ B ŏ̬ B

How relevant are the other rules that were proposed to deal with duple verse? The first base rule, allowing a stress to realise a beat, is of course fundamental to all English metre. The promotion rule is sometimes used in triple verse; the following lines, for instance, may be read without any special emphasis on 'didst' once the strong triple rhythm of the poem has been established:

(107) Though human, thou didst not deceive me,
   o B ŏ B̄ ŏ B   o [B]
  Though woman, thou didst not forsake
    o B ŏ B̄ ŏ B [o B]

(Notice that, in isolation, these lines could be read as four-beat duple verse, with 'didst' realising an offbeat.) Not surprisingly, this is an uncommon occurrence, since it requires an exceptionally long string of unstressed syllables, and a triple rhythm is much more potent than a duple rhythm in encouraging normally unstressed syllables to take a stress when a beat is required. Analysing a sample of 2,700 lines in triple metres, Tarlinskaja (1976) found that stresses in beat position occurred 98.6 per cent of the time (p. 273, Table 36; average of final column); although her use of foot-prosody results in a confusion of pairing and promotion, the high percentage shows that both these deviations are rare. (The equivalent figure for duple verse in tetrameter lines is 83 per cent (p. 260, Table 25; average of column 10).)

Demotion, on the other hand, is frequent. The type which occurs in duple verse – the realisation of an offbeat by a single stressed syllable – can, of course, occur only in the freer forms of triple metre which allow single offbeats. In such forms, a demoted stress functioning as an offbeat in fact maintains the rhythmic swing of the line more fully than a single nonstress would do. Compare the following line by Swinburne with my rewriting:

(108) In the sweet low light of thy face, under heavens untrod by
       ŏ   B   ŏ   B   ŏ   B
       the sun

[108a] In the sweet delight of thy face, under heavens untrod by
        ŏ   B   o B   ŏ   B
        the sun

In both, the triple metre is insistent enough to take the single offbeat in its stride, but there is a degree of temporal equivalence between a stress and two nonstresses that makes the first line run more smoothly. The syllabic movement slows down, but the rhythmic pace from beat to beat remains steady. This principle underlies strict accentual imitations of the Latin hexameter:

(109) Silvery fish, wreathed shell, and the strange lithe things
       B   ŏ B   ŏ   B   ŏ   B   ŏ   B
       of the water
       ŏ   B o

It is a pleasing rhythmic device, but one which tends to divert attention from what is being said to the sheer musicality of the line. In [108a], on the other hand, the rhythm performs a little skip at the single offbeat, hastening the arrival of the second beat, and enlivening the movement.

Demotion also occurs in double offbeats, however; the following are

typical examples, with the appropriate deviation symbols to indicate
which syllable is demoted:

(110) And his dark secret love
         ŏ   B   ö   B
       Doth thy life destroy

(111) And now you've gay bracelets and bright feathers three!
     o   B   ö   B   ŏ   B   ö   B

It is also possible, when the triple set is very strong, for both syllables in
the offbeat to be demoted, though this is rare, and creates considerable
tension – whether one chooses to squeeze the words into the rhythmic
pattern, or to disrupt the regular metre:

(112) And the sheen of their spears was like stars on the sea,
      When the blue wave rolls nightly on deep Galilee
      ŏ   B   ö   B   ŏ   B   ŏ B

Tarlinskaja (1976, p. 134) finds only ten examples of two stressed
syllables constituting an offbeat in 1,046 lines of triple metre by Scott.

More than anything else, it is the use of demotion that creates the
feeling in so much triple verse that the natural rhythm of the language
is being dominated by the patterns of the metre (see 4.4): the strong
metrical set often encourages the reader to make demotion a matter of
pronunciation, and actually to subdue the stress in contravention of the
norms of speech. However, the vigorously insistent set can also be an
asset: it can be pitted against natural speech rhythms to create a high
degree of tension and a sense of great energy. Much of Browning's
verse in triple metre, for example, invites by its content and syntax a
reading with strong speech rhythms that repeatedly crush the metre
only to have it spring back into shape again:

(113) Sure you were wishful to speak?
      B   ŏ   B   ŏ   B   [o B]
      You, with brow ruled like a score,
      B   ö   B   ŏ   B   [o B]
      Yes, and eyes buried in pits on each cheek,
      B   ŏ   B   ŏ   B   ŏ   B
      Like two great breves, as they wrote them of yore,
      B   ö   B   ŏ   B   ŏ   B
      Each side that bar, your straight beak!
      B   ö   B   ŏ   B   [o B]

The vitality of Browning's narrator would be lost if we allowed the
triple metre to override the vigorous speech rhythms here, though it is
important to note that the metrical rules are not broken, merely

stretched to the limit by the linguistic substance. The effect is very different from the free use of traditional metres by a writer like Frost, which creates the opposite impression, a kind of relaxed wandering beyond the bounds.

As is the case with duple verse, demotion can occur before the first beat as well as in the course of the line. Here are some examples of line-openings in 'How they Brought the Good News from Ghent to Aix':

(114) I sprang to the stirrup, and Joris, and he
     o B

(115) 'Speed!' echoed the wall to us galloping through
     ŏ B

(116) Not a word to each other; we kept the great pace
     ŏ B

(117) Neck by neck, stride by stride, never changing our place
     ŏ̋ B

(118) And one eye's black intelligence, – ever that glance
     ŏ̈ B

Browning uses all but the most deviant of the possible options, and a rewriting of the last line will show that even that option – two demotions in a double offbeat – can be accommodated if the same emphasis is given to the word 'eye':

[118a] One dark eye's black intelligence, – ever that glance
      ö̈ B

Metrical set is all-important here: a line like (117) in isolation does not reveal its triple structure, but once the reader is attuned to the rhythm of the poem, the necessary demotions will be automatically perceived. We can specify the set by means of a metrical pattern with an obligatory initial offbeat, o4B; an offbeat rule with a strong preference for double offbeats; and a demotion rule which allows all the options we have discussed both before the first beat and between beats.

We can state this demotion rule in its fullest form as follows:

Demotion rule (triple verse)

A stressed syllable, or an unstressed syllable and a stressed syllable (in either order), or two stressed syllables, may realise an offbeat between two stresses, or after a line-boundary and before a stress

The ordering of the eight options gives an approximate indication of degrees of complexity: a single stressed syllable is the first option, since it is one of the least complex kinds of demotion; then we have −s +s and +s −s, the first of which is less complex than the second, partly because a stress is more often subordinated to a following than a preceding stress (figures cited by Tarlinskaja, 1976, pp. 132–3, support this ordering); and the double demotion of two stresses, as the most disruptive, is placed last. All of these can occur in two environments, between two stresses and at the beginning of a line before a stress, of which the former is given first in the rule as less complex. Stricter forms of triple metre, of course, make use of a demotion rule which excludes one or more of the later options given here. However, so many other factors are at work, including the exact nature of the metrical set and the morphological and syntactic structures of the actual words, that this ordering cannot be regarded as absolute.

As in duple verse, the rule does not allow for demotion at the end of the line, and rewritings of triple lines suggest that this is correct:

(119) Touch her not scornfully;
      B   ŏ   B   ŏ
      Think of her mournfully
      B   ŏ   B   ŏ

                +s   +s
[119a] Touch her with soft hands

                +s −s +s
[119b] Touch her with tender hands

                +s +s −s
[119c] Touch her with soft fingers

The extra stresses here disrupt the triple movement entirely, and the only environment in which they might not do so is in strongly run-on lines, when the line-boundary would, in effect, disappear. The environment for the operation of the demotion rule, therefore, is exactly the same for triple metre as it is for duple.

There remains one deviation rule to consider: the implied offbeat rule. Not surprisingly, this is rarely made use of in triple verse: we are less likely to feel that a pause enforced by successive stresses is doing duty for a double offbeat than for a single offbeat. It can only occur without distorting the rhythm when a powerfully dominating metrical set has been established, producing very marked beats, as is the case in popular rhymes:

(120) Early to bed, early to rise
     B ŏ B ŏB ŏ B

The effect of an unrealised offbeat in literary verse can be gauged from the following rewriting:

(121) They, with the gold to give, doled him out silver
     B   ŏ B ŏ' B ŏ B o

[121a] They, with the gold, doled him out silver
     B   ŏ B ŏB ŏ B o

Because of the natural division of the four-beat line into two two-beat units, and the syntactic break at this point, it is possible to read [121a] naturally and maintain the underlying rhythm; it does, however, have the effect of encouraging a chanted reading, and this would be the only way of preserving the rhythm if it occurred in a less favourable environment. It is probably most accurate to regard its occasional use as part of the freedom allowed to a certain type of highly rhythmical verse, in which offbeats can be realised by two, one, or no syllables, and to state as a general rule that strict triple verse does not make use of implied offbeats. The pairing conditions also have no place in triple metre, of course; their whole *raison d'être* is the pattern of alternation between single beat and single offbeat.

Traditional prosody attempts to distinguish between 'dactylic' and 'anapaestic' metres, the distinction once again hinging on the expected patterns at line-opening and line-end: fully dactylic verse would have a metrical pattern that begins with a beat and ends with a double offbeat, and anapaestic verse the opposite. However, many other combinations occur without being felt to be oddities; in fact, Tarlinskaja finds in her sampling of triple verse that the majority of lines begin in neither of these ways, but with a single offbeat (1976, p. 272, Table 35). It is as well to refrain from using terms which suggest that two of the many possibilities have some kind of canonic status simply because they can be divided into 'feet'. The consistent use of different realisations in different parts of the line can easily be reflected in the rules; one common form of triple verse, for instance, would be represented by the following version of the offbeat rule:

> *An unstressed syllable may realise an initial offbeat; two unstressed syllables may realise a non-initial offbeat*

Of the five rules developed to account for duple metre, then, triple metre shares three (the base rules and the promotion rule), has its own variant of another (the demotion rule), and lacks the fifth; and it observes none of the duple verse conditions. The distinction is not absolute, however, and the rules reflect this by making it possible to derive lines in either duple or triple metre, or from anywhere on the spectrum between them, from exactly the same metrical patterns.

To an even greater degree than is the case with duple metre, the rules for triple metre fall short of providing a machine for processing strings of syllables to produce metrical judgements. The freedom implied by the numerous options of the demotion rule is to some extent illusory, because the poet has to handle his linguistic material with great care to make sure that his use of these deviations is not disruptive of the underlying rhythm. The rules for the freest triple metre state, in effect, that between two stresses any one or two syllables can realise an offbeat, whether −s, +s, −s −s, −s +s, +s −s, or +s +s, but there is an important implicit qualification: 'provided that a strong enough set for triple verse is established and maintained'. And this means, 'provided that certain limits are observed on the use of the later deviations, and of linguistic structures which pull away from the metrical forms which they embody.' Perhaps a much more elaborate metrical theory, married to a detailed phonological theory, would be able to specify those limits explicitly. For the time being we have to fall back on the ear to tell us when the poet has overstepped the borders of metricality – or, rather, has begun to travel in the no-man's-land around its edges – by mismatching the rhythms generated by morphology and syntax with the rhythms created by the metre, or by making too free with the deviations allowed by the rules. When we do sense this, however, our set of rules ought to be able to tell us exactly where and how it has happened; where the strain is being felt, why the joints are coming apart. This is why it is important to be as clear as possible about the different rhythmic processes involved, and the differing degrees of complexity they create. It is important, too, to evolve a method of metrical analysis which will make it possible to examine the relationship between metrical and linguistic structures, which is the subject of the next chapter. We shall find there that this relationship is complicated enough in duple verse, and no attempt will be made to grapple with the problems posed by triple verse.

7.10 COMPLEXITY AND TENSION

The metrical style of a body of regular English verse, whether it be that of a period, a poet, a section of a poet's oeuvre, or a single poem, can be characterised by a selection from the general set of rules and conditions, and any idiosyncracies can be indicated within the framework provided by that set. The smaller and more homogeneous the body of verse, the more detailed the specification of its metrical characteristics can be, right down to the single line, in which it is possible to say exactly what rules are being used and what conditions being observed at every point. Although the characteristics of metrical styles vary in several ways, one general feature has been implied in our discussion so far: the variation from simple to complex. By a simple metrical style we mean one in which the selection of deviation rules produces a highly regular rhythmic alternation, and by a complex style one in which regular alternation is frequently challenged. And we have ordered our rules so that, by and large, the more often a later rule is used the more complex the metrical style. Thus we might say that Dryden's metre is relatively simple, since he strictly limits his use of the later deviation rules, while Milton's is complex, because he freely takes advantage of them. Similarly, an individual line can be classed roughly on a scale of complexity according to the deviation rules it makes use of. The following lines from Shakespeare's *Sonnets* are in an approximately increasing order of complexity, and will also serve to illustrate some combinations of the rules we have been considering:

Base rules only

$$
\begin{array}{lllllllll}
\text{-s} & \text{+s} & \text{-s} & \text{+s-s} & \text{+s} & \text{-s} & \text{+s} & \text{-s} & \text{+s}
\end{array}
$$

(122) By chance, or nature's changing course untrimmed

$$
\begin{array}{ccccccccc}
\text{o} & \text{B} & \text{o} & \text{B} & \text{o} & \text{B} & \text{o} & \text{B} & \text{o} & \text{B}
\end{array}
$$

Double offbeat option of second base rule

$$
\begin{array}{lllllllll}
\text{+s} & \text{-s} & \text{-s} & \text{+s} & \text{-s} & \text{+s} & \text{-s} & \text{+s} & \text{-s} & \text{+s}
\end{array}
$$

(123) Vaunt in their youthful sap, at height decrease

$$
\begin{array}{cccccccc}
\text{B} & \text{ŏ} & \text{B} & \text{o} & \text{B} & \text{o} & \text{B} & \text{o} & \text{B}
\end{array}
$$

Promotion

$$
\begin{array}{lllllllll}
\text{-s} & \text{+s} & \text{-s} & \text{-s} & \text{-s} & \text{+s} & \text{-s} & \text{+s-s} & \text{+s}
\end{array}
$$

(124) And often is his gold complexion dimmed

$$
\begin{array}{ccccccccc}
\text{o} & \text{B} & \text{o} & \bar{\text{B}} & \text{o} & \text{B} & \text{o} & \text{B} & \text{o} & \text{B}
\end{array}
$$

Demotion (mid-line)

$$\overset{-s}{}\quad\overset{+s}{}\quad\overset{-s}{}\quad\overset{+s}{}\quad\overset{-s}{}\quad\overset{+s}{}\quad\overset{+s}{}\quad\overset{+s}{}\quad\overset{-s}{}\quad\overset{+s}{}$$

(125) Nor Mars his sword, nor war's quick fire shall burn

o   B   o   B   o   B   ȯ   B   o   B

Demotion (initial)

$$\overset{+s}{}\quad\overset{+s}{}\quad\overset{-s\ +s}{}\quad\overset{-s\ +s-s}{}\quad\overset{+s}{}\quad\overset{-s}{}\quad\overset{+s}{}$$

(126) Rough winds do shake the darling buds of May

ȯ   B   o   B   o   B o   B   o   B

Implied offbeat and double offbeat

$$\overset{-s\ +s-s\ +s}{}\quad\overset{+s}{}\quad\overset{-s}{}\quad\overset{-s\ +s}{}\quad\overset{-s\ +s}{}$$

(127) As testy sick men when their deaths be near

o   B o B ŏ B   ŏ   B   o B

Promotion, implied offbeat, and double offbeat

$$\overset{-s}{}\quad\overset{+s}{}\quad\overset{-s}{}\quad\overset{-s}{}\quad\overset{-s}{}\quad\overset{+s}{}\quad\overset{+s}{}\quad\overset{-s-s}{}\quad\overset{+s}{}$$

(128) At random from the truth vainly expressed

o   B   o   B̄   o   B ŏ B   ŏ   B

Demotion, double offbeat, and implied offbeat

$$\overset{+s}{}\quad\overset{+s-s}{}\quad\overset{+s}{}\quad\overset{-s}{}\quad\overset{-s}{}\quad\overset{+s}{}\quad\overset{+s}{}\quad\overset{-s}{}\quad\overset{+s}{}$$

(129) Love alters not with his brief hours and weeks

ȯ   B o   B   ŏ   B ȯ B   o   B

Two double offbeats and two implied offbeats

$$\overset{-s}{}\quad\overset{+s}{}\quad\overset{-s}{}\quad\overset{-s\ +s}{}\quad\overset{+s}{}\quad\overset{-s}{}\quad\overset{-s\ +s}{}\quad\overset{+s}{}$$

(130) As subject to Time's love, or to Time's hate

o   B   ŏ   B   ȯ B   ŏ   B   ȯ B

The final example is probably at the limit of complexity tolerated in this particular metrical style.

The role of conditions also needs to be taken into account in considering complexity. To impose a condition on a rule in a particular metrical style is to allow its operation only in circumstances which minimise the complexity of the deviation it permits. Thus none of the Shakespeare lines quoted contains an implied offbeat without an accompanying double offbeat; such a deviation would produce a line too complex to be accepted in this style. Conditions other than the ones formulated in this chapter may operate in a particular poem; for instance the implied offbeat rule may have an attached condition prohibiting its occurrence immediately after the first beat (see above, pp. 174–5). A metrical set which includes conditions on the rules will therefore usually represent a simpler metre than one which does not, unless the poet, or literary convention, has imposed an idiosyncratic condition which increases complexity. The initial inversion conditions, which control the inclusion or omission of initial optional offbeats, are something of a special case, since they are more concerned with the maintenance of the syllable count than with simplicity, and in the case of the rarely-used trochaic inversion condition, complexity is actually increased when the condition is observed.

We cannot construct a linear scale of complexity; readers do not carry a mental measuring-device with which to grade the lines they read, and an imprecise indication of the contribution made by various rules and conditions to the complexity of a line is in fact an accurate representation of the reader's metrical responses. Linguists are more likely now to accept that grammar has indeterminate areas than they were in the heyday of generative theory, and metre is certainly no more sharply defined than syntax. It is not obvious that example (123) is less complex than (124); the double offbeat is perhaps on a different axis of complexity from that on which promotion and demotion are judged. Similarly, we cannot be precise about the degree of complexity which a particular poem or style will tolerate. Most long poems include occasional lines that are much more complex than the norm, like (130) above, and there is no point in trying to decide whether the rules should exclude any or all of these, thereby reflecting their exceptional status, or whether they should include any or all of them, at the risk of suggesting that they are typical. We can sum up a metrical style by indicating which rules and combinations of rules are made use of frequently, which occasionally, and which never; it will not be a quantifiable account, but it will be an adequate representation both of the metre and of the reader's sense of it. An equivalent in syntax might be the varying degrees of complexity possible within grammatical sentences; there is no specific point at which the addition of one more relative clause to a string of relative clauses will render a sentence unacceptable in normal usage, but an accumulation of such clauses will make it very difficult to understand. Similarly, the use of several deviations in a line, while not breaking any rule, may make the metre difficult to read and to perceive.

Furthermore, complexity cannot be separated from a number of other ingredients in the more general psychological experience we have been calling 'tension' (see 4.1). Firstly, in assessing the tension of a given line, the part played by the metrical set established by the whole poem is crucial. A line which in a poem of Milton's would confirm the complex metrical set might, if it occurred in a poem of Dryden's, strike the ear as totally out of place. The opposite is conceivable, too: a line, or at least a group of lines, in Dryden's metrical style might create tension of a kind in a poem by Milton through their unwonted regularity. A complex metrical style has a relatively high level of general tension, but increases of tension in individual lines will be difficult to achieve: the dislocation created, say, by a double offbeat in a simple style may be experienced as greater than that created by an implied offbeat in a more complex style. While complexity, however hard to define, is an absolute quality measured against a norm outside the poem in question, tension is relative to the immediate metrical context, and this makes it an even more elusive attribute.

Another important source of tension is the relationship between the metrical and linguistic structures, which will be discussed in the following chapter; a given deviation rule will produce differing degrees of tension depending on the actual words and syntactic formations in which it is embodied. In addition, there are rhythmic considerations that operate equally in prose and verse – rhetorical rhythms, one might call them – to create a sense of satisfaction or unease: for instance, cumulative sequences of words with an increasing or decreasing number of syllables (see Nash, 1980, pp. 81–2, and *passim*). The content of the poetry also has a strong effect: to take one example, a realistic speaking voice will pull against the regularities of the rhythm, while a lyrical utterance will seek a harmonious accommodation with the metre. Nursery rhymes invite the subordination of all metrical variation to an insistent regularity; dramatic verse invites the subordination of the metrical pattern to the natural rhythms of speech. The difference between four-beat and five-beat rhythms also enters the picture: we noted in Chapter 5 that the former is more tolerant of deviations because of its more prominent underlying rhythm, and some complex realisations can create very little tension, or can even reduce it. In the following lines, the deviations set up a relaxed, jaunty rhythm (in this case, with parodic intent), because we are encouraged to read with a very regular beat:

(131) Between the end of the *Chatterley* ban
      o B   o B   ŏ   B ŏ   B
    And the Beatles' first LP
       ŏ   B   o   B   ŏB   [o B]

Such effects are particularly strong in dipodic verse: see the example by Kipling quoted above (4.7, (66)). In the pentameter, however, deviations almost always increase tension, which is another source of the subtlety of which this metrical form is capable. When it comes to line-junctures, on the other hand, the tension created by run-ons in four-beat verse is, as we have noted, greater than that in five-beat verse, because the metrical break being challenged by the syntax is more marked.

Tension of a different kind can inhere at the level of the larger rhythmic grouping as well, notably the line. The placing of syntactic breaks, for instance, may not only affect the level of tension at particular points, but determine the rhythmic quality of the line as a whole. We have seen already (5.5) how a pause after the second beat of the pentameter tends to create a line with a clear rhythmic balance, which we can indicate as 2:3; a pause after the third beat, 3:2, though less conducive to a strong rhythmic pattern, also divides the line into relatively evenly balanced units. Pope states it as a rule (which he does not always observe) that the pause in the pentameter occurs after the fourth, fifth, or sixth syllable (see Adler, 1964, pp. 5–6), and Johnson asserts that 'the noblest and most majestic pauses which our versification admits, are upon the fourth and sixth syllables' (*The Rambler*, No. 90). A pause which isolates the first and last beat in a 1:4 or 4:1 division, on the other hand, creates a unit with a less simple rhythmic organisation and less fluent movement. If such a line occurs in verse which by a preponderance of the other type of line has established a metrical set incorporating the more even division as a preference, it will produce an increase in tension.

It is interesting to consider the role of the pairing formations, and the rhythmic patterns they bestow on the line, in this context. That *diabolus in prosodia*, the 'second-foot inversion', which is the earliest possible occurrence of stress-initial pairing in an iambic line, produces an opening of $-s +s +s -s -s +s \ldots$, and within this, the sequence $+s -s -s +s$ tends to form a separate unit, thereby creating a hiatus after the first beat, and an unbalanced 1:4 line. Stress-final pairing, on the other hand, is frequently employed to open the line with $-s -s +s +s \ldots$, since this, as a self-sufficient rhythmic grouping, divides the line 2:3. Turning to the end of the line, we find a similar situation. While the prohibited 'final inversion', $\ldots -s +s +s -s$, tends to isolate the final beat of the line, a stress-final pairing, $\ldots -s -s +s +s$, produces a more satisfying 3:2 division. Statistics confirm these preferences:

Tarlinskaja's tabulation of the occurrence in iambic pentameters of stress-final pairing, which she terms 'juncture inversion', shows that its commonest appearance is at the beginning of the line, and that for many poets its use at line-end matches or surpasses in frequency its use at both of the possible positions within the line (1976, pp. 285–6, Table 44). This is in strong contrast to stress-initial pairing, which occurs most readily in the middle two of its four possible positions (pp. 283–4, Table 43), dividing the line into 3:2 or 2:3 by the pause between the two stresses. The iambic initial inversion, the commonest of all these variations, also tends to create a clear 2:3 balance. In the strict four-beat line, too, stress-final pairing occurs most frequently at line-opening and line-end, where it helps to divide the line into two equal rhythmic units (see Bailey's figures, 1975b, p. 46):

(132) Where the rough mountain track divides

To silent valleys on all sides

It will be obvious that tension is an aspect of verse rhythm even less amenable to quantification than complexity. When so many variables operate together, it is unrealistic to expect a metrical theory to specify exact degrees of tension on a numerical scale; the most one can demand is that it provide a way of explaining the reader's experience of tension, whether at particular points or over larger stretches of verse.

I have emphasised so far in this section the imprecision in the reader's judgements of metre, and the necessary reflection of this in the rules. It will be as well to end with a demonstration that in some respects the reader's judgements are extremely sharp, and that the proposed rules and conditions mirror that sharpness. The stricter the metrical style, the clearer such judgements become, and it will be a useful exercise, therefore, to subject a line by Pope to various transformations, observing the rhythmic effect of each one. I give the line with the preceding four lines; each example should be read in its place after these four lines in order to re-establish the appropriate metrical set (ideally, the whole poem – the *Epistle to Arbuthnot* – should be read first):

(133) Whether in florid impotence he speaks,
　　　　 And, as the prompter breathes, the puppet squeaks;
　　　　 Or at the ear of Eve, familiar toad,

Half froth, half venom, spits himself abroad,
In puns, or politics, or tales, or lies
o   B   o   B o B̄   o   B   o   B

Although widely accepted in pentameter verse, feminine endings are uncommon in Pope's pentameters, and if the metrical set is well established, the following will be experienced as an increase in tension:

[133a] In puns, or politics, or tales, or stories
o   B   o   B o B̄   o   B   o   B o

Another variant which, measured against absolute standards, is highly regular, but which is anomalous in Pope's, as in most, iambic pentameters is the following:

[133b] Spewing puns, or politics, or lies
B o   B   o   B o B̄   o B

This line fails to observe the iambic inversion condition to which Pope strictly adheres; it drops the initial offbeat without a following double offbeat. Such a line would sound less odd among Chaucer's iambic pentameters, because of his acceptance of 'headless' lines; in Pope's verse it strongly increases the tension, though it is no more complex than the original.

What about the following line?

[133c] In puns, or plays, or a fine tale, or lies
o   B   o   B   ŏ B ô B   o   B

If not unacceptable, it is clearly approaching the frontier; there are in fact very few examples of stress-final pairing in the *Epistle*, and nearly all occur at the beginning of the line. And we move distinctly into the border area when we introduce stress-initial pairing:

[133d] In politics, or puns, stories or lies
o   B o B̄   o   B   ô B   ŏ   B

This is metrically the equivalent of (128), which as we saw is by no means the limit of complexity in Shakespeare's *Sonnets*. But such lines in Pope's verse, and there are a few, are experienced as the momentary adoption of a less rigorous, though still recognisable, metrical style. If the pairing conditions were ignored, however, we would be justified in assuming a change in pronunciation or an error in transcription:

[133e] In puns, or politics, or stories, or lies
o   B   o   B o B̄   o   B   ŏ   B

[133f] In puns, politics, or tales, or lies
o   B   o̊ B o B̄   o   B   o   B

The addition or omission of a single unstressed syllable in these examples is sufficient to render the line too complex to satisfy the ear attuned to Pope's controlled, syllabically exact, rhythmic forms.

All these variants can be read as some kind of pentameter, as the scansion indicates, and would be acceptable in the context of a looser pentameter style. There is, however, another kind of deviation where the borderline transgressed is more rigid; the result in this case is not a complex pentameter, but a line which is not a pentameter at all. It is an important task of a metrical theory to indicate this kind of borderline, and to distinguish it from the unacceptability created by too great a degree of complexity. This type of deviation may not be very marked in terms of the number and disposition of syllables, but is clearly discernible by the ear. If, for instance, we drop an unstressed syllable that is one of the three permitting promotion to occur, the result is the loss of a beat:

[133g] In puns or politics, tales or lies
o   B   o   B o̊   B   o   B

The scansion shows the only possible metrical pattern that can be realised by this line: a four-beat rhythm with one double offbeat. In some free metrical styles, a four-beat line among five-beat lines could be accepted as a deliberate variation from the prevailing metre; in Pope's verse it is unthinkable. Nor is it necessary to drop a syllable from the line to create this degree of irregularity: the following line has ten syllables, but also allows only four beats, and, what is worse, begins to slip into a triple rhythm completely at odds with the pentameter's duple alternations:

[133h] In parties, politics, stories, or lies
o   B   o   B o̊   B   o̊   B

The rhythm can be equally upset by the introduction of an extra beat, though once more the syllable count may remain unaffected:

[133i] In puns, politics, or rhyme, tales, and lies
o   B   o̊ B o B̄   o   B   o̊ B   o   B

Or, without even a possibility of eliding a syllable to save the pentameter:

[133j] In puns, party-games, or rhyme, tales, and lies
o   B   o̊ B o B   o   B   o̊ B   o   B

There are, of course, many other combinations of ten stressed or unstressed syllables which would be totally unacceptable in Pope's verse, but these examples will be enough to show that however flexible the rules may seem in some directions, there are other directions in which a line can travel only a very short distance before it plunges into metrical chaos, or, what is sometimes worse, a totally different rhythm. It is these sharp distinctions which prove the existence of a subtle but firm sense of metrical structure shared by poets and readers, and it is on this basis that any adequate account of metrical form must be built.

Notes

1. In deriving these comparative statistics from Tarlinskaja's tables, one has to ignore the column relating to 'inversion within the first foot', which does not produce a pairing formation (see section 7 of this chapter). It is partly this treatment of initial inversion and stress-initial pairing as a single phenomenon ('trochaic substitution') which has led to the widespread underestimation of the relative frequency and importance of stress-final pairing in English verse.
2. For a discussion of the frequent occurrence of this pattern in English verse, see Scripture (1928).
3. Groves (1979, Appendix) cites 80 examples of such 'headless' lines from Shakespeare's plays.

Chapter 8

Metrical rules and the structures of language

Metrical rules of the kind proposed in the previous chapter constitute no more than a framework within which to locate and analyse rhythmic effects. They are intended to represent the way in which stretches of the English language are perceived as rhythmic forms, but they do not offer a means of processing strings of syllables in a mechanical way to produce descriptions of their metrical structure. They could not be translated into a computer programme which would make possible a sifting of lines into metrical and unmetrical, or simple and complex – let alone good and bad. In other words, they rely for their application to English poetry on the experience and sensitivity of the user; what they offer the metrical analyst is a way of going about his task. Chapter 10 will provide some examples of the kind of statement about verse which they make possible.

One of the reasons why the rules fall short of full explicitness is that they ignore most of the finer details cf linguistic structure: exact phonetic properties, hierarchies of stress, placing of word boundaries, and morphological and syntactic organisation. It might be argued that this shortcoming vitiates the whole approach, that the hardest task of metrical theory is precisely to relate the complexities of language to the simplicities of metrical form; and it is true that much of the discussion of metre from a linguistic point of view has centred on just this problem. The needs of the poetry reader and critic are not those of the linguist, however; an account of poetic rhythm which related systematically the details of phonetic, phonological, syntactic, and perhaps semantic theory to a metrical framework of the kind we have been considering would be extraordinarily complex, and accessible only to the specialist. Moreover, much of its complexity would arise from the task of making explicit the reader's responses to his own language; a valuable enterprise, to be sure, but not one which will solve the problems about verse form which have faced generations of readers and critics. The way forward lies rather in the further exploration of the territory we have been examining; this is the metrical theorist's own domain, and only the phonologist can relate it fully to a linguistic theory. (There are signs, in fact, that phonological theory is developing towards metrical theory; a recent study of English stress (Giegerich, 1980), for instance, proposes – with no reference to verse – rules for spoken English that closely parallel metrical rules governing implied offbeats, promotion, and demotion.)

Our framework, then, offers a way of looking at the rhythms of poetry but still asks of the student of metre that he relate the patterns it identifies to the language he knows. In this chapter I shall consider some aspects of the relationship between metrical rules and the structures of English, as manifested in the practice of poets since Chaucer, but I shall not attempt to formalise these in further rules, nor am I aiming at anything like comprehensiveness or definitiveness. As with many of the metrical rules and conditions, we shall find that the regular features of this relationship spring as much from the need to avoid the most dominating rhythmic patterns – four-beat groups, falling rhythms, triple movements – as they do from the desire to create rhythmic patterns. I shall concentrate primarily on the iambic pentameter, as the metrical form which has most successfully escaped this kind of domination while retaining all the potency of a distinctive and simple rhythmic structure. A further advantage will be that the reader will have a constant metrical set against which to test individual lines (though it is always advisable to re-establish the set by reading some regular verse before each example). The theories and revised theories, proposals and counter-proposals of the generative school of metrical analysis – which will no doubt continue unabated – have shown that the relationship between metre and language is a highly complex one, not to be reduced to a few simple rules, and the necessarily *ad hoc* mode of procedure in the discussion that follows will perhaps clarify the nature and certainly highlight the degree of the problem.

8.1 INDEFINITE STRESS

The output of the metrical rules is a very simple sequence expressed in terms of a single binary feature ±s, which we have been calling the *stress pattern*; the actual verse line is a complex arrangement of phonemes, syllables, words, and syntactic units, with great variety in stress contour, placement of pauses, and rhythmic movement. A totally explicit metrical theory would have to make use of a third level in scansion above that of +s and −s showing all these details, in accordance with one or other phonological theory, and to provide a set of rules defining the relationships between them. But such an account would not only be so complicated as to be unmanageable; it would also obscure the true nature of the relationship between metrical and linguistic structures, which is not one that is amenable to fixed rules. As an illustration, let us examine the most obvious simplification contained in our metrical rules, the reduction of a highly varied stress contour, reflecting the morphological and syntactic structures of the language, to a sequence of stressed and unstressed syllables.

For most syllables in English no problem arises, since the choice between +s and −s is obvious to any speaker of the language. Most nouns, independent verbs, adjectives, and adverbs − what are sometimes called 'major-category' or 'open-class' words − have one main stress, which, whatever its place in the stress hierarchy of the phrase or sentence, functions metrically as +s (we shall consider some exceptions to this generalisation in section 3). Conversely, many monosyllabic words whose function is in some sense auxiliary − 'minor-category' or 'closed-class' words − are clearly to be regarded as −s, and to these we can add most of the syllables in polysyllabic words which do not take the main stress. Thus there can be no question about the scansion of the following lines:

$$\overset{+s\ -s}{\underset{B\quad \delta}{\text{(1) Rapine}}}\ \overset{-s}{\underset{}{\text{and}}}\ \overset{+s}{\underset{B\ \ o}{\text{Wrong}}}\ \overset{-s}{\underset{}{\text{and}}}\ \overset{+s}{\underset{B\ \ o\ B}{\text{Fear}}}\ \overset{-s\ +s}{\underset{}{\text{usurped}}}\ \overset{-s}{\underset{o}{\text{her}}}\ \overset{+s}{\underset{B}{\text{place,}}}$$

```
    +s −s   −s       +s   −s    +s  −s +s      −s    +s
(1) Rapine and Wrong and Fear usurped her place,
    B    ð    B   o   B   o B           o    B
```

```
    −s   −s +s  +s −s  +s −s +s −s    +s
And a bold, artful, surly, savage race
ŏ    B   ŏB  o   B  o   B  o    B
```

But not all syllables can be so unequivocally categorised. The location of the beats in the following lines is not in doubt, but the exact nature of the offbeats is not so easily decided:

```
(2) One rose, a rose that gladdened earth and sky,
    B       B        B            B          B
One rose, my rose, that sweetened all mine air
B       B           B            B         B
```

A reader who wishes to give these lines a weighty, deliberate delivery to underline the poignancy would stress many of the offbeats, allowing the process of demotion to keep the metre within bounds; the second line, for instance, might be read as follows:

+s   +s   +s +s   −s   +s −s   +s   +s +s

One rose, my rose, that sweetened all mine air

ó   B   ó   B   o   B o   B   ó   B

On the other hand, a performance which aimed at lightness and regularity might minimise the stress on the offbeats, producing a line with no deviations:

−s   +s   −s +s   −s   +s −s   +s   −s +s

One rose, my rose, that sweetened all mine air

o   B   o   B   o   B o   B   o   B

A metrical theory which incorporated fine phonological detail would have to account for these variations by means of a set of options; but even this would be untrue to the rhythmic reality, which is that as far as the metrical *structure* of the line is concerned, the variations are of little significance. The rhythmic framework provided by the beats is firm enough to allow freedom in the realisation of the offbeats; if the reader chooses to stress them, demotion will take care of the rhythmic alternation, assisted by the unchanging syntactic relations. The difference will be one of rhythmic character, but the metre itself will not come under any threat. It is not, therefore, a series of options, but a genuine freedom; as far as the metre is concerned, the ear is simply not as sensitive to increases and decreases of stress in these positions as in some others.

It is possible to use scansion to prescribe or record particular ways of reading a line, as in the two scansions of the same line above, but its fundamental purpose is to reveal the metrical structure that underlies *any* satisfactory performance, so we need a way of showing the variability of some of the offbeats in our example. It is true that this freedom is theoretically implied by a scansion showing only beats and offbeats, since any offbeat realised by a syllable between two stressed syllables (or the other environments in which demotion is possible) can tolerate different degrees of stress; but what we are concerned with here is a specific conjunction of metre and language where this metrical freedom is available to a syllable which at the same time is allowed by the syntactic structure and semantic content to vary in its stress. Since this variability is an aspect of the pronunciation of the words, we show it in the stress pattern above the line, and we use the symbol s to represent an *indefinite stress*; rather than being stressed or unstressed, such syllables can be thought of as 'stressable'. A full scansion of (2) would be as follows, showing the maximum amount of freedom permitted by the rhetorical and syntactic structures of the language:

```
 s   +s   −s  +s    −s    +s  −s   +s    −s     +s
One rose, a rose that gladdened earth and sky,
 o   B    o   B     o    B    o    B     o      B

 s   +s    s  +s    −s    +s  −s   +s     s    +s
One rose, my rose, that sweetened all mine air.
 o   B    o   B     o     B  o    B      o    B
```

All the other offbeats, of course, are realised directly by nonstresses, since the language allows no other pronunciation. Notice that in the case of an indefinite stress we indicate no deviation under the word; the simplest metrical realisation is a possibility, though the demands of the poetry, as interpreted by a reader, may carry pronunciation towards a demoted realisation. If we had to scan the lines without showing indefinite stresses, we would have to choose in each case whether or not to show a fully stressed syllable plus demotion, though this is not in fact a *metrical* decision at all.

Indefinite stressing is not confined to the offbeats; the converse situation obtains between two nonstresses, where a syllable is free to vary in stress and still realise a beat, thanks to the possibility of promotion. We show this possibility in exactly the same way:

```
                     s                          s
(3)  Oh, Love, what is it in this world of ours
      o    B      o  B o  B̄   o    B    o B o

                      s
     Which makes it fatal to be loved? Ah why
       o    B     o   B o  B̄  o  B         o    B

                         s
     With cypress branches hast thou wreathed thy bowers,
       o    B     o     B    o    B    o     B      o  B o

                       s
     And made thy best interpreter a sigh?
       o    B     o   B  o  B    o B̄ o B
```

In this example, the indefinite stresses can be given some weight by the reader, or left as unstressed and allowed to function as beats through promotion, all the emphasis then falling on the other stresses. To give a full scansion of these lines, it would be necessary only to add two more indefinite stresses in offbeat position on 'Oh' and 'Ah'; everything else in the stress pattern is already implied by the metrical pattern and deviation symbols.

Occasionally, sense and syntax permit two adjacent syllables to function together as indefinite stresses, permitting even greater variability. Traditional scansion of the following line implies that the same pair of words receives exactly opposite stress patterns:

     x /   x / x / x   / x   /
(4) I know *when one* is dead and *when one* lives

A sensitive reading, however, is likely to give them both the same pronunciation, either with all four syllables unstressed, allowing promotion on the first 'one' and the second 'when', or with all four stressed, allowing demotion on the first 'when' and the second 'one' – or something in between these alternatives. The only way to register this freedom is by means of indefinite stresses:

            s s   s s
(*4*) I know when one is dead and when one lives
           o B̄   B̄ o
           ȯ B   B ȯ

In a case like this, it becomes necessary to indicate which of the possible realisations of the metrical pattern implied by the indefinite stresses are appropriate; it is unlikely, for instance, that pairing would occur. (Strictly speaking, these restrictions should be shown in the stress pattern, since they are the product of the particular syntactic and semantic features of the line in question, but this would mean introducing new formal conventions of a very specialised kind.) It is important to realise that the use of indefinite stress is not merely as a shorthand for a set of alternatives; it is a distinctive rhythmic phenomenon dependent on the existence of a regular metre, which is experienced no matter how the line is pronounced. There is no clear dividing line between the readings shown in the scansion of (*4*): since the beats and offbeats are always realised by the same syllables, there is no metrical reason for the distinction, and the brain need not make it either.

One can give a general account of the kinds of monosyllable which are prone to receive indefinite stress in the appropriate metrical environment; syntactically they usually occupy a position between those with full lexical independence and those which function only as auxiliaries, and include pronouns, conventional adjectives which do not add much information to that provided by the noun, verbs of being and becoming, verbs which are subordinate parts of larger verbal units, and, in general, prepositions, conjunctions, and interjections. But it is impossible to reduce the occurrence of indefinite stress to rules, since it depends so much on the specific linguistic context in which the word appears. The same is true of indefinite stress in polysyllables, though the situation here is a little clearer, since there are two distinct types of polysyllable involved. The first is the polysyllabic minor-category word, in which the main stress can be weakened:

s
(5) And few, amid the rural tribe, have time
B

Here we are likely to have some sense of a stress on the syllable in question, yet a rapid reading will create a rhythm virtually identical to that produced by three unstressed syllables. The second type is the major-category word in which a significant degree of stress falls on a syllable other than the one taking the main stress, usually separated from it by an unstressed syllable in accordance with the alternating tendency of the language:

s
(6) Creature so fair his reconcilement seeking
B

This is a more accurate reflection of the reader's experience than would be given either by a straightforward realisation of a beat by a stress, or by a promoted nonstress. In many polysyllabic words, however, there is only the slightest degree of secondary stress, and it is more accurate to regard such syllables as unstressed. Compounds, whose stress contours pose special problems, will be dealt with separately in section 8 of this chapter.

How does the language accommodate this freedom in pronunciation? To understand this fully we need to return for a moment to the discussion of stress hierarchies in 3.3. There we observed that the hearer's sense of a stress contour depends a great deal on his awareness of the phonological structure of the words and of the syntactic structure of the sentence, and that it can operate in the absence of physical cues for stress. This means, for example, that the stress relationships of *amid* or *reconcilement*, or of the sentences in (2) and (3), will be perceived whether or not they are fully manifested in terms of pitch, duration, and volume, leaving the spoken realisation some freedom to vary according to the demands of the verse. When the fixed stress contour of the sentence coincides with the metrical set, such variable stresses are given a special character: the two perceptual schemata reinforce one another, so that a syllable whose level of stress is undetermined by either is given a kind of freedom unknown outside the structures of regular verse. Its rhythmic status is doubly guaranteed, so to speak, and its actual pronunciation in a given performance can be determined entirely by the reader's sense of semantic and aesthetic needs.

In some contexts, a stress that might be variable in prose is forced to function in only one way by the metre. Thus if we rewrite the second line of (2) as follows, the metre induces a pronunciation of 'my' without a stress:

> +s   −s   −s +s
> [2a] Give me my rose, that sweetens all the air
> B   ǒ   B

The syllables on either side of a promoted or demoted syllable also allow of no variation; the most natural reading of the following line gives no stress to 'me':

> −s   −s   −s
> (7) Or that your prowess can me yield relief
> o   B̄   o

The stress of a minor category polysyllable behaves in a similar way; if the metrical context allows it, it can be indefinite, but there are times when it has to function as a nonstress, like the second syllable of 'upon' in the following line:

> −s   −s −s   +s
> (8) And I will comment upon that offence
> o   B̄ o   B

If one allows 'upon' any stress in its normal place, instead of throwing it all forward to 'that', one is likely to end up thinking, like Booth (1977, p. 293), that the line is prose; what is true is that the simultaneous promotion of the first syllable of 'upon' and the denial of stress to the second creates a significant degree of tension (which an ingenious critic might regard as emblematic of the self-deprecation being expressed). When a minor category disyllable of this kind is used in a double offbeat, however, there is no rhythmic pressure on the first syllable, and the word functions without difficulty as two nonstresses:

> +s   +s   −s −s
> (9) Constant, mature, proof against all assaults
> B ǒ   B   ǒ

Spenser uses the second of these formations as part of the lulling rhythmic spell cast by Despair:

> (10)   Sleep after toil, port after stormy seas,
>
> Ease after war, death after life does greatly please

It is as if all energy has been drained away, leaving the prepositions listless and stressless. Yet the same word can provide a metrically essential stress, and a sense of strenuousness, when required:

> (11)   He left me: I called after him aloud

There are also times when the indefiniteness of a stress in a minor category word allows two possible scansions, and the line hovers between them, blurring the metrical pattern. In such cases, we need to show both possibilities in the scansion:

> (12)   That comes to all, but torture without end

> (13)   Pride, Malice, Folly against Dryden rose

As in the case of adjacent indefinite stresses, this is not a matter of clear alternatives, but of a range of possibility which is experienced however the line is read – though the fact that in this case it involves different placings of the beat renders the effect more complex and the rhythmic tension more pronounced. It is this capacity of the stronger syllable in a minor category polysyllable to function metrically either as a stress or a nonstress that makes it so difficult to handle in fully explicit rules; it is not surprising that, as we saw in 2.2, it creates problems for the metrist who tries to pin down once and for all the Protean substance of language.

8.2 SENSE AND THE STRESS PATTERN

If the stress contour of a sentence were determined entirely by the

phonological structure of its words and the syntactic structure in which
they are situated, a fully explicit metrical theory might be more than a
fond hope; but as the discussion of indefinite stress will already have
made clear, the sense makes a contribution to the gradations of stress
which defies representation in a set of rules. I am concerned in this
section with those cases where the meaning clearly imposes its own
hierarchy of stresses on the neutral stress contour of words and
sentences, one of the most intractably problematic areas of metrics,
though also one of the most illuminating.[1] I shall refer to any such
special stressing as *emphatic stress*, including what is often called
'contrastive stress'.

We can start by examining the different guises which can be adopted
by the same word under the influence of meaning and metre; the
personal pronoun *I* as used by Keats in *The Fall of Hyperion* will serve
as an illustration. In our first example it is unequivocally a nonstress:

(14) Onward I looked beneath the gloomy boughs

Here the metre demands a nonstress as part of the double offbeat in an
initial inversion, the semantic emphasis is on 'Onward' and 'looked',
and the rhythm of the language, as always, encourages the avoidance
of successive stresses. The next example also invites an unstressed
pronunciation for rhythmic and semantic reasons:

(15) Then to the west I looked, and saw far off

The metrical structure, however, does not demand a nonstress: if there
were semantic reasons for giving some degree of stress to 'I' no
dislocation would follow, only a slowing down of the movement. If this
were the case the scansion would indicate an indefinite stress; but since
the variability is only a theoretical possibility and is not likely to enter
into a reading, we show the syllable as unstressed. In the following
example, the pattern is reversed, and the pronoun occurs between two
nonstresses, again allowing variability of stress. But the sense suggests
an unstressed pronunciation, realising a beat through promotion:

(16) So old the place was, I remembered none

It would, however, be possible to scan the line with an indefinite stress
to permit a deliberate, metrically regular, reading. And in the next

example, indefinite stress is probably the most accurate way of indicating the range of possible pronunciations:

(17) 'The other vexes it.' Then shouted I,

Spite of myself . . .

Since it occurs in one of the environments of the promotion rule, between a nonstress and a line-boundary, the pronoun is metrically free to take any degree of stress, and the sense and inverted syntax invite some degree of emphasis, though it is not the task of the scansion to prescribe how much. The next example also offers the reader a choice, this time between two scansions, depending on the placing of emphatic stress:

(18) That I am favoured for unworthiness

By stressing 'I', the first reading emphasises that it is the poet who is favoured, while the second throws the emphasis on to the favouring itself. However, the most natural reading is perhaps to give all three words a weak pronunciation, producing a stress pattern of three nonstresses and allowing promotion to occur:

That I am favoured for unworthiness

This allows the main emphasis in the line to fall where the sense suggests it should, on 'unworthiness'. Finally, we can look at an example where the rhythmic pulse tips the balance; I give it first as it might be read in a prose context:

(19) Though I breathe death with them it will be life

It is an acceptable metrical reading, the pairing conditions being satisfactorily met; but the rhythm both of the language and of the verse discourages implied offbeats where alternative readings are possible, and here may induce sufficient stress on the pronoun to allow it to take a beat:

^{−s}   ^{+s}   ^{+s}   ^{+s}
Though I breathe death with them it will be life
o   B ŏ   B

The pronoun needs just enough weight to bring it level with the following word, and must not take away from the important contrastive stress on 'death', set as it is against 'life' later in the line. This freedom to give personal pronouns a little extra weight to avoid rhythmic irregularity is capitalised on by many poets. The most satisfactory performance of the following line, for instance, is probably as shown; in representing emphatic stress, I use an underlined s in the stress pattern, especially where the emphasis is for purposes of contrast:

^{−s} <u>s</u>.^{+s}   <u>s</u>   <u>s</u> <u>s</u> ^{−s} ^{−s} <u>s</u>   <u>s</u>
(20) If I lose thee, my loss is my love's gain
o B ŏ   B   ŏ B · ŏ   B   ŏ B

This means giving both 'I' and 'thee' sufficient stress to make them equivalent to 'lose', thereby allowing demotion to occur, and stressing the first 'my' but not the second, so that the double contrast – 'my' with 'my love's' and 'loss' with 'gain' – is fully brought out. The effect is of five even stresses, lingering on the painful thought of personal loss, followed by a double offbeat and two more even stresses, this time separated by an implied offbeat, to round off the line with a firm (if spurious) assertiveness.

What we see in these examples is that semantic and metrical demands are constantly in operation together, moulding the neutral contours of stress provided by syntax and phonology, and that the particular prosodic usefulness of lexical categories like the pronoun lies in the degree to which they are able to bend according to these demands. Even syllables whose lexically-determined stress is indisputably strong can function as nonstresses in appropriate semantic and metrical contexts (we shall encounter some instances in the following section). But the working relationship of sense and metre is not always such a harmonious one, and it will be instructive to look at a series of examples in which the emphatic stresses are somewhat more imperious and the metrical requirements somewhat more stringent.

Sometimes, the semantic demands simply heighten the regularity of the rhythm, as in the third line of this example:

(21) Why shouldst thou, Night, abuse me only thus,
That every creature to his kind dost call

^{−s}   s ^{−s}   <u>s</u> ^{−s} ^{+s} ^{−s} <u>s</u> ^{−s} <u>s</u>
And yet 'tis thou dost only sever us?
o   B   o   B   o   B   o   B   o B

The three emphatic peaks of this line are all already in metrically stressed positions; 'thou' (the same force already described), 'sever' (as opposed to uniting), and 'us' (in contrast to all other creatures). The result is a mutual reinforcement between the strongly insistent rhythm, expressive of the speaker's emotional state, and the semantic weight on particular points of complaint. There are also instances where the semantic demands impose a metrical interpretation on the line different from that implied by the neutral stress contour; in the following example 'undo' requires an initial emphatic stress to contrast it with 'do', and the result is a line with pairing instead of a nondeviant realisation of the metrical pattern:

(22)   [. . .] so God shall uncreate,
                   +s   s   −s −s
            Be frustrate, do, undo, and labour lose
                      B ŏB   ŏ

Sometimes complexity is considerably increased by a necessary emphatic stress, as in the following line (where I give both the scansion demanded by the sense and below that the much simpler scansion that would be appropriate if there were no semantic contrasts):

            −s   −s   s   +s   −s   +s   −s   −s   s   +s
(23) Lest to you hap, that happened to me here
       ŏ   B ŏ B   o   B   ŏ   Bŏ B
       o   B̄   o   B   o   B   o   B̄   o   B

The semantic influence on metre is even more important when the metricality of the line *depends*, as it does in none of the above examples, on the use of emphatic stress. In the following line, a reading which paid only scant attention to the meaning, and none to the metre, might treat the pronoun 'I' as an unstressed syllable:

                              −s −s +s   −s
(24) And what is't but mine own when I praise thee?
       o   B o   B̄   o B   ŏ   B   o

The result, as shown, is a four-beat line with one double offbeat and a feminine ending. It occurs, however, in a sonnet by Shakespeare, and there is a clear emphasis on 'I' and 'thee', the terms which the poet is claiming to regard as identical. This yields a regular iambic pentameter with a smooth demotion:

                                          s   +s   s
            And what is't but mine own when I praise thee?
                 B o   B̄   o   B   o B ŏ   B

Milton furnishes an example in which an emphatic 'that' is demanded, or else the line slithers into a triple rhythm:

(25) God so commanded, and left that command
ŏ   B   o   B   ŏ   B ô B   o   B

A line in which all the beats are carried by emphatic stresses, and the only major lexical item is demoted, is the following:

(26) Yet he broke them, ere they could him
o   B   ŏ   B   o   B   o   B

In lines like these, to misread the metre is to miss the sense.

One might expect poets to avoid using strong emphatic stresses on syllables which, metrically, require demotion, but this is not the case, and the reasons for this apparent perverseness have a bearing on the general question of the relationship between rhythmic structures and phonetic details. The first line of (21) demands some degree of emphasis on 'me', which is a demoted syllable, and the following example from 'Verses on the Death of Dr Swift' is even clearer:

(27) For how can stony bowels melt
       In those who never pity felt;
       When *we* are lashed, *they* kiss the rod
o   B   o   B   ŏ   B   o   B

There can be no doubt about the contrastive stress here, because the italics are Swift's own; yet the second emphasis falls on a syllable which has to be demoted to preserve the metricality of the line. What comes to the rescue of the reader here is the variety of ways in which stress in English can be manifested. In discussing this subject in 3.2 we noted that pitch, volume, duration, and sound-quality can all function as cues for stress, and that of these, pitch and duration are the most effective. This means that it is possible to give a word a special semantic emphasis by pronouncing it with a different pitch-contour from that used in unemphatic speech; indeed, this is the natural way to create such an emphasis. In the case of 'they' above, it is by pronouncing it at a higher pitch (and possibly with greater volume) than 'kiss' that we give it a contrastive emphasis, not necessarily by any greater duration. The importance of this is that the higher pitch is less likely to attract a beat; the syllable remains temporally equivalent to its neighbours, and its syntactic subordination to the verb that follows is still perceived, allowing demotion to occur in the normal way. This possibility of separating the stress-cues, and allowing the rhythm to be controlled largely by duration while meaning is controlled by pitch, is one which poets and their readers tend to use instinctively. However, it should be noted that it can only save the metre when there are semantic reasons for the special emphasis: since the perception of stress contours is not based on the physical properties of the sounds themselves, an unmetrical line for which syntax and meaning offer only one reading cannot be rendered metrical by tricks of the voice. Of course, tension is increased at such moments, as the two features of stress that usually work in conjunction are pulled apart; but tension itself is a valuable expressive resource. For example, the powerfully appropriate tension in the penultimate lines of the first two stanzas of Donne's 'Hymn to God the Father' is not only semantic but metrical, the word 'not' receiving an emphatic stress, while the metre (and the pun on the poet's name) demands a stress on the last word. The use of a pitch emphasis allows a blurred rhythm that hovers between two realisations of the metrical pattern:

$$\qquad\qquad\qquad -s \quad\ s \quad\ \underline{s} \quad +s$$
(28) When thou hast done, thou hast not done

Emphasis by pitch also permits an alternative reading of (22): the semantic opposition manifested by the first syllable of 'undo' can be expressed in this way, leaving the second syllable with a durational stress that corresponds to the phonological structure of the word and takes the beat:

$$\qquad\qquad\quad +s \quad \underline{s} \quad +s$$
(22) Be frustrate, do, undo, and labour lose

There are times, however, when even this flexibility is not sufficient to prevent the metrical and rhetorical structures from colliding. Let us look at two rather similar lines, the first by Shakespeare and the second by Keats:

$$\qquad\qquad\qquad\ s \qquad\qquad\qquad\quad s$$
(29) How can I then be elder than thou art

$$\qquad\qquad\qquad\ s \qquad\qquad\qquad\ s$$
(30) Bright star! Would I were steadfast as thou art

Both lines imply a contrast between 'I' and 'thou', with the appropriate emphatic stress, but the result in both cases is a 'final inversion' and an unmetrical, four-beat line. This is because 'thou' is preceded by two nonstresses which we have no option but to treat as a double offbeat (unlike Keats's other final inversions, discussed earlier), and followed by a verb which takes very little stress and so cannot function as a final beat. In a different semantic context, the stress pattern of 'thou art' could be reversed, producing a perfectly acceptable line:

[30a] Bright star above, as steadfast as t̄hou art,

Thou canst not match my own prolonged desire

But in (29) and (30), a single reading which attempted to do justice to both metre and sense would have to effect some sort of compromise by minimising the emphasis on 'thou', perhaps by using pitch rather than the other stress cues, and giving 'art' sufficient duration to allow it to attract a beat. Two lines from Donne's tenth Elegy which have given rise to a great deal of metrical heartsearching for similar reasons are the following:

(31) So, if I dream I have you, I have you

(32) Makes me her medal, and makes her love me

The reader can consult the debate between Stein (1956) and Chatman (1956b) over the pronunciation and scansion of these lines, which, if it does not settle the question, at least proves that it is far from easy to settle. One conclusion, however, may be drawn from our discussion: it appears that the weighting of stresses demanded by the sense does not entirely displace the neutral stress contour produced by phonology and syntax, and that the variable which determines the role of that neutral contour in the total rhythmic effect is the metre. When, as in (24)–(26), the requirements of the sense coincide with the requirements of the metrical structure, in opposition to the neutral stress contour, the latter is present only as a shadow in the background, pulling against the rhythmic alternations and thereby slightly increasing the tension. When there is some degree of conflict between emphasis and metre, however, as in (27)–(32), it is the implicit neutral contour which preserves rhythmic regularity, and the counter-demands of the sense which create tension. The result is a rhythmic complexity greater than that produced by straightforward deviations, and one which can add a dimension to the reader's experience of the language unavailable outside metrical verse.[2] We have focused on obvious examples, but it is likely that the three-way relationship among the rhythmic demands made by syntax and phonology, metre, and meaning operates continuously as one of the sources of the special density and richness imparted to language by regular verse.

8.3 METRICAL SUBORDINATION

In discussing the stress contours of English (3.3) we gave some attention to the principle of hierarchical organisation and the consequent subordination of certain stressed syllables to others within the linguistic structure. I wish to make use of the concept of subordination in a freer way than would be tolerated in a linguistic study, but one which will be more useful to the reader of poetry than the strict application of a particular phonological theory. It will be recalled that subordination is a reflection of syntactic relations, and holds between stresses within a single syntactic unit; thus the stressed syllable of an adjective is usually subordinate to the stressed syllable of a following noun, and the same is true of the relation between a verb and a noun functioning as its object. In addition to this, the final stress of a sentence is usually the predominant one. It must be emphasised once more that subordination is not simply a matter of one syllable's being pronounced longer, louder, or at a higher pitch than another, but of a perceived relationship within the syntactic structure, ultimately related to habitual muscular actions but in a given case not necessarily manifested by physical means at all. This fact is crucial to an understanding of poetic rhythm.

For the most part, subordinated stresses need not be distinguished in rules or scansion. A stress which is subordinated will, of course, have a rhythmic effect which is slightly different from that created by an unsubordinated stress; this kind of difference will be considered later in the chapter, as will the special problems posed by subordination within compounds. Nor do words which sometimes function as stresses and sometimes as nonstresses concern us here; they have been discussed in the previous sections. But there remain cases in which the stress on a subordinated syllable is not reduced to a nonstress, even though the syllable occurs in a position in which we would expect only a nonstress. I gave some examples of this apparent contravention of the metrical rules in 7.4, and argued that it would be best not to handle it within the metrical rules; we can now take up those examples, which are typical of many more from all periods in the history of iambic verse, for further consideration:

       +s   −s +s   +s
(33) Drawn of fair peacocks, that excel in pride

       +s −s +s   +s
(34) Flows in fit words and heavenly eloquence

       +s   −s   +s   +s
(35) Damn with faint praise, assent with civil leer

       +s   −s +s   +s
(36) Deep as first love, and wild with all regret

Nor is this formation a peculiarity of the five-beat line:

       +s   −s +s   +s
(37) Love you ten years before the flood

The anomalous stresses in these examples are all clear cases of syntactic subordination, and of only one type of subordination at that: a monosyllabic adjective followed by a noun with a stress on its first (or only) syllable. It is obvious that subordination is crucial to our sense that these lines do not transgress the metrical bounds, since it allows the first stressed syllable to be perceived as part of a double offbeat. When a line is rendered metrical by virtue of syntactic subordination, a phenomenon which I shall call *metrical subordination*, the symbol [s] can be used in the stress pattern; the metrical pattern and deviation symbols can then be shown beneath the line as if the syllable were a nonstress:

       +s   −s [s] +s
(*33*) Drawn of fair peacocks, that excel in pride
       B   ŏ   B

On the other hand, where a syntactically subordinated stress functions normally in the metre as a full stress, no indication is given in the scansion. Other syntactic structures in this formation are much less common, but when they do occur they usually show at least the same degree of subordination:

           [s]
(38) Proud to catch cold at a Venetian door
       B   ŏ   B

(39) Read or read not what I am now essaying
B   ŏ   B

In the first example, the verb is subordinated to its object (and the conventional nature of the collocation increases the subordination); while in the second the negative takes an emphatic stress, and the repeated verb is subordinated to it. In either case, the syllable in question might more accurately be shown as a nonstress, though the degree of stress which it retains is a choice to be made by the reader. The inclusion in some metrical theories of a rule which deletes a stress before another stress in the same phrase (see Magnuson and Ryder, 1971; and Chisholm, 1977) is an attempt to deal with metrical subordination, but by extending the principle to all phrases in all metrical formations it does as much harm as good: in stress-initial pairing, for instance, such de-stressing would be fatal to the metre. Even as an optional rule it would misrepresent the very specific circumstances under which metrical subordination occurs. (The classical approach, of course, does not offer any way of dealing with this phenomenon, except by labelling it 'trochee + spondee'.)

It is also noticeable that all these examples occur in the same position in the line, as the second syllable of a double offbeat in an initial inversion; and this reflects an overwhelming preference in the verse tradition, ignored in the theories just mentioned. One reason for this is that the equivalent formation later in the line produces the highly deviant sequence of two stresses, a nonstress, and two further stresses, the effect of which we shall consider below. A second reason, however, is suggested by the somewhat surprising list of poets who use this device frequently. Tarlinskaja's statistics (1976, p. 287, Table 45, last 4 columns) show not only that it forms a relatively high proportion of all the strong deviations used by such rhythmically liberated poets as Donne, Swinburne, and Browning, but also that it is quite common in the strict pentameters of Thomson and Pope. The writers whose metrical styles fall somewhere between these extremes, however, are more likely to avoid it: Shakespeare, Wordsworth, and Byron use it very sparingly.[3] Why should this be so? We can assume that in poets like Pope and Thomson it occurs almost exclusively at the beginning of the line, and it is to the metrical possibilities at this point that we must look for an answer. The stricter the verse, the stronger and more clear-cut the metrical set; and strict iambic pentameter includes as a sharply-defined possible opening the initial inversion sequence +s −s

−s +s . . . It is no doubt because this expectation is so strong a part of the set in highly regular verse (which is to say that it creates no metrical tension when it occurs) that it can also be satisfied by the sequence +s −s [s] +s . . . This pattern has therefore become one of the available alternatives enshrined by convention at the start of the iambic line, in spite of its potential disruptiveness. In metrical styles of middling freedom, however, it is less easy to interpret such a sequence as an initial inversion, because there is no strong metrical set to prevent the subordinated stress from attracting a rhythmically destructive extra beat; while in the very freest styles, a movement in the direction of a sixth beat is itself among the available options.

Metrical subordination does sometimes occur after the beginning of the line, however. Here too it is most likely within a strongly defined +s −s −s +s pattern, occurring after a distinct pause:

                                    [s]
(40) While late bare earth, proud of new clothing, springeth
           B   ô   B   ŏ   B

                          [s]
(41) To expiate which sin, kiss and shake hands
           B ô B   ŏ

The increase in tension when this occurs is considerably greater than at the line-opening, and may push the line to the borders of metricality, though such extremity can be used for expressive purposes:

                            [s]
(42) For precious friends, hid in death's dateless night
           B   ô B   ŏ   B

Any sensitive reader will register this line as metrically complex, the tension occurring especially on the crucial word 'death's'; the metre demands that its syntactic subordination to the noun phrase that follows be as fully manifested as possible by an unemphatic pronunciation, while the meaning, and the clustering of consonants, require that it be given special weight. Metrical subordination of this kind testifies to a relatively free metrical style, and even then can be used only rarely if the five-beat foundation of the metre is not to be disturbed. Pope appears to limit his use of it to the line-opening, though one exception is a line which, rather unfairly, he makes deliberately monstrous with its help:

(43) A needless Alexandrine ends the song
                              [s]
      That, like a wounded snake, drags its slow length along
         B ô B   ŏ   B

Since the metrical subordination here is more of a fiction than a reality – 'slow' requires too much semantic emphasis to be weakened – this Alexandrine can scarcely be read without seven beats.

Naturally, we find a greater number of such variations (and even more extreme ones) in dramatic verse, where the impression of impassioned speech may be more important than the maintenance of a regular rhythmic pulse. The ghost of King Hamlet is given a line which relies on subordination for its metricality:

(44) I could a tale unfold whose lightest word
[s]
      Would harrow up thy soul, freeze thy young blood
      B   ŏ   B   ŏ   B

A metrical theory based on foot-divisions would see such a variation as merely the substitution of a trochee and a spondee in the last two feet, but if one responds to the rhythm as a continuity one feels that the strong pull of the language against the second half of the metrical pattern takes one to the limits of regular metrical form. Shelley, whose metrical style is highly distinctive in the liberties it takes, makes quite free use of metrical subordination later in the line. The following examples all come from *Adonais*:

[s]
(45) And one with trembling hands clasps his cold head
      B   ŏ   B   ŏ   B

[s]
(46) Fresh leaves and flowers deck the dead season's bier
      B   ŏ   B   ŏ   B

[s]
(47) All baser things pant with life's sacred thirst
      B   ŏ   B   ŏ   B

And the generous limits of Milton's metrical style let it in, here nicely illustrative in the way it overfills the rhythmic space:

[s]
(48) In narrow room nature's whole wealth, yea more
      B   ŏ   B   ŏ

Metrical subordination most commonly occurs on the second syllable of the double offbeat, but sense and syntax sometimes produce the same phenomenon on the first syllable. In the following line, the two occurrences of 'beaus' take emphatic stress, and it is more natural to subordinate 'banish' than to demote the first word:

     s   [s]   s
(49) Beaus banish beaus, and coaches coaches drive
         B   ŏ   B

Or a choice can be offered between initial inversion and an initial double offbeat; I show the latter in the following example:

       [s]
(50) Make the soul dance upon a jig to heaven
         ŏ   B ŏ B

This is perhaps a smoother way of reading the line than emphasising 'Make' and subordinating 'soul'; indeed, we might regard 'Make' as a wholly unstressed auxiliary verb rather than an instance of subordination. Emphatic stressing can create the same situation: in the second line of (51) all the emphasis is on 'looks' (spoken with an ironic inflection) while 'Hero' is merely an unemphatic repetition of 'she':

(51) Wherewith she yielded, that was won before;
       [s]   s
    Hero's looks yielded, but her words made war
     ŏ   B   ŏ B

A similar choice may be offered in mid-line:

               [s]
(52) Though in her lids hung the sweet tears of May
       B   ŏ   B ŏ B

Here we may prefer to make use of the subordination of 'hung', as shown, rather than that of 'sweet'. Many metrical theories attempt to classify the stressed syllables of the language into various types for the purpose of formulating rules; as these examples suggest, however, the specific conditions of a particular line (in terms of both rhythm and meaning) can induce *any* monosyllable or disyllable to lose some or all of its stress. (The main stress in a word of more than two syllables is unlikely to be subordinated or destressed, since there is usually only one possible alignment with the metrical pattern, in which the main stress realises a beat.)

Do any metrical formations other than the double offbeat capitalise on syntactic subordination in this way? The question is not relevant to the commonest environment for offbeats, between two stresses, because demotion allows even a full stress in this position (though a subordinated stress naturally provides a smoother realisation); and the same is true of an initial offbeat before a stress. Metrical subordination cannot occur as part of the environment of a promoted nonstress, since this requires genuine nonstresses. But there is one situation where a subordinated stress might be tolerated, though a full stress is not: in a feminine ending. As a stress is normally subordinated to a *following* stress, examples will be rare, but one instance is Byron's couplet addressed to Southey, which uses subordination of a kind for comic effect; the penultimate word takes the emphasis, leaving the name stranded at the end as a weakly stressed syllable:

(53) Gasping on deck, because you soar too high, Bob,

And fall, for lack of moisture, quite a dry Bob!

When John Murray objected to the obscenity (a 'dry-Bob' is a coital act without ejaculation), Byron lessened the insult but increased the metricality by removing 'Bob' from both lines. A final theoretical possibility, parallel to double demotion in triple verse, is a double offbeat realised by *two* subordinated syllables. Not having come across one in other people's lines, I offer my own:

[54] If Derby Road develops as foretold,

East Street's new houses never will be sold

This is, at least, readable, if the subordination of 'Street' to 'East' and 'new' to 'houses' is exploited; though I could be accused of cheating, since names that use 'Street' function as if they were compounds.

If the subordinated stress in the formation we have been considering is replaced by a full stress, the line reaches a degree of deviation which we might wish to call unmetricality. Nevertheless, there is no sharp boundary here between the metrical and the unmetrical, and such a line will still have a closeness to the metrical pattern which other possible sequences of syllables would lack: it observes the syllable count, it does not fall into any other common metrical pattern, and it carries at least an echo of the more acceptable double offbeat with subordinated stress. Moreover, the effect it has in five-beat verse is of adding a beat to the line, which, as our earlier discussions have shown, is less dangerous to the pentameter than losing a beat, and less upsetting to the rhythm than a similar addition would be to four-beat verse. So we should not be surprised to find that such lines do occur on occasion, especially in the verse of writers who enjoy testing the limits of the normal metrical forms of English. Browning, for instance, bends it to his own purposes in the vigorous pentameter verse of 'Fra Lippo Lippi', creating exceptional six-beat lines:[4]

(55) Hands and feet, scrambling somehow, and so dropped
     B   o   B ŏ   B   o   B   o   B̄   o   B

(56) Clench my teeth, suck my lips in tight, and paint
     B   o B ŏ B   o B o B   o   B

Here syntax and sense prevent subordination of 'feet' and 'teeth', though this is what the metre requires, and the pause encourages an implied offbeat even though there is no accompanying double offbeat. In the second case, we may prefer to rely on the subordination of 'suck' to make the line an example of initial inversion with postponed compensation, a more metrical, but perhaps less expressive, rendering of the line:

                        [s]
     Clench my teeth, suck my lips in tight, and paint
     B   o B   ŏ   B

Another of the great metrical experimenters in the English tradition, Spenser, uses the same device to heighten the tortured grief of Fradubio's lament:

(57) Wretched man, wretched tree; whose nature weak
     B   o   B   ŏ B   o   B   o   B o B

It can be used to create in the context of five-beat verse an evenly balanced line with three beats matching a further three, and hints of unrealised beats at mid-line and line-end:

(58) Beauty, strength, youth, are flowers but fading seen;
     B   o   B   ŏ B   o   B   o B o B

     Duty, faith, love, are roots, and ever green
     B o B   ŏ B   o   B   o   B o B

Or a striking pattern of three pairs of beats can emerge; this contributes to the memorability of one of Milton's best-known lines:

(59) Weep no more, woeful shepherds, weep no more
     B   o   B ŏ B o   B   o   B   o B

(The alternative is metrical subordination of the stress in 'woeful', to create a more regular pentameter with postponed pairing; sense and syntax allow this, but it greatly weakens the line's insistence.) A further situation in which it is difficult to avoid a six-beat reading is that of a line which contains more than one possible environment for metrical subordination, and there is no good reason for the preferential treatment of any one of these:

    (60) The deep groves and white temples and wet caves

One of the three adjectives would have to be metrically subordinated to achieve a five-beat line, but as all are parallel they all demand the same degree of emphasis. To pick one out arbitrarily would be invidious, and a momentary expansion of the metre to accept six beats is the only linguistically acceptable solution.

Let us now pursue further the question of what actually happens when we read a line which relies on metrical subordination. The tension created is greater than that occasioned by what might appear a very similar situation, demotion in the double offbeat of triple verse. Compare Pope's original with my rewriting in triple verse:

    (61)   View him with scornful, yet with jealous eyes,
           And hate for arts that caused himself to rise;

           +s   −s   [s]   +s
           Damn with faint praise, assent with civil leer,
           B   ŏ   B
           And without sneering, teach the rest to sneer.

    [61]   View him with scornful and terrible eyes,
           And hate him for methods that caused him to rise;
           +s   −s   +s   +s
           Damn with faint praise and assent with a leer,
           B   ŏ̇   B   ŏ B   ŏ B
           Teach, without sneering, how others may sneer.

In the rewritten version, the dominating triple rhythm allows 'faint' to function as part of the offbeat without greatly upsetting the smoothness of the line; whereas in the original it is felt as more prominent, and the tension is more markedly increased. On the other hand, the subordinated syllable is not perceived as being of the same order of prominence as it would be if it realised a beat:

          −s   −s   +s   +s
    [61b] Or with faint praise, assent with civil leer
           ŏ   B   ŏ B

The effect of metrical subordination is probably another instance of what we have called rhythmic blurring: the beat is not precisely located, and its force spreads into the adjacent syllable, momentarily blunting the sharpness of the rhythmic alternation. This effect is only possible because the deviation does not push the line towards any other common rhythm; in fact, metrical subordination can stiffen a line which might otherwise fall into a triple rhythm, as the following rewriting shows:

                          [s]
(62)   Hold like rich garners the full-ripened grain
       B   ŏ   B   ŏ   B ŏB o   B

[62a] Hold like a garner the full-ripened grain
       B   ŏ B   ŏ   B   ŏ   B

The rewritten version, as the scansion indicates, falls into a four-beat triple rhythm; in the original, the retardation caused by the subordinated stress is sufficient to keep this rival rhythm at bay.

We indicate metrical subordination in the stress pattern because it is an aspect of the relationship between the complex phonological and syntactic structures of the language and the simpler set of possibilities generated by the rules. By showing it at this level, we also imply that, however the verse is read, some rhythmic pressure will be experienced on the normal stress contours of the language. We may wish to minimise this tension between the regularity of the set and the irregularity of the language by giving the syllable in question the least degree of stress consistent with normal English pronunciation, or to heighten it by the opposite means; but it should be remembered that subordination is determined by syntactic considerations which can operate without physical embodiment, and that the power of the reader over the structure of verse is therefore limited. The pronunciation we give to any line is also circumscribed by the larger metrical context, and by all the other features of the poem; there is no point in reading Pope as though he were Shelley, or *Paradise Lost* as though it were *Pericles*.

8.4 DOUBLE OFFBEATS AND ELISION

In this and the following three sections we shall take up the various ways set out in Chapter 7 of realising the beats and offbeats of duple verse as stresses and nonstresses, and examine the complications entailed by the embodiment of this stress pattern in actual specimens of the English language. A straightforward example we have already touched on is the option in the second base rule which allows an offbeat to be realised by two unstressed syllables in duple verse. We have seen that in the strictest accentual-syllabic verse, a double offbeat is accepted only when paired with an implied offbeat, or after an initial beat; in such cases, preservation of the syllable count is crucial, and the rhythm is least complex when the two syllables in the offbeat are fully articulated as separate rhythmic units. In other duple verse environments, which are our concern in this section, the two nonstresses of a double offbeat function as a substitute for a single nonstress, and the degree of metrical tension they produce has the opposite relation to their phonetic and syntactic characteristics: the more rapid and homogeneous the pronunciation they invite, the more smoothly can they function in the rhythmic alternation. Two unreduced vowels, a clustering of consonants, or an intervening syntactic pause, all encourage the perception of two discrete syllables, and the increased complexity of a double offbeat; while a syllable which tends to disappear in pronunciation, or two vowels which run into one another, create a rhythmic effect closer to that of a single offbeat. I have already emphasised that there is no sharp distinction here (see 7.2); the double offbeat slides by insensible degrees into the single offbeat, and even an attempt at a rough distinction depends on the pronunciation one chooses to employ. To illustrate the gradations of this scale, I quote a dozen lines from a passage of *The Prelude*, with the syllables of the relevant offbeats in italics:

(63) The oth*er that* was a god, yea many gods

(64) That once *in the* stillness of a summer's noon

(65) Which yet I understood, artic*ulate* sounds

(66) Went hurr*ying* o'er *the il*limitable waste

(67) *To ex*hilarate the spirit, and to soothe

(68) A stone, and in the opp*osite* hand, a shell

(69) Had gi*ven fore*warning, and that he himself

(70) Had fall*en in* presence of a stud*ious* friend

(71) He seemed an Arab of the Bed*ouin* tribes

(72) While this was utt*ering*, strange as it may seem

(73) Of the un*wield*ly creature he bestrode

(74) Why, gifted with such *powers* to send abroad

The order here is an approximate progression from indisputable double offbeats to single offbeats with only a slight suggestion of an additional syllable, and it would be artificial to draw a dividing line at any point in the sequence. The rules which determine the rhythmic salience of any syllable are phonetic, not metrical, rules, and therefore not our direct concern; but in order to demonstrate the relationship between the two domains it will be useful to make a few general observations about the phonetic properties that are involved. We can begin with a distinction between the two ways in which a sequence of sounds may occupy a status somewhere between one and two syllables, which I shall call *contraction* and *coalescence*. (We are not concerned here with alternative pronunciations or historical changes involving the complete loss of a syllable: in such cases the metrical options are clearly defined.)

Contraction occurs when an unstressed vowel before a consonant may be pronounced very lightly or omitted altogether, and the lines already quoted can be used to exemplify some of the phonetic features which make this possible. The reduced vowel [ə] is most susceptible of contraction since it is already attenuated. Thus the penultimate syllable of 'articulate' in (65), if it is pronounced with an unreduced vowel, is less easily contracted than the equivalent syllable of 'uttering' (72), which has [ə] in the same position. Furthermore, there seems to be more freedom to contract a vowel when there is an adjacent consonant of a type which will allow it to take over a part of the vowel's rhythmic function. If the consonant that follows is a continuant (a continuous sound, as opposed to the instantaneous sound of a plosive), especially a sonorant (*r, l, m,* or *n*), its duration allows it to function to some degree as a surrogate vowel; this means that the rhythmic structure of the word or phrase is not totally transformed if the vowel is omitted, since a shadow of the missing syllable remains. Examples above are 'opposite' (68) and 'uttering' (72). A preceding continuant can also share this rhythmic role, as in 'given' (69) and 'fallen' (70), and the vowel in such cases need not be followed by a second continuant – *spirit*, for instance, is often monosyllabic. We may note finally that the disappearance of a vowel between two consonants creates new neighbours which may or may not prove compatible: try reading examples (63) and (64) with any of the italicised vowels missing, and you will find that articulatory organs which obey English speech habits are unhappy with the resulting succession of sounds. 'Opposite' in (68) also creates slight phonetic discomfort if the vowel is omitted, because the unvoiced *p* does not lead easily into the voiced *s* (phonetically [z]); and in (69) the sequence of *v* and *n* which would result from the dropping of the second vowel of 'given' is not a normal conclusion to a syllable (note how much easier it would be if the second consonant could be shifted to the next syllable, as in *given away*). On the other hand, the combination of consonants that is left when the middle vowel of 'uttering' (72) is not pronounced is a very natural one in English, hence the ease with which contraction occurs to make it a disyllabic word – with the slight duration of the *r* to adumbrate the missing syllable.

The other way in which the distinction between one and two syllables can be diminished, which I am calling 'coalescence', is by the running together of two adjacent vowels, at least one of them unstressed, whether between two words or within a single word. Coalescence can be divided into two broad categories. One of these is almost the converse of contraction, in that the first vowel plays a rhythmic role similar to that of a consonant. The *i* of 'studious' (70), for example, can be pronounced as a full vowel, producing a trisyllabic word, or as the consonant *y* (in strict phonetic terms, the semivowel or glide [j]), yielding a disyllabic word with only a suggestion of an additional syllable. In 'hurrying' (66), the process is thwarted by the similarity of the two vowel sounds, and the join is not as seamless. In (71), 'Bedouin' can have three syllables, or two plus a vestigial third manifested as [w]. This type of coalescence occurs easily between a word ending in *y* and one beginning with a vowel: one example which poets are fond of is *many a* pronounced as two syllables. The second type of coalescence involves the flowing of one vowel into the next to create a diphthong or a triphthong; examples of this happening between words are 'the illimitable' (66), and 'To exhilarate' (67). In careful speech such words retain most of their individual syllabic force, but a rapid pronunciation brings them closer to a single syllable. Within the word, the process is smoother: 'unwieldly' (73) and 'powers' (74) can be pronounced with four and two syllables respectively, or by the coalescence of the adjacent vowels, with three and one. In fact, this type of coalescence is often made easier by the use of the chameleon sounds [w] and [j], and the effect is then not clearly distinguishable from that of the first type.

Contraction and coalescence, then, are essentially principles of latitude in English pronunciation, allowing variations in speed and style of utterance; although I have used examples from verse, the same points could be made from specimens of normal speech. Such freedom is invaluable to the poet attempting to accommodate the substance of the English language to a regular metrical pattern. Sometimes the complete dropping of a syllable, whether by contraction or coalescence, or in an alternative pronunciation sanctioned by convention, is shown in print by the poet, publisher, or editor:

(75) And gan t'augment her bitterness much more

(76) Extreme, and scatt'ring bright, can love inhere

(77) Who for his pains is cuff'd, and kick'd

Such abbreviations shift camps as the centuries pass: easy colloquialisms become poetic affectations; essential guides to pronunciation turn into superfluous ornaments. But they pose no problem for the reader or prosodist, who can pronounce or scan the line without paying any attention to the missing syllable, unless there are reasons to suspect an error or a different printing convention. But when, in the absence of any graphic indication, there are metrical reasons for regarding a syllable as carrying less than full syllabic weight, we need to invoke a metrical practice which is merely a conventionalised form of the phonetic phenomenon we have been discussing, though it goes by a host of forbidding names – 'syncope', 'apocope', 'synaloepha', and 'synaeresis' among them. I am appropriating the most familiar of these terms, *elision*, to do duty for all types, and am concerned only with the distinction between elision by contraction and elision by coalescence. The former can be shown by means of a bracketed symbol in the stress pattern:

$$\quad\;\; +s \quad (s) -s \quad +s$$
(78) And shuddering still to face the distant deep
$$\qquad\;\; B \quad\; o \quad\;\; B$$

And elision by coalescence requires a symbol uniting two vowels:

$$\qquad\qquad\quad +s \quad -s \quad +s$$
(79) With throngs promiscuous strow the level green
$$\qquad\qquad\quad B \quad o \quad\; B$$

By indicating elision in the stress pattern we imply that it creates a slight degree of tension at that level, though we can leave unchanged the symbols below the line which show the simplest realisation of the metrical pattern. When the pronunciation is so natural as to create no tension, however, there is little point in showing elision; 'powers' in (74) could be shown as a simple monosyllable.

The choice between showing a double offbeat or an elision in the scansion can be an unreal one, and the important feature is the inherent elidability of the phonetic material, not the actual pronunciation. Tennyson said of his use of 'tired' in 'The Lotos-Eaters' that it was 'neither monosyllabic nor disyllabic, but a dreamy child of the two' (quoted in *Poems*, ed. Ricks, p. 431); while the hint of a triple rhythm within the duple metre of Marvell's 'wingéd chariot hurrying near' will be felt whatever pronunciation one gives the middle two words. There is, however, one general guide to the reader and scanner, already mentioned in the previous chapter: the observance or nonobservance of pairing conditions. In verse which does not observe the double offbeat condition, the poet is free to introduce additional unstressed syllables, as long as the duple rhythm is not threatened; for instance, it is clear from the first few examples among the lines from *The Prelude* quoted earlier that the double offbeat condition is not being strictly adhered to, and it seems appropriate, therefore, to invoke elision only when the pronunciation naturally vacillates between one and two syllables, as in two or three of the later examples. Sometimes the choice is between a double offbeat and a triple offbeat, in which case we can assume that elision is implied, as in this line from the same passage:

(80) Gathering upon us; quickening then the pace
    B   ŏ B

It remains true that most of the unpaired double offbeats in Wordsworth's verse exhibit some degree of contraction or coalescence in a normal pronunciation; in other words, they are not the most rhythmically deviant type of double offbeat, and Wordsworth himself may have regarded all of them as being, at least in theory, elidable. Browning, on the other hand, frequently introduces unelidable double offbeats into duple verse, as many as three (and on occasion even four) in a single pentameter (see Hatcher, 1928, Ch. 6):

(81) From the terrible patience of God? 'All which just means
     ŏ   B ŏ B   ŏ B

A poet who is observing a strict syllable count, however, will ensure that every unpaired extra syllable is elidable. In scanning such verse, therefore, we can show double offbeats only when the pairing conditions are met; otherwise two syllables in an offbeat must be contracted or coalesced. Such poets use elision only when it is phonetically appropriate, of course, with the slight qualification that poetic convention sometimes exerts an influence as well. Coalescence across word-boundaries, for instance, which is not the smoothest form of elision, may have met with wide approval because of its impeccable classical and European pedigreee; even Pope uses it, and objects, mimetically, to verse which does not do so:

(82) Though oft the ear the open vowels tire

And the treatment of *h* as a vowel in such elisions may have more to do with Latin precedent than English pronunciation; one is certainly not surprised to find it in verse as steeped in the classics as Milton's:

(83) Night's hemisphere had veiled the horizon round
　　　　　　　　　　　　　　B　　o　B

There is one context in which double offbeats, without elision and without an accompanying implied offbeat, sometimes occur in verse which is otherwise relatively strict: when the two nonstresses are separated by a syntactic break. The situation here is usually the reverse of elision, since the pause helps to keep the two nonstresses apart, and the result is to create in effect two shorter lines, the first with a feminine ending. It is almost exclusively used in dramatic verse, especially where there is a change of speaker:

(84) Wake Duncan with thy knocking: I would thou couldst
　　　　　　　　　　　　　　　　　ŏ

(85) Out of this fearful country!
　　　　　　　　　　　　　　Behold, sir King
　　　　　　　　　　　　　ŏ

Milton, for all his metrical variety, does not use this licence in the epic poems nor in *Samson Agonistes*, but *Comus* contains several examples (see Weismiller, 1972, pp. 1041–4):

(86) Alone and helpless! Is this the confidence
　　　　　　　　　　　ŏ

As we have noted (5.3), there is a tendency to avoid feminine endings that are not followed by a syntactic boundary; that is, the preference for a break between the two syllables in an unpaired and unelided offbeat extends to the interlineal domain.

In all the examples of elision quoted, the elided syllable has an unstressed syllable on at least one side; that is, it is part of what would be, without the elision, a double (or triple) offbeat. A syllable with stresses on both sides is not a likely candidate for elision; for one thing, most such syllables function as an offbeat between two beats. But even when the metre accepts adjacent stresses, as in demotion or pairing formations, elision is uncommon between the stresses, and one reason for this lies in the rhythmic character of the language. Although the rhythmic configurations of speech have no metrical pattern underlying them, the general tendency towards an alternating sequence of stress and nonstress functions in a somewhat similar way. A rapid pronunciation of 'never again' may involve the contraction of the second syllable of 'never', creating an alternation; but such a contraction is not as likely in the phrase 'never advertise', where it would only disrupt the alternating sequence. Poets responsive to the needs of the language are unlikely to demand such elisions in verse, except in cases where the elided form is very common in its own right. One such example in the English tradition is the elided pronunciation of *heaven*,[5] which is almost always used in verse like Milton's as a stressed monosyllable, even in the context of demotion or implied offbeats:

(87) That shook Heaven's whole circumference, confirmed
          B   ŏ   B

(88) Heaven's cheerful face, the lowering element
       ŏ   B

(89) And Heaven's high arbitrator sit secure
          B   ŏ   B

(90) Of those Heaven-warring champions could be found
        ŏ   B   ô B

None of these lines would be metrical by Milton's standards if 'Heaven' were disyllabic. Nevertheless, he retains the right to use it as a disyllable on occasion: in the following example, its second syllable brings the line into conformity with the implied offbeat condition:

(91) Pleased, out of Heaven shalt look down and smile
       B   ŏ   B   ŏ   B ô B   o   B

As this last example suggests, elision, like all metrical and prosodic options, is governed by one strong constraint; it can occur only when this makes possible the realisation of the appropriate metrical pattern. Where the metrical pattern demands two syllables, elision cannot occur, as in (82). The following line could be a three-beat line with elision:

(92) Still clutching the inviolable shade
     o   B   ŏ   B   ŏ   B

But its context makes it clear that it realises a five-beat pattern by means of promotions, and takes advantage of neither of the possible elisions:

(92) Still nursing the unconquerable hope,
     Still clutching the inviolable shade
     o   B   o   B̄   o Bo B̄ o   B

Poets occasionally flaunt this metrical opportunism in a single line:

(93) Being had, to triumph, being lacked, to hope
     o   B   o Bo   Bo B   o   B

Lines like this are a further demonstration that the reader's response to rhythm is not a response merely to objective details of sound: one does not have to read the two occurrences of the word in different ways, since the metrical context allows the same pronunciation – emphasising neither alternative – to realise in one case an offbeat, in the other a beat and an offbeat.

To end this discussion, some characteristic lines from *Paradise Lost* will illustrate the rhythmic variety which can be created, even in strictly syllabic verse, by a poet who takes advantage of the freedom offered by the elidability of many English syllables:

(94) Shade above shade, a woody theatre
                        Bo B̄

     Of stateliest view. Yet higher than their tops
     B   o   B   B   o   B̄

     (s)
     The verdurous wall of Paradise up sprung;
     B   o   B

          (s)
     Which to our general sire gave prospect large
     B   o   B

Into his nether empire neighbouring round.
   B   o   B   o   B

And higher than that wall a circling row
 B o   B̄

Of goodliest trees loaden with fairest fruit
 B   o   B

One does not have to be on the lookout, as one reads, for syllables in need of elision; Milton has already done the work in choosing the right metrical and phonetic conditions, and only a reasonable sensitivity to the stress-timed rhythm of English is necessary. Some readers, it is true, will want to emphasise the syllabic regularity of Milton's verse by eliding phonetically wherever possible; while others will prefer to bring out its rhythmic variety by the opposite means; but the difference does not amount to much. We have observed that when contraction or coalescence occurs, a trace usually remains of the missing syllable, and this makes its own contribution to the rhythmic vitality of the verse. There is no point in taking sides in a debate between eliders (who brandish historical evidence) and non-eliders (who, like Saintsbury, champion the 'trisyllabic foot'); the language itself effects the necessary compromise. Once more, we are responding not to centiseconds of syllabic duration, but to the structure of words, and that structure is something which we, as speakers of English, remain aware of over a wide latitude in actual pronunciation: words which are variable as to number of syllables are always perceived as such, not one thing at one time and quite a different thing at another. In scansion, however, it makes good sense always to show elision in verse which forbids extra unstressed syllables except when they occur in compliance with the double offbeat condition or when they are phonetically (or conventionally) elidable; to do otherwise is to ignore not only a principle according to which the poem was written, but more importantly, one of the most delicate features of the verse's rhythmic texture.

8.5 PROMOTION AND DEMOTION

The promotion of nonstresses to the role of a metrical beat seems to be a phenomenon very little affected by the linguistic structures in which it occurs, which is not surprising in this, the least marked of metrical deviations. We can accept any three nonstresses as realising a sequence of offbeat, beat, offbeat, though, as we have seen, we do not necessarily experience the beat as sharply localised on the middle syllable unless this syllable is slightly more prominent than its neighbours. Promotion can occur in the case of three monosyllables:

(95) This thought is as a death, which cannot choose

One or more syllables can be part of a polysyllable:

(96) Who, doomed to an obscure but tranquil state

(97) No hungry generations tread thee down

Or all three syllables can be part of the same word:

(98) Through Eden took their solitary way.

We have also noted examples where two of the three syllables constitute an entire word ((8)–(10) of this chapter). In all these examples one can sense the natural alternating rhythm of English co-operating with the metre in the promotion of the middle nonstress; this is particularly noticeable in the case of polysyllables, since a syllable at one remove from the main stress – like the first syllable of 'generations' in (97) – will often carry some degree of secondary stress. If in the case of monosyllables the syntax encourages a slightly greater emphasis on the promoted syllable, the result will naturally be smoother; thus 'as' in (95) is a somewhat easier promotion than 'an' in (96). Poetic practice reflects even such slight differences: Tarlinskaja (1976, pp. 252–3, Table 14) found that in her sample, most poets used articles less frequently in the position of the beat than any other type of monosyllable. Promotion and elision are often interconnected; in (98), for instance, 'solitary' has to be read as a four-syllable word, because if it is reduced to three, promotion is impossible, the line loses a beat, and one of the most finely controlled of all concluding paragraphs in English literature comes down with a bump.

Nor is promotion a respecter of syntactic boundaries, as the following examples testify:

(99) To rear the column, or the arch to bend

(100) No uttered syllable, or, woe betide!
　　　　　　　o B̄ o

(101) Of a surpassing brightness. At the sight
　　　　　　　　o　　B̄　o

We can give these pauses as unhurried a treatment as we like without losing the effect of promotion – which is not surprising when we consider that promotion also occurs, as the rule indicates, when there is nothing at all before or after the promoted nonstress, that is, at line-opening or line-end. One further point to note is that if either of the outer syllables is given extra weight, the metre itself is not threatened; it is shifted towards the different, more complex, formation of pairing. If, for instance, we wish in (95) to stress 'is' more strongly than the following two syllables, the beat is attracted towards it, and stress-timing both encourages a pause after 'thought' and speeds up 'as a':

　　+s　　　+s −s −s
(95) This thought is as a death, which cannot choose ·
　　　B　　　ôB　ǒ

There are not two hard-and-fast alternatives here: some blurring of the rhythm is possible in a normal reading, though as soon as one tries to identify the rhythmic pattern, say by tapping, one is forced to opt one way or the other. Hesitation between the two can, however, be experienced as rhythmic tension:

(102) Of darkness visible so much be lent
　　　　　o B̄　o　　B
　　　　　ǒ　　Bô　B

Here the need to give 'so' a certain degree of emphatic stress prevents the smooth operation of promotion, while the need to keep it subordinate to the more strongly emphasised 'much' inhibits pairing. The result is a rhythmic uncertainty which is felt in any reading of the line.

Demotion, too, occurs in a variety of linguistic contexts, and can operate over syntactic boundaries. Here are some examples:

(103) If I could joy in aught, sweet interchange
　　　　B　　　　　　　ô　B

(104) A thousand wings, by turns, blow back the hair
　　　　　B　　　　　ô　　　B

(105) Fare ill, lie hard, lack clothes, lack fire, lack food?
　　　 ŏ　 B　 ŏ　 B　 ŏ　　 B　　 ŏ　 B　 ŏ　 B

(106) The long day wanes; the slow moon climbs; the deep
　　　　 B　 ŏ　 B　　　 B　 ŏ　 B

(107) The still, sad music of humanity
　　　　 B　 ŏ　 B

(108) And that must sleep, shriek, struggle to escape
　　　　　 B　　 ŏ　　 B

It will be evident that, although these are all acceptable by the demotion rule, and not the kind of line we would want to exclude from pentameter verse, they do vary in rhythmic tension. When the middle of the three stresses is naturally subordinate to either or both of its neighbours, the pattern fits closely into the alternating pattern of the metre (which is also the preferred rhythm of English speech). Thus in (103) the adjective is subordinate to the noun, and it is natural to give 'aught' an emphatic stress, so tension is kept to a minimum. The relevant phrases in (104) might be pronounced differently in a different rhythmic context (try 'A thousand helpers blow back Linda's hair'), but what comes most easily here is a relatively stronger stress on 'turns' and 'back' than on 'blow'. In (105) the natural subordination of a verb to a following adverb or noun, especially at the end of a clause, creates an exceptionally slow but highly regular series of alternations. Tension is perhaps greater in (106), though the number of demotions is smaller, and the syntax does not demand pauses. This is because we cannot subordinate the middle stresses to both partners; as nouns they dominate their preceding adjectives, and need at least as strong a stress as 'long' and 'slow' to avoid giving these adjectives a false semantic salience (this day and moon are not being differentiated from any others). The nouns are in their turn subordinate to the verbs that follow, however, so that the principle of alternation is partly saved, and the rhythm endures not a breach but an expansion.

Example (107) illustrates a common structure for this metrical formation, two adjectives and a noun, though of a type which insists on full weight being given to both adjectives and which slows down the rhythm even more than the preceding examples. Sense as well as syntax encourages us to pause between 'still' and 'sad', which almost has the effect of inducing an extra beat on the latter syllable. Some other combinations of double adjective and noun have a much slighter effect on the rhythm because they can be taken as a single phrase without pauses: 'ten low words', 'fine red hat'. In such cases the second two words form a subsidiary unit within the phrase, and the subordination of the second adjective to the noun is therefore more strongly felt. The rhythm is even more markedly slowed in (108), where three verbs of equal importance occupy the pattern. Read as prose, the three stresses would certainly all function as rhythmic peaks; in the context of duple verse, it may be possible to suppress the beat on the middle syllable in some way. However, as with extreme cases of metrical subordination, it may be more accurate to say that we sometimes accept six-beat lines in pentameter verse, though only under certain very special conditions which we have learned to recognise. But perhaps an even more accurate report on the psychological experience of reading such a line would be that the rhythm is suspended when we come to those three stresses; that our ear accepts what happens as the equivalent of two beats and an offbeat, but that it does not locate these events precisely. It is, in other words, a further example of the blurring of the rhythm such as we find in the opposite phenomenon, three equally unstressed syllables, though it has a more pronounced effect on the movement of the line.

These differences in the tension produced by demotion as a result of different linguistic structures are, of course, often used expressively. Milton can convey both smooth and rough movements by means of demotion, using syntactic structures that fit snugly into the metrical pattern for the first and catalogues that resist subordination for the second:

> (109) Now came still evening on, and twilight gray
>   ò   B   ò B
>   Had in her sober livery all things clad
>   B   ò   B
>
> (110) O'er bog or steep, through strait, rough, dense, or rare,
>   B   ò   B
>   With head, hands, wings or feet pursues his way
>   B   ò   B

It is, of course, possibly to multiply monosyllables in a list even further and still keep technically within the metrical rules; a line beloved of prosodists is Milton's

> (111) Rocks, caves, lakes, fens, bogs, dens, and shades of death
>   ò   B   ò   B   ò   B   o   B   o   B

Although the line can be 'saved' by the rules, no sensitive ear can hear it as a normal pentameter. Nor is there any point in trying to make it sound like one by emphasising particular words, as is sometimes suggested; the line stands as an example of Milton's stretching of his verse to the limits of metricality (though it should be noted that it does not take the far more disruptive step of introducing a rival metre), and we can share with him some intellectual satisfaction in knowing that in theory it breaks no rules. (The mimetic appropriateness of the suspension of clear metrical structure at this point is obvious.) It is interesting to observe that Milton follows the practice of the classical hexameter in ending the line with a reassertion of the metrical norm; and Tennyson, another self-conscious metrist who learned a great deal from Latin verse, does the same in a line which clearly imitates Milton's:

> (112) Rain, wind, frost, heat, hail, damp, and sleet, and snow
>   ŏ   B   ŏ   B   ŏ   B   o   B   o   B

None of these examples tempts the reader to give the middle stress *more* weight than the outer two, and so upset the alternation; when such lines do occur, they make special demands on the reader, as in the following:

> (113) Big as a Jew's head cut off at the nape
>   B   ŏ   B   o   B̄

We have to give 'Jew's' and 'cut' as much weight as 'head', and leave 'off' unstressed so that 'at' can take the next beat by promotion. This reading does not contradict the norms of the language, and, it may be added, serves to bring out most fully the perverse passion of Browning's Bishop. Metrical needs do not always serve expressive needs in this way, however; in the following example, the sense demands a slow, emotionally-charged, enunciation, while the strong four-beat metre of the poem insists on a brisker movement to allow demotion:

> (114) For while the tired waves, vainly breaking,
>   o   B   o   B   ŏ   B   o   B   o
>   Seem here no painful inch to gain

If the reader is seduced into giving even a hint of a second syllable to 'tired', 'waves' insists on a beat to itself, and the rest of the line becomes a metrical embarrassment.

This is not the limit of tension between the stress pattern demanded by syntax and meaning and the principle of alternation, however; it sometimes appears that the demoted stress is actually stronger than one of the stresses that realise the beats:

(115) Here on this spot of earth. Search, Thea, search
          B   ŏ   B

(116)   Is that an angel there
       That holds a crown? Come, blessed brother, come!
       B   ŏ   B

It is difficult to see what natural reading could render these lines acceptably rhythmical by means of demotion. The repeated injunctions in (115) must be given strong emphasis, and the use of pitch as in examples (27) and (28) will not serve, while 'Thea' is obviously spoken as an unemphatic address to a companion. Similarly, in (116) the third syllable of the trio is part of an address, and could only be given as strong a stress as the previous two if an unusual emphasis on the adjective were semantically justified. We are in fact once more on a borderline between two metrical variants; the dramatic force of these lines is probably better conveyed by a reading that allows the third stress to be metrically subordinated, as in example (49) above:

                                    [s]
(*115*) Here on this spot of earth. Search, Thea, search
          B   ŏ B   ŏ

It should be clear that in examples like these we are dealing primarily with syntactic relations themselves, and only secondarily with the patterns of sound by which those relations manifest themselves. Thus in Milton's line, (111), it is the syntax which gives the succession of nouns equal weight, and no sleight of pronunciation can override that structure; the freedom to use different cues for stress so helpful in cases of semantic emphasis and contrast is of no avail here. Nor is the relationship between syntax and metre easily reducible to rules; we should not assume from (115) and (116), for instance, that a sentence break after the first stress will always make demotion difficult. Let us rewrite a very ordinary example of demotion to explore this point (I quote a few earlier lines to establish the metrical context):

(117)   [...] 'twas my joy
       With store of springes o'er my shoulder hung
       To range the open heights where woodcocks ran
       Along the smooth green turf. Through half the night
       B   ŏ   B

[117a] Along the turf. Smooth lawns were ranged around
       B   ŏ   B

[117b] Along the turf. Smooth green embankments rose
           B   ò   B

Only the second rewriting markedly affects the rhythm, because in the first it is still possible to subordinate 'smooth' to 'lawns' and so preserve the feeling of alternation. In [117b], however, 'smooth' is not subordinated to the next word, and comes closer to attracting a beat to itself, creating a significant increase in tension. One could multiply examples of the interaction of metrical and linguistic form indefinitely, but it is more important to ensure that we have the right terms in which to discuss such examples than it is to catalogue them.

The demotion of syllables before the first beat is affected by the linguistic substance of the line in similar and self-evident ways, and it will not be necessary to do more than furnish some examples, illustrating that the stronger the stress on the syllable in question in relation to what follows, the more difficult it is to discount it from the rhythmic structure, and therefore the greater the tension:

(118) Keen pangs of love, awakening as a babe
            ò   B

(119) Love alters not with his brief hours and weeks
            ò   B

(120) Say, vagrant Muse! their wiles and subtle arts
            ò   B

(121) Thee, Serpent, subtlest beast of all the field
            ò   B

(122) Hide, hide them, million-myrtled wilderness
            ò   B

In (118) and (119) the natural subordination of the first stress to the second makes these openings not very far removed from the normal iambic opening, and the rhythm, though it is slow to get under way, is not threatened. This cannot happen in (120), however, where 'Say' attracts a beat by its emphasis and syntactic isolation; the most rhythmical reading is perhaps to treat the stress on 'vagrant' as metrically subordinated and allow a double offbeat, or at least to blur the rhythm in this direction. However, in (121) this way out is prevented both by the sense ('Thee' and 'Serpent' each demand a stress) and by the linguistic structure of the sentence ('Serpent' is not subordinated), while the repetition in (122) categorically insists that both syllables receive the same degree of stress. As with some of the more extreme occurrences of demotion within the line, such examples can be regarded as legitimate stretchings of the metre, temporary suspensions of the rhythmic alternation which do not carry the verse into the foreign territory of another metre, but offer the language a chance to enforce the claims of its own rhythmic nature against those of a simple pattern of beats and offbeats.

8.6 PAIRING AND SYNTAX

The most disruptive variation in regular styles of duple metre is the pairing of stresses and nonstresses in the familiar patterns +s +s −s −s and −s −s +s +s, and it is not surprising, therefore, to find that the actual linguistic material used in these formations is crucial to their rhythmic effect. We shall consider first the less common form, stress-initial pairing, which the classical approach terms 'inversion'. In order to understand the preference shown by poets for certain syntactic structures in this formation, we need to examine with some care the metrical dangers which it is constantly courting. Consider the following two examples from the same poem:

> (123) At Sestos Hero dwelt; Hero the fair
>   B ǒ   B ǒ
>
> (124) When Venus' sweet rites are performed and done
>   B ǒ B   ǒ

In the first example, the sense and syntax invite a strong stress on each of the syllables taking a beat, and the implied offbeat occurs naturally in the pause between the syntactic units. But in the second example, the adjective 'sweet' is subordinate to the noun 'rites' in normal pronunciation, and in order to bring out the five-beat structure of the line, it is necessary to give the first word an emphasis which is somewhat artificial in view of the conventionality of the epithet. If one does not do this, the line slips into a jaunty triple rhythm; indeed, it would be perfectly acceptable in the context of free four-beat triple verse:

> When Venus' sweet rites are performéd and done
> o B ǒ˘   B   ǒ B ǒ   B

We have seen that this kind of demotion is very common in triple verse.

The possibility of a quite different rhythm asserting itself constitutes a greater threat to the integrity of the metre than a straightforward increase of tension would do, and the practice of poets shows that there is a general tendency to avoid a syntactic organisation which subordinates the first stress to the second in this formation. Since the final stress in a phrase is very rarely subordinated, a common way of achieving this is to separate the stress by some kind of syntactic break, as in (123). There is no danger of the first stress becoming a demoted member of a double offbeat, and the implied offbeat takes its place naturally in the syntactically determined pause between the stresses, throwing into prominence the familiar rhythmic unit, $+s -s -s +s$. In (124), on the other hand, the syntactic subordination of the first stress to the second, the tendency of the language to avoid successive stresses, and the absence of any syntactic boundary between the stresses, all conspire to tip the rhythm in the direction of a triple movement. This threat can be utilised to heighten the emphasis on a pair of stressed monosyllables, since a reading sensitive to the demands of the metre has to give them equal weight in order to prevent the slide into an alien rhythm (though it is a risky procedure, relying as it does on the fallible reader rather than the immutable structures of the language):

(125) And trouble deaf heaven with my bootless cries

(126) As testy sick men when their deaths be near

The strain involved in supporting the metre is apparent; Booth (1977, p. 180) finds (125) 'metrically puzzling', and we have already noted the expressive effectiveness of its jarring rhythm (pp. 13–14).

Some metrical analysts build the preference for a syntactic break in this formation into their rules (for example, Chisholm, 1977; Kiparsky, 1977): but it is a feature not so much of the metrical structure as of the interplay between the constraints of the metre and the variables of the language. A few more examples will give some indication of the range of possibilities:

(127) What words had passed thy lips, Adam severe

(128) A little boat tied to a willow tree

(129) The eagle soars high in the element

(130) To shun the heaven that leads men to this hell
                                   B   ŏ   B   ŏ

(131) Bold nature that gives common birth
       To all products of sea and earth
       B ŏ   B   ŏ

There is no danger of subordination in (127); both stresses take full
weight, the final phrase has the familiar +s −s −s +s shape, and the
dislocation is as slight as it can be in this formation. Although (128) has
no punctuation between the stresses, there is again a syntactic break,
this time a phrase boundary, preventing subordination and allowing a
pause for an implied offbeat. A comma here would be legitimate, but
the metre itself encourages the correct pronunciation, with the
emphasis on 'boat' rather than the adjective that precedes it. The
danger of misreading is greater in (129), where at first one may be
tempted to make 'soars' subordinate to 'high', and to treat 'in the
element' as a quite separate phrase, a danger which is increased by the
possibility of reading 'element' as a triple line-ending:

(*129*) The eagle soars high in the element
         o B   ŏ'   B   ŏ   B ŏ

But of course what is required is full weight on 'soars' and a pause
before 'high', which is to be read as part of a single phrase to the end of
the line, where promotion provides the final beat. The need to read the
line as a pentameter thus clarifies the syntax. Metrical demands also
heighten the semantic colouring in the next example (130); a
misplaced emphatic stress on 'men' would produce a four-beat line,
whereas the proper emphasis on 'leads' yields a firmly conclusive
pentameter. (An alternative reading is to dispense altogether with the
stress on 'men' – the sense of which is almost 'us' – and to promote 'to'.)
There is perhaps less semantic justification for the metrically necessary
emphasis on 'all' in (131), though the more insistent four-beat rhythm
provides stronger metrical stiffening than a five-beat rhythm would; a
further problem here is the placing of word-boundaries, which will be
discussed in the following section.

In free uses of the pentameter, such as dramatic blank verse, it is
possible to find lines in which the only way of avoiding a four-beat
triple rhythm is to give an unstressed syllable an artificial stress in order
to create a pairing formation:

                          +s
(132) To see thy Antony making his peace
       Bŏ   B   ŏ

This may have sounded less abnormal to Shakespeare than it does to us, since there is evidence to suggest that secondary stress has declined in prominence since the sixteenth century (see Dobson, 1968, p. 445); it is noticeable that the syllables in question are usually ones which might attract such a stress (Groves, 1979, pp. 55–6, 151–3, cites a number of Shakespearean examples in which this is the case). Similar pronunciation changes may also account for the following lines from Shakespeare's *Sonnets* and from *Paradise Lost* respectively:

(133) The forward violet thus did I chide
                          +s
                 B ŏ̂ B   ŏ

(134) Which but th'Omnipotent none could have foiled
                      +s
                B ŏ̂ B   ŏ

It is possible, as Groves argues from a different point of view, that in some styles of pentameter – notably in dramatic verse – a strong internal pause can function like a line-ending in allowing promotion of a nonstress (we have already seen that in the matter of additional nonstresses a line-internal break can have the same effect as a line-ending):

(135) Under my battlements; come you Spirits
               –s –s
           o B̄   ŏ B

A quite different way of avoiding the danger posed by stress-initial pairing with subordination is exemplified by the following lines:

(136) He in the first flower of my freshest age
       B ŏ   B ô B   ŏ

(137) Break with the first fall: they can ne'er behold
       B   ŏ   B ô B   ŏ

(138) Ah, but a man's reach should exceed his grasp
               s   s
       B   ŏ B ô B   ŏ

In these examples, there is strong subordination of the first stress to the second (made stronger in (138) by the contrastive stress on 'reach'); but there is no danger of a triple rhythm asserting itself, because in each case the stress-initial pairing is preceded by an initial inversion which produces a legitimate double offbeat and prevents the subordinated stress from itself becoming part of an unwanted double offbeat. At worst, the effect approaches that of three successive nonstresses, with some blurring of the line's second beat. A rewriting of (138) will illustrate what would happen if the initial inversion were absent:

[138a]   A living man's reach should exceed his grasp
        o B ŏ́   B   ŏ B   o B

The only way to combat this four-beat reading would be a wholly unnatural emphasis on 'man's', and even then the absence of any syntactic or semantic justification for the emphasis would render it merely a matter of sound – and as we have repeatedly had cause to observe, our response to rhythm is not merely a response to the sound.

Turning now to the reverse formation, stress-final pairing, we can again note the effect of a syntactic break between the two stresses:

(139)   We'll visit him, and his wild talk will show
              ŏ   B   ô B

(140)   With frantic gesture and short breathless cry
            ŏ   B   ô B

In the first of these, the implied offbeat falls between an adjective and its noun while in the second it falls between two equivalent adjectives separated by a slight syntactic break (which could be represented by a comma). Once more there is a difference in rhythmic effect, but it is now in the opposite direction, and the reason for this is quite clear: the risk of one of the stresses losing its weight and combining with an adjacent nonstress to create a double offbeat and a triple rhythm is now located in the *second* of the stresses. Subordination of the first to the second stress, as in (139), is now harmless, since a double offbeat already exists before the two stresses; but a syntactic break between the stresses, as in (140), creates the possibility that the second stress will be subordinated to a later stress, and suffer demotion within an unwanted double offbeat. Add to this the fact that the ear has already accepted one double offbeat in the line and is therefore not averse to accepting another, and it becomes obvious why in this formation poets usually avoid syntactic breaks, or, more generally, subordination of the second stress. The alternative rhythm which lurks around a line like (140) is again that of a four-beat triple-metre line with demotion:

      With frantic gesture and short breathless cry
       o   B   o B   ŏ   B   ŏ̈   B

Of course, Shelley's line can be defended on expressive grounds: we are forced to give 'breathless' a strong stress to preserve the metre, and the resulting tension is entirely appropriate to the meaning. Other writers encourage careful emphasis on a pair of adjectives by the same method; Spenser and Shakespeare, for instance:

(141) Our lovely lasses, or bright shining brides
      o B o B ŏ   B ŏ B

(142) When to the sessions of sweet silent thought
     B ŏ B   ŏ   B ŏB

Both these run a strong risk of being misread: Spenser's adjectives are relatively conventional, and hence do not seem to deserve the weight which the metre requires them to carry; and Shakespeare has implanted such a strong suggestion of a triple metre by means of two double offbeats, that it demands a firm thrust against that rhythm on 'silent' to save the line. In the first example the result is a slight awkwardness, in the second a sudden focusing on an apparently tautologous adjective, which gains from the added attention drawn to it by the demands of the metre. Nor are these the most extreme examples of lines which require deliberate stiffening as we read: the following can only be understood metrically as examples of stress-final pairing, but the triple rhythm is knocking hard at the door:

(143) From hence your memory death cannot take
            ŏ B ŏ B

(144) By night he fled, and at midnight returned
          ŏ   B ŏB

(145) My eyes to fathom the space every way
          ŏ   B ŏB

The explanation for such lines may lie partly in the diminishing importance of subsidiary stressing in English pronunciation already alluded to (we shall reconsider (144) in this light in section 8 below), or in a more deliberate style of verse delivery than is current at present; but perhaps the most significant fact about them is their uncommonness in all periods.

The most frequent syntactic units making up the pair of stresses in this formation, therefore, are the ones most avoided in its mirror image: adjective+noun or verb+noun. Noun+verb is less common, because the direction of subordination is often from the latter to the former, creating the unwanted triple effect, as a construct will show (the first scansion represents the more natural rhythm):

[146] Alas, if the worm eats the fruit, it dies
     o B   ŏ   B   ŏ̆   B o B
     o B   ŏ·   B ŏB   o   B o B

If a break between the stresses does occur, the danger of a triple rhythm can be averted by ensuring that the second stress is not a subordinated part of the syntactic unit that follows:

(147) Productive in herb, plant, and nobler birth
              ŏ   B ŏ B

(148) But bare of laurel they live, dream, and die
               ŏ   B ŏ B

(149) With his broad, bright, and dropping orb were gone
           ŏ   B ŏ B

Another way of avoiding the danger is to follow pairing with a promoted nonstress:

(150) And wit was his vain, frivolous pretence
           ŏ   B ŏ B o B̄

Here there is no possibility that the first syllable of 'frivolous' will be rhythmically weaker than the third, and so create a triple rhythm. It is clear that we are not dealing with distinctions that could be captured in simple rules requiring or prohibiting syntactic boundaries between the stresses, but with the specific circumstances of individual lines, in which metrical, phonological, syntactic, and semantic properties all play a part.

As we noted in discussing its rhythmic properties, stress-final pairing is especially common at the opening and closing of the line. The metrical freedom of the line-opening means that a double offbeat is less likely to suggest a triple rhythm, and the first two stresses in the line are less likely to belong to different syntactic units than later pairs. Pope, in whose metrical practice stress-final pairing is relatively rare, quite often uses it at this point:

(151) And the long labours of the *toilette* cease
         ŏ   B ŏ B

Position, syntactic structure, and phonetic substance – together with the tendency to extend 'long' in speech to emphasise its meaning – all make this the least disruptive of implied offbeats, and the slowing down of the rhythm a very gentle process (too gentle for the sense, we may feel – until we learn what the 'long labours' are). Compare this to

the opening of one of Shelley's most savage lines, where alliteration
joins with metrical and syntactic necessity to give strident emphasis to
the stressed words:

(152) Till they drop, blind in blood, without a blow
       ŏ   B ŏ B

Some reasons for the favouring of the line-end for stress-final pairing
have already been suggested, but a further one is that in this position
the danger of slipping into another rhythm is least present, since the
second stress is followed by a line boundary:

(153) I wished the man a dinner, and sat still
             ŏ   B ô B

Even when emphatic stress creates a reversal of subordination, it is too
late in the line to shift the rhythm into triple gear (the italicisation in
this example from *Don Juan* is Byron's own):

(154) She loved her lord, or thought so; but *that* love
                ŏ   B ô B

    Stress-final and stress-initial pairings can occur in sequence, the
middle stress doing duty in both formations (see pp. 178–9 above).
This happens most smoothly when the syntactic structures match the
metrical structures, three strong stresses realising the three successive
beats:

      +s   +s   +s
(155) Of the wide world, dreaming on things to come
      ŏ   B ô B ô B   ŏ

          +s   +s   +s   −s
(156) This day, when my soul's form bends toward the east
          ŏ   B ô B ô B   ŏ

      +s   +s   +s
(157) And the fleet shades glide o'er the dusky green
      ŏ   B ô B ô B   ŏ

We are more used to treating three successive stresses as beat, offbeat
by demotion, and beat, and if the middle stress is syntactically
subordinate to its neighbours, this reading – which results in a
four-beat line – is hard to resist:

[155a] Of the great wide world and of things to come
       ŏ   B   ŏ   B   ŏ   B   o B

Browning does occasionally write a line like this:

(158) From the old cold shade and unhappy soil

The reader has the option of a four-beat line (which, as we have seen, Browning seems to have accepted as an occasional variant in pentameter verse), or a somewhat artificial stress on the monosyllabic adjectives. On the other hand, the same trio of words that realise three beats in (155)–(157) could equally well realise two if the metre demanded it, though the rhythmic effect would be different – a smoother, more rapid flow, with less individual highlighting of each item:

[155b] Of all the wide world, dreaming endless dreams
        o B   o B   ò   B o B   o   B

In comparing stress-initial and stress-final pairing, it may seem that the latter is at a disadvantage in preferring to do without a syntactic break, and hence a possible pause, at the point at which the implied offbeat occurs. However, it is worth recalling our earlier comparison of the two formations in 7.6: we noted that stress-final pairing often makes use of a blurred rhythm, capitalising on subordination of the first to the second stress to move the −s −s +s +s pattern some way towards −s −s −s +s, with promotion of the middle nonstress. A syntactic break between the stresses prevents this rhythmic drift, creating a harsher jolt (as in Shelley's lines (140) and (152) above). In stress-initial pairing, on the other hand, subordination would have to occur in the opposite direction to create a similar effect (we noted a possible example in (130)), and it is more usual to find the implied offbeat clearly localised between the two stresses, causing a more marked displacement of the beat. It is not surprising, therefore, that stress-final pairing is the more common type, and is especially favoured by poets who prefer smooth rhythms. Pope's use of stress-final pairing with subordination can be associated with his use of metrical subordination (see section 3 above), since both rely on syntactically and therefore phonologically weakened stresses to stretch the metre without snapping it; what he tends to avoid are forms which require sharply defined implied offbeats and their attendant disruption of the easy movement of the line.

8.7 PAIRING AND WORD-BOUNDARIES

Even more delicate in their rhythmic effect than syntactic boundaries are word-boundaries. We do not normally pause between words unless there are syntactic reasons to do so, yet it appears that even the difference between, say, two monosyllables and an apparently identically stressed disyllable can have rhythmic consequences. We have already discussed the role of word-boundaries in creating rising and falling rhythms (4.6), but there is evidence that they play a less obvious part in the realising, or thwarting, of metrical structures. Consider the following examples of stress-final pairing:

(159) And growing still in stature the grim shape

(160) Remembering not, retains an obscure sense

These lines have an identical pattern of stresses and nonstresses, yet the type of pairing in (159) where the middle two syllables of the formation ('the grim') belong to different words, is much more common than that in (160), where they are part of the same word ('obscure') – a feature which I shall call *linkage*. Tarlinskaja (1976, p. 286, Table 44) finds only 24 clear examples of stress-final linkage (which she calls 'autonomous polysyllables in juncture inversions') in some 13,000 lines of nondramatic iambic pentameter verse from Spenser to Swinburne; and there are no examples at all in her samples of over 600 lines each by Spenser, Jonson, Dryden, Pope, Thomson, Byron (*Childe Harold*), Browning, Tennyson, Rossetti, and Swinburne. (This contrasts with 1,939 examples of stress-final pairing *without* linkage – *loc. cit.*, total of column 6.) Bailey (1975b, p. 43), investigating syllabically strict tetrameter verse with its tighter restraints, found no clear examples in 2,762 lines. Creek's figures (1920, p. 86) for the placement of 'iambic words' (i.e. words with a pattern of nonstress–stress) also show that they very rarely occur in this relation to the metrical structure. These differences are too great to be statistically explained by the higher frequency with which the sequence −s +s is realised in the language by pairs of monosyllables rather than by disyllables. It is important, however, not to overstate the case; such formations *do* occur in the work of a variety of writers, in all parts of the line, and when they do the rhythmic movement is not destroyed.

Here are several examples, with the authors named, and the linkage
indicated:

(161) To set the exact wealth of all our states (Shakespeare)
ŏ   B   ŏ   B

(162) Shall behold God, and never taste death's woe (Donne)
ŏ   B   ŏ   B

(163) Through the pure marble air his oblique way (Milton)[6]
ŏ   B   ŏ   B

(164) He clothed the nakedness of austere truth (Wordsworth)
ŏ   B   ŏ   B

(165) Some people prefer wine – 'tis not amiss (Byron)
ŏ   B   ŏ   B

(166) Another clipped her profuse locks, and threw (Shelley)
ŏ   B   ŏ   B

(167) Of abrupt thunder, when Ionian shoals (Keats)
ŏ   B   ŏ   B

(168) The complete fire is death. From partial fires (Empson)
ŏ   B   ŏ   B

Before we consider the significance of this restriction and the
exceptions to it, we need to give some attention to the traditional way
of dealing with lines like (161)–(168) by treating them as the product
of historical changes in pronunciation. Some examples from earlier
periods can be explained in this way; there is independent evidence from
orthoepists in the sixteenth and seventeenth centuries that certain
disyllables could be stressed on either the first or the second syllable
(see Dobson, 1968, pp. 446–8). Metrical analysts who assume that all
verse aspires to a condition of absolute regularity invoke this 'variable
stress' or 'recession of accent' in order to deny completely the
existence of stress-final linkage (it is one of the weapons wielded by
Van Dam, 1900, in his bid to fit all Shakespeare's lines to his
Procrustean prosody); and the same assumption underlies historical
studies of pronunciation which use lines with apparent linkage as
evidence for stress shifts (see Kökeritz, 1953, Appendix 2, for
example). But if the poetry of earlier periods were really studded with
disyllables that could be freely pronounced with initial or final stress,
we would expect far more lines like the following one from *The Faerie
Queene*:

(169) Then came hot July boiling like to fire

To give 'July' the modern pronunciation with a final stress renders the line far less regular than any of examples (161)–(168), whereas an initial stress produces an acceptable line:

+s −s

Then came hot July boiling like to fire

o   B   o   B o   B o   B̄   o B

In such a case, it is legitimate to argue that the line constitutes evidence of an earlier pronunciation of *July* with initial stress; and there is in fact supporting evidence outside verse for this pronunciation of the word (see Dobson, 1968, p. 447). Such lines, however, are rare; and discussions of 'recession of accent' invariably concentrate on the more common phenomenon of stress-final linkage.

A metrical set for alternating rhythm will always exert pressure on the two middle syllables of a syntactically unified pairing formation to blur or exchange their stresses; it is, of course, the language's resistance to this interference with its internal structures that creates the tension associated with the device of pairing (though the metre is only heightening a tension in the language itself between lexically-determined stress patterns and a rhythmic preference for alternation). Analysts who invoke 'variable stress' to account for every occurrence of linkage are finding (or inventing) historical reasons for yielding to this pressure; and even when there is independent evidence for a change in accentuation the modern reader may prefer the tension of a pairing formation to the oddity of an obsolete pronunciation. Even if we could be certain that *complete* was always given an initial stress in Elizabethan English, we might still choose to give it its modern pronunciation in the following line:

−s   +s   +s

(170) A maid of grace and complete majesty

o   B o B

There are, it is true, a few polysyllables in present English which yield to the alternating pressure of the metrical set. We have already noted that the relatively weak stress of minor category polysyllables permits some variability; examples (12) and (13) in section 1 of this chapter show how words like *without* and *against* can lose their internal stress contrast within what would otherwise be a stress-final pairing with linkage. Another type of polysyllable with some degree of variability is the word with a detachable prefix; the following lines invite a reading with prefix and stem given the same degree of stress to permit demotion instead of pairing (in the first example, I include the preceding line to show the neutral stress pattern of a similar word when it co-operates with the metrical alternation):

(171) Thou dost beguile the world, unbless some mother.

For where is she so fair whose uneared womb

(172) The pangs of disprized love, the law's delay

Disyllables in which the weaker syllable retains some degree of secondary stress can operate in the same way to avert pairing with linkage:

(173) I met a traveller from an antique land

Since a word's present pronunciation is a product of its phonological history, there is a blending of synchronic and diachronic perspectives at moments like this (as there is, in other ways, at every moment of our reading of the texts of the past): one cannot be sure whether an inherent feature of the modern pronunciation is being capitalised on, or an older pronunciation is being brought back to life by the pressures of the verse form. In the end, the problem of 'variable stress' is not simply one of historical reconstruction, but of a balance of tensions created by the deliberate (and unavoidable) mismatching of metrical form and linguistic structure. If we assume that stress-final linkage is a valid and valuable rhythmic variation, much of the apparent evidence for alternative pronunciations disappears, together with the need to invoke them.

Even without recourse to theories of pronunciation change, however, the evidence of a general tendency to avoid linkage in stress-final pairing is plentiful. What we are dealing with, therefore, is a particular relationship of word-boundaries to metrical pattern that occurs too rarely to be accepted as a normal feature of the metrical tradition (which is what the Halle–Keyser rules imply – see especially Halle and Keyser, 1971b, pp. 169–71), but too often to be completely excluded by a metrical theory (which is the effect of the rules proposed by Chisholm, 1977) or to have major theoretical claims based on its absence (as is done by Kiparsky, 1977). There is evidently a rhythmic difference between the two types, not very noticeable when a direct comparison is made, but marked enough to be revealed in the practice of poets over large bodies of verse; weak enough to be ignored in freer styles, but strong enough to be the basis of a condition in stricter metres. The need that so many commentators and editors have felt to explain away the linked form by invoking pronunciation changes, while accepting the unlinked form without question, is itself further evidence of the perceptual reality of the distinction.

What then is the precise difference in rhythm between the two forms, with and without linkage? Let us repeat our first examples:

(*159*) And growing still in stature the grim shape

(*160*) Remembering not, retains an obscure sense

We noted in the previous section that in examples like (159) there may be some rhythmic seepage from 'grim' (which is subordinated to 'shape') to 'the', taking us a little way towards the rhythmic pattern in which 'grim' would be weakened and 'the' would become the focal point of the beat. To go further and allow the beat actually to shift to the normally unstressed syllable would, of course, be a highly unnatural reading, but it would at least do no damage to the *lexical* structures involved. In (160), on the other hand, there can be no such rhythmic blurring, since the lexical identity of 'obscure' depends on the contrast of stress between the syllables. So this can be nothing other than a full-blooded instance of an implied offbeat between two syntactically connected words, with the maximum rhythmic tension of which this deviation is capable. One can imagine an apprentice poet stressing every second syllable of his line to make sure he has written a correct iambic pentameter, and passing (159) in spite of the oddly stressed 'the' in such a reading, while rejecting (160) because of the way it reverses the stress pattern of 'obscure'. This is, of course, a crude notion of the poet at work, but this elementary procedure may not be unrelated to the nuances of rhythmic intuition which have kept such lines out of Spenser's or Pope's poetry.

Discussions of linkage have usually been confined to stress-final pairing, which is traditionally viewed as a completely different phenomenon from stress-initial pairing. If the two formations are related, as I have argued, we would expect to find in the other type a similar avoidance of linkage across the middle two syllables, and an investigation of this possibility will throw a little more light on the problem of word-boundaries and pairing. The picture is complicated, however, by the preference in stress-initial pairing for a syntactic break between the stresses, allowing a natural pause to do duty for the implied offbeat, and creating a relatively discrete rhythmic unit over the following four syllables, the familiar +s −s −s +s. When the first stress and nonstress of this pattern belong to the same word, the lexically-determined contrast is part of its distinctive shape, and so there is no tendency to blur it. An example already quoted will show how naturally linkage occurs under these conditions:

$$+s \qquad +s\ -s \quad -s$$
(123) At Sestos Hero dwelt; Hero the fair
$$\quad\quad\quad\quad\quad\ \text{B}\ \ \text{ŏ}\quad \text{B}\ \ \text{ŏ}$$

The regularising effect of a pause between the stresses is evident even when the syntactic break in this position is relatively slight, as long as some integrity is allowed to the rhythmic pattern that follows it (though the third example below was still harsh to Johnson's ears, judging from his complaints about it in *The Rambler*, No. 86):

(174) We shall be called purgers, not murderers
$$\quad\quad\quad\quad\quad\quad \text{B}\quad \text{ŏ}\ \text{B}\quad\quad\quad \text{ŏ}$$

(175) The light whose smile kindles the universe
$$\quad\quad\quad\quad\quad\quad\quad\quad \text{B}\ \text{ŏ}\ \text{B}\quad\quad \text{ŏ}$$

(176) And the soft wings of peace cover him round
$$\quad\quad\quad\quad\quad\quad\quad\quad \text{B}\quad \text{ŏ}\ \text{B}\ \text{ŏ}$$

The more frequent use of linkage in stress-initial than in stress-final pairing is substantiated by Tarlinskaja's statistics (1976, pp. 283–4, Table 43): in the same body of verse referred to earlier, she finds 172 stress-initial linkages, compared with 465 occurrences of monosyllables (the equivalent figures for stress-final pairing being 24 and 1,939).[7] Her figures also show that polysyllables occur frequently in initial inversion: here too the +s −s −s +s pattern has a rhythmic identity which accommodates lexical stress contrasts with perfect ease. (In the stricter conditions of tetrameter verse, however, there seems to be a stronger restriction: Bailey (1975b, p. 45) finds only one stress-initial linkage in his sample, and Tarlinskaja's count for four-beat verse (1976, p. 261, Table 27) points in the same direction.) However, in order to assess the degree of symmetry between the two forms of pairing, we need to isolate stress-initial linkage which occurs without a preceding syntactic break, for it is only under such circumstances that there might be found a tendency towards blurring which linkage would prevent. Unfortunately, none of the statistical studies mentioned makes this separation, but my own investigation suggests that this type of stress-initial linkage is at least as rare as its stress-final equivalent (and one must take into account the fact that there is a larger stock of stress-initial words available in the language). Kiparsky (1977) may be overstating the case in claiming that Shakespeare never uses stress-initial linkage when there is not at least a phrase boundary to the left, but it is certainly very unusual in his work. Stress-initial pairing without a pause between the stresses is, in any case, not very common because of the danger of creating a triple-rhythm four-beat line discussed in the previous section, but when it does occur it is nearly always without linkage:

(177)   The first sort by their own suggestion fell
          B   ŏ B   ŏ

The pressure to avoid stress-initial linkage is also shown in the behaviour of polysyllables with relatively weak or variable stresses, as is the case with words like *without* and *antique* in the reverse formation. In the following line, we are tempted to reduce 'almost' to two equally weak stresses, and to put all the semantic weight on the next word, rather than to give utterance to an uncompromising stress-initial pairing with linkage (though a dramatic reading might justifiably prefer the latter):

(178)   Yet in these thoughts myself almost despising
                          B   o B̄   o B
                          B   ŏB   ŏ   B

But, as with stress-final linkage, there is no absolute prohibition: examples of stress-initial linkage without a preceding syntactic break are to be found in poetry of all periods, especially in freer styles of pentameter. Wyatt and Surrey furnish instances:

(179)   The vain travail hath wearied me so sore
          B   ŏ B   ŏ

(180) The swift ⌈swallow⌉ pursueth the flies small
        B ŏ   B   ŏ

Possible examples from Shakespeare's dramatic verse include the following:

(181) And much ⌈different from the man he was
        B   ŏ B   ŏ

(182) We are the queen's ⌈abjects⌉, and must obey
        B   ŏB   ŏ

Milton, as we noted in Chapter 2 (p. 48), has a few such lines:

(183) Which tasted works ⌈knowledge⌉ of good and evil
        B   ŏ   B   ŏ

(184) Of this round world, whose first ⌈convex⌉ divides
        B   ŏ B   ŏ

As one might expect, Browning's liberal pentameters include occasional lines of this sort:

(185) And years make men ⌈restless⌉ – they needs must see
        B   ŏ B   ŏ

(186) Ungenerous thrift of each ⌈marital⌉ debt
        B   ŏ   B ŏ

The last two examples illustrate the triple-rhythm threat that attends this formation: 'men' and 'each' require a somewhat self-conscious stressing to preserve the pentameter structure.

Once again, the explanation for such lines from earlier periods may lie in changes of pronunciation, but examples like these do not constitute proof of such changes, and it appears to be a reasonable conclusion that, once the effect of syntax is taken into account, stress-initial linkage is like its mirror image in being rare but not unknown. The slight rhythmic difference that is at stake here can be illustrated by comparing a stress-initial pairing without linkage (and without a syntactic break) with a rewriting that introduces linkage:

(187) Methought I heard some old man of the earth
        B   ŏ B   ŏ

[187a] Methought I heard some old ⌈woman⌉ of earth
         B   ŏ B   ŏ

In [187a] the need to press straight on to the rest of the word, with its inbuilt stress contrast, seems to heighten the challenge to the rhythm, whereas the self-sufficiency of 'man' in the original allows the voice to do some rhythmic adjusting. The distinction between self-arrested and disyllabic stress discussed in 3.2 may be pertinent here too: in the following version of the line the need to move on to the second syllable of the linking word is not as urgent because the stress is self-arrested, and the result is perhaps a little more rhythmically relaxed:

[187b] Methought I heard some old stranger of earth
B   ô   B   ŏ

Notice that one result of the restrictions on linkage in both types of pairing is that the inner stress of the formation must be a monosyllable, except, in the case of stress-initial pairing, when it follows a syntactic break. Since a demoted stress, too, can only be a monosyllable (setting aside the special problem of compounds), it is possible in a theory based on strong and weak positions to state that in strict duple verse all full stresses which occur in weak positions are monosyllables, apart from those which follow syntactic breaks (as is done, for instance, by Kiparsky, 1975). Such a 'rule' is a good example of a merely abstract generalisation which obscures the metrical features that underlie it; what is more, it offers no distinction between metrical and unmetrical lines, since the description applies not only to all the former but also to a large number of the latter.

It will be worth pursuing the question of linkage into one more metrical province: that of postponed pairing and postponed compensation. The linking word normally forms a bridge between the pair of offbeats and the pair of beats (in whichever order they occur), but in the case of postponed pairing these are separated by at least two syllables. Do the restrictions on linkage apply to this formation, and if so, at which point?

In stress-initial postponement, linkage seems to cause no increase in tension when it involves the double offbeat; an example already discussed is the following:

(188) How many bards gild the lapses of time!
B   ô B   o B   ŏ

However, it does appear to increase the irregularity when it involves the syllables immediately after the implied offbeat: the following

rewriting runs less easily as a pentameter than the original, and is
rhythmically more like examples (179)–(186):

[188a] How many bards ⌐burnish¬ lapses of time
          B   ŏ B o   B   ŏ

In a metrical theory based on the filling of weak and strong positions,
this distinction will show up as an avoidance of word-initial stressed
syllables in weak position when preceded by a stressed syllable, as in
[188a], or in (179)–(186), but an acceptance of a similar stress when
preceded by a nonstress, as in (188) (see above, p. 48). Kiparsky
(1977, p. 201) quotes in illustration several lines of Milton's in which
linkage occurs in the latter context, the majority of them involving
initial inversion with promotion and postponed compensation:

(189) To the ⌐garden¬ of bliss, thy seat prepared
     B̄   o   B   ŏ

Once again, by ignoring the underlying rhythmic distinctions involved,
the abstract formulation gives a false impression of the nature of the
regularities observed: what is in fact avoided is linkage involving the
beat after an implied offbeat, so the restriction does not apply to the
double offbeat in postponed pairing, and is irrelevant to postponed
compensation.

In the stress-final formation, postponed pairing is so rare that the
additional tension created by linkage is scarcely significant, but the
same distinction does seem valid; if one of the two rewritten examples
below can be said to increase the metrical dislocation of the original, it
is the second, in which the linkage precedes the implied offbeat:

(190)   Your business is not to catch men with show
               ŏ   B o B ŏ B

[190a] Your business ⌐expects¬ to catch men with show
              ŏ   B   o B ŏ B

[190b] Your business does not ⌐invite¬ men with show
              ŏ   B o B ŏ B

The placing of word boundaries in postponed pairing therefore
suggests that the constraints on linkage in all types of pairing are the
result of the unusual rhythmic conditions created by an implied offbeat
which fails to coincide with a syntactic break, and that the double
offbeat is a relatively harmless partner in the affair.

In general, it seems safe to conclude that stress-final and stress-initial pairing are very much alike in the conditions they impose on word-boundaries when the four syllables of the formation function together as a single rhythmic unit, and that the reasons in both cases are the same. The infrequency of stress-final linkage, therefore, cannot be explained as an avoidance of 'inversion across foot-boundaries', as is sometimes done by metrists who employ a classical approach (for instance, Tarlinskaja, 1976, p. 150; Kiparsky, 1977): the same avoidance of linking words occurs in stress-initial pairing when the syntactic circumstances are equivalent, even though in this case the 'inversion' occurs within the 'foot'. The discussion by Kiparsky (1977) of the role of the phrase boundary in metrical rules suggests that this analysis could be extended to less close linkages than that of the word, and it might be possible to formulate *linkage conditions* to account for the restrictions observed in certain metrical styles. This type of constraint on the relationship of linguistic and metrical structures is an illuminating instance of the fine discriminations that constitute the metrical knowledge acquired by poets and readers within the English tradition, analogous to those tiny features of syntax and phonology which, though we do not become aware of them unless they are pointed out by a linguist, we scrupulously observe whenever we speak our own language.

8.8 COMPOUNDS

The relationship between metrical patterns and linguistic structures becomes particularly problematic in those cases where a close match is not possible. Not every linguistic formation slips easily into an alternating or triple rhythm, but poets are understandably loath to exclude any of the resources of their language from their verse. With regard to duple verse, the most important body of individual words which comes into this category consists of certain types of compound, and these words have consequently been the subject of much metrical debate. A satisfactory metrical theory should at least facilitate accurate identification of the problems they cause.

In compounds formed from two monosyllabic words, the second word is usually subordinated to the first but retains some degree of stress (see the discussion in 3.3), and the easiest way to use them in verse is in contexts which permit an indefinite stress on this syllable:

$$+s \qquad s \quad +s$$
(191) But later ages' pride, like corn-fed steed
$$ B \quad o \quad B$$

$$ +s \qquad s \qquad +s$$
(192) And burn the long-lived Phoenix in her blood
$$ B \qquad o \qquad B$$

$$ +s \qquad s \quad +s$$
(193) Old knights, and over them the sea-wind sang
$$ B \qquad o \qquad B$$

Any degree of stress on the second element of the compound, up to equality with the first, can be accommodated here, since demotion is always possible. Disyllabic compounds also occur quite often in situations like the following:

$$ +s \qquad -s \qquad -s \ -s \ +s$$
(194) Or ever sleep his eye-strings did untie
$$ B \qquad o \qquad \bar{B} \quad o \quad B$$

$$ +s \quad -s \qquad -s \qquad -s \ +s$$
(195) Fair seed-time had my soul, and I grew up
$$ B \qquad o \qquad \bar{B} \qquad o \quad B$$

I have shown the second element as unstressed, but if it is given sufficient stress to attract a beat the line does not become unmetrical:

$$ +s \qquad +s \qquad -s \ -s \ +s$$
(*194*) Or ever sleep his eye-strings did untie
$$ B \quad \overset{\circ}{o} \quad B \qquad \overset{\vee}{o} \quad B$$

It is probably accurate to say that the two patterns merge, and some blurring of the rhythm occurs: we have already noted that this seems to be a common feature of stress-final pairing, but that it is rare in the stress-initial variant because of the problems posed by subordination when the two stresses are part of the same phrase. If both stresses belong to the same compound, however, these problems do not arise, because it is the second element that is subordinated – there is no threatening triple rhythm in (194) as there is in (128)–(131).

Something similar happens in lines like the following, in which two scansions are again possible, depending on whether the second item in the compound is treated as a stress or a nonstress, and a reading may include hints of both:

(196) Thy beauty's shield, heart-shaped and vermeil dyed
$$ B \qquad \overset{\circ}{o} \qquad B \qquad o$$
$$ B \quad \hat{o} \ B \qquad\qquad \overset{\circ}{o}$$

(197) And green wood-ways, and eyes among the leaves
$$ B \qquad \overset{\circ}{o} \qquad B \quad o$$
$$ B \quad \overset{\circ}{o} \ B \qquad\qquad \overset{\vee}{o}$$

'Wood-ways' occupies a position in which a simple polysyllable would be rare because of the constraints on linkage discussed in the previous section; but it is precisely its status as a compound, with some degree of rhythmic independence for each of its components, that makes it acceptable here.

When the second item of a disyllabic compound does not fall in a metrical position which tolerates either stress or nonstress, however, the degree of unease with which it occupies its place depends on the nature of the compound. Familiar compounds which have virtually become single lexical items will function happily when a stress–nonstress sequence is demanded, but will cause difficulties if only two stresses will suit the metre. On the other hand, rare or newly-minted compounds in which both elements carry a heavy semantic burden will do best in the latter context. Compare the following lines by Keats:

$$-s \quad -s \qquad +s \qquad +s$$
(198) Of fruits and flowers, and bunches of knot-grass

$$-s \qquad\quad -s \quad +s \qquad +s$$
(199) Not pined by human sorrows, but bright-blanched

Unless the line is to lose a beat, the final syllable in these examples must have a stress as strong as its predecessor; and we find this much easier in the case of 'bright-blanched' than 'knot-grass'. Pronunciation changes may be responsible for some of our problems; a disyllabic compound was more likely in early modern English to have a secondary stress (see Dobson, 1968, pp. 445, 830–34), and Renaissance poetry seems particularly rich in compounds that demand two strong stresses, where we would give only one:

(200) And an earth-quake, as if it straight would lose

(201) As the death-bed whereon it must expire

(202) By sudden onset: either with Hell-fire

(203) By night he fled, and at midnight returned

There is, of course, a certain degree of fluidity at the borderline between the categories of compound and phrase, reflected in orthographic uncertainties both now and in the past; Thorpe's 1609 printing of Sonnet 73, for instance, gives 'twi-light' and 'Sun-set' but 'death bed', and in Sonnet 62 both 'selfe-love' and 'selfe love' occur. In forms of verse in which a strong rhythm dominates the linguistic material, compounds can more happily provide two beats; an example used in Chapter 4 provides an illustration:

(204) Sing a song of sixpence
      B   o B   o Bŏ B

Yeats uses a four-beat line with the fourth beat unrealised in 'The Cap and Bells' to create a strong rhythmic pulse, which is powerful enough to push the main stress on to the second element in a compound:

(205) But the young queen would not listen;
                                 s   +s
      She rose in her pale night-gown
      o B   ŏ   B   o   B   [o B]

Bailey (1975a) recorded ten speakers reading the poem, and notes that nine 'appeared to move the stronger stress to the second element' of 'night-gown' (p. 26).

The poet who wishes to use a compound which has successive stresses plus an additional unstressed syllable – like *dog-owner* or *land-grabber* – has to pick his way even more carefully, since the commonest treatment of the disyllabic compound, demotion of the second stress, is denied him in duple metre. If the compound can be treated simply as a stress and two nonstresses, which will only be possible if it has become familiarised and is acting as a single word, there is no problem. Kiparsky (1977, p. 221) notes that in Shakespeare words like *bedfellow* and *torchbearer* are consistently treated in this way:

                                      +s −s −s
(206) I have this twelvemonth been her bedfellow
                                          B o B̄

(It is interesting to note, however, that the words Kiparsky mentions occur most frequently at line-end, which suggests that the final syllable is most easily promoted when it has no competing syllable, however weak, after it.) Pope seems to be relying on this pronunciation in the following line, though the unfamiliarity of the compound makes it difficult to suppress the second stress:

              +s   −s   −s   −s
(207) Each word-catcher that lives on syllables
        B   o   B̄   o

As this example suggests, a freshly-coined compound, where both elements requre some emphasis, does not sit happily in this position: it results in a stress-initial pairing without a syntactic break between stresses (without even a full lexical boundary), and a disruptive linkage of the kind discussed in the previous section. Magnuson and Ryder (1970) find no examples of this type of compound in this relation to the metre in Shakespeare's sonnets, and Beaver (1976) finds only two in nearly 1,500 lines of Donne's verse.

Such compounds function more easily in metrical environments which permit the first stress to be demoted:

(208) Thy hair soft-lifted by the winnowing wind

(209) Self-empire, and the majesty of love

Alternatively, each stress can take a beat in a pairing formation:

(210) To dry the rain on my storm-beaten face

(211) But that two-handed engine at the door

(212) Of the soon-fading jealous Caliphat

The danger here is that the subordinated second stress will be weakened to a nonstress, creating a double offbeat with the nonstress that follows, and succumbing to a triple rhythm. If 'storm' is given too much emphasis in (210), this is what happens; and it is even harder to avoid this temptation in the following line, where an iambic inversion has already introduced a double offbeat and a suspicion of tripleness:

(213) They are the daughters of sky-ruling Jove

Once again, historical changes in the pronunciation of compounds may make it harder for us to give such lines the reading they deserve.

The most difficult of these compounds to match with a duple metre are probably those that occupy an intermediate position between the completely assimilated type whose natural pattern of stresses is

+s −s −s, and the type in which both words clearly carry a strong stress, +s +s −s. Kiparsky (1977, p. 222) notes the complete absence of certain compounds from Shakespeare's verse, including *hedge-sparrow*, *cock-pigeon*, and *grave-maker*, which may have fallen between the stools in this way. The natural home of all trisyllabic compounds of this type, whatever the degree of subordination, is triple verse, in which the second two syllables function easily as a double offbeat:

(214) He paid what he could with his ill-gotten pelf
    o B   ŏ B   ŏ B   ŏ B

In this discussion of compounds, as in the earlier sections of this chapter, we have been focusing on some of the fine detail of the relationship between a relatively simple metrical form (the sequence of stresses and nonstresses generated by the metrical rule upon the foundation of a given metrical pattern and underlying rhythm) and the complex gradations and hierarchies of the actual stress contours and rhythmic progressions produced by linguistic structures and semantic content. The discussion could be prolonged indefinitely, since every lexical and syntactic formation has its characteristic sound pattern, and every phrase and sentence its range of possible semantic colourings which receive expression at least in part through stress and rhythm. It will be enough if this consideration of some aspects of the topic has demonstrated not only that the relationship is complicated, but also that it is not haphazard.

Notes

1. Emphatic stress has posed problems for many metrical theories: see, for instance, the disagreements between Stein (1956) and Chatman (1956b), or between Halle & Keyser (1966, 1971b) and Magnuson & Ryder (1970), or Beaver's shifting position in successive studies (1968a, 1969, 1971a, 1976).
2. An interesting account, along these lines, of the rhythmic multiplicity that can be implied by a single line of regular verse is given by Scott (1980, pp. 5–7). The subject is discussed further in 9.6 below.
3. It is interesting to note that in the four-beat verse studied by Bailey (1975b), metrical subordination occurs occasionally in his samples from most poets before the twentieth century, but not at all in Eliot, Auden, or Graves (p. 75, Table II).
4. Hatcher (1928, p. 91) calls this 'one of the most numerous of Browning's variations', and cites several examples.
5. In one of the first published discussions of English metre, this word caused problems because of its common contraction to a monosyllable: see Harvey & Spenser (1579–80, pp. 98–9), and Attridge (1974, pp. 146–7).

6. Though there are several examples in *Comus* and the first three books of *Paradise Lost*, there are no clear examples in Milton's later work, suggesting that he became increasingly sensitive to the rhythmic effect of this formation (and also that it cannot be explained away by pronunciation changes) – see Bridges (1921, pp. 70–73) and Sprott (1953, pp. 136–7).

7. Since Tarlinskaja includes initial inversions in her totals, it is necessary to subtract these in order to reach figures for stress-initial pairing.

Part Four: Practice

Chapter 9

The functions of poetic rhythm

In asking why English verse is characterised by particular rhythmic properties, and in looking for ways of talking precisely about those properties, I have constantly implied, but given no specific attention to, possible answers to a different question: what is the function of rhythmic organisation as an aspect of poetic language? Since the most obvious distinction between prose and verse is a rhythmic one, it is a question that confronts the function of poetry itself as a form of language and art, and to discuss it in detail, without taking anything for granted, would demand another book. Let us merely remind ourselves what such a study would entail: it would be an attempt to explain why the practice of organising a very small selection of the features of the spoken language into a strictly limited set of patterns has manifested itself over a range of verbal activity from the most infantile to the most sophisticated, in a variety of cultural contexts from the most elite to the most popular, and in a historical continuum that shows no signs of coming to an end; and why specimens of language ordered in this way have been almost universally acknowledged to possess a power and an appeal not shared by any other linguistic productions. By contrast, all I shall be doing in this chapter is bringing under brief scrutiny some widespread views of the functions of rhythm in verse, in order to relate more fully the foregoing theoretical account to the actual practice of poetry, before I turn to an even more pragmatic approach in Chapter 10.

But first, some further disclaimers are necessary. I shall make no attempt to single out a main function of rhythm; I assume that the aural organisation and movement of a poem's language operates in a variety of ways to determine, deepen, or complicate its 'effect' (a word which will have to do duty for the elusive tissue of mental and physical events involved in and produced by the reading of a poem); and although it will be convenient to separate out some of these strands, it must be remembered that they do not function in isolation, but interact with one another and with all the other elements of the poem: I shall say scarcely anything, for instance, about the manifold ways in which syntax and word-order contribute to impressions of movement and rhythm. It must also be borne in mind that literature is characterised as much by its subversion of prevailing norms as by its obedience to them, and a traditional rhythmic function, like any other literary function, can be turned on its head in the unique situation of a particular text. As in the book as a whole, I shall confine myself almost entirely to metrical verse, though much of what follows will have implications for nonmetrical verse. Though the discussion will reflect the account of metre I have given in earlier chapters, it will not illustrate the functions of individual rhythmic formations and variations; many of these will be evident already, and the passages to be considered in the following chapter will exemplify some of them further. As an additional limitation, I shall be concerned only with the importance of rhythm for the reader, though there is ample evidence for its formative role in the act of writing.[1] Nor shall I summarise or make specific reference to the mass of critical and theoretical discussion of this subject: that too would demand a separate study. What follows is largely speculative, and leaves behind the realm of empirical evidence and testable hypothesis within which we have so far tried to confine ourselves.

Although we have observed the rootedness of English metrical structures in the nature of the English language, we have also seen how these linguistic characteristics are modified by general principles of rhythmic form, and by more conventional features of the literary tradition. To examine the functions of rhythm in poetry is to ask how this process of modification invests the language's rhythmic properties with additional potency, and our attention must therefore be directed towards the distinctiveness which metre imparts to language, rather than to the common ground between them. We shall consider in this chapter a number of respects in which verse differs from other manifestations of language, making use of a broad categorisation whose inevitable element of arbitrariness will, I hope, be outweighed by its expository convenience. We can make an initial distinction between *semantic* and *nonsemantic* functions of poetic rhythm, that is, between those aspects which operate within the same space as the meanings of the poem's words, whether to reinforce, limit, expand, or modify them, and those which operate on some other axis, contributing to the total working of the poem but not to its 'meaning' in the narrow sense. This distinction corresponds roughly to a distinction that can be drawn between two ways in which verse challenges the arbitrary but indissoluble link between signifier and signified on which the linguistic sign, as envisaged by Saussure, depends: the first by creating the illusion of a peculiarly intimate connection between the physical stuff of language and its meanings rather than a conventionally guaranteed coexistence, and the second by insisting on, and taking advantage of, that arbitrariness. The first four sections of this chapter will deal with semantic functions, the last two with nonsemantic functions.

9.1 ICONIC FUNCTIONS

In considering the semantic functions of poetic rhythm, we are enquiring into the various ways in which the substance of language, perceived as a dynamic phenomenon, can itself contribute to meaning, independently of the signifying procedures of the words for which it provides a physical vehicle. We can subdivide these functions into two: those which are *externally* oriented, and work by establishing relations between the linguistic artefact and the world beyond it other than those determined by the normal processes of signification; and those which are *internally* oriented, and work by highlighting or linking elements within the poem and thereby modifying its semantic texture. This section and the two that follow it will be concerned with the former, and section 4 with the latter. We shall look first at what can be termed *iconic* functions; that is, devices which depend on some perceptible resemblance between the physical properties of language and external reality.

Faced with the unprofitable task of commenting on the part played by rhythm in the meaning of a poem, critics often turn to the notion of 'imitative form', but the apparent safety of this refuge among the shifting sands of metrical analysis may exist only in the eager imagination of the commentator and the lazy assent of his reader. The monitory specimen of such criticism given by Dr. Johnson, one of the few trustworthy guides in this treacherous territory, cannot be quoted too often. Johnson imagines his straw critic, Dick Minim, praising some lines from *Hudibras*:

> Honour is like the glassy bubble,
> Which costs philosophers such trouble;
> Where, one part crack'd, the whole does fly,
> And wits are crack'd to find out why.

> In these verses, says Minim, we have two striking accommodations of the sound to the sense. It is impossible to utter the first two lines emphatically without an act like that which they describe; *bubble* and *trouble* causing a momentary inflation of the cheeks by the retention of the breath, which is afterwards forcibly emitted, as in the practice of *blowing bubbles*. But the greatest excellence is in the third line, which is *crack'd* in the middle to express a crack, and then shivers into monosyllables.

> *The Idler, No. 60*

The parody is, unfortunately, not very far removed from what still passes at times for acceptable literary criticism.

We cannot banish the notion of imitative effects from criticism, however, though we can attempt to clarify it. I propose to make a rough distinction between two ways in which the perceived physical properties of language can function iconically in poetry, which I shall call *mimetic* and *emblematic* devices. Mimetic devices take effect as an immediate part of the reading activity, and need not reach consciousness as a separate semantic mechanism; they contribute to that sense of heightened meaning which we can experience even when we cannot explain it. Emblematic devices, on the other hand, provide relations between the linguistic substance and the larger world only by means of a conscious intellectual act; shaped poems and numerological structures are obvious instances, and a simple metrical example would be a poem on the Trinity in triple metre. The distinction is not between 'natural' and 'conventional' effects, since all literature – and all language – achieves meaning only through convention, but rather between naturalised and nonnaturalised conventions. As a result, the dividing line between the two types is subject to historical fluctuation; there may have been a time when readers responded to numerological patterns with the same unconscious immediacy with which we respond to some rhythmic patterns, and the visual dimension of the text, which at present keeps a foot in both camps, has had, from this point of view, a chequered history.[2]

The iconic resemblances discerned in poetry by commentators are often emblematic rather than mimetic, since criticism, driven by the imperious need to create a metatext to set beside the original text, will often seize upon the features of a poem most easily pointed to and talked about, instead of attending scrupulously to the act of reading and the mental habits on which it is based. I am not suggesting that we exclude emblematic interpretation from the critical repertoire, but that we recognise it for what it is – and that we recognise further that, since there is no limit imposed by the actual processes of reading, the number of emblematic devices which can be ascribed to a text is infinite. Why not look for emblematic appropriateness in the number of words in each sentence, or in the patterns made by letters with tails, or in the use of earlier or later sections of the alphabet? A further dimension is added by metaphorical slippage, as Johnson was well aware: 'The fancied resemblances, I fear, arise sometimes merely from the ambiguity of words; there is supposed to be some relation between a *soft* line and *soft* couch, or between *hard* syllables and *hard* fortune' (*Life of Pope*). It is largely the prevailing conventions of criticism, not those of literature, which render some emblematic interpretations more plausible than others: we may find ourselves accepting an emblematic analysis of a rhythmic feature not because it tallies with our experience of the poem, but because it conforms to our notions of what such an analysis is empowered to say. A problem remains, however, in that our reading of a line may be permanently altered by an emblematic analysis (even one we find implausible); it is partly in this fashion, of course, that the practice of criticism can push iconic devices over the dividing line between the emblematic and the mimetic. One way in which emblematic devices can function as a genuine part of the reading activity is by drawing attention to the role of convention itself; if, for instance, we were to encounter in a poem the word *grass* printed in green ink, any pleasure we experienced would not arise because the text represented so realistically the colours of the real world, but because it played with the norms of textual representation. This would not be a semantic contribution to the poem, however; it is closer to the type of function we shall discuss in section 6 of this chapter.

As far as rhythm is concerned, the emblematic function which has been most important in the history of verse is a general one, located in the fact of metrical organisation itself: the Neoplatonic notion that language which obeys the rules of a strict metre represents an ideal reality governed by order and harmony. The heading of the final book of St Augustine's *De Musica* (tr. Taliaferro, 1947, p. 324) presents this idea in a nutshell: 'The mind is raised from the consideration of changeable numbers in inferior things to unchangeable numbers in unchangeable truth itself.' Associated with this view is the feeling that metrical regularity purges language of its haphazardness and redundancy, an attitude eloquently expressed by Sidney (1595, sig. C4^r): 'The senate of poets hath chosen verse as their fittest raiment, meaning, as in matter they passed all in all, so in manner to go beyond them: not speaking (table-talk fashion, or like men in a dream) words as they chanceably fall from the mouth, but peising [weighing] each syllable of each word by just proportion according to the dignity of the subject.' Though our own explanations are likely to be in terms of psychological needs rather than glimpses of God, the sense of a more orderly language created by the intensive formalising procedures of metre undoubtedly remains a valued feature of regular verse, and we shall return to it in discussing the nonsemantic dimension of metrical patterning in section 5.

Turning to mimetic devices, in which the iconic representation of the world beyond the poem is part of the reading process, we find the path of criticism still beset with dangers. One is the ease with which it is possible to misrepresent the physical properties of language that enter the activity of reading, not only in the kind of impressionistic metaphor already alluded to ('strident consonants', 'smooth vowels', and the like), but also in descriptions which confuse visual and aural properties, impose theoretical divisions on continuous movement, or fall prey to one of a dozen other common misconceptions about the linguistic medium and the ways in which it is perceived. Total eradication of this source of error would demand a more definitive account of English than linguistic science has so far produced, but the discussion in Chapter 3 will have given some idea of the kind of information that is available and valuable to the literary critic. One point which will be worth reiterating, because it is assumed in much of the discussion in this chapter, is that in the analysis of verse, all references to the physical properties of language are references to its *perceived* properties, and not its objective phonic or graphic substance.

Another danger is the temptation to ascribe directly to the sounds and movements of poetic language a semantic weight and precision which they do not independently possess. The perceived features of language are semantically neutral, and they can only participate in the meaning of a poem by virtue of literary convention. An icon, although it is unlike a pure sign in that it embodies a physical similarity, still depends on learned associations; the difference between a red triangle arbitrarily signifying a major road ahead and a black cross iconically representing a crossroads is not that the latter can be interpreted without any reference to convention – a driver who knew nothing at all about the system of road-signs would be in as great danger of meeting with an accident after the cross as after the triangle. Thus to relate a rapid succession of syllables to a rapid movement in the world at large, for instance, is to rely on a learned strategy of poetic interpretation, however habitual it may have become. Given, then, that both the signs of language and the mimetic devices of poetry are conventional modes of representation, it is not surprising that the system which is more deeply ingrained takes precedence over the peculiarly poetic mode. If there is a contradiction between the meaning of the linguistic sign and the iconic suggestions of its physical properties, the latter are usually ignored; after all, poets have not lost much sleep over the fact that *big* is a little word with a short, close vowel, and *tiny* a longer word with an open diphthong. (Mallarmé, it is true, felt that *jour* and *nuit* had inappropriate vowel sounds – see *Crise de vers* – but this did not prevent him from using these words successfully in his poetry.) Another important point is that the semantic force of imitation is far less specific than the signified meanings of language; any sense of precision in a mimetic effect is likely to be the contribution of the linguistic system rather than the iconic resemblances. We need to take care, too, that we do not claim for the properties of language resemblances to features of the external world with which they have nothing substantial in common. Once again, Johnson's good sense is worth attending to: 'The representative power of poetic harmony consists of sound and measure; of the force of syllables singly considered, and of the time in which they are pronounced. Sound can resemble nothing but sound, and time can measure nothing but motion and duration.' (*The Rambler*, No. 94.) Any other kind of resemblance is likely to be emblematic, since it must rely on features of the verse less central to the experience of reading than sound and movement, or on the metaphorical slippage mentioned earlier.

Although the imitation of external sounds in the sounds of language is frequently mentioned in the detailed criticism of poetry, unquestionable instances are not easy to identify. The overwhelming majority of the sounds that occur in verse have no mimetic function, and operate normally as constituents of conventional linguistic signs, or, at most, call up associations with other signs within the system. If we are to respond, say, to / s / not just as one phoneme entering into significant relations with others, but as a noise produced by the expulsion of air through the teeth which may in its physical characteristics resemble other noises, the text must in some way bring this aspect of language into the reader's interpretative activity. Two ways of doing this are by strongly patterning the sounds, and by drawing attention at the level of content to the manner in which they are produced. Nabokov uses both of these in the opening of Humbert Humbert's narration in *Lolita*:

(1) Lolita, light of my life, fire of my loins. My sin, my soul.
     Lo-lee-ta: the tip of the tongue taking a trip of three steps
     down the palate to tap, at three, on the teeth. Lo. Lee. Ta.

The extravagant aural patterning of the first two sentences induces a strong consciousness of the sounds as sounds, and the third sentence then draws attention to the goings-on within the mouth, producing an acute awareness of the tongue-tip's action in pronouncing *t* and *th* eighteen times in twenty-two words. The pleasure to be derived from this bravura performance is not that of a precise piece of description, but that of a showman's trick, and its function is to alert us to the narrator's fascination with and expertise in language, his fusion of verbal and sexual delight. It is against such indisputable examples that more doubtful imitative effects should be tested.

Our strict concern, however, is with the second of Johnson's categories, the imitation of motion and duration by the rhythm of language, and here again we need to proceed with the utmost caution. 'It is scarcely to be doubted', warns Johnson in the same essay, 'that on many occasions we make the music which we imagine ourselves to hear, that we modulate the poem by our own disposition, and ascribe to the numbers the effects of the sense.' On the other hand, mimetic effects of rhythm are probably more common and more powerful than those of pure sound, with which they are often confused. A poem may or may not encourage a heightened response to the individual sounds it uses – we feel that Keats invites it more than Dryden, say – but all poetry, including free verse, produces a heightened response to the movement of language. If we say that a line of verse sounds like the ticking of a clock, what we probably mean is that it imitates the regular pulses which characterise the rhythm of that sound:

$$\overset{-s\ +s}{}\ \overset{-s\ +s}{}\ \ \ \ \overset{-s\ +s}{}\ \ \ \ \overset{-s\ +s}{}\ \ \ \overset{-s\ +s}{}$$
(2) When I do count the clock that tells the time

The repeated / k / and / t / help largely to focus attention on the stressed monosyllables which represent the clock's (perceptually) stronger ticks; the fact that they are unvoiced plosives which may be felt to have some similarity to the sound referred to is only secondary, and perhaps an emblematic rather than a mimetic feature. In the passage from *Lolita*, the reader's consciousness of the tongue's dance within the oral cavity is heightened by the prominent rhythm, which emphasises the stress-timed nature of English by keeping the numbers of intervening syllables to the limits observed by regular verse:

(*1*) The tip of the tongue taking a trip of three steps down the
palate to tap, at three, on the teeth.

As a more typical example of mimetic rhythm, we may consider the opening of Lawrence's nine-line poem, 'Brooding Grief':

(3) A yellow leaf from the darkness
Hops like a frog before me.
[s]
Why should I start and stand still?

I was watching the woman that bore me

The poem opens in a simple metre, making use of the base rules alone: each stress is separated from its neighbour by one or two nonstresses, realising a three-beat metrical pattern (or four-beat with one beat unrealised). But the third line ends unexpectedly with two consecutive stresses, and there is no easy way of relating these to a metrical pattern. Either the first would have to be metrically subordinated, as shown, which preserves the three-beat pattern but contradicts the semantic emphasis, or both would have to be given weight, to allow the line an extra beat through the agency of the most complex of deviations, an implied offbeat. Note how a continuation of the previous rhythm would have a quite different effect:

[3a] Why should I start and stiffen?

The uncertainty, which comes about only because a strict metrical set is rapidly established, and which no manipulation of the voice can overcome, is crucial to the effect: the rhythm, in a quite literal sense, 'stands still', as the alternating pattern is momentarily suspended, before beginning again with even greater regularity in the following line. Though it has no mimetic function, the double alliteration on 'start' – 'stand' – 'still' heightens attention to the stressed syllables responsible for the change in movement. It will be evident that the rhythm provides nothing but regular motion of a certain kind and sudden stasis: the words as linguistic signs imbue the sequence with specific meaning, though this meaning is in its turn reinforced and perhaps generalised by the rhythm. (The halt of 'stand still' also has a structural function, closing the first section of the poem and providing a pivot on which the time sequence turns; this function of rhythm is the subject of section 4 below.) This is not a particularly subtle instance of rhythmic imitation, which is why it is relatively easy to discuss; as an example of a more difficult question, one might ask whether the placing of 'Hops' after an enjambment can be regarded as imitative, since in this case the rhythmic formation would pass unremarked if it did not embody a semantically striking word.

By their very nature, as largely unconscious elements in the reading process whose function is merely to intensify or modify the meanings already given by the language, true mimetic effects remain for the most part inaccessible to conscious appraisal and precise analysis. In proportion as the reader becomes aware of them, and is able to pinpoint their operation, so they tend towards the emblematic. This is especially true of effects of sound: the more overtly imitative they are, the more they strike the reader's notice, and the less directly and immediately they function to suggest qualities of the outside world. We enjoy the heightened awareness of the sounds of *language* produced by Tennyson's 'murmuring of innumerable bees', but it is unlikely that any reader hears, as he pronounces the words, a distant buzzing. (Humbert's paean to Lolita is a special case, because in denying the reader his habitual and comfortable unconsciousness of the organs whereby he speaks, the language actually heightens attention to its subject matter.) Rhythmic effects can work in this way too; Pope's famous demonstrations of mimetic rhythm in the *Essay on Criticism* can be savoured because they *are* demonstrations, momentarily bringing to consciousness our usually automatic responses to the movements of the spoken language. In cases like these, the degree to which iconic resemblances fall short of precise imitation is probably as important as the degree to which they achieve it, and they belong properly with our consideration of nonsemantic functions in section 6.

9.2 AFFECTIVE FUNCTIONS

Plato's view of the distinctiveness of poetic language, it will be recalled, was that it possesses a special power to induce emotional responses; for him this was a reason for banishing poets from the republic, but the notion of metre as a means of increasing the affective force of language has survived without pejorative overtones to become one of the most prevalent conceptions of it. Yet it is difficult to account for this common view in terms of iconic functions: it is true that they add semantic intensity and complexity to language, but when one thinks of the deeper levels of mental experience with which poetry is assumed to engage, they appear to operate at a relatively superficial level. Let us turn yet once more to Johnson for guidance: 'The measure or time of pronouncing may be varied so as very strongly to represent, not only the modes of external motion, but the quick or slow succession of ideas, and consequently the passions of the mind.' (*The Rambler*, No. 94) It is precisely the 'passions of the mind' that we are concerned with in this section, and to which I am applying the broad term 'affective': the emotions, attitudes, and modes of thought that constitute mental experience (and the bodily experience that feeds and realises it). Is it possible to develop Johnson's suggestion that the movement of verse can represent not only the outside world but this inner world as well?

A human voice reading a line of poetry sounds much more like other human voices speaking in other situations than it does any non-human sound, such as the galloping of a horse or the rushing of a brook. The most immediate kind of representational power which poetic rhythm possesses, therefore, is one which we ignored in our discussion of iconic functions: the ability to reflect not the external reality being spoken of but the rhythms that characterise the act of speaking itself; and as these rhythms frequently serve to express the speaker's mental state, they are an obvious source of affective signification in poetry. Using C. S. Peirce's well-known categorisation of signs, one might regard a rhythmic feature that functions in this way as an *index* of extraverbal reality, rather than an icon; that is, it signifies something other than itself not because it resembles that other thing, but because it is a direct product of it.

We should not, however, assume that every distinguishable emotion produces a distinguishable mode of speech movement. Harding (1976, Ch. 8) provides an illuminating discussion of this characteristic of rhythm, arguing that 'rather than according directly with particular emotional states, rhythm reflects – or, more properly, is itself part of – the energy conditions that accompany emotion' (p. 101), and that 'our expressive movements, including our speech rhythms, reflect levels of energy and the ways in which it is being deployed – smoothly and steadily, restlessly, hesitantly, explosively, with strong determination, with cumulative force' (p. 114). Although Harding feels that the term 'energy' used in this way may be only a metaphor, it accords well with the view of syllable and stress production that we considered in Chapter 3, and relates closely to theories of musical rhythm which ascribe to sequences of tension and release the power to arouse emotion of an undifferentiated kind (see Meyer, 1956, pp. 13–42). But Harding, in his concern to relate verse to ordinary human utterances, fails to make a crucial distinction: between the habitual imposition of various kinds of rhythmic movement upon the language in normal speech, and the *embodiment* of such rhythms in the structural properties of the language in verse. In other words, the full expressive use of poetic rhythm involves not a mere imitation of speech in the name of 'realism', but the selection of linguistic forms that, as we read (or empathise with someone else's reading), engage directly with the fundamental modes of energy expenditure that characterise emotional and attitudinal conditions. Verse makes intrinsic to language what is usually extrinsic, and in so doing, sets the language of poetry apart from other uses as much as it unites it to them.

A simple example will make this clearer. The poem by Lawrence already mentioned ends as follows:[3]

(4)   I was watching the woman that bore me
     Stretched in the brindled darkness
     Of the sick-room, rigid with will
     To die: and the quick leaf tore me
     Back to this rainy swill
     Of leaves and lamps and traffic mingled before me.

It would be merely an exercise of emblematising fancy to claim that the final line iconically represents the scene referred to: that the regular rhythm evokes the pattern of street-lamps, say, or that the alliteration conveys the sound of falling rain. Yet the form of the language does seem highly appropriate, and the embodiment of emotion in characteristic speech rhythms offers an explanation. In 3.4 we noted the habitual use by English speakers of a regular rhythm with pronounced beats to express certain moods – suppressed anger or weary distaste, for instance – and the last line of Lawrence's poem not only invites this kind of reading because of the evident emotional state of the imagined speaker, but enforces it by the rhythmic (and syntactic) structures of the language itself. Rhythmic tension is high in the antepenultimate line, owing to the strong pause after two syllables and the demoted stress on 'leaf', which, coming after a double offbeat, almost persuades us that it is part of a pairing formation:

    To die: and the quick leaf tore me
     o B   ŏ   B   ŏ   B   o

The following line eases the tension and leads into the only five-beat line in the poem, whose rhythmic regularity, strong alternations of stressed and unstressed syllables (supported by alliteration and a simple syntactic structure), and final hint of the triple rhythm that has played throughout the poem, all contribute, together with its unusual length, to an isochronic insistence that embodies a slow, steady release of affective energy:

    Back to this rainy swill
     B   ŏ   B   o   B
    Of leaves and lamps and traffic mingled before me
     o B   o   B   o   B o B   ŏ   B   o

A consciously dramatic reading would, of course, capitalise on these features, but the important point is that they are built into the language of the poem, and even a flat or silent reading must engage with them; the rhythmic effects inhere not in the actual sounds of an individual performance, but in the linguistic structure itself.

This is not to say that rhythmic regularity always carries an emotional charge, let alone this quality of emotion; even in the Lawrence example the contribution made by the movement is very generalised (disgust? bitterness? resignation?), and can coexist with a variety of interpretations of the poem. As always, the semantic properties take the lead, and may or may not be reinforced or modified by the formal properties. In other poems, with other words, very similar rhythms may appear powerfully expressive of very different psychological states: after all, we may fall into rhythmically regular speech under the pressure of delight, or affection, or bewilderment.

Although for convenience we can refer to these characteristic patterns and dispositions of energy as *affective rhythms*, we must remember that they lie deeper than specific emotions and mental states (as is indicated by the powerful but unparticularised emotional quality of much nonprogrammatic music). In their capacity to embody a range of mental conditions, rhythmic forms are, so to speak, overdetermined, and it is perhaps part of their function in poetry to broaden the scope of purely lexical meanings by relating them to a less specific substratum of affective energy.

There may appear to be a clear distinction between poetry that uses rhythm in this way to embody the mental state of a fictive speaker and poetry that uses rhythm to imitate not the word but the world; in practice, however, the two functions merge, since a poem that imitates external reality in its rhythmic form may at the same time be embodying that very habit of speech: we often impose on our utterances physical features which mimic the subject of our words – as when we speak rapidly while talking of a quick succession of events, or slowly while describing a sluggish movement. In such cases, we may well be simultaneously expressing some quality of emotion: not just a rapid set of occurrences, but the associated excitement; not merely leaden motion, but the boredom it produces. So the rhythm of Florimel's lyrical praise of Perdita imitates the grace of her movements, as is often observed, but it also embodies his rapture; while Tennyson's long day waning and Marvell's winged chariot hurrying both represent mental states rather than the passage of time. The regularity of (2) is more interesting as a reflection of the speaker's mood than of the operation of clockwork; and we may feel that the rhythm of the phrase 'stand still' in (3) does not merely imitate the speaker's movements, but adumbrates the psychological shock given overt expression later in the poem: the irruption of self-consciousness into the lulling cocoon of memory.

Nor does there have to be an imagined speaker whose speech rhythms are embodied in the line for it to convey mental conditions in this way. There is more to Milton's description of Satan in prospect of Eden than a mimetic representation of the movements of his facial muscles:

(5) Thus while he spake, each passion dimmed his face
    Thrice changed with pale, ire, envy, and despair,

Which marred his borrowed visage, and betrayed
Him counterfeit, if any eye beheld.
For heavenly minds from such distempers foul
Are ever clear. Whereof he soon aware,
Each perturbation smoothed with outward calm.

We sense in the first four lines the jagged rhythms of vigorous and conflicting emotions, syntactic complexity abetting metrical complexity, and then a reimposition of regularity; but in whose speech do we locate these rhythms? It is not, after all, the narrator whose emotions are in conflict or who puts on a false smoothness. Nor is affective embodiment of this decentred sort limited to local effects: the metrical style of a whole work or oeuvre may suggest certain modes of utterance and hence certain mental dispositions. The metre of *Paradise Lost* in its entirety is characterised by rhythmic variety within the bounds of strict rules, strengthening the impression conveyed by other stylistic features of abundant mental energy deployed with firm deliberateness (though it does not add to our understanding of the poem to situate these features in the imagined mind of a 'narrator', or 'the poet', or 'Milton'). The rhythms of Donne's *Satires*, on the other hand, with their disregard of the stricter metrical rules, are less expressive of the control and organisation of mental experience than of vigorous spontaneity. It seems, then, that rhythmic form in poetry can provide a foundation for any evocation of psychological conditions, whether mediated by a dramatic speaker or not; in this way, too, poetic language transcends (or undermines) the naturalistic representation of real speech.

Affective functions are probably more universal, and more potent in extending the range of depth of linguistic meaning, than iconic functions; and if rhythmic expressiveness goes beyond convention at any point, it is here. Precise imitation of the external world offers the reader little more than amusement and admiration, like realistic bird-calls in a symphony or *trompe-l'oeil* details in a painting; the most powerful rhythmic functions in verse exist at a less conscious level, and it is an attractive thought that the rhythms of poetry may harness those deeper dispositions towards the patterned retardation and release of energy that underlie the expression of emotional states, whether they are interpreted as features of an imagined speaker's utterance or as an affective colouring without a personal locus. Traditional metrical forms occupy a special place in this area of rhythmic function: though nonmetrical verse has all the potential for iconic effects that metrical verse has – perhaps even more, since it can range more freely in its search for imitative devices – and can embody a variety of affective speech rhythms, it is the approximation to *regular* rhythms, and the consequent play of arousal and satisfaction, which engages the deepest sources of affective behaviour: those neural and muscular periodicities that generate all mental and physical activity.

9.3 ASSOCIATIVE FUNCTIONS

Whereas an iconic effect relies on some physical resemblance between language and the rest of the world (an analogy I used earlier was a black cross representing a crossroads), and an affective rhythm serves as an index of a mental state (in the way that skid-marks indicate a dangerous bend), an *associative* connection – which Peirce rather misleadingly called 'symbolic' – is one which depends entirely on an acquired disposition to relate diverse phenomena (like the red triangle which signifies a major road). That is to say, convention is responsible not merely for sanctioning as meaningful one out of many similarities between a linguistic form and external reality, as is the case with iconic representation, but for instituting a connection where there is no basis in resemblance at all. Among the conventions of language, the equivalent distinction is between *motivated* signs – those which make use of onomatopoeia, for instance – and the *unmotivated* or arbitrary signs that constitute the bulk of our speech; iconic effects in poetry can be said to increase the degree of motivation in language, while associative effects extend the system of unmotivated signs. Of course, there is a large area of poetic signification in which the resemblances between poetic devices and the reality with which we associate them are so slight that a judgement as to whether they are merely fortuitous, or perhaps just pegs on which, historically, conventional associations have been hung, is impossible (and perhaps empty). Attempts to ascertain exactly the degree of motivation in language founder in the same zone of uncertainty.

Because literary associations become so thoroughly naturalised, we are more likely to underestimate than overestimate their importance, and to think that we are responding to iconic relations when we are simply obeying long-established habits of association. As an example, let us take the response which triple metre evokes in most readers today: we are likely to feel that it is peculiarly suited to light, humorous verse, and unsuited to a serious engagement with the painful aspects of experience. There seems to be justification for this reaction in the nature of the rhythm itself: the double offbeats make for a light, rapid movement with both a mimetic and an affective dimension; the insistence of the rhythm tends to override natural speech patterns and so limit emotional expressiveness; and there is a certain artificiality about the linguistic structures that have to be used in order to avoid the alternating stress contours that characterise the language. Cowper's 'Poplar-Field' if often criticised for such reasons:

(6) Twelve years have elapsed since I first took a view
     Of my favourite field and the bank where they grew;
     And now in the grass behold they are laid,
     And the tree is my seat that once lent me a shade.

Yet we cannot simply dismiss this poem as an example of the unfortunate results of using a metre inappropriate to the subject. Not only was it much admired, it was also much imitated: Hollander, in his suggestive study of metrical conventions (1975, Ch. 9), shows that the use of triple metre as a medium for sober, reflective writing flourished in the nineteenth century side by side with its use for comic and satiric verse. We must conclude that the element of purely conventional association in our response to this metre is substantial, and that there is nothing frivolous or jaunty in a triple movement *per se*. Once these associations are evoked, however, the iconic and affective consequences of the metrical characteristics already mentioned come into play – but we can never be certain that we are not ascribing to them semantic powers for which the initial associations alone are responsible.

Rhythmic associations are therefore primarily associations with other poems or other manifestations of rhythm. A triple rhythm sounds cheerful because we associate it with the triple rhythms of all the cheerful poems in such metres that we know; if, however, current literary tastes were different, and we were steeped in the tradition of 'The Poplar-Field' and its successors, we might have very different associations, and find them equally natural.[4] The contribution made by the rhythms of *The Prelude* to the total effect of that poem depends crucially on their relation to the rhythms of *Paradise Lost*; and *The Prelude* has in its turn provided rhythmic nuances that echo through later poetry, all the more powerfully, perhaps, when they do so without reaching consciousness. It is likely, too, that familiarity with *The*

Prelude colours our reading of *Paradise Lost*: the unconscious faculty
which responds to the subtleties of rhythm does not acknowledge
anachronism. At the other extreme from associations which we never
become aware of, or which masquerade as inherent properties of the
rhythm, are the self-conscious intertextual associations of pastiche and
parody.

The metrical form brings other poems to mind in a more general
sense, too: it acts as a signal that the language we are reading is the
special language of poetry, a 'frame', in I. A. Richards's words,
'isolating the poetic experience from the accidents and irrelevancies of
everyday existence' (1924, p. 112). A poet who for a time tried to
combat this specialisation of poetic language was Wordsworth, and in
the 'Preface' and 'Appendix' to *Lyrical Ballads* he acknowledges that
the associations of metre in the mind of the reader constitute a barrier
to this enterprise; in reply, Coleridge devoted most of Chapter 18. of
Biographia Literaria to a demonstration that the links between the use
of metre and certain kinds of language are so intimate that the reader
cannot but be disappointed if the expectations which are aroused by
the presence of metrical form receive no satisfaction. The strength of
these general associations of regular verse form is also witnessed by the
need to combat them that is experienced in poetic revolutions: they
bring a tradition forcefully to mind, and to reject them is to reject that
tradition. This is true of specific metres, too; the iambic pentameter is a
legitimate target for populist poetic reformers not because of its
inherent properties (its 'hegemonic stance towards the ordinary
language of men', say), but because of its traditional associations with
'high art'. And quite apart from these ideological reasons for the heave
to break the pentameter, poets who choose to remain within its chains
have to contend with the extraordinary difficulties of writing in a
rhythmic form already intimately associated with the verse of Chaucer,
Shakespeare, Milton, Pope, and Wordsworth – to go no further.

Another variety of conventional association is the kind which
enables verse to be pronounced 'musical' or 'beautiful'. The sounds of
speech have no intrinsic aesthetic properties, except of the most
obvious kind: a regular rhythm is in some sense more musical than an
irregular rhythm, but it is not a sense which is at all helpful in the
criticism of poetry. And even the conventional distinctions between
'musical' and 'harsh' sounds count for very little except in conjunction
with a subject-matter which draws attention to them – in which case it
is usually possible to be more precise about the semantic features

which are receiving reinforcement by the sound. The fact that verse is more highly patterned than prose, and some poems more highly patterned than others, is less important as an attribute of 'beauty' than as a feature of organisation, and will be discussed as such in section 5; and there are more useful analogies to be drawn with music than those based on vague notions of melodious utterance, one of which will be touched on in the same section.

9.4 EMPHASIS AND CONNECTION

Rhythm participates in the greater semantic density of poetic language not only by establishing its own connections between the poem and the physical and mental world, but also by functioning within the poem as a formal network that acts directly upon the semantic level by emphasising or connecting individual elements in the text. One obvious mode of rhythmic emphasis is the use of variations to create local tension: when the language slips smoothly past on the wings of a regular rhythm no word or sequence receives prominence (an asset in some kinds of song-like verse); but a deviation in an established rhythm thrusts itself into the reader's attention in a way that is impossible in prose. This practice is endemic in poetry at every level, from the individual syllable or word rendered salient by rhythmic tension to the line or stanza set apart by its metrical scheme. The last line of the following stanza forces itself on the attention not only by virtue of the semantic contrast with what has gone before but also by the rhythmic shift which it performs:

(7)   They change to a high new house,
          o   B   ŏ   B   ŏ   B
        He, she, all of them – aye,
        B   ŏ B   ŏ   B
        Clocks and carpets and chairs
        B   ŏ   B   ŏ   B
        On the lawn all day,
          ŏ   B   ŏ B
        And brightest things that are theirs . . .
        o   B   o   B   ŏ   B
        Ah, no; the years, the years;
          ŏ   B   o B   o   B
      Down their carved names the raindrop ploughs.
        ŏ   B   ŏ B   o B   o   B

Five lines of regular rhythm with an easy triple lilt produced by a double offbeat in each line give way to a transitional line with a rhythmically arresting initial demotion and with no hint of tripleness, and this leads to a full four-beat line opening with a stress-final pairing, which, as a deviation foreign to triple verse, firmly establishes the weightier duple rhythm. The greatest metrical tension in the line occurs at the implied offbeat, creating an emphasis on the two stressed monosyllables, which underlines their challenge to the entire set of ideas presented in the opening five lines. Emphatic variations often function mimetically or affectively as well: the phrase 'stand still' in (3) is an example we have already considered, and in this stanza the opening nostalgia and the closing grief are embodied in appropriate rhythmic modes.

Rhythm serves to connect as well as to isolate: it acts as a kind of internal rhyming device juxtaposing elements in the poem which may not be linked by logic or surface meaning. Blake's 'London' is an example of a poem in which rhythmic repetitions function very closely with syntactic parallels not only to give the text cohesion and memorability, but to enhance its range and depth of meaning. We may note first that in the third stanza there are two phrases characterised by three strong beats alternating with single offbeats, a predominantly falling movement, and a possessive construction matched in a particular way to this rhythmic pattern:

(8) How the chimney-sweeper's cry
            B   o   B   o   B
     Every blackening church appals,
     And the hapless soldier's sigh
            B   o   B   o   B
     Runs in blood down palace walls.

Rhythm, syntax, and rhyme all contribute to the equation of two phenomena which might seem to have no logical connection. In the next stanza these phrases are echoed by a third, to bring into the same sphere another form of exploitation:

     But most through midnight streets I hear
     How the youthful harlot's curse
            B   o   B   o   B

And the next line brings this succession of parallels to its climax by using exactly the same rhythmic and syntactic structure to relate these images of suffering to a kind of sorrow considered by the society under attack to be totally unrelated to and unaffected by them:

> Blasts the new-born infant's tear
> B   o   B   o   B

Another motif, rhythmically and syntactically an abbreviated form of this one, is interwoven with it. Wheras the longer phrase refers directly to human sufferers, the shorter one brings together diverse features of the city, and through them the forms of oppression which they represent and endure. It is announced in the opening lines of the poem, and emphasised both by its semantic prominence and the immediate repetition:

> I wander through each chartered street
>   B   o   B
> Near where the chartered Thames does flow
>   B   o   B

It is echoed in 'blackening church', 'palace walls', and 'midnight streets', and makes its climactic appearance in the final words of the poem, which fuse two kinds of procession that might be seen in those streets, and two fundamental, and normally opposed, human experiences:

> And blights with plagues the marriage hearse
>   B   o   B

Rhythmic echoes no doubt work subliminally for the most part, and only when they are made obvious by such means as Blake uses do we become conscious of them. But it is one of the distinguishing characteristics of verse, and of the habits by which we read it, that changes or repetitions in the rhythmic texture are experienced not as the random and contingent by-products of a signifying system, but as part of the signifying process itself.

Rhythmic and metrical changes also serve as articulators of larger structural patterns, contributing to the meaning of the poem by signalling and reinforcing thematic shifts (as well as increasing the structural unity of the poem, a point to be discussed in the following section). We have already noted how the suspension of the regular rhythm in the third line of Lawrence's 'Brooding Grief' acts as a pivot in the time sequence of the poem, and changes in metre accompanying changes in subject or mood are too familiar to need illustration here:

an example discussed in 10.2 is the last stanza of Hardy's lyric, 'The Voice'. On a large scale, metrical variation can provide an internal organisation that emphasises contrasts of mood and content without loss of overall coherence: Tennyson's *Maud* and McDiarmid's *A Drunk Man Looks at the Thistle* are examples of long poetic monologues that make sensitive use of this dimension of metre, and one of its most highly-developed manifestations is the pattern of blank and rhymed verse, prose, and interspersed lyrics in a play like *A Midsummer Night's Dream* or *The Tempest*.

9.5 PATTERN AND COHESION

All the functions of metre we have looked at so far can be broadly classified as modes of semantic reinforcement or modification: the rhythmic features operate in the same field as the meanings conveyed by the words, whether to strengthen or to modify them. This has proved to be the type of metrical function most amenable to critical discussion, since rhythm is thereby assimilated to a notion of poetry as an expression of certain truths about the world beyond it with a subtlety or forcefulness denied to nonpoetic language. Although this approach credits poetry with a certain kind of distinctiveness – a specially dense use of language signalled, and in part created, by metre – it provides only for an intensification of the main business of ordinary language: the communication of meaning from one individual human consciousness to another. We have seen that one function of metre is in fact to prise meaning away from the notion of a single speaker, but we need to go further than this in considering its power to distance poetry from ordinary language and ordinary experience: we need to examine the ways in which poetic rhythm might operate quite separately from the semantic content of the lines it marshalls, preventing us from taking that semantic content as a simple statement about a familiar reality perceived in familiar ways. In regular verse, metre is not something that is called upon only in moments of expressive need, but a constant presence, sanctifying or stigmatising the language it marks as different. We shall be concerned in this section and the next with two complementary views of the nonsemantic functions of rhythm, derived ultimately from two conceptions of art: as the provider of reassuring experiences of order, and as the challenger of settled assumptions.

The feature of verse that most obviously distinguishes it from other uses of language is the degree to which it is patterned and organised; this has a semantic dimension, both as an emblem of harmony and as a network of internal connections, which has already been noted, and a nonsemantic dimension, which derives from the high valuation set upon order and unity themselves as aesthetic properties. We experience a fairly straightforward kind of gratification when we encounter the language that belongs to the contingencies of our daily existence clothed in a formal garb which raises it above that casual flux, its substance and not just its verbal systems submitting to strict rules. Although it is a long way from this elementary satisfaction to the sophisticated pleasures derived from a highly intricate metrical scheme, perhaps interlaced with verbal repetitions and echoes of sound, as in *Pearl* or Spenser's *Epithalamion*, they are undoubtedly related: patterning is ubiquitous in art, and the needs it serves are at once too obvious and too obscure to permit discussion here. We may note, however, that one result of this assumption of order is the greater memorability of metrical language, and that this in turn makes possible the subtle web of associations among poems that we have already discussed; in this way, the existence of order and pattern contributes indirectly to poetry's semantic richness.

A related purpose served by metrical ordering is the creation of a unified and discrete linguistic object, inviting apprehension as a formal entity, quite apart from its semantic import. The unit and integrity of a text are enhanced by the use of an unchanging metrical form, and even more so by an unchanging metrical style – the same rules used with the same frequency in the same parts of the line, the same preferences for certain types of linguistic formation in the fulfilment of metrical conditions, and so on. Rhythmic characteristics are an aspect of the remarkable consistency which makes it possible for the reader to feel that the opening and ending of, say, *Paradise Lost* or *The Ring and the Book* are parts of the same poem, standing complete in itself and separate from every other production in the English language. On the other hand, metre can also be used to articulate internal structure, and in this way increase a work's formal organisation – a simple example would be the Alexandrine that closes the Spenserian stanza. As we have seen, these rhythmic functions usually serve a semantic purpose as well, but it is important to note that they need not do so; a formal pattern may contradict patterns of meaning, and some modern poetry uses rhythmic cohesion as the major unifier of semantically unrelated or conflicting elements.

So far we have been considering the structuring function of metre without paying any attention to the dimension of time, as if a poem could be apprehended in a single instant. There is a sense in which a formally organised text does transcend the inevitably sequential nature of the reader's experience of it, memorably expressed by St Augustine: 'So it is that a metrical line is beautiful in its own kind although two syllables of that line cannot be pronounced simultaneously. The second is pronounced only after the first has passed, and such is the order of procedure to the end of the line, so that when the last syllable sounds, alone, unaccompanied by the sound of the previous syllables, it yet, as being part of the whole metrical fabric, perfects the form and metrical beauty of the whole.' (*De Vera Religione*, XXII, 42; tr. Nuttall, 1967, p. 45) However, the contribution made by metre to the wholeness of a poem can also be understood in dynamic terms: rhythmic ordering provides both an onward impetus and a series of resting places along the way, and it may participate in the closure of a text by bringing that onward movement to a satisfying end (or, by not doing so, heighten the abruptness with which the work stops). It performs this function in two ways, which were mentioned in the discussion of rhythmic perception in 4.1: firstly, and most obviously, in conjunction with line-lengths, rhyme schemes, and stanza forms, by setting up expectations of formal patterns requiring completion, and secondly, by means of the continual fluctuations in tension which characterise linguistic rhythm. Although it can be said in one sense to be highly unified, verse in which there is very little rhythmic tension – that is, verse in which the metrical pattern is realised by only the simplest rules, and in which linguistic structures accord very closely with metrical structures – not only lacks the expressive resources of iconic and affective rhythms, but offers little sense of onward movement from syllable to syllable and line to line:

(9)   My mind to me a kingdom is;
          Such present joys therein I find,
      That it excels all other bliss
          That earth affords or grows by kind.
      Though much I want which most would have,
      Yet still my mind forbids to crave.

Though in this stanza there are strong patterns to be fulfilled, the rhythm has very little life to it, and this is because the phonological and syntactic forms fall plump into the slots of the metrical alternation, without extending or challenging the regular beat. Of course, the life can go out of verse at the other extreme, too: if the language fails to make any contact at all with an underlying rhythm, it puts itself equally out of reach of the dynamic momentum afforded by sequences of tension and relaxation.

Rhythm contributes to the sense of momentum not just on its own, but also in the interplay between the rhythmic sequence and the other sequential features of the poem; the continuous confirming or contradicting of metrical expectations overlaps with other patterns of expectation and satisfaction to impel the verse forward and to delay a sense of closure. Metrical relaxation may occur at a point at which the syntactic pressure for continuation is high (the obvious example is enjambment), or vice versa (the syntactic pause within the line); rhythmic parallelism may be accompanied by syntactic variation, or syntactic repetition by metrical changes; a stanza may end with a structural resolution but leave strong semantic expectations; iambic openings and masculine endings may encourage a rising rhythm while the contours of words and phrases encourage a falling one. All such effects may contribute to the meaning of a poem, whether through imitation, affective embodiment, emphasis, or connection; but they also have an important nonsemantic function, creating a form that is experienced not as a static object but as a sequential progression, alternately disturbing and satisfying, challenging and calming, and usually ending with a sense, however momentary, of conflict resolved. Music offers a close analogy: a composer can draw on a common stock of melodic, harmonic, and rhythmic material to create a series of expectations at several levels, whose simultaneous fulfilment is postponed until the end of the work. The satisfaction experienced at the close of a heroic couplet, for instance, is not merely the sum of the separate satisfactions provided by the completion of patterns in meaning, syntax, metre, and rhyme, but the experience, on reaching the final word of the couplet, of *simultaneous* completion at all these levels. And a poem as a whole may achieve completeness by setting up a series of expectations, whether emotional, narrative, syntactic, logical, rhetorical, or formal, which are only completely and simultaneously fulfilled at the end.[5] One way in which the rhythm can contribute to the experience of closure is by refusing a metrical pattern its fullest realisation until the final lines; an example is Jonson's lyric, 'Her Triumph', where tensions of syntax, imagery, rhetoric, and metre are all finally resolved in the simple directness of the famous final line:

(10) O so white! O so soft! O so sweet is she!

This is not to say that closing lines are necessarily more regular than others (though a statistical survey might show that this is indeed a general tendency), but that the small charge of satisfaction produced by the full realisation of a rhythmic scheme is one element which may be used in the orchestration of expectations and satisfactions that constitutes the dynamic ordering of a poem.

9.6 FOREGROUNDING AND TEXTUALITY

The major tradition in the discussion of metrical function is founded on the assumption that a work of art is characterised, perhaps defined, by its unusual unity and cohesion, and metre is understood as contributing to the closeness of the links, both between the forms of language and its meanings and among the various parts of the poem, that establish this satisfying unity. It is a tradition with a long history, finding expression in terms of order and decorum in classical rhetoric and its Renaissance successors, remaining potent in Augustan notions of artistic rules and imitative effects, and receiving a powerful new impetus in the Romantic theories of organic form which today still dominate aesthetic thought and responses to art. In this century, however, an apparently opposed view has gained strength, one which sees metre as a means of unsettling the fixities normally sustained by language and challenging our assumptions of order and cohesion in the world and in ourselves. The approaches to rhythmically ordered language that we have considered in the previous sections tend to treat its distinctiveness from other uses of language as a means towards or a product of its special semantic and aesthetic status; this approach, however, regards that distancing itself as a prime function of poetic rhythm.

The first body of theory to examine systematically the differences between poetic and nonpoetic language was Russian Formalism, which laid emphasis on verse not as a means whereby language can transcend the ordinary world, but as a verbal practice which reinvigorates attention to language itself, and to the way in which language constitutes that ordinary world as part of our experience.[6] We grow accustomed to the speech we use and hear around us every day, and take for granted the easy passage from words to ideas; the strange, organised language of poetry de-automatises and defamiliar-ises that response, foregrounds the language itself rather than its subject, establishes a set towards the medium and not the message, and interrogates the connections between sounds and meanings. Poetry represents not a minimisation of the arbitrariness obtaining between signifier and signified, as a semantically oriented approach to verse would imply, but an enforcement and exploitation of it; our rush for meaning is impeded, and we are obliged to acknowledge the independence and value of the linguistic properties we are usually so eager to leave behind.

All formal devices in poetry serve this function by furnishing the text with elements that cannot be incorporated into the kind of interpretation we habitually give to linguistic utterances.[7] In our literary theory and criticism we all too easily ignore this dimension and fall back on semantic properties or ideological content, and the common emphasis on mimetic effects of rhythm typifies this retreat from what is distinctive about the language of literature. But even within the domain of formal devices, metre should not simply be regarded as one defamiliarising feature among many: it counters singleness and simpleness of meaning in a particularly forceful way, by organising and foregrounding not those elements of language which have a semantic function – words and sentences, and the phonemes or distinctive features out of which these are constructed – but the presemantic carrier of speech, the rhythmic progression of stressed and unstressed syllables. It is because it belongs to this fundamental level of language that it can function so powerfully to imitate and embody the outer and inner world, and to focus attention or provide cohesion within the poetic structure, but it is for this reason too that it can challenge so effectively the unconscious ease with which we habitually produce and consume our language.

More recently, critical theory has witnessed a development of this position which makes an even greater separation between the language of literature – or more generally of the written text – and other modes of discourse, and which lays an even stronger emphasis on its function as a subverter of the linguistic conventions by which we make our world, and, some of its proponents would argue, are made ourselves. The post-structuralist view of the literary text as the site of an unending interplay of unsettled meanings would seem to leave little room for the notion of metrical verse as the moulding of speech rhythms into regular forms to create a distinctive poetic voice.[8] However, we have at many points in this study been obliged to question the assumption that verse is a representation of an individual's spoken words, and in this chapter it has been constantly evident that the value of metre lies in its capacity to render language unlike the language of daily communication, whether in its potency, its patterning, or its self-consciousness as a conventional system. Metre is perhaps not as unsusceptible to these modes of criticism as may appear at first sight, therefore, and though this is an issue too large to do more than broach here, it may be worth raising briefly some of the points which an approach of this kind would need to develop. In doing so, we shall retrace some of the earlier arguments of this book, but in a new perspective.

Throughout this study we have been aware of a Scylla and a Charybdis: on one side the danger of identifying metre with the actual physical characteristics of particular utterances (a rock against which musical scansion and instrumental measurements run the risk of being dashed), and on the other side the danger of abstracting metrical structure too far from the spoken language (a whirlpool which generative metrics finds it hard to avoid). But a safe course can be navigated by relying on the fundamental nature of language rhythm itself: a sequence of controlled variations in the release of energy, experienced both physiologically and psychologically, which underlies all our speech activities. If the linguistic structure of an utterance is such that this sequence occurs in accordance with an elementary regular rhythmic form, the result is an increased consciousness not only of the physical substance of language but of the motive force of speech itself. And because in such cases the connection between the linguistic structure and the underlying rhythm is built into the sentence (via the muscular habits possessed by all speakers of the language), and is not imposed on the utterance from outside, it exists prior to and apart from any individual performance.[9] If the engagement is complex in nature, if there is a degree of variability in the interlocking of linguistic structures and underlying rhythms, that too is a feature of the verbal material itself, as perceived by anyone familiar with the tradition of English verse; for instance, when we feel that a metrical beat is blurred, or that rhythmic tension is heightened, that blurring and that tension are properties of the line which cannot be evaded in any reading which stays within the normal pronunciation of English. Elision, too, derives from an inescapable conjunction between metrical and linguistic structures: certain groups of sound lack clear definition as either one or two syllables, and though they can function rhythmically in both ways, it is always with a hint of their intermediate status. Indefinite stress is also a product of the interaction of language and metre, and its special character is perceived in any mode of pronunciation. The importance of inherent structural properties can also be seen in the way that syntactic organisation determines rhythmic patterns: the subordination of an adjective to a following noun, for instance, is a rhythmic relationship which can be overlaid by semantic emphasis but cannot be abolished by it. As we have seen, beneath the patterns of emphatic stress the neutral contours derived from syntactic relations continue to have their say: if a line is metrical only because emphatic stresses override the neutral pattern (see Ch. 8, examples (24)–(26)), there remains a degree of instability about its rhythms; and conversely, if the requirements of emphatic stress conflict with the metre (see Ch. 8 (27)–(32)), the line may be rescued from unmetricality by the underlying neutral stresses. In all these cases, it is the presence of a metrical set that confers on the language a degree of rhythmic (and semantic) complexity beyond the reach of the ordinary spoken language.

Reading a line of metrical verse aloud, therefore, is not simply a matter of choosing one interpretation and rejecting others: the fact of optionality itself is a characteristic of the rhythm, and remains effective whatever shades of stressing the line receives. There is, in other words, a range of acceptable readings, none of which can fully articulate the complexities of the rhythm and its relations with the other levels of verse, but all of which will engage with the underlying rhythm and thereby in some degree reflect those complexities. If you prefer to emphasise the regularity of the metre, the resolute irregularity of the language will be felt pulling against you; if you let speech rhythms have their head, the periodicity of the beat will exercise a counter-claim: both readings, however, will register the inherent tension of the line. Current taste, influenced by the rise of free verse, favours the latter style of delivery, but such preferences relate only to surface features. Although metrical verse insists on being read aloud, it insists equally that its organisation of the language belongs to a deeper level than the sounds produced by any particular mode of recitation.

An individual reading can never be a total realisation of a metrical line, just as a play can never find its full existence in a single performance or production: its potential is completely fulfilled only in the sum of all the readings which the language and the conventions of literature make possible – or have made possible, or will make possible. Metrical structure, however, can charge a single reading with rhythmic implications that go beyond itself, and it is perhaps this which gives metrical language its reputation for qualities of density, complexity, and subtlety: it enables us to hear not a speech, but speech. Another way of putting this is that metre, by freeing the spoken language from its univocal straitjacket, invests it with the kind of openness and multiplicity that is normally the special prerogative of the written text. The critical task facing the metrical analyst is not to decide on the 'best' or 'right' way of reading each line, so that it can be located in the mouth of an imaginary speaker; it is rather to determine the limits of variability fixed by the line's metrical structure, and to indicate the part played by that strictness, and the freedom within it, in the working of the poem. Metrical verse does not represent an approximation to 'the speaking voice', if we understand by that the direct imitation of a specific utterance on a specific occasion: that singleness is exactly what it enables language to escape from. By putting his words into the hands of a pre-existing metrical scheme, an external organising force from which no syllable can escape, the poet makes a willing surrender of the liberty that is fundamental to ordinary speech, and in so doing exchanges the expressive potential of the individual utterance for that of the literary institution within which his poem takes its place. Metre acknowledges – and enforces – the fact that literary language is not the language of daily discourse, and that the 'meaning' of a literary text is not to be located in some authorially underwritten intention or critically validated interpretation, but in what the text itself does for its readers, or, more accurately, in what its readers are able to do with, and within, the linguistic structures by which it is constituted. A literary work contains many voices, some of which find their most telling mode of expression in its rhythms, including, perhaps, both the voice of divine order and the voice of human doubt.

Notes

1. The following statements are representative of many more: 'Now this is very profound, what rhythm is, and goes far deeper than words. A sight, an emotion, creates this wave in the mind, long before it makes words to fit it' (Virginia Woolf, 1926, p. 247); 'I know that a poem, or a passage of a poem, may tend to realise itself first as a particular rhythm before it reaches expression in words, and that this rhythm may bring to birth the idea and the image' (T. S. Eliot, 1942, p. 28); 'I feel that poetry comes from the basic rhythmic structures of one's body or mind' (Richard Eberhart, 1973, p. 42); 'Even before it is ready to change into language, a

poem may begin to assert its buried life in the mind with wordless surges of rhythm and counter-rhythm' (Stanley Kunitz, 1978, p. 284).

2. The reading of classical verse in England depended for centuries on a response to the visual features of a text whose aural manifestation was largely unmetrical; see Attridge (1974, Part One).

3. I give the text of the poem as published in *Amores* (1916); for the *Collected Poems* of 1928 Lawrence changed 'traffic' to 'the city street', lengthening the final line still further, but diminishing its rhythmic insistence.

4. Lotman (1976, pp. 54–5) produces some interesting Russian examples of the historical changes in associations which rhythmic forms can undergo.

5. The most valuable discussion of this aspect of poetic form is by B. H. Smith (1968, Ch. 1 and 2); its musical analogue is fully explored by Meyer (1956).

6. With regard to the study of verse rhythm, the most important of the Formalists were Jakobson, Tomashevskij, and Tynjanov; a useful survey of their work is given by Erlich (1955, Ch. 12).

7. Other aspects of verse which work apart from and often counter to the semantic and rational aspect are rhyme (see Wimsatt, 1954) and the visual dimension (see Hollander, 1975, Ch. 12). For a full discussion of the devices of formal artifice which set poetry apart from ordinary discourse, see Forrest-Thomson (1978).

8. See, for instance, the defence by Donoghue (1980), in reviewing some examples of deconstructive criticism, of the common assumption that 'in reading a poem you think of the words on the page as a transcription of a voice speaking'.

9. One of the few metrical analysts to acknowledge this is Scott (1980), who questions the 'peculiar assumption that the scanner is duty bound to push verse towards a single and definitive existence, which is the *recited* existence of verse' (p. 5).

Chapter 10

Rhythm at work: some examples

To undertake an account of the major metrical forms of a language is to attempt a description and explanation of something with which readers of poetry in that language are already deeply familiar; the only proper test of the foregoing chapters, therefore, lies well beyond the covers of this book. But before handing over a set of newly designed tools, it is common practice to offer potential users a glimpse of them at work, however artificial the showroom environment in which the demonstration takes place. The examples in this chapter constitute a fairly random selection from the range of verse forms employed in English poetry, unavoidably wrenched from the contexts which give them a large part of their value and meaning, and discussed with regard to one or two aspects of the contribution made by rhythm to the total poetic effect. In arranging these examples, I have paid no attention to chronology, in the belief that the juxtaposition of comparable uses of rhythm from different periods would be more illuminating than a historical survey. In the chapter as a whole, and in the individual sections, the order is roughly from freer to stricter forms, but the disparate ingredients of poetic rhythm prevent any possibility of linear progression. The scansions given are not intended to be complete or definitive; in particular, I have often shown only one metrical realisation where an indefinite stress implying a range of possibilities would have been more accurate, but also more complicated, and irrelevant to the point at issue. Although my concern, strictly speaking, is with metrical verse, I begin with two examples of nonmetrical verse which draw on some of the resources of regular rhythmic form.

10.1 NONMETRICAL VERSE

(1) Gasholders, russet among fields. Milldams, marlpools that lay
    unstirring. Eel-swarms. Coagulations of frogs: once, with

branches and half-bricks, he battered a ditchful; then sidled
away from the stillness and silence.

Ceolred was his friend and remained so, even after the day of
the lost fighter: a biplane, already obsolete and
irreplaceable, two inches of heavy snub silver. Ceolred let it
spin through a hole in the classroom-floorboards, softly, into
the rat-droppings and coins.

After school he lured Ceolred, who was sniggering with fright,
down to the old quarries, and flayed him. Then, leaving
Ceolred, he journeyed for hours, calm and alone, in his
private derelict sandlorry named *Albion*.

Geoffrey Hill, *Mercian Hymns*, VII:
'The Kingdom of Offa'.

It is all too easy to take a piece of nonmetrical language and find
rhythmic ingenuities in it; the characteristic mixture of repetition and
variety in the movement of English produces flows and eddies, echoes
and inversions, that would look like the work of a skilful designer if
they were not ubiquitous. Much discussion of the rhythms of literary
prose or free verse falls into this trap, and it is difficult to know how to
avoid it when the only certain rhythmic effects are the obvious and
therefore uninteresting ones. One precaution is to attempt such an
analysis only with writing which possesses a distinctive aural character
recognisable among the myriad other arrangements of the syllables of
English; this is true of Geoffrey Hill's set of prose-poems, *Mercian
Hymns*, and the above example is typical of the sequence in its
scrupulous control of rhythmic form.

It is obvious that nonmetrical language does not make use of beats in
the same way as its rhythmically regular counterpart; nevertheless, the
peaks of energy on stressed syllables still function as the carriers of a
fundamentally stress-timed rhythm, and prose that invites careful
enunciation by its sense and sound-patterns can exhibit many of the
functions of rhythmic form discussed in the previous chapter. In the
opening paragraph of this poem, the language is at its most
concentrated and unprosaic, blending the eighth and twentieth
centuries in a depiction of Offa's boyhood haunts; this feeling of
powerful compression is achieved partly by the sensory density of the
images, partly by the ellipses of syntax, and partly by the management

of sound and movement. The patterns of alliteration and assonance need no comment, but these are allied to a less evident rhythmic structure which also contributes to the sense of an intensified language. The large proportion of strongly-stressed syllables and the limitations on the number of nonstresses between them heighten the stress-timing tendency of the language, so that scansion in terms of beats and offbeats is not altogether misleading:

> Gasholders, russet among fields. Milldams, marlpools that lay
> B   ŏ   B   ŏ   B   ŏ B   o   B   ŏ   B
> unstirring. Eel-swarms. Coagulations of frogs: once, with
> o   B o   B   ŏ   B̄ o B   ŏ   B   ŏB   o
> branches and half-bricks, he battered a ditchful; then
> B   ŏ   B   B   ŏ   B   ŏ   B   ŏ
> sidled away from the stillness and silence.
> B   ŏ   B   ŏ   B   ŏ   B o

The rhythm that emerges here is a familiar one in English poetry: the consistent separation of beats by single or double offbeats. There is only one instance of a triple offbeat, and the two implied offbeats occur naturally at strong pauses. Otherwise, the only irregularity occurs on the word 'Coagulations'. The scansion I give shows the promotion of the second syllable, which carries a secondary stress, to a beat; this is undoubtedly how the rhythm would make itself felt in regular verse, but as prose it probably reads more naturally without a beat, creating a temporary disturbance in the steady sequence of alternations, a sudden stutter of syllables testifying to the ugliness and fascination of the scene it refers to.

The rhythmicality of the passage contributes to its semantic and affective intensity, evoking the young Offa's absorption in the surroundings of his 'kingdom'; but its effects can be more fully specified. When we examine the grouping of the words, we find that the predominant rhythm is falling: most of the more significant words begin with a stress ('Coagulations' being a notable exception), and because of the syntactic omissions, sentences and phrases begin immediately with important nouns. This is an intensifying device used throughout *Mercian Hymns*, to the extent that a falling rhythm becomes part of the work's metrical signature, contributing to its cohesion and distinctiveness. One variety of this rhythm is especially noticeable in this paragraph: the compound whose second syllable carries some degree of secondary stress, preventing the falling rhythm from picking up speed – examples here are 'milldams', 'marlpools', 'Eel-swarms', and perhaps 'half-brick'. After its slow opening, however, the paragraph does speed up, as we turn to an account of Offa's actions on a particular occasion: the rhythm becomes more relaxed as the syntax reverts to normality, and the final clause uses a regular four-beat triple rhythm, heightened by alliteration and assonance, for the boy's escape (its smoothness perhaps masking the unease – reminiscent of Wordsworth's in 'Nutting' – which the action has aroused).

We register a change of tone as the second paragraph begins: the diction and syntax are nonpoetic (the model is the school story), and this in itself encourages a reading which plays down rhythmic alternations, so there is no temptation to give secondary stresses and minor category words any weight. The result is that the stresses are separated by anything between four nonstresses and none at all, producing the distinctive irregularity of ordinary speech:

+s −s   −s −s +s   −s   −s +s   −s s−s s −s   −s +s
Ceolred was his friend, and remained so, even after the day
−s   −s +s   +s −s
of the lost fighter

A rapid run of syllables is brought to a halt by two successive stresses, where stress-timing abruptly slows down the rhythm and emphasises the ambiguous phrase 'lost fighter'. Note that we are free to give the initial syllables of 'even' and 'after' any degree of emphasis, as there is no metrical set to limit us; the nearest equivalent in metrical verse is indefinite stress, and I have used the same symbol. (Strictly speaking, the stress contour of a nonmetrical sequence like this should be shown according to a detailed phonological system, not in the simplified pattern we have been using for regular verse.) Note, too, that the effect of the successive stresses after a pair of nonstresses is different from that of stress-final pairing, although the pattern is the same: there is no pressure from an alternating set to blur the rhythm, and no foregrounding of the linguistic substance as the result of tension. Sense and syntax also determine the movement of the next phrase, which reverts to a rapid syllabic sequence, and then decelerates as the object is fixed (anti)climactically in the schoolboy's small-scale world:

−s +s −s   −s +s   −s+s   −s−s −s   −s −s +s −s   −s   +s+s   −s −s
a biplane, already obsolete and irreplaceable, two inches of
+s −s   +s   +s −s
heavy snub silver

The last six words, with their concentration of stresses, linger over the highly prized model, in strong contrast to the cruel effortlessness of its despatch suggested in the easy regularity of the rhythm that follows:

> Ceolred let it spin through a hole in the classroom-floorboards,
> B   o   B   o   B   ŏ   B   ̌ o   B   o   B   o
> +s   −s −s −s   −s +s   −s   −s   −s   +s
> softly, into the rat-droppings and coins

The sentence itself softly trails away into the rhythms of ordinary speech. (There are not, of course, two distinct types of movement in the poem, as the use of two different sets of symbols might suggest; they merge seamlessly with one another, like the poem's disparate fields of reference.)

The final paragraph continues the deployment of variable speech rhythms, their casualness contrasting ironically with the forcefulness of 'flayed', rendered an alien word in this schoolboy diction by the omission of the expected 'alive':

> +s −s   +s   −s +s−s   +s   −s   −s −s   +s −s−s   −s   +s
> After school he lured Ceolred, who was sniggering with fright,
> +s   −s   −s+s   +s   −s   −s   +s   −s
> down to the old quarries, and flayed him

But the poem ends with a return to rhythmic regularity: two syntactically highlighted occurrences of the pattern +s −s −s +s, familiar from duple verse, are followed by a final assertion of the falling rhythm (in both duple and triple forms):

> +s   +s   −s   −s +s   +s   −s   −s+s
> Then, leaving Ceolred, he journeyed for hours, calm and alone,
>   B   o   B   ŏ   B   ŏ   B o   B   ŏ B
>
> in his private derelict sandlorry named Albion
>   ŏ   B   o   B   ŏ   B   o   B   ŏB ŏ

If we stress 'named', as implied by this scansion, an appropriate pause is induced by stress-timing before the climax of 'Albion' – a final expansion of the juvenile world, from a make of truck to a real kingdom. (In fully regular verse, this pause would be experienced as an implied offbeat, though it is somewhat inaccurate to represent it as such here.) This use of heightened regularity to terminate the poem produces an experience of closure which encourages the reader to interpret the final sentence as in some way a culmination of or conclusion to what has gone before, and not just an addendum; as, perhaps, an image of the lonely satisfactions of power (or fantasies of power) generated by the unleashing of violence and vengeance.

If it is to be something other than prose, prose-poetry must make the fullest use of the inherent rhythmic properties of the language. It cannot rely, as free verse can, on externally imposed interruptions to heighten the reader's consciousness of movement and duration; it can, however, take advantage of the onward flow of prose in its achievement of rhythmic subtlety. The degree to which *Mercian Hymns* does so is accidentally demonstrated by two quotations which appear in an essay on Hill (Bloom, 1976, pp. 243–4) with the original compositor's line-divisions preserved in the new setting, transforming the block of prose into free verse: the result is the total destruction of the language's rhythmic power. The range of movement in this poem is great – from the haphazard patter of rapid narrative to the firm structure of a four-beat triple rhythm – yet it is held together by the continuity of the prose form and by the larger rhythmic organisation; and this simultaneous variety and cohesion at the level of rhythm plays no small part in the poem's fusion of a diversity of material into a single complex poetic experience. Above all, the use of rhythm to intensify the semantic dimension of the poem – mimetically, affectively, emphatically – is a major element in the investiture of a child's unremarkable experience with the breadth and singularity of an autocratic ruler's.

(2)   The river's tent is broken; the last fingers of leaf
       Clutch and sink into the wet bank. The wind
       Crosses the brown land, unheard. The nymphs are departed.
       Sweet Thames, run softly, till I end my song.
       The river bears no empty bottles, sandwich papers,
       Silk handkerchiefs, cardboard boxes, cigarette ends
       Or other testimony of summer nights. The nymphs are
           departed.
       And their friends, the loitering heirs of city directors;
       Departed, have left no addresses.
       By the waters of Leman I sat down and wept . . .
       Sweet Thames, run softly till I end my song,
       Sweet Thames, run softly, for I speak not loud or long.
       But at my back in a cold blast I hear
       The rattle of the bones, and chuckle spread from ear to ear.

                                   Eliot, from *The Waste Land*, III:
                                              'The Fire Sermon.'

As we have seen, a sense of rhythmic regularity in English, of stresses functioning as beats, is created when the number of unstressed syllables between stresses is for the most part limited to one or two, and further heightened when the beats fall into groups corresponding to common underlying rhythms; this establishes in the reader's mind a metrical set, which simplifies the stress contrasts of the language and makes possible certain limited syllabic variations. But there is a border area, where regularity remains only half-realised, and a shadowy metrical set prevents sense and syntax from wholly determining the rhythmic character of the line, but does not in itself govern the movement of the verse. Many 'free verse' poets operate in this territory, and Eliot is one who is quite explicit about his rhythmic preferences: 'The ghost of some simple metre should lurk behind the arras in even the "freest" verse; to advance menacingly as we doze, and withdraw as we rouse' (1917, p. 187). What Eliot is describing is only one variety of nonmetrical verse (and, given the reassurance that simple rhythms usually have to offer, employing a curious metaphor to do so), but he is clearly preaching what he practises. In this example, even the lines which are not quotations from or variants of lines of earlier verse show a distinct preference for single nonstresses between stresses, spiced with a fair number of double nonstresses and a few instances of three nonstresses or none. There is only one sequence of four nonstresses ('testimony of'), and none with more. The result is a rhythm distinctly different from that of prose, heightened by a division into lines that correspond roughly to the favoured lengths of regular English verse (all but one have between nine and fourteen syllables), by the quotations from metrical poetry, and by the diction and content. If any metrical set were to emerge it would be for five-beat lines, but since the five-beat grouping demands strict adherence to the normal deviation rules, the variations here are sufficient to keep regularity just out of reach. As a result, the lines establish associations with the tradition of English verse, but in an oblique and ironic way, neither committing the poem to that tradition, nor wholly challenging it. In scanning such lines, we can indicate beats when there is some foregrounding of rhythmic regularity (though judgements as to when this occurs are highly subjective):

> The river's tent is broken; the last fingers of leaf
> o B o   B   o   B   ŏ   B   ðB   ð   B
>   −s −s   −s   +s   +s   −s   +s
>
> Clutch and sink into the wet bank. The wind
> B   o   B

+s −s   −s +s   +s   −s +s
Crosses the brown land, unheard. The nymphs are departed.
                                    o B   ŏ   B o

But Eliot does more than half-reproduce the rhythms of the iambic
tradition, he reproduces some of its famous lines; and it is instructive to
observe how they are transformed by their new context. Spenser's line,
in its setting in 'Prothalamion', relies on two demotions and a
promotion for its metrical acceptability as an iambic pentameter:

Sweet Thames run softly, till I end my song
    ŏ   B   ŏ   B   o B̄ oB   o   Ḃ

In the context of Eliot's verse, without the pressure of a strong metrical
set, we may be inclined to interpret it differently: although syntax and
the alternations of speech rhythm keep the originally demoted stresses
weak, the beat on 'till' may disappear. But however the line is
experienced, its rhythm is part of the poem's contrast between
twentieth-century and Elizabethan England: whether as a pentameter
demanding a slightly artificial pronunciation to retain its shape, or as a
familiar line distorted by its modern surroundings. On its second
appearance, any inclination to promote 'till' is further weakened, not
only because the preceding comma has disappeared, but also because
it follows a regular four-beat line in triple verse (imitating the
rhythmical opening of Psalm 137 in the Authorised Version) and
therefore tends itself towards a four-beat pattern:

By the waters of Leman I sat down and wept . . .
    ŏ   B   ŏ   B   ŏ B   ŏ   B
Sweet Thames, run softly till I end my song
    ŏ   B   ŏ   B   ɤ̆   B   o B

This shrinkage of the original metrical form is confirmed by the next
line, which provides the additional beat needed to restore the
pentameter rhythm:

Sweet Thames, run softly, for I speak not loud or long
    ŏ   B   ŏ   B   ɤ̆   B   o B   o B

The other variant of a well-known line is an even more distorted echo.
Instead of Marvell's regular iambic tetrameter,

But at my back I always hear,
  o B̄   o   B   oB o   B

Eliot's line is a pentameter – or would be a pentameter if the metrical
set were strong enough to encourage the perception of stress-final
pairing:

But at my back in a cold blast I hear
o B̄   o B   ŏ   B   ò B   o B

As it is, the five-beat rhythm remains only a familiar ghost behind the arras, one of the multiplicity of associations which constitute in large measure the poem's mode of meaning.

10.2 FOUR-BEAT VERSE

(3) Bidderes and beggeres faste aboute yede
    Till hire bely and hire bagge were bretful ycrammed;
    Flite thanne for hire foode, foughten at the ale.
    In glotonye, god woot, go thei to bedde,
    And risen up with ribaudie as Roberdes knaves;
    Sleep and sleuthe seweth hem evere.
    Pilgrymes and Palmeres plighten hem togidere
    For to seken Seint Iame and Seintes at Rome;
    Wenten forth in hire wey with many wise tales,
    And hadden leve to lyen al hire lif after.

Langland, *Piers Plowman*, B-text,
'Prologue', 40–49 (ed. Kane and Donaldson, 1975)

This is not the place to speculate about the relationship between the poetry of the fourteenth-century alliterative revival and Anglo-Saxon verse; let it suffice to say that the basic structure of a line divided into two parts, usually with two beats in each, is shared, as is the use of alliteration to mark the beats, and that the similarity between the forms and the later four-beat line seems unlikely to be mere coincidence. Uncertainties about pronunciation make it impossible to discuss metrical details with any confidence but it is legitimate to ask what such verse can offer to readers relying wholly on the rhythmic qualities of modern English.

Langland used the alliterative line with unusual freedom, though our example does not show the widest variations which his verse exhibits. Even here it is obvious, however, that the metre has a rhythmic character quite different from that of the regular four-beat line; even if we assume that final −e was not pronounced, the number of unstressed syllables between major stresses in this example varies from none to four, and this is too great a range to create the alternating rhythm by which we identify regular verse. The 'beats' of this metre are not peaks of energy balanced against equivalent valleys, but isolated alps jutting up from foothill ranges; and the perception of particular syllables as keystones in the rhythmic structure is encouraged not by a metrical set but by the device of alliteration. In scansion we can do no more than show the stress pattern (in the usual simplified form) and the location of the beats and mid-line divisions:

```
 -s    +s-s  -s  +s    +s    +s   -s  -s +s
In glotonye, god woot, go thei to bedde,
   B          B      ·  B           B
 -s    +s-s -s   -s  +s-s  -s -s   +s -s  -s   +s -s
And risen up with ribaudie as Roberdes knaves;
   B          B          ·   B            B
 +s   -s    +s     +s -s    -s  +s -s
Sleep and sleuthe seweth hem evere.
   B       B      · B          B
```

Langland's usual practice, as in this example, is to alliterate only the first three of the four beats; and there is usually some degree of syntactic break between the two halves of the line to counter the unifying pressure of the alliterative pattern. At times the offbeats are predominantly double, creating what Saintsbury calls an 'anapaestic underhum', but no firm metrical set is established, and the verse lacks the expressive potential of variation from a strict norm. This means that promotion and demotion, as they occur in the main tradition of accentual-syllabic verse, are not possible; it often requires something of a conscious effort – at least for the modern reader – to place the beats on the alliterated syllables and not on supernumerary stresses:

```
       +s      +s    +s        +s        +s
For to seken Seint Iame and Seintes at Rome;
   B      B        ·      B           B
 +s     +s        +s      +s   +s  +s
Wenten forth in hire wey with many wise tales
   B              B    ·        B      B
```

In the light of these demands for heavy stressing on selected syllables, the traditional name, 'strong-stress metre', seems an appropriate one.

The wisest course for the modern reader is probably to concentrate on the vigorous speech rhythms, and let the metre fend for itself; the rhythmic strength of Langland's verse lies in its energetic freedom, not in the tight control of metrical form. The main structural component is the line, which is usually a single syntactic unit with a strong pause at the end and an internal articulation into half-lines; the alliteration, normally encompassing the first three beats of the line (though with considerable variation), helps to bind the line, and set it apart from its neighbours. The alliterated beats naturally give expressive emphasis to the words on which they occur, and in this passage the narrator's anger is allowed to explode in terms like 'bely', 'bagge', 'Flite', 'foughten', 'glotonye', 'ribaudie', and 'sleuthe'. This is not language raised to a higher pitch of orderliness, but speech granted extra force by the highlighting of significant words, and cumulative power by the succession of discrete but parallel units of rhythm, sound, and sense.

> (4)   I have met them at close of day
>   Coming with vivid faces
>   From counter or desk among grey
>   Eighteenth-century houses.
>   I have passed with a nod of the head
>   Or polite meaningless words,
>   Or have lingered awhile and said
>   Polite meaningless words,
>   And thought before I had done
>   Of a mocking tale or a gibe
>   To please a companion
>   Around the fire at the club.
>   . . . .
>   I write it out in a verse –
>   MacDonagh and MacBride
>   And Connolly and Pearse
>   Now and in time to be,
>   Wherever green is worn,
>   Are changed, changed utterly:
>   A terrible beauty is born.
>
>   Yeats, from 'Easter, 1916'

The four-beat line in modern English is typically used to create a prominent rhythmic structure, reducing the full range of speech movement to a relatively simple contour. But in 'Easter, 1916', Yeats uses a form of the line which allows speech rhythms to impel and shape the verse, even though the potential for rhythmic simplicity is preserved. The foundation of this form is a metrical pattern of three realised beats followed by an unrealised beat, although it must be said immediately that the rhythmic freedom of the verse subdues this structure to the point where the unrealised beat is only a dim presence; as there are no realised fourth beats at all, there is no strong expectation for one, and the experience is quite different from, say, that of the 4.3.4.3 stanza. Perhaps the best way of putting it is that as we move from one line to the next, the absence of a fourth beat produces a slight degree of tension, and this tension contributes to the unease that hovers about even the apparently ordinary descriptions in the opening of the poem. (See Ch. 4, example (22), for another use of this form.) The variation in nonstresses between beats – usually two or one, occasionally none – further diminishes the prominence of the rhythm, and prevents a clear triple or duple movement from emerging:

> I have met them at close of day
> ŏ   B   ŏ   B   o   B   [o B]
> Coming with vivid faces
> B   ŏ   B   o   B o   [B]
> From counter or desk among grey
> o   B   ŏ   B   ŏ   B   [o B]
> Eighteenth-century houses.
> B   o   B   ŏ   B   o   [B]

The sense of a four-beat structure is given some support by the use of rhyme and syntax to suggest a division into quatrains, though their prominence is reduced by the many imperfect rhymes, the run-ons within the quatrain, and the absence of any typographical differentiation. A very slight rewriting will show how close the verse comes to the full four-beat rhythm, but at the same time how sharp is the distinction it maintains:

> I have met them all at close of day
> ŏ   B   o   B   o   B   o   B
> Coming with vivid faces
> B   ŏ   B o   B o   [B]
> From counter or desk among the grey
> o   B   ŏ   B   o   B   o   B
> Eighteenth-century houses.
> B   o   B   ŏ   B   o   [B]

The addition of a syllable in the first and third lines produces a common metre stanza, and the verse acquires a jauntiness far removed from the sober, unemphatic quality of the original. Notice how the insertion of 'the' in line 3 alters the character of the strong run-on that follows: in this version we can read straight on with no sense of tension, the underlying rhythmic structure providing the experience of a metrical break. In the original, however, there is the shadow of an unrealised beat to contend with; we can scarcely pause between the two adjectives (since the first qualifies the whole of the phrase that follows), yet to read straight on is to squeeze out entirely the unrealised beat.

Having subdued the underlying rhythm to this degree, Yeats is unable to make very much use of demotion and promotion, since these variations depend on the establishment of a strong alternating metrical set. In the first passage above, there are no demoted stresses, and only one promoted nonstress. (This occurs on the last syllable of 'companion', and is more theoretical than real, since the dominance of speech rhythm produces a two-beat line, with only the faint rhyme on the last syllable suggesting a third point of prominence.) The use of stresses to realise almost all the beats, and of a varying number of nonstresses between them, produces a rhythm with many similarities to that of medieval strong-stress metre, but with three beats to a line instead of four. Yet when it becomes appropriate for the underlying rhythm to emerge strongly into the open, as in the final lines of the poem (the second passage quoted), it does so very readily; promotion is made possible by, and emphasises, the chant-like quality of the new mode of utterance, with its simple cumulative syntax and pauses at line ends:

> I write it out in a verse –
> o   B   o   B   ŏ   B   [o B]
> MacDonagh and MacBride
> o   B   o   B̄   o   B   [o B]
> And Connolly and Pearse
> o   B   o B̆ o   B   [o B]
> Now and in time to be,
> B   ŏ   B   o   B   [o B]
> Wherever green is worn
> o B o   B   o   B   [o B]

The aptness of this metrical form for the poem is obvious. It allows both the easy flexibility of the detached observer's meditation and the intense rhythmicality of the admirer's incantation. It enacts the transformation which is its subject: the quotidian becomes the remarkable, the casual becomes the compulsive. The local effects are just as telling, such as the emphasis given to 'grey', with all that it implies, by the tension of the run-on already described, or the emblematic awkwardness of the implied offbeat in

> polite meaningless words,
> B   ŏ   B

repeated to bring home the banality. Perhaps the most remarkable effect is in the two lines that end the poem (having occurred earlier in a slightly different version). The first of these is unusual in implying two scansions, one derived from the strong-stress aspect of the metre, the other from its accentual-syllabic, rhyming aspect:

Are changed, changed utterly
o   B   ŏ   B   ôB ŏ   [B]
o   B   ó   B o B̄   [o B]

No single reading can satisfy these contradictory demands, and the resulting rhythmic tension thrusts the line into prominence, enacts its own difficult transition, and embodies a strong, though unspecific, emotional response. A line which retained the rhythmic shape of its predecessors would have a totally different effect:

Are changed in every way
o   B   o   B   o   B

The closing line presents the results of the change, rhythmically as well as semantically: it is almost songlike in character, with its upbeat, triple rhythm, firm stresses, alliteration, and perfect rhyme:

A terrible beauty is born
o B ŏ   B   ŏ   B

The adjective reflects the speaker's continuing detachment from the events he is contemplating, but the rhythm informs us that at another level all doubts are silenced.

(5) Woman much missed, how you call to me, call to me.
    Saying that now you are not as you were
    When you had changed from the one who was all to me,
    But as at first, when our day was fair.

    Can it be you that I hear? Let me view you then,
    Standing as when I drew near to the town
    Where you would wait for me: yes, as I knew you then,
    Even to the original air-blue gown!

    Or is it only the breeze, in its listlessness
    Travelling across the wet mead to me here,
    You being ever dissolved to wan wistlessness,
    Heard no more again far or near?

      Thus I; faltering forward,
      Leaves around me falling,
    Wind oozing thin through the thorn from norward,
      And the woman calling.

                         Hardy, 'The Voice'

The regular use of a triple rhythm is relatively rare in English poetry, and to modern ears at least has a trick of reducing emotional complexities to pleasant jinglings. Hardy is one of the few poets who have found darker expressive possibilities in it, as this example testifies. The first stanza presents the dead woman's call without any expressed doubts as to its reality, and this apparent certainty is matched by the simple realisation of the metre:

> Woman much missed, how you call to me, call to me,
> B   ŏ   B   ŏ   B   ŏ   B   ŏ
> Saying that now you are not as you were
> B   ŏ   B   ŏ   B   ŏ   B
> When you had changed from the one who was all to me,
> B̄   ŏ   B   ŏ   B   ŏ   B   ŏ
> But as at first, when our day was fair.
> B̄   ŏ   B   ŏ   B   o   B

It is the familiar 4 × 4 structure, and the triple metre is almost wholly regular; that is, a strong preference is shown for double offbeats, and little use is made of promotion and demotion. (Implied offbeats, it will be remembered, are in any case foreign to triple metre.) The metrical pattern alternates between 4B and 4Bo, a form with which we are already familiar in duple verse (see Ch. 4, examples (48) and (54)), and one which encourages a falling rhythm, further encouraged here by the repeated phrase in line 1. Only at the very end of the stanza does Hardy avail himself of the possible methods of muting a triple rhythm, by substituting a single offbeat for the expected double offbeat. Yet the rhythm does not dominate the language; it is rapid, but not insistent. One reason is that it is achieved by the use of syntactic sequences that fall naturally but not mechanically into triple patterns, rather than by polysyllables with their stronger contrast between stress and nonstresses (apart from two disyllables, the entire stanza is monosyllabic). The fact that the stanza is a single sentence also provides some syntactic justification for the rapid movement. The affective speech rhythm which the verse embodies is relaxed and freely-flowing: it has neither the tension nor the heavy beats that characterise different kinds of emotional stress. The repetition at the end of the first line contributes to the stanza's tone of wonderment – we say a thing twice if we find it hard to believe – and mimetically introduces a hint of the repeated cry itself, with a triple rhythm that suggests a sound dying away (echoed two lines later in an attenuated form by means of a rhyme which merely drops the phrase's first consonant).

The opening of the second stanza continues the smooth rhythm, though it is slightly ruffled by the pause after the question, and the attitude expressed is no longer quite so confident; the third line, too, pauses tensely at its midpoint:

> Can it be you that I hear? Let me view you then,
>   B   ŏ   B   ŏ   B   ŏ   B   ŏˑ
> Standing as when I drew near to the town
>   B   ŏ   B   ŏˑ   B   ŏ   B
> Where you would wait for me: yes, as I knew you then
>   B̄   ŏ   B   ŏ   B   ŏ · B   ŏ

At the end of the third line here, the stress which the sense demands on 'then' increases the tension (as Leavis pointed out when discussing the poem in *New Bearings*), since the rules of triple metre do not permit demotion in this position. There follows a line which presents the strongest threat to the metre so far, in the occurrence of four nonstresses between the first two beats. Either we give them all syllabic value, which suspends the metre for this part of the line, or we use elision, which preserves the metre, but creates a different kind of tension:

>   (s)   ⁻s
> Even to the original air-blue gown!
>   B   ŏ   B ŏ   B   ŏ   B

The end of the line deviates in the opposite direction, though less markedly: as in all three of the longer stanzas, the last offbeat is monosyllabic, but in this case it involves a degree of demotion as well, creating a final cadence with a slower, heavier movement.

This rhythmic change in the last line-and-a-half of the stanza does not have any iconic reference to the air-blue gown, though it does work affectively: the speaker is no longer bemused by an aural image but excited by a visual one, and the words lose their easy flow for the sharper contours of emotional utterance. The rhythmic tension helps to convey a sense that the visitation is not only a cause for joy, but a cause (and ultimately the result) of deep sorrow; and when the vision evaporates and the poet faces the objective reality of his situation the rhythm actually becomes easier again, at least for a while. Hardy makes the triple rhythm at the start of the third stanza expressive of a kind of feebleness of energy; it is possible, and appropriate, to read the first line with ten unstressed and only two fully stressed syllables, leaving promotion to take care of the other beats:

                         +s   +s
    Or is it only the breeze, in its listlessness
    B̄   ŏ   B̄   ŏ   B   ŏ   B   ŏ

We have not returned to the lilting melody of the first stanza, however:
in the lines that follow, two strong monosyllables require demotion:

    Travelling across the wet mead to me here,
    B   ŏ   B   ŏ   B   ŏ B
    You being ever dissolved to wan wistlessness
    B   ŏ   B   ŏ   B   ŏ̈   B   ŏ

And at the end of the stanza, where the reality of loss is fully
acknowledged, the rhythm seems to be on the verge of collapse:

    Heard no more again far or near
    B   o   B   ŏ̈   B   o   B

There are no straightforward double offbeats: two of the offbeats are
single, implying a shift to duple metre, and this makes the demotion in
the other offbeat difficult to sustain. A slight rewriting of the line is
revealing:

    Heard of no more again far off or near
    B   ŏ   B   ŏ̈   B   ŏ   B

Here the triple rhythm is enforced by the indisputable double offbeats,
and 'again' now functions easily as a double offbeat with demotion.

    Hardy then makes a rhythmic move which must startle even the
deafest ear: the collapse threatened at the end of the third stanza takes
place, and as the speaker tries to sum up his position and finds only
uncertainty, so the rhythm falters forward without attaining any clear
shape. The first line begins with an upbeat, as no previous line has
done, and follows this with a pair of beats separated by an implied
offbeat, suggesting a duple rhythm; then there follow a tremor of the
lost triple rhythm, the first feminine ending of the poem, and the first
unrealised beat:

    Thus I; faltering forward
    o B ŏ B   ŏ   B   o   [B]

We are in a different rhythmic world; this is, of course, the voice of the
speaker in full self-consciousness, and we realise that all that has gone
before is in quotation marks. The second line is in regular duple metre,
and provides a context within which we could have interpreted the
previous line, but now it is too late:

> Leaves around me falling
> B   o B   o B o   [B]

Nor are we allowed to settle into the new metre, because the third line returns us to the rhythm of the first three stanzas: triple verse with a tense demotion on 'oozing', and a single offbeat before the final beat, like the last line in each of the earlier stanzas:

> Wind oozing thin through the thorn from norward
> B   ŏ   B   ŏ   B   o   B o

Nevertheless, it belongs to the structure of the stanza as well: it is the fully realised line of the short metre pattern (3.3.4.3), and its feminine ending, rhyming with the first line, is in contrast with the triple rhymes of the previous stanzas, contributing to the sense that this stanza is a kind of withered remnant of those. We seem to have progressed – or regressed – from the compelling vision of a dead woman to the harsh ordinariness of a wet and windy field, but the last line springs one more surprise, insisting again on the reality of the voice, in the shortest, simplest line of them all. To fit its metrical structure into the short metre form, one would have to promote the first syllable, but perhaps the most natural reading is one which shrinks the phrase to two beats:

> And the woman calling
> ŏ   B   o   B o

The earlier lyrical, perhaps slightly fanciful, rhythm allowed us to treat the voice from the past as mere hallucination; but this stark rhythm cannot be so easily explained away.

> (6) Sweetest love, I do not go
>   For weariness of thee,
> Nor in hope the world can show
>   A fitter love for me;
>   But since that I
> Must die at last, 'tis best
> To use myself in jest
>   Thus by feigned deaths to die.
>
> Yesternight the sun went hence,
>   And yet is here today,
> He hath no desire nor sense,
>   Nor half so short a way:
>   Then fear not me,

But believe that I shall make
Speedier journeys, since I take
More wings and spurs than he.

Donne, 'Song: "Sweetest love, I do not go" ',
stanzas 1–2

The examples of metrical freedom we have considered so far have been almost entirely in the use of realisation rules; but the metrical pattern itself can be a source of fruitful variation. If one is going to make frequent use of deviation, it is probably just as well to keep to a familiar metrical pattern, since a shifting framework will not provide the necessary firm scaffolding; but a regular metrical style can employ a changing metrical pattern without running the danger of rhythmic collapse. Donne is a master of this correlation: his surface rhythms move towards and away from the metrical pattern while his metrical patterns move away from and towards the simple underlying rhythms. The result is verse which ranges from baroque elaboration to lucid simplicity, from the energy of vigorous speech to the calm continuities of song. In this example, the main site of variation is the metrical pattern, and the syllables remain for the most part content with regular alternations (though, as we shall see, they are not unaffected by shifts in the underlying form of the verse). The opening four lines employ the simple 4.3.4.3 structure for a relaxed, assured assertion:

Sweetest love, I do not go
B̄ o   B   o B̄   o   B
  For weariness of thee,
   o   B o B̄   o   B [o B]
Nor in hope the world can show
B̄ o   B   o B   o   B
  A fitter love for me
  o B o B   o   B [o B]

The only deviation used is the least complex one, promotion, which by preventing strong alternations, contributes to the quiet confidence of the utterance. Notice that the metrical pattern has initial offbeats only in the second and fourth lines, and no final offbeats; this enhances the rhythmic simplicity by providing each line with a final beat and each half of the quatrain with an initial beat, and by easing the progression from line to line within each half, while articulating the division between the two halves.

The second part of the stanza introduces a less comforting notion (though its ostensible purpose is to reassure), and the steady movement receives a slight shock. This is experienced not in the use of rhythmic variation within the line, but by a change in the metrical pattern to a two-beat line followed by three three-beat lines, accompanied by a shift from an *abab* rhyme scheme to *abba*. Though it is not until the last line that deviation is used to disturb the progress of the rhythm and provide a local emphasis, the quatrain as a whole has the effect of moving into a new key for the statement of a second, more sombre, subject:

> But since that I
> o B   o B
> Must die at last, 'tis best
> o   B o B   o   B
> To use myself in jest
> o B   o B o B
> Thus by feigned deaths to die.
> ŏ B   ŏ B   o B

Because of the shortness of the first line, the absence of any full four-beat units, and the strong run-ons, there is no clear sense of unrealised beats; in fact, the syntactic structure encourages the emergence of a counterpointed four-beat rhythm to threaten the grouping determined by the line-divisions, and there is even a half-rhyme to reinforce the alternative alignment:

> But since that I must die at last,
> o   B   o B o   B o B
> 'Tis best to use myself in jest
> o   B   o B   o B o   B

The result is a metrical uncertainty that belies the assurance of the statement, and creates a peculiar tension in the final line, which we are tempted to regard as another four-beat unit by promotion of the first syllable:

> Thus by feigned deaths to die
> B̄   o   B   ŏ B   o B

However we read the line, the ambiguity of the metrical pattern imbues 'thus' with an uneasy, hesitating quality, as if the logic of the argument it expounds falters in the moment of utterance.

The second stanza begins with a whimsical analogy that proclaims a return to the mood of confidence, and the rhythm is appropriately smooth:

> Yesternight the sun went hence,
> B o B   o B o   B

And yet is here today,
  o   B   o   B   o B   [o B]
He hath no desire nor sense,
  B   o   B̄   o B   o   B
Nor half so short a way
  o   B   o   B   o   B   [o B]

Again promotion helps to keep the rhythm light, and the first line of
each pair runs easily into the second. Then, once more, the short line
brings a sense of modulation, as the speaker turns to his own promised
return, and this time a new rhythmic effect is used to undermine the
assured prediction that follows. Our expectation is that the sixth line
will begin with a single offbeat, like all the even-numbered lines so far,
and this seems to receive confirmation in the word 'But'. However, this
is followed immediately by another nonstress, implying a double
offbeat, though one which breaks the metrical rules so far observed by
being unpaired and unelidable:

Then fear not me,
  o   B   o   B
But believe that I shall make
 ŏ   B   o B   o   B

At least the line does contain the anticipated three beats – but the
following line throws even this into doubt, since it unexpectedly and
unambiguously contains four beats, and appears to begin with an initial
inversion that implies the normal iambic conventions:

Speedier journeys, since I take
  B   ŏ   B   o   B   o B

The only way to match these two lines is to use an initial promotion in
the first and elision in the second, and reinterpret the metrical pattern
as a fundamentally four-beat one, involving an unrealised beat in the
last line:

Then fear not me,
  o   B   o   B
But believe that I shall make
 B̄   o B   o B   o   B
   −s
Speedier journeys, since I take
  B   o   B   o   B   o B
More wings and spurs than he.
 ŏ   B   o   B   o   B   [o B]

We do not, of course, experience poetic rhythm in this doggedly
analytic and linear way; what we are aware of (perhaps only very

dimly) is some subterranean disturbance finally under control in the last line, whose clear shape reassuringly echoes that of the stanza's second and fourth lines.

In case this seems an oversubtle account of the working of rhythm, it is worth looking at the equivalent pairs of lines in later stanzas. In the two stanzas that follow, these lines exhibit exactly the same ambiguity as the line with 'But' (and the line with 'Thus' in the first stanza): we can scan them as four-beat, but there is a strong inclination in reading them to treat the first two syllables as a double offbeat (and now there is no indisputable four-beat line to provide guidance):

> But come bad chance,
> And we join to it our strength
> $\bar{\text{B}}$ o B   o $\bar{\text{B}}$ o   B
> And we teach it art and length
> $\bar{\text{B}}$ o B   o B o   B
> Itself o'er us to advance.

> It cannot be
> That thou lov'st me, as thou sayst,
> $\bar{\text{B}}$ o   B   o $\bar{\text{B}}$ o   B
>   s̱   s̱
> If in thine my life thou waste,
> B o   B   o B   o   B
> Thou art the best of me.

Only in the fifth and final stanza does metrical certainty return: the first line of the pair is once more ambiguous in precisely the same way, but the second has four unequivocal beats, allowing the poem to close with a revival of its early confidence:

> But think that we
> Are but turned aside to sleep;
> $\bar{\text{B}}$ o B   o B o   B
> They who one another keep
> B   o B   o B   o   B
> Alive, ne'er parted be.

It is worth adding that, in spite of the poem's title, both the rhythmic shaping of the whole work and the local effects of uncertainty and tension would be lost in a musical setting that imposed the same metrical framework on each stanza.

(7) Gr-r-r – there go, my heart's abhorrence!
    Water your damned flower-pots, do!
    If hate killed men, Brother Lawrence,
    God's blood, would not mine kill you!
    What? your myrtle-bush wants trimming?
    Oh, that rose has prior claims –
    Needs its leaden vase filled brimming?
    Hell dry you up with its flames!

Browning, 'Soliloquy of the Spanish
Cloister', stanza 1

We have looked at examples of unchanging metrical patterns realised by a varying number of syllables and of varying metrical patterns realised according to syllabically strict rules; this example is rigorous in both respects, but illustrates a third kind of metrical freedom. Most of Browning's verse employs a fixed metrical pattern and obeys the conventions of accentual-syllabic metre; but it proclaims its liberty by exploiting to the full the rhythmic variety permitted within those confines. The result is a distinctive mode of verse, in which the irregular rhythms of speech, rather than finding expression through the variety of metrical configurations, seem pitted against the authority of the metre. This effect is particularly marked when the metrical form is one characterised by rhythmic insistence; I have already quoted examples of Browning's trochaic and triple metres (Ch. 7, examples (102) and (113)–(118)), and this passage exemplifies one of the most insistent of all metres, trochaic verse in a 4 × 4 structure.

The metrical pattern is once more the familiar alternation of 4B and 4Bo with an *abab* rhyme scheme, here arranged into eight-line stanzas. The verse uses all the duple metre rules, and observes the pairing conditions and the trochaic initial inversion condition. Besides employing the most complex deviations, an unusual freedom for trochaic verse, the poem is written in a language which makes its own strong rhythmic demands – one need look no further than the first syllable for an example. Although the opening line is a very simple realisation of the metrical pattern, it insists on being read in a way which does not tamely submit to the regularising power of the metre:

G-r-r-r – there go, my heart's abhorrence!
B   ò   B   o B   o B o

The second line allows full expressive emphasis on 'damned flower-pots' by making use of an implied offbeat, and the rhythm is kept from falling into the swing of a ballad or a nursery rhyme by its observation of the pairing conditions:

Water your damned flower-pots, do!
B   ŏ́   B   ŏ̂ B   o   B

The syllabic regularity of the verse prevents us from treating 'flower' as a disyllable, which we might do in a looser metrical style. The third line is even more deviant: the succession of four strong stresses allows a dramatically free reading to treat the language as prose, but a recognition of the metrical structure encourages a more subtle articulation, making full use of the expressiveness of metrical tension. It is an example of that rare formation, trochaic initial inversion:

        s   [s]
If hate killed men, Brother Lawrence
o   B ŏ̂ B   o   B   o   B   o

The semantic emphasis falls on 'killed', permitting the metrical subordination of 'men'. The rules and conditions are all observed, but it remains a rhythmically exceptional line, its metre stretched to contain a vigorous speech-rhythm, and it is characteristic of Browning that he should do this not by liberating himself from metrical rules, but by using an option made possible more by the conventions of syllabic prosody than by the realities of rhythm (see 7.8 above). The savage undertone continues in the next line, and is again caught in a deviant form: this time a stress-initial pairing at the beginning of the line (there are thus four different openings in so many lines):

              s   s
God's blood, would not mine kill you!
B   ŏ̂ B   ŏ   B ŏ̂ B

Again, the line needs care in reading if its violent emotion is to be expressed without losing the four-beat pattern: strong stresses on the opening exclamation (necessary also to realise the beats, since there is no syntactic break between them), and contrastive emphasis on 'mine' and 'you'. There is, of course, a stress on 'kill', but as it is repeated from the previous line it cannot be emphatic, and demotion occurs without too much difficulty.

The tone changes as the second quatrain begins: the speaker mincingly imitates what he takes to be his enemy's thoughts, and the rhythm provides the perfect vehicle. Lines 5–7 are more regular than the previous three lines, the only deviations being two demoted beats, and only the second of these disturbs the evenness of the alternations:

What, your myrtle-bush wants trimming?
B   o   B   o B   ŏ   B   o
Oh, that rose has prior claims –
B   o B   o Bo   B
Needs its leaden vase filled brimming?
B   o B   o B   ŏ   B   o

We have already observed examples in both conversational speech and poetry of rhythmic regularity serving to express controlled but powerful emotion (pp. 73–4 and 297). The calm is of course the lull before the storm, which bursts in the last line, apparently shattering the regular rhythm. But close attention reveals that this is not quite so: a contrast is being drawn between the watered plants and a waterless fate; an emphatic stress therefore falls on 'you', allowing demotion on the second word:

s
Hell dry you up with its flames!
B   ŏ B   o   B̄   o   B

Other stanzas of the poem also use rhythmic complexity for climactic endings; stanza 2, for instance, closes with these lines:

What's the Latin name for 'parsley'?
What's the Greek name for Swine's Snout?

The superb scorn with which the speaker rewords to himself Friar Lawrence's conversational offering is expressed in part by the rhythmic deformation that the model endures while its syntax remains unchanged. Because an emphatic stress falls on 'Greek' in contrast to 'Latin', 'name' can be metrically subordinated as part of a double offbeat, allowing a stress-final pairing which culminates in a blaze of magnificent, alliterated hatred:

s   [s]
What's the Greek name for Swine's Snout?
B̄   o   B   ŏ   B   ŏ B

Few poets demand as much attention to their use of metre as Browning does, and probably not many readers are willing to give it. It must be realised that what is at stake is not some abstract notion of metrical correctness, but the only way in which the close but tempestuous relationship between metre and speech rhythm in Browning's verse can be properly appreciated and, more important, fully felt.

(8) Never pain to tell thy love
Love that never told can be,
For the gentle wind does move
Silently, invisibly.

I told my love, I told my love,
I told her all my heart;
Trembling, cold, in ghastly fears,
Ah, she doth depart.

Soon as she was gone from me,
A traveller came by
Silently, invisibly;
O, was no deny.

Blake, from the Notebook

One of the simplest forms in English poetry – in one sense of the word 'simple' – is the 4 × 4 duple stanza which makes free use of initial offbeats and unrealised beats, and thereby resists classification as iambic or trochaic, tetrameter or trimeter. The use of such an elementary form suits this poem's character as a moral fable, a paring down to essentials of a complex human event in order to enforce it as an illustration of a general truth, without taking away any of its complexity. That truth, I take it, is one which Blake frequently expounds: love in all its true power is something one dare not frankly show to the world; only the method of indirection, of secrecy, meets with acceptance. Blake's use of a form in which society commonly encapsulates its truisms – in hymns and in children's rhymes – in order to attack those truisms is another example of the associative function of metrical form: here the purpose is to expose what it brings to mind, rather than to claim kinship.

The rules by means of which this poem's metre can be specified are appropriately simple. The base rules are used without the option allowing double offbeats; and though promotion occurs normally, neither the demotion rule nor the implied offbeat rule apply. In other words, the general set is cut off after the third rule, indicating a metre that realises the underlying rhythm with unusual directness. The 4 × 4 rhythmic structure allows unrealised offbeats in the usual places in the first and third lines, and the metrical pattern can therefore be stated as follows:

((o)) B o B o B ([o B])

But a simple metre does not mean a lack of expressive resources. Blake's poem starts with two lines in the most direct realisation of the metrical pattern possible, contributing to the aphoristic force of the injunction and perhaps concealing the bitter irony that lies beneath it:

Never pain to tell thy love
B o B o B o B
Love that never told can be
B o B o B o B

The epigrammatic effect is heightened by the chiasmus (never tell:love/love:never told) and the anadiplosis it contains (love/Love). The realisation of all four beats in the second line, where an unrealised beat might have occurred, supports this symmetrical arrangement, and sets up expectations for the rest of the poem. Then there is a striking change: the next two lines have a much less forthright rhythm, relying on promotion to keep the movement quick and light (although there are eight beats again, there are only five stresses):

For the gentle wind does move
B̄ o B o B o B
Silently, invisibly
B o B̆ o B o B̆

The rhythm clearly suits the content, but the logical connection implied by 'For' is not clear to the reader: we have moved off at a tangent from the apparent obviousness of the opening sentiments into a mysterious region which the rest of the poem will have to account for.

After the generalised moral comes the exemplification in personal experience, and the rhythm changes once more: the voice again becomes emphatic, this time in an insistent rising rhythm based on pairs of monosyllables mirroring the obsessive repetition, and using initial offbeats for the first time:

I told my love, I told my love,
o B o B o B o B
I told her all my heart
o B o B o B [o B]

The fourth beat we have been led to expect does not come this time; instead, there is a tense pause, followed by the climactic line of the poem:

Trembling, cold, in ghastly fears
 B   o   B   o   B   o   B

This line is as metrically simple as the opening lines of the poem, but the relation of the linguistic structures to the metrical pattern is very different. The opening word – hardly the expected response to a confession of love – abruptly reverses the rising rhythm of the previous two lines, and in place of the unified or medially divided structure, this line has a break after the first offbeat, followed by an isolated, and therefore prominent, monosyllable. Instead of the expected rhyme with the first line, 'love' is answered by 'fears'. The rhythmically simple final line tells the inevitable consequences in equally simple language, now in the present tense, as if the moment is continually relived:

Ah, she doth depart
 B   o   B̄   o   B   [o B]

It should perhaps be reiterated that no claim is being made about Blake's consciousness of these metrical details; what we are trying to explain is why the reader finds the poem compelling – why, for instance, the seventh line is experienced as such a powerful climax. The explanation can be pursued further, in fact. If we look at the second stanza as a whole, we notice that, as so often with 4×4 structures, especially with unrealised beats, a dipodic tendency is present. The repeated 'told' demands a particularly strong stress, since this is the point being emphasised, and Blake has this word fall, naturally enough, in those places where the primary beat would normally occur:

I told my love, I told my love,
 o B   o b   o B   o b

I told her all my heart
 o B   o b   o B   [o b]

But the third line destroys this dipodic rhythm completely, and it is specifically on the word 'cold' that the dislocation occurs, since it demands as much weight as the first stress. This helps to account for the way in which the line, and one word in particular, stands out from the rhythmic sequence, in spite of the regular realisation of the metre. The highlighting of the line is sealed by the reinstatement of the dipodic rhythm immediately after it, to continue strongly to the end of the poem.

The opening line of the final stanza has a regular rhythm but no words which require special emphasis, as if the trauma of the second stanza is now over; the events have been replaced in the past, and the poet's ironic control is reasserted:

> Soon as she was gone from me
> B   o   B   o   B   o   B

The rhythm lightens still further in the second line, which has only one strong stress, preparing us for a repetition of the poem's gentlest line, now moved into the pivotal third line position:

> A traveller came by
> o   B o B̄   o   B   [o B]
> Silently, invisibly
> B o   B̄ o B o B̄

The mysterious wind of the first stanza has now received embodiment in a type of human individual, the secretive lover so hated by Blake. The effect of the rival's very different approach needs no elaborate statement: the metre is again reduced to essentials, and this time the syntax with it, for the baldest enunciation of willing acceptance:

> O, was no deny.
> B   o   B   o B   [o B]

The silence in which the final beat occurs is as eloquent as any of the sounds that have preceded it.

10.3 FIVE-BEAT VERSE

> (9) They flee from me that sometime did me seek,
>   With naked foot stalking in my chamber.
>   I have seen them gentle, tame, and meek,
>   That now are wild, and do not remember
>   That sometime they put themself in danger
>   To take bread at my hand; and now they range,
>   Busily seeking with a continual change.
>
>   Thanked be fortune, it hath been otherwise
>   Twenty times better; but once in special,
>   In thin array after a pleasant guise,
>   When her loose gown from her shoulders did fall,
>   And she me caught in her arms long and small,
>   Therewithal sweetly did me kiss,
>   And softly said, 'Dear heart, how like you this?'

It was no dream: I lay broad waking.
But all is turned thorough my gentleness
Into a strange fashion of forsaking;
And I have leave to go of her goodness,
And she also to use newfangleness.
But since that I so kindly am served,
I would fain know what she hath deserved.

Wyatt, 'They flee from me . . .'

Wyatt's metrical intentions remain one of the most enduring of prosodic mysteries, and I have no solution to offer. Instead, I shall confine myself to asking how a modern reader can approach the rhythms of Wyatt's most famous poem, armed only with ordinary metrical skills and his grasp of the present-day equivalent of Wyatt's language. The experience of a multitude of readers testifies to the poem's continuing vitality; it is unlikly, therefore, that its rhythms are unsuccessful, whether or not they are what Wyatt or his audience heard. Most modern readers prefer Wyatt's original to Tottel's regularised version (though the pendulum of taste may swing again), but it is some comfort to know that so soon after the poet's death an editor should have found his metre odd.

It is immediately obvious that the poem does not establish a four-beat metrical set, as much of Wyatt's poetry does; but it cannot be said either that it establishes a five-beat set. Some of the lines are recognisable as iambic pentameters according to the normal rules (though the syntactic and lexical structures do not always co-operate with the metrical scheme); for example:

In thin array after a pleasant guise
o   B   o B ŏB   ŏ   B o   B

And she me caught in her arms long and small
o   B o B   ŏ B   ŏB o   B

And she also to use newfangleness
o   BŏB   ŏ B   o B   oB̄

Moreover, if we take the initial offbeat of the metrical pattern to be optional and assume that the pairing conditions do not apply, many more lines are rendered acceptable, such as the following:

I have seen them gentle, tame, and meek
B o   B   o   B   o B   o   B

Busily seeking with a continual change
B ŏ   B   o   B̄   ŏ   B ŏ   B

Twenty times better; but once in special
B   o   B   ŏ B   ŏ   B   o   B ŏ

If we read a selection of these lines in succession, they are regular
enough to establish a five-beat metrical set: in the course of the poem,
however, we have to contend with lines like the following, which are
perceived most naturally as four-beat lines:

That now are wild, and do not remember
o   B   o   B   o   B   ŏ   B
That sometime they put themself in danger
o   B   ŏ   B   o   B   o   B   o

It is the presence of lines like these that unsettles the sense of regularity
established by the clear five-beat lines, and renders ambiguous
other lines which might be perceived as five-beat in a more
homogeneous context. The line that follows these two could be read as
a pentameter:

To take bread at my hand; and now they range
o   B   ô   B   ŏ   B   o   B   o   B

but coming where it does, it is more likely to be understood as a third
example of four-beat verse:

To take bread at my hand; and now they range
ŏ   B   ŏ   B   o   B   o   B

It would be a waste of time to look for a metrical structure common
to all those lines, because the reader's experience is that they are
metrically different – and that it remains a satisfying poem. Whether
further research in metrical and phonological history will throw light
on Wyatt's intentions is a separate question; what matters here is that
the poem (unlike, say, Browning's 'Soliloquy') does not benefit from
attempts to read it as consistently regular accentual-syllabic metre.
The reader has to be true to the rhythms of the language, and let the
passages of regular metre emerge of their own accord. Thus the
opening two lines fall naturally into a five-beat duple rhythm, the only
disturbance coming, perhaps appropriately, with the unpaired implied
offbeat before 'stalking':

They flee from me that sometime did me seek,
o   B   o   B   o   B   o   B̄   o   B
With naked foot stalking in my chamber
o   B o   B ô B o   B̄   o   B   o

Another regular pentameter is the following, and there is no doubt that its rocking rhythm contributes to the satisfaction it expresses:

> And softly said, 'Dear heart, how like you this?'
>   o   B   o   B   ŏ   B   o   B   o   B

The following line, on the other hand, gets some of its power from its avoidance of a regular pentameter rhythm: it hovers between a four-beat and a five-beat pattern:

> It was no dream: I lay broad waking
>   ŏ   Bŏ B   o B   ŏ   B o
>   B ŏ B ŏ B

Yet to put it in these terms is perhaps to impose inappropriate metrical grids on the line; we experience it simply as a rhythmic sequence which refuses to fall into an alternating pattern (and is not encouraged to do so by any metrical set), and which therefore gives primacy to the speech rhythm embodied in its disposition of stresses and nonstresses. The assertion is so forcefully felt not because of rhythmic tension (which is more properly a feature of strict verse forms), but because of its slow, emphatic movement:

> −s   −s   +s   +s   −s +s   +s   +s −s
> It was no dream: I lay broad waking

The result of the poem's rhythmic variation is that every line operates on its own terms; the ear may be haunted by familiar rhythms from time to time, but it seems right that in an account of lost bliss it should never be granted the satisfaction of a regular metre.

(10) That time of year thou mayst in me behold
      When yellow leaves, or none, or few, do hang
      Upon those boughs which shake against the cold,
      Bare ruined choirs, where late the sweet birds sang.
      In me thou seest the twilight of such day
      As after sunset fadeth in the west,
      Which by and by black night doth take away,
      Death's second self, that seals up all in rest.
      In me thou seest the glowing of such fire
      That on the ashes of his youth doth lie,
      As the death-bed whereon it must expire,
      Consumed with that which it was nourished by.
        This thou perceiv'st, which makes thy love more strong,
        To love that well which thou must leave ere long.

                                        Shakespeare, Sonnet 73

Shakespeare's *Sonnets* observe the normal rules and conditions of the iambic pentameter, with very few exceptional lines, and demonstrate one facet of the metre that has shone at the centre of the English verse tradition for so long. Sonnet 73 has already had many pages of critical commentary lavished upon it (see, for example, Nowottny, 1962, pp. 76–86; Booth, 1969, pp. 118–30; R. Fowler, 1975, pp. 93–120), but for this very reason it will be a valuable exercise to consider it from a strictly metrical point of view. It opens with three lines that invite a relatively unemphatic reading, the natural alternations of the stress contour producing a regular five-beat duple rhythm without any effort, and an easy rising movement:

> That time of year thou mayst in me behold
>   o B   o   B   o   B   o   B o B
>
> When yellow leaves, or none, or few, do hang
>   o   B o   B   o   B   o   B   o   B
>
> Upon those boughs which shake against the cold
> o B̄   o   B   o   B o B̄   o   B

The relaxed flow of the rising rhythm is challenged slightly by the falling contour of 'yellow', a word which also introduces the first sensory quality in the poem, but that vivid colour is half taken away by what follows in the line, and the rhythm reverts to its rising movement. It is a movement broken by pauses, matching the hesitant syntax and the slightly anomalous pattern of contrasts (yellow leaves against no leaves against few leaves), and suiting the ambivalence of the season, and the human experience it stands for. The rising rhythm continues in the third line, which has only three strong stresses.

The next line takes a startling metaphorical leap within the simile, and this is accompanied by a shift to a more deviant rhythm, suggestive of an intensification of emotion:

>   +ŝ
> Bare ruined choirs, where late the sweet birds sang
> ò   Bo   B   o   B   o B   ò   B

The rising rhythm is obstructed by the initial strong stress; and the syntactic relation of the first word to the second, parallel adjectives qualifying the same noun, means that the demotion is in no way made smooth by natural subordination. The first unstressed offbeat is realised by a minimum of phonetic substance, since 'ruined' is not strongly disyllabic, and indeed the next word has a similar complex vowel which, by elision, is treated as one syllable. The whole phrase therefore achieves rhythmic salience, helping to establish this as the dominant image of the quatrain, though it is stated in only three words. In the remainder of the line, this picture of the bleak present is succeeded by an evocation of a happier past, and the rhythm immediately softens into regularity, ending with a phrase of three stresses which, although it provides a firm close to the quatrain, does not, because the middle stress is syntactically subordinated to the last, disturb the evenness of movement. The clustering of stresses at the beginning and end of the line, with their very different rhythmic effects, reinforces the contrast between the two states in question.

The sense of a return to the opening with which the second quatrain begins is produced not only by its place in the sonnet structure and by the semantic repetition, but also by a return to the regular rising rhythm, although at the end of the line this shifts into a different movement by way of a pairing formation:

> In me thou seest the twilight of such day
> o   B   o   B   o   B   ŏ   B ŏ B

It is not, however, a strongly marked pairing, since the rhythm is blurred in the direction of the alternative reading:

> ... twilight of such day
>   B o   B̄   o   B

The two lines that follow retain the smooth movement, though 'black' is given some prominence by its occurrence as an offbeat, slowing the line down on its most ominous word:

> As after sunset fadeth in the west,
> o B o B o   B o   B̄   o B
> Which by and by black night doth take away
> o   B o   B ŏ   B   o   B   o B

Then once more the final line of the quatrain opens with an initial demotion on a word that demands attention, and thereby opposes the pressure of the metre. In addition, the clustering of consonants forces a pause between 'Death's' and 'second', and alliteration and assonance highlight the phrase still further, and echo through the remainder of the line:

> Death's second self, that seals up all in rest
> ŏ   B o   B   o   B   o B o B

As in its counterpart in the first quatrain, the line moves from a salient three-word, two-beat phrase into a smooth, predominantly rising rhythm, but this time it is not for a nostalgic vision of the past but a look forward to what seems a desired consummation.

The third quatrain opens with another new beginning that repeats earlier ones, this time an exact reproduction of the rhythm, and many of the words, of the first line of the second quatrain; and it too is followed by a regular line, using only promotion to lighten the movement:

> In me thou seest the glowing of such fire
> o   B   o   B   o   B   ŏ   B ŏB
> That on the ashes of his youth doth lie
> o B̄   o B o B̄   o B   o   B

But the pattern of recurrence is broken when the idea of death, which has been pressing more and more forcefully into the poem, is introduced a line earlier; and it occurs this time not with a demotion but a stress-final pairing. Moreover, the two beats fall on the two components of a compound (see the discussion above, pp. 277–8), requiring, for the modern reader at least, an unusual emphasis on the whole word. The rest of the line, and the closing line of the quatrain, falls into a weak alternating rhythm with only three more strong stresses, as if enacting the expiration they refer to, or, more accurately, embodying the affective rhythms of a speaker losing his determination and energy:

> As the death-bed whereon it must expire,
> ŏ   B   ŏ B   o B̄ o B̄ o B
> Consumed with that which it was nourished by
> o   B   o   B̄   o B̄ o B   o   B̄

The closing couplet will be read by different readers in different ways. The three quatrains, with their parallels in meaning and rhythm, clearly invite consideration as a progression, even though the sonnet does not advance logically through them. If we have responded mainly to the growing power of the idea of death in each restatement, and to the increasing negativity of winter, night, and extinguished ashes, the predominant feeling will be one of self-denigration and spiritual desolation, and the couplet will express the poet's glad surprise at the young man's love: 'That you should continue to love me at this juncture is evidence of the strength of that love.' On the other hand, if we have also responded to the increasing concentration of the imagery in terms of its physical and temporal scope, to the intensifying colours from autumn leaves to sunset to glowing embers, and to the increasing intellectual complexity of the metaphors, we may feel that there is a further sense to the couplet: 'For the very reason that I have not long to live, my life takes on a kind of growing intensity which inspires your love.' However we find ourselves understanding it, there is no doubt that the relation of the couplet to the body of the poem is far from simple and far from single, and we may note the contribution of the metre to this multiplicity of meaning. After an ambiguous 'This', referring back to the whole web of ideas and feelings without doing anything to guide us in interpreting them, the rhythm settles once more into a steady rising movement; but since several of the offbeats are realised by indefinite stresses, there is considerable freedom – built into the structure of the verse – for variations in emphasis and intonation:

> s   s   s   s
> This thou perceiv'st, which makes thy love more strong,
> B   ŏ   B   o   B   o   B   o   B
>
>   s   s   s
> To love that well which thou must leave ere long
> o   B   o   B   o   B   o   B   o   B

It is not just a matter of two clear interpretations, but of a range of meanings which the metrical and syntactic forms refuse to limit; it makes little sense to ask, 'What does the speaker *really* mean?' Metre can be highly effective not only in enforcing precision, but in leaving options open.

> (11)   Pleasures the sex, as children birds, pursue,
>   Still out of reach, yet never out of view,
>   Sure, if they catch, to spoil the toy at most,
>   To covet flying, and regret when lost:
>   At last, to follies youth could scarce defend,
>   'Tis half their age's prudence to pretend;
>   Ashamed to own they gave delight before,
>   Reduced to feign it, when they give no more:
>   As hags hold sabbaths, less for joy than spite,
>   So these their merry, miserable night;
>   Still round and round the ghosts of beauty glide,
>   And haunt the places where their honour died.
>   See how the world its veterans rewards!
>   A youth of frolics, an old age of cards,
>   Fair to no purpose, artful to no end,

> Young without lovers, old without a friend,
> A fop their passion, but their prize a sot,
> Alive, ridiculous, and dead, forgot!

Pope, 'Epistle to a Lady', 231–248

By severely limiting the kind and number of metrical deviations he uses, Pope closes off certain possibilities in the realm of rhythmic expressiveness, but gains access to others. The precision, economy, and control which his poetry conveys is partly an effect created by the metre; it is rigorously syllabic (to the extent of avoiding feminine endings), which is to say that it strictly observes both pairing conditions, and although it makes use of all the deviation rules, it does so sparingly and only when the rhythmic tendencies of the language can act in concert with the metre. This puts Pope's verse at a far remove from the speaking voice, of course, but its sprightly rhythms offer their own substitute for what seem by contrast the lumbering movements of conversation: an apparently direct embodiment of mental agility and lucidity. A strict metre of this sort can, of course, degenerate into sing-song (though the danger is not as great as in four-beat verse), and Saintsbury put Pope low in his metrical league-table for this reason. But once we are attuned to the finer details of the metre, any sense of monotony disappears: it is alive with small shifts and tensions, and any strongly repetitive passage is there for a purpose. Because of the firm outline of the five-beat grouping, marked off by rhyme and terminal pause, Pope can make use of the rhythmic balance of the whole line as a source of subtle variation – a source unavailable to a writer like Milton, whose line-units are not a prominent part of the reader's metrical set. It is this aspect of Pope's verse on which we shall focus in discussing the example.

One of the most common rhythmic line-structures in Pope's pentameters, common enough (and salient enough) to form part of the metrical set, is that exhibited by the first three lines:

> Pleasures the sex, as children birds, pursue,
> B   ŏ   B   o   B   o   B   o   B
> Still out of reach, yet never out of view,
> B   ŏ   B   o   B   o   B̄   o   B
> Sure, if they catch, to spoil the toy at most
> B   ŏ   B   o   B   o   B   o   B

It is an elementary and frequently-occurring pattern which we have already discussed (see pp. 142–3): the line is divided by a pause (often marked by punctuation) into a two-beat section and a three-beat section, but the latter's relative speed and lightness makes it more nearly equivalent to the first in rhythmic terms than their different lengths would suggest. In all these lines, the movement of the underlying rhythm in the first section is kept particularly slow by the use of initial inversion, which rhythmically spaces out the first two beats; and in the second line, the second section is rendered especially quick by its central promoted nonstress. The verbal repetition in this second line increases the equivalence of the two parts still further: one would only have to pronounce 'never' as 'ne'er' to achieve an exact correspondence of rhythm. However, the extra light syllable is crucial to the metrical structure, since it provides the second section with its central beat and its accelerated underlying rhythm (note that the same words, 'out of', realise an offbeat in the first section and a beat plus offbeat in the second). This line-structure is often used, as here, to give a witticism added bite: a slow start, as the trap is laid, and a quick finish as it is sprung. Let us call it, in Pope's hands at least, a *sprung* pentameter.

The fourth line shows how a slight rhythmic difference can create a quite distinct line-structure: there is still a 2:3 division of beats, but because the third and not the fourth beat is realised by promotion, the second section does not fall into the rapid movement of the sprung line:

To covet flying, and regret when lost
  o B o   Bo   B̄   o B   o   B

Instead, the rhythm creates what we might call a *balanced* pentameter, in which the first two and last two beats are realised by stresses and the middle beat is realised by a promoted nonstress. The balanced line is still usually divided by a pause between the second and third beats, though this is no longer an essential feature, since the three successive nonstresses at the centre act as a structural divider. The character of the balanced line is quite different from that of the sprung line: the medial promoted nonstress acts as a kind of pivot, and the speed of the sections on either side is roughly the same. The effect is less that of winding up and release than of thesis and antithesis, and the sense is frequently concentrated into two significant words on each side of the central beat. It is a useful structure with which to close a group of lines, providing a firm and settled ending, and is more suited to this position than the sprung pentameter, with its quicker, unemphatic second section. The line in question does in fact round off the first four lines of the paragraph (Pope is of course sensitive to the natural tendency of couplets to group themselves in pairs), and the next line begins a new four-line group. The rhythm of these four lines is highly regular, with only a couple of promotions to vary the firm alternation of stress and nonstress; the first three make little use of internal structuring, while the group closes once more on a balanced line:

> At last, to follies youth could scarce defend,
> o B   o B o   B   o   B   o B
> 'Tis half their age's prudence to pretend;
> o   B   o B o   B o   B o B
> Ashamed to own they gave delight before,
> o   B   o B   o   B   o R   o B
> Reduced to feign it, when they give no more.
> o B   o B   o   B̄   o B   o   B

This regularity gives the lines a rhythmic sobriety which matches the grimmer vision they offer.

The emotional intensity of the poetry is growing, and the group of lines that follows shows an increase in metrical variation. It begins with a balanced line whose rhythm acquires a distinctive colouring through the additional emphasis given to each half, the first by means of a demotion, and the second by means of two contrastive stresses; the weight on each side of the balance is increased, as it were:

> As hags hold sabbaths, less for joy than spite
> o   B   ŏ   B   o   B̄   o   B   o   B

This is followed by a sprung line whose lively rhythm seems to join in the mockery it expresses, especially since it is quickest and lightest on the word 'miserable':

> So these their merry, miserable night
> o   B   o   B o   B o B̄ o B

It is not an entirely relaxed rhythm, however: the structure is rendered less simple than that of the earlier sprung lines by the occurrence of the pause *after* the offbeat, and by the closely-knit syntax, which prevents the intonational signalling of the division; and the refusal of any elision to 'miserable' produces a slightly self-conscious pronunciation. Pope follows this with an obviously mimetic line in which every beat is realised by a full stress, and there are no pauses; and once more ends the four-line group with a balanced pentameter, whose simple rhythm perhaps allows pity as well as humour:

Still round and round the ghosts of beauty glide,

  o   B   o   B   o   B   o   B   o   B

And haunt the places where their honour died

o   B   o   B o $\bar{\text{B}}$ o   B o   B

The next paragraph is welded into a six-line whole by the use of varied line-structures. The theme is announced with a strongly sprung line, enforced by initial inversion and a promotion on the fourth beat in spite of the absence of any marked pause:

See how the world its veterans rewards! ˙

B   ŏ   B   o   B o $\bar{\text{B}}$ o   B

The irony of the statement becomes fully apparent only in the lines that follow, however. The first of these uses stress-final pairing (relatively rare in this strict metrical style) to bring out the contrast beneath the apparent parallel:

A youth of frolics, an old age of cards!

o   B   o   B   ŏ   B   ŏB   o   B

Youth is given the easy rhythm, age the distorted one. There follow two matching sprung lines, their structure again heightened by initial inversion and promoted fourth beats, and, like the second line of the passage, by repeated phrases between the major beats:

Fair to no purpose, artful to no end,

B   ŏ   B   o   B   o $\bar{\text{B}}$ o   B

Young without lovers, old without a friend

B   ŏ   B o   B   o $\bar{\text{B}}$ o   B

By this means, the rhythm is virtually broken into two-beat units, which function like repeated phrases in music to build up a sense of expectation. This is amply rewarded in the remarkable power of the final couplet, bringing the paragraph to a close on two balanced lines, in which each side is charged with the same weight, not only of phonetic substance, but of explosive emotional force:

A fop their passion, but their prize a sot,

o B   o   B o $\bar{\text{B}}$ o   B   o   B

Alive, ridiculous, and dead, forgot!

o B   oBo $\bar{\text{B}}$ o   B   o   B

The strength of feeling cannot be missed, but its exact quality resists categorisation: one is tempted to say that it is a fusion of intense scorn with equally intense compassion. Such a union could occur only at the deepest level of affective experience, well below the specific emotions represented in the vocabulary we use; and, if the general arguments of this study have any validity, it is precisely to this profound level that we can trace the creative and transforming power of poetic rhythm.

Appendix

Rules and scansion

METRICAL RULES: THE GENERAL SET

The following is a summary in verbal and formal terms of the metrical rules that constitute the general set for English accentual-syllabic verse. References are given to the main discussions of individual topics.

Underlying rhythm and metrical pattern

The *underlying rhythm* (4.2) is normally a four-beat or a five-beat unit, shown as 4B, 5B. These units may form larger *rhythmic structures*, shown as 4 × 4, 5 × 2, etc.

The *metrical pattern* (4.3) consists of an alternation of beats and offbeats, realising an underlying rhythm, and arranged in lines. The fourth beat of a four-beat rhythm, with or without the preceding offbeat, may be *unrealised*.

The following symbols are used in stating the metrical pattern:

B: beat
o: offbeat
(o):   optional offbeat: neutral preference
⟨o⟩:   optional offbeat: preference for inclusion
((o)):   optional offbeat: preference for omission
[B]:   unrealised beat
([B]):   optional unrealised beat

Thus four-beat verse with obligatory initial offbeats and optional feminine endings has the metrical pattern:

   o B o B o B o B (o) or o4B(o)

Stanza forms are abbreviated by indicating realised beats only; for instance:

4.4.4.4:	long metre
4.3.4.3:	common metre or ballad stanza
3.3.4.3:	short metre
6.7:	poulter's measure

Realisation rules and conditions

All regular metres make use of the base rules and some or all of the deviation rules; stricter duple metres may impose one or more of the conditions. The later the rule, or option within a rule, the more complex the line produced by it will tend to be.

Formal conventions

In the formal statements of the rules that follow the verbal statements, the following symbols are used in addition to those given above:

+s:	stressed syllable } as constituents of the *stress*
−s:	unstressed syllable } *pattern*: see below
#:	line-boundary (initial or final)
x → y:	x may realise y
x → y / a__b:	x may realise y when the former occurs between a and b
(x):	additional option: neutral preference
⟨x⟩:	additional option: preference for inclusion
((x)):	additional option: preference for omission
x,y:	alternative options
ø → x / a__b:	x may be implied between a and b

Options which include bracketed items are ordered *later* than options which do not.

Duple metre

BASE RULES (7.2)

(1) *Beat rule*
    A stressed syllable may realise a beat.
    +s → B

(2) *Offbeat rule*
    One (or two) unstressed syllables may realise an offbeat.
    −s ((−s)) → o

Expanded:
(i) (single offbeat) $-s \to o$ (preferred)
(ii) (double offbeat) $-s -s \to o$
(For verse which varies freely between single and double offbeats, the
form of the rule is $-s (-s) \to o$.)

DEVIATION RULES

(3) *Promotion rule* (7.3)
An unstressed syllable may realise a beat when it occurs
between two unstressed syllables, or with a line-boundary on
one side and an unstressed syllable on the other.
$-s \to B / -s, \#$ ____$-s, \#$
Expanded:
(i) $-s \to B / -s$ __$-s$
(ii) $-s \to B / -s$ __ $\#$
(iii) $-s \to B / \#$ __ $-s$
[(iv) $-s \to B \#$ __$\#$]
Option (iv) applies only to a line consisting of a single nonstress; its
operation is therefore only hypothetical, though it is not
counter-intuitive.

(4) *Demotion rule* (7.4)
A stressed syllable may realise an offbeat when it occurs
between two stressed syllables, or after a line-boundary and
before a stressed syllable.
$+s \to o / +s, \#$ __ $+s$
Expanded:
(i) $+s \to o / +s$ __ $+s$
(ii) $+s \to o / \#$__ $+s$

(5) *Implied offbeat rule* (7.5)
An offbeat may be implied between two stressed syllables.
$\emptyset \to o / +s$ __ $+s$

CONDITIONS

(1) *Pairing conditions* (7.6)
(a) *Implied offbeat condition*
An implied offbeat may occur only (i) when it is
immediately preceded or followed by a non-final double

offbeat; or (ii) in observance of an initial inversion condition.

(b) *Double offbeat condition*

A double offbeat may occur only in observance of (i) the implied offbeat condition, or (ii) an initial inversion condition.

(2) *Initial inversion conditions*

(a) *Iambic opening* (7.7)

An optional initial offbeat may be omitted only if the first beat is immediately followed by a double offbeat.

(b) *Trochaic opening* (7.8)

An optional initial offbeat may be included only if the first beat is immediately followed by an implied offbeat.

The domains of conditions may not overlap.

Triple metre (7.9)

BASE RULES

(1) *Beat rule:* as for duple metre.

(2) *Offbeat rule*

Strict triple metre

Two unstressed syllables may realise an offbeat

$-s -s \rightarrow o$

Free triple metre

Two unstressed syllables (or one) may realise an offbeat

$-s \langle -s \rangle \rightarrow o$

Expanded:

(i) $-s \rightarrow o$

(ii) $-s -s \rightarrow o$ (preferred)

DEVIATION RULES

(3) *Promotion rule*: as for duple metre

(4) *Demotion rule*

A stressed syllable, or an unstressed syllable and a stressed syllable (in either order), or two stressed syllables, may realise an offbeat between two stresses, or after a line-boundary and before a stress.

$(-s) +s, +s -s, +s +s \rightarrow o / +s, \# \_\_\_ +s$

Expanded:
(i)   +s → o / +s __ +s
(ii)   +s → o / # __ +s
(iii) −s +s → o / +s __ +s
(iv)   −s +s → o / # __ +s
(v)   +s −s → o / +s __+s
(vi)   +s −s → o / # __ +s
(vii) +s +s → o / +s __ +s
(viii) +s +s → o / # __ +s

Stress pattern

The realisation rules generate a sequence of syllables marked +s and −s; however, a full description of the syllabic characteristics involved in the rhythmic perception of the line includes some further possibilities. Other types of syllable may replace +s or −s in the output of the rules, but only under the specific conditions discussed in Chapter 8:

s: indefinite stress; may replace either +s or −s (8.1)
s̲:   emphatic stress; may replace +s (8.2)
[s]: metrically subordinated stress; may replace −s (8.3)
(s): elision by contraction; the syllable is omitted (8.4)
⁺s, ⁻s: elision by coalescence; may replace +s or −s (8.4)

These symbols are used in the statement of the *stress pattern*, which is a simplification of the linguistically determined *stress contour* brought about by the perception of a regular rhythm.

SCANSION

The scansion of a line provides a graphic representation of the relationship between the metrical pattern and the stress pattern; that is, it shows which metrical rules are employed at particular points to realise beats and offbeats. It therefore directly reflects the way in which the line is perceived as rhythmically regular, indicating the degree and exact nature of metrical deviation at every stage. In addition to the symbols representing the metrical pattern and stress pattern, the following *deviation symbols* are used:

ŏ: double offbeat
B̄:   promotion

   ŏ: demotion

   ᴧ: implied offbeat

   ᴕ̆, ᴕ̈, ᴕ̇: double offbeat with demotion

   ᴕ̈:   triple offbeat

Full scansion shows the stress pattern above the line, and the metrical pattern with deviation symbols beneath it:

     +s −s   [s]   +s   −s   +s (s) −s+s −s −s
(1) Gilding pale streams with heavenly alchemy
     B   ŏ   B   o   B   o B   o B̄

However, the stress pattern can be fully specified without showing +s and −s, since the absence of a symbol will indicate the most straightforward realisation implied by the metrical pattern and deviation symbol:

         [s]   (s)
(*1*) Gilding pale streams with heavenly alchemy
     B   ŏ   B   o   B   o B   o B̄

The grouping of words and syllables can also be shown above the line, to draw attention to the presence of *rising* or *falling rhythms* (4.6):

(2) I wake and feel the fell of dark, not day

or to indicate the occurrence of *linkage* affecting the operation of a deviation rule (8.7):

(3) A proud woman not kindred of his soul
     B ŏ B   ŏ

Bibliography

Where two dates are given, the one after the author's name is the date of first publication, and is used for reference in the text.

Abercrombie, David (1964a) 'A phonetician's view of verse structure' in *Studies in Phonetics and Linguistics* (London, 1965), 16–25

Abercrombie, David (1964b) 'Syllable quantity and enclitics in English' in *Studies in Phonetics and Linguistics* (London, 1965), 26–34

Abercrombie, David (1967) *Elements of General Phonetics* (Edinburgh)

Abercrombie, David (1971) 'Some functions of silent stress' in *Edinburgh Studies in English and Scots* ed. A. J. Aitken, Angus McIntosh, and Hermann Pálsson (London), 147–56

Abercrombie, Lascelles (1923) *Principles of English Prosody* (London)

Adams, Corinne (1979) *English Speech Rhythm and the Foreign Learner* (The Hague)

Adler, Jacob H. (1964) *The Reach of Art: A Study in the Prosody of Pope* University of Florida Monographs, Humanities, No. 16 (Gainesville, Florida)

Albrow, K. H. (1968) *The Rhythm and Intonation of Spoken English* Programme in Linguistics and English Teaching, Paper 9 (London and Harlow)

Allen, George D. (1972) 'The location of rhythmic stress beats in English: an experimental study' *Language and Speech* **15**, 72–100, 1979–95

Allen, George D. (1975) 'Speech rhythm: its relation to performance universals and articulatory timing' *Journal of Phonetics* **3**, 75–86

Allen, George D. and Hawkins, Sarah (1978) 'The development of phonological rhythm' in *Syllables and Segments* ed. Alan Bell and Joan Bybee Hooper (Amsterdam), 173–85

Allen, W. Sidney (1964) 'On quantity and quantitative verse' in *In Honour of Daniel Jones*, ed. D. Abercrombie *et al.* (London), 3–15

Allen, W. Sidney (1965) *Vox Latina: A Guide to the Pronunciation of Classical Latin* (Cambridge)

Allen, W. Sidney (1969) 'The Latin accent: a restatement' *Journal of Linguistics* **5**, 193–203

Allen, W. Sidney (1973) *Accent and Rhythm: Prosodic Features in Latin and Greek: A Study in Theory and Reconstruction* (Cambridge)

Arnold, G. F. (1957) 'Stress in English words' *Lingua* **6**, 221–67, 397–441

Attridge, Derek (1974) *Well-weighed Syllables: Elizabethan Verse in Classical Metres* (Cambridge)

Attridge, Derek (1979) 'Dryden's Dilemma, or, Racine Refashioned: the problem of the English dramatic couplet' *The Yearbook of English Studies* **9**, 55–77

Augustine, Saint (1947) *De Musica* tr. R. C. Taliaferro, *Writings of St Augustine*, Vol. 2 (New York)

Bailey, James (1975a) 'Linguistic givens and their metrical realization in a poem by Yeats' *Language and Style* **8**, 21–33

Bailey, James (1975b) *Toward a Statistical Analysis of English Verse: The Iambic Tetrameter of Ten Poets* (Lisse)

Baker, Sheridan (1960) 'English meter *is* quantitative' *College English* **21**, 309–315

Barkas, Pallister (1934) *A Critique of Modern English Prosody (1880–1930)* Studien zur Englischen Philologie, 82 (Halle)

Barnes, Mervin and Esau, Helmut (1978) 'English prosody reconsidered' *Language and Style* **11**, 212–22

Barnes, Mervin and Esau, Helmut (1979) 'Gilding the lapses in a theory of metrics' *Poetics* **8**, 481–7

Baum, Paull Franklin (1952) *The Other Harmony of Prose: An Essay in English Prose Rhythm* (Durham, North Carolina)

Beardsley, Monroe C. (1972) 'Verse and music' in *Versification: Major Language Types*, ed. W. K. Wimsatt (New York)

Beaver, Joseph C. (1968a) 'A grammar of prosody' *College English* **29**, 310–21

Beaver, Joseph C. (1968b) 'Progress and problems in generative metrics' *Papers from the Fourth Regional Meeting of the Chicago Linguistic Society* ed. B. J. Darden, C-J. N. Bailey, and A. Davison (Chicago), 146–55

Beaver, Joseph C. (1969) 'Contrastive stress and metered verse' *Language and Style* **2**, 257–71

Beaver, Joseph C. (1971a) 'Current metrical issues' *College English* **33**, 177–97

Beaver, Joseph C. (1971b) 'The rules of stress in English verse' *Language* **47**, 586–614

Beaver, Joseph C. (1973) 'A stress problem in English prosody' *Linguistics* **95**, 5–12

Beaver, Joseph C. (1974) 'Generative metrics: the present outlook' *Poetics* **12**, 7–28

Beaver, Joseph C. (1976) *The Prosody of John Donne* (mimeograph)

Bever, Thomas G. (1970) 'The influence of speech performance on linguistic structure' in *Advances in Psycholinguistics*, ed. G. B. Flores d'Arcais and W. J. M. Levelt (Amsterdam), 4–30

Blenerhasset, Thomas (1578) *The Second Part of the Mirror for Magistrates,* in *Parts Added to 'The Mirror for Magistrates'*, ed. L. B. Campbell (Cambridge, 1946)

Bloch, Bernard (1950) 'Studies in colloquial Japanese, IV: phonemics' *Language* **26**, 86–125

Bloom, Harold (1976) *Figures of Capable Imagination* (New York)

Bolinger, Dwight L. (1965) 'Pitch accent and sentence rhythm' in Bolinger,

Forms of English: Accent, Morpheme, Order, ed. Isamu Abe and Tetsuya Kanekiyo (Cambridge, Mass.), 139–80

Boomsliter, Paul C. and Creel, Warren (1977) 'The secret springs: Housman's outline on metrical rhythm and language' *Language and Style* **10**, 296–323

Boomsliter, Paul C., Creel, Warren and Hastings, George S. (1973) 'Perception and English poetic meter' *PMLA* **88**, 200–208

Booth, Stephen (1969) *An Essay on Shakespeare's Sonnets* (New Haven)

Booth, Stephen (1977) (ed.) *Shakespeare's Sonnets* (New Haven)

Bracher, Frederick (1947) 'The silent foot in pentameter verse' *PMLA* **62**, 1100–107

Braden, Gordon (1978) *The Classics and English Renaissance Poetry: Three Case Studies* (New Haven)

Bridges, Robert (1909) 'A letter to a musician on English prosody' in *The Structure of Verse: Modern Essays on Prosody* ed. Harvey Gross (Greenwich, Conn., 1966), 86–101

Bridges, Robert (1921) *Milton's Prosody, with a Chapter on Accentual Verse & Notes* revised final edn. (Oxford)

Brinsley, John (1612) *Ludus Literarius; or, the Grammar Schoole* ed. E. T. Campagnac (Liverpool and London, 1917)

Brooks, Cleanth and Warren, Robert Penn (1938) *Understanding Poetry* (New York)

Brown, Calvin S. (1965) 'Can musical notation help English scansion?' *Journal of Aesthetics and Art Criticism* **23**, 329–34

Brown, Warner (1908) *Time in English Verse Rhythm: An Empirical Study of Typical Verses by the Graphic Method* Archives of Psychology, No. 10 (New York)

Burling, Robbins (1966) 'The metrics of children's verse: a cross-linguistic study' *American Anthropologist* **68**, 1418–41

Burling, Robbins (1970) *Man's Many Voices: Language in Its Cultural Context* (New York)

Bysshe, Edward (1702) *The Art of English Poetry* facsimile edn. (Menston, 1968)

Cable, Thomas (1972) 'Timers, stressers, and linguists: contention and compromise' *Modern Language Quarterly* **33**, 227–39

Cable, Thomas (1973) 'A garland of pomposities: comment on Halle–Keyser prosody' *College English* **34**, 593–5

Cable, Thomas (1976) 'Recent developments in metrics' *Style* **10**, 313–28

Campbell, Robin and Wales, Roger (1970) 'The study of language acquisition' in *New Horizons in Linguistics* ed. John Lyons (Harmondsworth), 242–60

Campion, Thomas (1602) *Observations in the Art of English Poesie* in *The Works of Thomas Campion*, ed. W. R. Davis (London, 1969), 287–317

Catford, J. C. (1977) *Fundamental Problems in Phonetics* (Edinburgh)

Chatman, Seymour (1956a) 'Robert Frost's "Mowing": an inquiry into prosodic structure' *Kenyon Review* **18**, 421–38

Chatman, Seymour (1956b) 'Mr Stein on Donne' *Kenyon Review* **18**, 443–51

Chatman, Seymour (1960) 'Comparing metrical styles' in *Style in Language* ed. T. A. Sebeok (Cambridge, Mass.), 149–72

Chatman, Seymour (1965) *A Theory of Meter* (The Hague)

Chisholm, David (1977) 'Generative prosody and English verse' *Poetics* **6**, 111–54

Chomsky, Noam (1957) *Syntactic Structures* (The Hague)

Chomsky, Noam and Halle, Morris (1968) *The Sound Pattern of English* (New York)

Classe, André (1939) *The Rhythm of English Prose* (Oxford)

Coates, Richard (1980) 'Time in phonological representation' *Journal of Phonetics* **8**, 1–20

Cone, Edward T. (1968) *Musical Form and Musical Performance* (New York)

Cooper, Grosvener W. and Meyer, Leonard B. (1960) *The Rhythmic Structure of Music* (Chicago)

Creek, Herbert L. (1920) 'Rising and falling rhythm in English verse' *PMLA* **35**, 76–90

Croll, Morris W. (1923) 'Music and metrics' in *Style, Rhetoric, and Rhythm: Essays by Morris W. Croll* ed. J. Max Patrick and R. O. Evans (Princeton, 1966), 430–6

Croll, Morris W. (1929) *The Rhythm of English Verse* in *Style, Rhetoric, and Rhythm: Essays by Morris W. Croll*, ed. J. Max Patrick and R. O. Evans (Princeton, 1966), 365–429

Crystal, David (1969) *Prosodic Systems and Intonation in English* (Cambridge)

Crystal, David (1975) 'Intonation and metrical theory' in *The English Tone of Voice: Essays in Intonation, Prosody and Paralanguage* (London), 105–24

Culler, A. Dwight (1948) 'Edward Bysshe and the poet's handbook' *PMLA* **63**, 858–85

Cummings, D. W. and Herum, John (1967) 'Metrical boundaries and rhythm-phrases' *Modern Language Quarterly* **28**, 405–412

Delattre, Pierre (1966) 'A comparison of syllable length conditioning among languages' *International Review of Applied Linguistics* **4**, 183–98

Derwing, Bruce L. (1973) *Transformational Grammar as a Theory of Language Acquisition* (Cambridge)

Devine, A. M. and Stephens, L. D. (1975) 'The abstractness of metrical patterns: generative metrics and explicit traditional metrics' *Poetics* **4**, 411–29

Dillon, George L. (1976) 'Clause, pause, and punctuation in poetry' *Linguistics* **169**, 5–20

Dillon, George L. (1977) 'Kames and Kiparsky on syntactic boundaries' *Language and Style* **10**, 16–22

Dobson, E. J. (1968) *English Pronunciation 1500–1700*, 2nd edn. (Oxford)

Donoghue, Denis (1980) 'Deconstructing deconstruction' *The New York Review of Books* Vol. 27, No. 10

Dougherty, Adelyn (1973) *A Study of Rhythmic Structure in the Verse of William Butler Yeats* (The Hague)

Draper, M. H., Ladefoged P. and Whitteridge, D. (1959) 'Respiratory muscles in speech' *Journal of Speech and Hearing Research* **2**, 16–27

Eberhart, Richard (1973) 'On rhythm' *Agenda* **11**, Nos. 2–3, 41–4

Eliot, T. S. (1917) 'Reflections on *vers libre*' in *To Criticize the Critic* (London, 1965), 183–9

Eliot, T. S. (1942) *The Music of Poetry* (Glasgow)

Epstein, Edmund L. and Hawkes, Terence (1959) *Linguistics and English Prosody* Studies in Linguistics Occasional Papers, No. 7 (Buffalo, New York)

Erasmus, Desiderius (1528) *De Recta Latini Graecique sermonis pronuntiatione* (Basle)

Erlich, Victor (1955) *Russian Formalism: History – Doctrine* (The Hague)

Finnegan, Ruth (1977) *Oral Poetry: Its Nature, Significance and Social Context* (Cambridge)

Fodor, J. and Garrett, M. (1966) 'Some reflections on competence and performance' in *Psycholinguistic Papers* ed. J. Lyons and R. J. Wales (Edinburgh), 133–79

Forrest-Thomson, Veronica (1978) *Poetic Artifice: A Theory of Twentieth-Century Poetry* (Manchester)

Fowler, Carol A. (1980) 'Coarticulation and theories of extrinsic timing' *Journal of Phonetics* **8**, 113–33

Fowler, Roger (1966a) ' "Prose rhythm" and metre' in *Essays on Style and Language* ed. Roger Fowler (London), 82–99

Fowler, Roger (1966b) 'Structural metrics' in *The Languages of Literature: Some Contributions to Criticism* (London, 1971), 124–40

Fowler, Roger (1968) 'What is metrical analysis?' in *The Languages of Literature: Some Contributions to Criticism* (London, 1971), 141–77

Fowler, Roger (1970) 'Against idealization: some speculations on the theory of linguistic performance' *Linguistics* **63**, 19–50

Fowler, Roger (1975) 'Language and the reader: Shakespeare's Sonnet 73' in *Style and Structure in Literature: Essays in the New Stylistics* ed. Roger Fowler (Oxford), 79–122

Fraser, G. S. (1970) *Metre, Rhyme, and Free Verse* (London)

Freeman, Donald C. (1968) 'On the primes of metrical style' *Language and Style* **1**, 63–101

Freeman, Donald C. (1969) 'Metrical position constituency and generative metrics' *Language and Style* **2**, 195–206

Freeman, Donald C. (1972) 'Current trends in metrics' in *Current Trends in Stylistics* ed. Braj B. Kachru and H. F. W. Stahlke (Edmonton, Alberta), 67–81

Fromkin, Victoria (1968) 'Speculations on performance models' *Journal of Linguistics* **4**, 47–68

Fry, D. B. (1964) 'The function of the syllable' *Zeitschrift für Phonetik* **17**, 215–21

Frye, Northrop (1957) 'Introduction: lexis and melos' in *Sound and Poetry* ed. Northrop Frye, English Institute Essays, 1956 (New York), ix–xxvii

Funkhouser, Linda Bradley (1979) 'Acoustic rhythm in Randall Jarrell's *The Death of the Ball Turret Gunner*' *Poetics* **8**, 381–403

Fussell, Paul (1954) *Theory of Prosody in Eighteenth-Century England* (New London, Conn.)

Fussell, Paul (1979) *Poetic Meter and Poetic Form* revised edn. (New York)

Gascoigne, George (1575) *Certayne Notes of Instruction*, in *Elizabethan Critical Essays*, ed. G. Gregory Smith (London, 1904), Vol. I, 46–57

Gay, Thomas (1978) 'Physiological and acoustic correlates of perceived stress' *Language and Speech* **21**, 347–53

Gerould, Gordon Hall (1932) *The Ballad of Tradition* (Oxford)

Giegerich, Heinz J. (1980) 'On stress-timing in English phonology' *Lingua* **51**, 187–221

Gimson, A. C. (1970) *An Introduction to the Pronunciation of English*, 2nd edn. (London)

Greenbaum, Sidney and Quirk, Randolph (1970) *Elicitation Experiments in English: Linguistic Studies in Use and Attitude* (London)

Gross, Harvey (1964) *Sound and Form in Modern Poetry: A Study of Prosody from Thomas Hardy to Robert Lowell* (Ann Arbor, Michigan)

Groves, Peter Lewis (1979) 'Shakespeare's prosody: a new approach to an old problem' PhD Dissertation, Cambridge University

Guéron, Jacqueline (1974) 'The meter of nursery rhymes: an application of the Halle–Keyser theory of meter' *Poetics* **12**, 73–111

Halle, Morris (1970) 'On meter and prosody' in *Progress in Linguistics: A Collection of Papers* ed. Manfred Bierwisch and Karl Erich Heidolph (The Hague), 64–80

Halle, Morris and Keyser, Samuel Jay (1966) 'Chaucer and the study of prosody' *College English* **28**, 187–219

Halle, Morris and Keyser, Samuel Jay (1971a) *English Stress: Its Form, Its Growth, and Its Role in Verse* (New York, Evanston, London)

Halle, Morris and Keyser, Samuel Jay (1971b) 'Illustration and defense of a theory of the iambic pentameter' *College English* **33**, 154–76

Halliday, M. A. K. (1967) *Intonation and Grammar in British English* (The Hague)

Hamer, Enid (1930) *The Metres of English Poetry* (London)

Harding, D. W. (1976) *Words into Rhythm: English Speech Rhythm in Verse and Prose* (Cambridge)

Harvey, Gabriel and Spenser, Edmund (1579–80) *Three Proper and wittie familiar Letters; Two other very commendable Letters* in *Elizabethan Critical Essays*, ed. G. Gregory Smith (London, 1904), Vol. I, 87–122

Hascall, Dudley L. (1969) 'Some contributions to the Halle–Keyser theory of prosody' *College English* **30**, 357–65

Hascall, Dudley L. (1971) 'Trochaic meter' *College English* **33**, 217–26

Hatcher, Harlan Henthorne (1928) *The Versification of Robert Browning* (Columbus, Ohio)

Hawkes, Terence (1962) 'The matter of metre' *Essays in Criticism* **12**, 413–21

Hawkes, Terence (1971) Review of George Faure *Les Éléments du rythme poétique en anglais moderne*, *Modern Language Review* **66**, 885–7

Hendren, J. W. (1936) *A Study of Ballad Rhythm with Special Reference to Ballad Music* Princeton Studies in English, 14 (Princeton)

Hendren, J. W. (1959) 'Time and stress in English verse with special reference to Lanier's theory of rhythm' *The Rice Institute Pamphlet*, 46, No. 2

Hewitt, Elizabeth Kennedy (1972) 'Prosody: a structuralist approach' *Style* **6**, 229–59

Hollander, John (1956) 'The music of poetry' *Journal of Aesthetics and Art Criticism* **15**, 232–44

Hollander, John (1975) *Vision and Resonance: Two Senses of Poetic Form* (New York)

Huggins, A. W. F. (1972) 'On the perception of temporal phenomena in speech' *Journal of the Acoustical Society of America* **51**, 1279–90

Isaacs, Elcanon (1920) 'The nature of the rhythm experience' *Psychological Review* **27**, 270–99

Jacob, Cary F. (1918) *The Foundations and Nature of Verse* (New York)

Jakobson, Roman (1960) 'Closing statement: linguistics and poetics' in *Style in Language* ed. T. A. Sebeok (Cambridge, Mass.), 350–77

Jespersen, Otto (1900) 'Notes on metre' in *The Structure of Verse: Modern Essays on Prosody* ed. Harvey Gross (Greenwich, Conn., 1966), 111–30

Jones, Daniel (1960) *An Outline of English Phonetics*, 9th edn. (Cambridge)

Kates, Carol A. (1976) 'A critique of Chomsky's theory of grammatical competence' *Forum Linguisticum* **1**, 15–24

Ker, W. P. (1928) *Form and Style in Poetry: Lectures and Notes*, ed. R. W. Chambers (London)

Keyser, Samuel Jay (1969a) 'The linguistic basis of English prosody' in *Modern Studies in English: Readings in Transformational Grammar* ed. David A. Reibel and Sanford A. Schane (Englewood Cliffs, New Jersey), 379–94

Keyser, Samuel Jay (1969b) 'Old English prosody' *College English* **30**, 331–56

Kiparsky, Paul (1975) 'Stress, syntax, and meter' *Language* **51**, 576–616

Kiparsky, Paul (1977) 'The rhythmic structure of English verse' *Linguistic Inquiry* **8**, 189–247

Knowles, G. (1974) 'The rhythm of English syllables' *Lingua* **34**, 115–47

Kökeritz, Helge (1953) *Shakespeare's Pronunciation* (New Haven)

Kozhevnikov, V. A. and Chistovich, L. A. (1965) *Speech: Articulation and Perception* tr. Joint Publications Research Service (Washington, D. C.)

Kunitz, Stanley (1978) 'Action and incantation' (interview with Harvey Gross), *Antaeus*, Nos. 30–31, 283–95

Ladefoged, Peter, Draper, M. H. and Whitteridge, D. (1958) 'Syllables and stress' *Miscellanea Phonetica* **3**, 1–14

Lakoff, George (1973) 'Fuzzy grammar and the performance/competence terminology game' *Papers from the Ninth Regional Meeting of the Chicago Linguistic Society* ed. C. Corum *et al.* (Chicago), 271–91

Langer, Suzanne K. (1953) *Feeling and Form* (London)

Lanier, Sidney (1880) *The Science of English Verse* (New York)

Leavis, F. R. (1932) *New Bearings in English Poetry* (Harmondsworth, 1972)

Leech, Geoffrey N. (1969) *A Linguistic Guide to English Poetry* (London)

Lehiste, Ilse (1970a) *Suprasegmentals* (Cambridge, Mass., and London)

Lehiste, Ilse (1970b) 'Temporal organization of spoken language' *Working Papers in Linguistics (Ohio State University)* **4**, 85–94

Lehiste, Ilse (1977) 'Isochrony reconsidered' *Journal of Phonetics* **5**, 253–63

Lehiste, Ilse (1979) 'The perception of duration within sequences of four intervals' *Journal of Phonetics* **7**, 313–6

Levin, Samuel R. (1973) 'A revision of the Halle–Keyser metrical theory' *Language* **49**, 606–611

Lewis, C. S. (1938) 'The fifteenth-century heroic line' *Essays and Studies* **24**, 28–41

Lewis, C. S. (1960) 'Metre' *Review of English Literature* **1**, 45–50

Liberman, Mark and Prince, Alan (1977) 'On stress and linguistic rhythm' *Linguistic Inquiry* **8**, 249–336

Lightfoot, Marjorie J. (1970) 'Accent and time in descriptive prosody' *Word* **26**, 47–64

Lotman, Yury (1976) *Analysis of the Poetic Text* ed. and tr. D. Barton Johnson (Ann Arbor, Michigan)

Lunney, H. W. M. (1974) 'Location of stress: Classe's experiment re-instrumented' *Zeitschrift für Phonetik* **27**, 320–7

Lusson, Pierre and Roubaud, Jacques (1974) 'Mètre et rythme de l'alexandrin ordinaire' *Langue française* **23**, 41–53

McClean, M. D. and Tiffany, W. R. (1973) 'The acoustic parameters of stress in relation to syllable position, speech loudness, and rate' *Language and Speech* **16**, 283–91

Magnuson, Karl and Ryder, Frank G. (1970) 'The study of English prosody: an alternative proposal' *College English* **31**, 789–820

Magnuson, Karl and Ryder, Frank G. (1971) 'Second thoughts on English prosody' *College English* **33**, 198–216

Malof, Joseph (1964) 'The native rhythm of English metres' *Texas Studies in Literature and Language* **5**, 580–94

Malof, Joseph (1970) *A Manual of English Meters* (Bloomington, Indiana)

Martin, James G. (1970) 'Rhythm-induced judgements of word stress in sentences' *Journal of Verbal Learning and Verbal Behavior* **9**, 627–33

Martin, James G. (1972) 'Rhythmic (hierarchical) versus serial structure in speech and other behavior' *Psychological Review* **79**, 487–509

Meyer, Leonard B. (1956) *Emotion and Meaning in Music* (Chicago)

Nabokov, Vladimir (1964) *Notes on Prosody and Abram Gannibal: From the Commentary to the Author's Translation of Pushkin's 'Eugene Onegin'* (Princeton)

Napoli, Donna Jo (1978) 'The metrics of Italian nursery rhymes' *Language and Style* **11**, 40–58

Nash, Walter (1980) *Designs in Prose: A Study of Compositional Problems and Methods* (London)

Needler, G. H. (1941) *The Lone Shieling: Origin and Authorship of the Blackwood 'Canadian Boat-Song'* (Toronto)

Netsell, R. (1970) 'Underlying physiological mechanisms of syllable stress' summary in *Journal of the Acoustical Society of America* **47**, 103–4

Nettl, Bruno (1956) *Music in Primitive Culture* (Cambridge, Mass.)

Newton, Robert P. (1975) 'Trochaic and iambic' *Language and Style* **8**, 127–56

Nowottny, Winifred (1962) *The Language Poets Use* (London)

Nuttall, A. D. (1967) *Two Concepts of Allegory* (New York)

Öhman, S. E. G. (1967) 'Word and sentence intonation: a quantitative model' *Quarterly Progress and Status Report* Royal Institute of Technology, Stockholm **2–3**, 20–54

Omond, T. S. (1921) *English Metrists* (Oxford)

Opie, Iona and Peter (1951) *The Oxford Dictionary of Nursery Rhymes* (Oxford)

Oras, Ants (1960) *Pause Patterns in Elizabethan and Jacobean Drama: An Experiment in Prosody* University of Florida Monographs, Humanities, No. 3 (Gainesville, Florida)

Patmore, Coventry (1857)*Essay on English Metrical Law* Appendix to *Poems* second collective edn. (1886), Vol. II, 215–67

Perry, John Oliver (1965) 'The temporal analysis of poems' *British Journal of Aesthetics* **5**, 227–45

Pike, Kenneth L. (1945) *The Intonation of American English* University of Michigan Publications in Linguistics, Vol. I (Ann Arbor, Michigan)

Prall, D. W. (1929) *Aesthetic Judgement* (New York)

Prall, D. W. (1936) *Aesthetic Analysis* (New York)

Puttenham, George (1589)*The Arte of English Poesie*, in *Elizabethan Critical Essays* ed. G. Gregory Smith (London, 1904), Vol. II, 1–193

Pyle, Fitzroy (1939) 'The rhythms of the English heroic line: an essay in empirical analysis' *Hermathena* **53**, 100–126

Pyle, Fitzroy (1968) 'Pyrrhic and spondee: speech stress and metrical accent in English five-foot iambic verse structure' *Hermathena* **107**, 49–74

Pyle, Fitzroy (1973) 'Chaucer's prosody' *Medium Aevum* **42**, 47–56

Quirk, Randolph and Svartvik, Jan (1966) *Investigating Linguistic Acceptability* (The Hague)

Quirk, Randolph, Greenbaum, Sidney, Leech, Geoffrey and Svartvik, Jan (1972) *A Grammar of Contemporary English* (London)

Ramus, Petrus (1564) *Libri Duo de Veris Sonis Literarum & syllabarum* (Paris)

Richards, I. A. (1924) *Principles of Literary Criticism* (London, 1967)

Robertson, Jean (1960) 'Sir Philip Sidney and his poetry' in *Elizabethan Poetry* ed. John Russell Brown and Bernard Harris, Stratford-upon-Avon Studies, 2 (London), 111–29

Robinson, Ian (1971)*Chaucer's Prosody: A Study of the Middle English Verse Tradition* (Cambridge)

Roubaud, Jacques (1971) 'Mètre et vers: deux applications de la métrique générative de Halle–Keyser' *Poétique* **7**, 366–87

Ruskin, John (1880) *Elements of English Prosody* (Orpington, Kent)

Saintsbury, George (1906–10) *A History of English Prosody from the Twelfth Century to the Present Day* 3 vols. (London)

Saintsbury, George (1910) *Historical Manual of English Prosody* introd. Harvey Gross (New York, 1966)

Sapir, Edward (1921) 'The musical foundations of verse' *Journal of English and Germanic Philology* **20**, 213–28

Schane, Sanford A. (1979a) 'Rhythm, accent, and stress in English words' *Linguistic Inquiry* **10**, 483–502

Schane, Sanford A. (1979b) 'The rhythmic nature of English word accentuation' *Language* **55**, 559–602

Schramm, Wilbur L. (1934) 'Time and intensity in English tetrameter verse' *Philological Quarterly* **13**, 65–71

Schwarz, Elias (1962) 'Rhythm and "exercises in abstraction"' *PMLA* **77**, 668–70

Scott, Clive (1980) *French Verse-art: A Study* (Cambridge)

Scripture, E. W. (1921) 'The nature of verse' *British Journal of Psychology* **11**, 225–35

Scripture, E. W. (1928) 'The choriambus in English verse' *PMLA* **43**, 316–22

Shapiro, Karl and Beum, Robert (1965) *A Prosody Handbook* (New York)

Shen, Yao and Peterson, Giles G. (1962) *Isochronism in English* Studies in Linguistics Occasional Papers, No. 9 (Buffalo, New York)

Shockey, Linda, Gregorski, Richard and Lehiste, Ilse (1971) 'Word unit temporal compensation' *Working Papers in Linguistics (Ohio State University)*, **9**, 145–65

Sidney, Sir Philip (1595) *An Apologie for Poetrie*, facsimile edn. (Amsterdam, New York, 1971)

Sinfield, Alan (1971) *The Language of Tennyson's 'In Memoriam'* (Oxford)

Smith, Barbara Herrnstein (1968) *Poetic Closure: A Study of How Poems End* (Chicago)

Smith, Egerton (1923) *The Principles of English Metre* (Oxford)

Smith, G. S. (1980) (ed. and tr.) *Metre, Rhythm, Stanza, Rhyme* Russian Poetics in Translation, No. 7 (Colchester)

Smith, H. L. (1959) 'Toward redefining English prosody' *Studies in Linguistics* **14**, 68–76

Snell, Ada L. F. (1918–19) 'An objective study of syllabic quantity in English verse' *PMLA* **33**, 396–408; **34**, 416–35

Sprott, S. Ernest (1953) *Milton's Art of Prosody* (Oxford)

Standop, Ewald (1975) 'Metric theory gone astray: a critique of the Halle–Keyser theory' *Language and Style* **8**, 60–77

Steele, Joshua (1775) *An Essay towards Establishing the Melody and Measure of Speech*, facsimile edn. (Menston, 1969)

Stein, Arnold (1956) 'John Donne's prosody' *Kenyon Review* **18**, 439–43

Stetson, R. H. (1905) 'A motor theory of rhythm and discrete succession' *Psychological Review* **12**, 250–70, 293–350

Stetson, R. H. (1923) 'The teaching of rhythm' *Musical Quarterly* **9**, 181–90
Stetson, R. H. (1945) *Bases of Phonology* (Oberlin, Ohio)
Stetson, R. H. (1951) *Motor Phonetics: A Study of Speech Movements in Action*, 2nd edn. (Amsterdam)
Stevenson, Charles L. (1970) 'The rhythm of English verse' *Journal of Aesthetics and Art Criticism* **28**, 327–44
Stewart, George R. (1922) *Modern Metrical Technique as Illustrated by Ballad Meter (1700–1920)* (New York)
Stewart, George R. (1924) 'A method toward the study of dipodic verse' *PMLA* **39**, 979–89
Stewart, George R. (1925a) 'The meter of the popular ballad' *PMLA* **40**, 933–62
Stewart, George R. (1925b) 'The iambic-trochaic theory in relation to musical notation of verse' *Journal of English and Germanic Philology* **24**, 61–71
Stewart, George R. (1930) *The Technique of English Verse* (New York)
Sumera, Magdalena (1970) 'The temporal tradition in the study of verse structure' *Linguistics* **62**, 44–65
Sutherland, Ronald (1958) 'Structural linguistics and English prosody' *College English* **20**, 12–17

Taranovsky, K. F. (1971) 'The rhythmical structure of Russian binary metres' in *Metre, Rhythm, Stanza, Rhyme* ed. and tr. G. S. Smith (Colchester, 1980), 20–30
Tarlinskaja, Marina (1976) *English Verse: Theory and History*, tr. from the Russian (The Hague)
Tedford, W. H. and Synnott, C. S. (1972) 'Use of the semantic differential with poetic forms' *The Psychological Record* **22**, 369–73
Thompson, John (1961) *The Founding of English Metre* (London)
Thomson, William (1923) *The Rhythm of Speech* (Glasgow)
Tovey, Donald (1910–11) 'Rhythm' *Encyclopaedia Britannica* 11th edn, Vol. 23, 277–80
Trager, George L. and Smith, Henry Lee (1951) *An Outline of English Structure* (fourth printing), Studies in Linguistics Occasional Papers, No. 3 (Washington, D.C., 1957)
Turner, Paul R. (1970) 'Grammar for the speaker and hearer' *Linguistics* **57**, 93–9

Uldall, Elizabeth T. (1971) 'Isochronous stresses in R.P.' in *Form and Substance: Phonetic and Linguistic Papers Presented to Eli Fischer-Jørgensen* ed. L. L. Hammerich *et al.* (Copenhagen), 205–10

Van Dam, B. A. P. (1900) *William Shakespeare: Prosody and Text* (London)
Van Draat, P. Fijn (1910) *Rhythm in English Prose* Anglistische Forschungen, 29 (Heidelberg)
Van Draat, P. Fijn (1912) 'Rhythm in English prose' *Anglia* **36**, 1–58, 492–538
Verrier, Paul (1909) *Essai sur les principes de la métrique anglaise* (Paris)

Wales, R. J. and Marshall, J. C. (1966) 'The organization of linguistic performance' in *Psycholinguistic Papers* ed. J. Lyons and R. J. Wales (Edinburgh), 27–95

Wallin, J. E. Wallace (1911–12) 'Experimental studies of rhythm and time' *The Psychological Review* **18**, 100–131, 202–222; **19**, 271–98

Wasserman, Earl R. (1940) 'The return of the enjambed couplet' *ELH* **7**, 239–52

Webbe, William (1586) *A Discourse of English Poetrie* in *Elizabethan Critical Essays* ed. G. Gregory Smith (London, 1904), Vol. I, 226–302

Weismiller, Edward R. (1972) 'Studies of verse form in the minor English poems' in *A Variorum Commentary on the Poems of John Milton, Vol. 2: The Minor English Poems* ed. A. S. P. Woodhouse and Douglas Bush, Part Three (London), 1007–1087

Weismiller, Edward R. (1975) 'Studies of style and verse form in *Paradise Regained*' in *A Variorum Commentary on the Poems of John Milton, Vol. 4: Paradise Regained* ed. Walter MacKellar (London), 253–363

Wells, Rulon (1960) Comments on Part 5, 'Metrics', of *Style in Language* ed. T. A. Sebeok (Cambridge, Mass.) 197–200

Whitaker, Harry A. (1968) 'Rules versus strategies as a distinction between competence and performance' *Working Papers in Phonetics (UCLA)* **10**, 172–90

Whitehall, Harold (1956) 'From linguistics to criticism' *Kenyon Review* **18**, 411–21

Wilson, Peter (1979) 'Reading a line metrically: the practical implications of using the Halle–Keyser system' *Language and Style* **12**, 146–57

Wimsatt, W. K. (1954) 'One relation of rhyme to reason' in *The Verbal Icon* (Lexington, Kentucky), 153–66

Wimsatt, W. K. (1970) 'The rule and the norm: Halle and Keyser on Chaucer's meter' *College English* **31**, 774–88

Wimsatt, W. K. and Beardsley, Monroe C. (1959) 'The concept of meter: an exercise in abstraction' *PMLA* **74**, 585–98

Winters, Yvor (1957) *The Function of Criticism: Problems and Exercises* (Denver)

Woodrow, Herbert (1909) *A Quantitative Study of Rhythm: The Effect of Variations in Intensity, Rate and Duration* Archives of Psychology, 14 (New York)

Woodrow, Herbert (1951) 'Time perception' in *Handbook of Experimental Psychology* ed. S. S. Stevens (New York, London), 1224–36

Woolf, Virginia (1926) Letter to Vita Sackville-West, 16 March, 1926, in *A Change of Perspective: The Letters of Virginia Woolf, Vol. III, 1923–8*, ed. Nigel Nicolson (London, 1977)

Wright, Thomas W. (1974) 'Temporal interactions within a phrase and sentence context' *Journal of the Acoustical Society of America* **56**, 1258–65

Youmans, Gilbert (1974) 'Test case for a metrical theory: "La Belle Dame Sans Merci"' *Language and Style* **7**, 283–305

Zirin, Ronald A. (1970) *The Phonological Basis of Latin Prosody* (The Hague)

Žirmunskij, V. (1925) *Introduction to Metrics: The Theory of Verse* tr. C. F. Brown, ed. E. Stankiewicz and W. N. Vickery (The Hague, 1966)

Sources of Examples

The following abbreviations are used: FQ – Spenser, *The Faerie Queene*; Son– Shakespeare, *The Sonnets*; PL – Milton, *Paradise Lost*; Prel – Wordsworth, *The Prelude* (1850 text); DJ – Byron, *Don Juan*; RB – Browning, *The Ring and the Book* (1868–9 text). Ballads are cited from Child's collection.

Chapter 1
1 FQ I 7 i
2 Shelley, 'To a Skylark'
3 Blake, 'Nurse's Song'
4 Hogg? 'God Save the King'
5 Wordsworth, 'The Solitary Reaper'
6 Yeats, 'Two Songs from a Play'
7 Arnold, 'Stanzas from the Grande Chartreuse'
8 Son 30
9 Shakespeare, 'The Phoenix and Turtle'
10 Blake, 'The Chimney Sweeper' (*Songs of Experience*)
11 Son 29
12 Son 55
13 Son 64
14 Marvell, 'To His Coy Mistress'
16 Milton, 'Il Pensoroso'

Chapter 2
1 Shelley, 'To a Skylark'
2 Donne, *Holy Sonnets*: 'Batter my heart . . .'
5 Donne, 'To His Mistress Going to Bed'
6 Keats, 'How many bards . . .'
11 Son 7
12 PL II 297
13 PL III 465
14 PL VIII 299
15 Son 147
16 Son 57
17 Son 132

Chapter 4
1 Donne, 'Song: "Go, and catch a falling star" '
2 Hogg, 'The Skylark'
3 Traditional
4 *As You Like It*, V iii
5 Traditional
6 Advertising jingle
7 Traditional
8 Marlowe, 'The Passionate Shepherd to His Love'
9 'The Lochmaben Harper', Child 192A
10 Byron, 'Stanzas: "Could love for ever..." '
11 Burns, 'To a Louse'
12 Traditional
13 'The Gay Goshawk', Child 96A
14 Wordsworth, 'She dwelt among the untrodden ways'
15 Grimald, 'To his Familiar Friend'
16 Gay, 'A New Song of New Similies'
17 Gray, 'Ode on the Death of a Favourite Cat'
18 Coleridge, *The Ancient Mariner*, 91–6
19 Ditto, 446–51
20 Traditional
21 Tennyson, 'The Lady of Shalott'
22 Roethke, 'My Papa's Waltz'
23 Traditional
24 'Mary Hamilton', Child 173A
25 Queen Elizabeth I, 'The doubt of future foes...'
26 Traditional
27 Traditional
28 Traditional
29 'Clerk Colvill', Child 42A
30 'The Gay Goshawk', Child 96B
31 Campion, 'Come, let us sound...'
32 Coleridge, *The Ancient Mariner*, 29–30
33 'Sir Patrick Spens', Child 58A
34 De La Mare, 'The Listeners'
35 Auden, 'Victor'
36 Blake, 'Nurse's Song' (*Songs of Innocence*)
37 Blake, 'The Divine Image'
38 Blake, 'Nurse's Song' (*Songs of Experience*)
39 Traditional
40 Traditional
41 'Sir Patrick Spens', Child 58A
42 Marvell, 'A Dialogue Between the Resolved Soul and Created Pleasure'
43 Shelley, 'The Sensitive Plant'

44 Traditional
45 Traditional
46 Traditional
47 Hood, 'The Bridge of Sighs'
48 Betjeman, 'The Irish Unionist's Farewell to Greta Hellstrom in 1922'
49 Traditional
50 Traditional
51 Clough, 'Say Not the Struggle Nought Availeth'
52 'The Wife of Usher's Well', Child 79A
53 Johnson, 'On the Death of Dr. Robert Levet'
54 Johnson, 'A Short Song of Congratulation'
55 Tennyson, *In Memoriam*, II
56 Sidney, *Astrophil and Stella*: Fourth Song
57 *The Tempest*, IV i
58 Longfellow, *Hiawatha*: 'Hiawatha's Departure'
59 'Thomas Rymer', Child 37A
60 'The Wife of Usher's Well', Child 79A
61 Traditional
62 Chesterton, 'The Rolling English Road'
63 Browning, 'A Toccata of Galuppi's'
64 Byron, 'To Thomas Moore'
65 Ditto
66 Kipling, 'The Long Trail'
67 Pound, 'In a Station of the Metro'

Chapter 5
 1 Chaucer, *General Prologue*, 14
 2 Son 65
 3 PL XII 645
 4 Pope, 'Epistle to Dr. Arbuthnot', 309
 5 Prel IV 327
 6 Yeats, 'Sailing to Byzantium'
 7 Anon., 'The Valiant Seaman's Happy Return to His Love' (C. Stone, *Sea Songs and Ballads*, Oxford, 1906)
 8 Gray, 'Elegy Written in a Country Churchyard'
 9 Byron, 'The Destruction of Sennacherib'
10 Burns, 'Ae Fond Kiss'
11 Browning, 'One Word More'
12 Jonson, *Cynthia's Revels*, V vi
13 Pope, 'Elegy to the Memory of an Unfortunate Lady'
14 Emily Brontë, 'The Old Stoic'
15 Kipling, 'If- -'
16 Marvell, 'The Garden'
17 Pope, 'To Mrs M. B. on Her Birthday'

18 Herbert, 'Easter'
19 Auden, *New Year Letter*, Part Three
20 Sidney, 'What tongue can her perfections tell?', *Arcadia*, Book III
21 Traditional
22 Prince, *Afterword on Rupert Brooke*, I
23 Herrick, 'To Dianeme: "Sweet, be not proud..."'
24 Herrick, 'When He Would Have His Verses Read'
25 Byron, *Beppo*, 10
26 Lovelace, 'The Grasshopper'

Chapter 7
1 'Robin Hood Rescuing Three Squires', Child 140B
2 'The Famous Flower of Serving-Men', Child 106
3 DJ IX 76
4 Auden, 'Victor'
5 Arnold, 'Requiescat'
6 Ditto
7 Ditto
8 'Tam Lin', Child 39F
9 Shelley, 'Lines Written in the Bay of Lerici'
10 Coleridge, *The Ancient Mariner*, 504
11 Tennyson, 'Ulysses'
12 *The Tempest*, I ii
13 Moore, 'Hark, the Vesper Hymn is Stealing'
14 PL I 142
15 Tennyson, 'Tithonus'
16 Hardy, 'The Newcomer's Wife'
17 'Lord Thomas and Fair Annet', Child 73C
18 Milton, 'Il Pensoroso'
19 Coleridge, *The Ancient Mariner*, 269
20 *The Tempest*, I ii
21 Burns, 'To a Mouse'
22 Tennyson, *Idylls of the King*: 'The Passing of Arthur', 34
23 FQ I iv 17
24 Dryden, *Absalom and Achitophel*, 869
25 Pope, 'Epistle to Dr. Arbuthnot', 201
26 Tennyson, 'Tears, Idle Tears'
27 DJ I 210
28 Pope, 'Epistle to Dr. Arbuthnot', 182
29 Traditional
30 Traditional
31 Traditional
32 Tennyson, 'Break, Break, Break'
33 *A Midsummer Night's Dream*, II i

34 Wyatt, 'My lute, awake . . .'
35 Donne, 'A Nocturnal upon St. Lucy's Day'
36 Shelley, 'To Night'
37 PL I 1
38 Tennyson, 'The Lady of Shalott'
39 *Romeo and Juliet*, IV iii
40 Wordsworth, 'Resolution and Independence'
41 Ditto
44 Keats, 'To Sleep'
45 Keats, 'Ode on Melancholy'
46 'Lord Ingram and Chiel Wyet', Child 66D
48 Browning, 'Fra Lippo Lippi', 91
49 Son 107
50 Milton, *Comus*, 438
51 'Sir Patrick Spens', Child 58A
52 'Clerk Saunders', Child 69G
53 Milton, 'L'Allegro'
54 Chaucer, *General Prologue*, 149
55 Ditto, 545
56 Surrey, 'Love that doth reign . . .'
57 Surrey, 'The soote season . . .'
58 Prel VI 27
59 Son 30
60 Keats, *The Eve of St. Agnes*, 364
61 Keats, 'Ode to a Nightingale'
62 Marvell, 'The Garden'
63 Thomson, *The Seasons*: 'Summer', 353
64 Browning, 'Fra Lippo Lippi', 179
65 Keats, 'How many bards . . .'
66 Donne, 'Mercurius Gallo-Belgicus'
67 Yeats, 'The Second Coming'
68 Donne, 'A Nocturnal upon St. Lucy's Day'
69 Tennyson, 'Mariana'
70 PL I 4
71 PL I 9
72 PL I 45
73 PL I 28
74 PL I 65
80 Chaucer, *General Prologue*, 294
81 Surrey, 'Norfolk sprung thee . . .'
82 *Richard II*, I iii
83 Keats, *Hyperion*, I 134
84 RB IV 290
86 Milton, 'L'Allegro'

87 Donne, *Holy Sonnets*: 'At the round earth's imagined corners ...'
88 RB X 2114
89 Son 116
90 Keats, *The Fall of Hyperion*, I 155
91 Marvell, 'The Garden'
92 Tennyson, 'Locksley Hall'
93 Ditto
94 Jonson, 'Epitaph on Elizabeth, L. H.'
95 Browning, 'Love among the Ruins'
96 Tennyson, 'The Lady of Shalott'
97 Donne, 'Song: "Go, and catch a falling star" '
98 Carew, 'Disdain Returned'
99 Shelley, 'To a Skylark'
100 Sidney, *Astrophil and Stella*: Fourth Song
101 *The Tempest*, V i
102 Browning, 'One Word More'
103 Browning, 'The Patriot'
104 *The Tempest*, V i
105 *Twelfth Night*, V i
106 Lawrence, 'Piano'
107 Byron, 'Stanzas to Augusta: "Though the day of my destiny's over" '
108 Swinburne, 'Hymn to Proserpine'
109 Kingsley, *Andromeda*, 118
110 Blake, 'The Sick Rose'
111 Hardy, 'The Ruined Maid'
112 Byron, 'The Destruction of Sennacherib'
113 Browning, 'Master Hugues of Saxe-Gotha'
114 Browning, ' "How They Brought the Good News from Ghent to Aix" '
115 Ditto
116 Ditto
117 Ditto
118 Ditto
119 Hood, 'The Bridge of Sighs'
120 Traditional
121 Browning, 'The Lost Leader'
122 Son 18
123 Son 15
124 Son 18
125 Son 55
126 Son 18
127 Son 140
128 Son 147
129 Son 116
130 Son 124

131 Larkin, 'Annus Mirabilis'
132 Auden, *New Year Letter*, Part Two
133 Pope, 'Epistle to Dr. Arbuthnot', 317–21

Chapter 8
 1 Crabbe, *The Village*, I 111–12
 2 Tennyson, *Idylls of the King*: 'Pelleas and Ettarre', 393–4
 3 DJ III 2
 4 *King Lear*, V iii
 5 Crabbe, *The Village*, I 25
 6 PL X 943
 7 FQ I vii 42
 8 Son 89
 9 PL X 882
10 FQ I ix 40
11 Prel V 133
12 PL I 67
13 Pope, *An Essay on Criticism*, 458
14 Keats, *The Fall of Hyperion*, I 297
15 Ditto, I 87
16 Ditto, I 65
17 Ditto, I 202
18 Ditto, I 182
19 Ditto, I 209
20 Son 42
21 Drayton, *Idea* (1619), Sonnet 37, 'Dear, why should you
     command . . .'
22 PL IX 944
23 FQ I ii 31
24 Son 39
25 PL IX 652
26 Jonson, 'An Epitaph on Master Vincent Corbett'
27 Swift, 'Verses on the Death of Dr. Swift'
28 Donne, 'A Hymn to God the Father'
29 Son 22
30 Keats, 'Bright star . . .'
31 Donne, 'Elegy 10: "The Dream" '
32 Ditto
33 FQ I iv 17
34 Dryden, *Absalom and Achitophel*, 869
35 Pope, 'Epistle to Dr. Arbuthnot', 201
36 Tennyson, 'Tears, Idle Tears'
37 Marvell, 'To His Coy Mistress'

83 PL IX 52
84 *Macbeth*, II ii
85 *The Tempest*, V i
86 Milton, *Comus*, 582
87 PL II 353
88 PL II 490
89 PL II 359
90 PL II 424
91 PL III 257
92 Arnold, *The Scholar-Gipsy*, 211–12
93 Son 52
94 PL IV 141–7
95 Son 64
96 Cowper, *The Task*, VI 908
97 Keats, 'Ode to a Nightingale'
98 PL XII 649
99 Pope, 'Epistle to Burlington', 48
100 Keats, *The Eve of St. Agnes*, 203
101 Prel V 80
102 Pope, *The Dunciad*, IV 3
103 PL IX 115
104 Pope, *The Rape of the Lock*, III 136
105 RB IV 649
106 Tennyson, 'Ulysses'
107 Wordsworth, 'Tintern Abbey'
108 Yeats, 'Among School Children'
109 PL IV 598–9
110 PL II 621
112 Tennyson, 'Saint Simeon Stylites'
113 Browning, 'The Bishop Orders His Tomb'
114 Clough, 'Say Not the Struggle Nought Availeth'
115 Keats, *Hyperion*, I 116
116 Tennyson, 'Saint Simeon Stylites'
117 Prel I 309–312
118 Coleridge, 'To William Wordsworth'
119 Son 116
120 Gay, *Trivia*, III 263
121 PL IX 560
122 Tennyson, 'Lucretius', 204
123 Marlowe, *Hero and Leander*, I 5
124 Ditto, I 320
125 Son 29
126 Son 140
127 PL IX 1144

Chapter 9
1 Nabokov, *Lolita*
2 Son 12
3 Lawrence, 'Brooding Grief'
4 Ditto
5 PL IV 114–20
6 Cowper, 'The Poplar-Field'
7 Hardy, 'During Wind and Rain'
8 Blake, 'London'
9 Edward Dyer, 'My mind to me a kingdom is'
10 Jonson, 'Her Triumph', *A Celebration of Charis*.

Appendix
1 Son 33
2 Hopkins, 'I wake and feel the fell of dark, not day'
3 Yeats, 'A Dialogue of Self and Soul'

Index

Bold figures indicate main entries. Authors of examples are indexed only where reference is made to their individual use of rhythm.